Images and Arms Control

# Images and Arms Control
## Perceptions of the Soviet Union in the Reagan Administration

Keith L. Shimko

*Ann Arbor*
THE UNIVERSITY OF MICHIGAN PRESS

1994   1993   1992   1991      4   3   2   1


*A CIP catalogue record for this book is available from
the British Library.*


Library of Congress Cataloging-in-Publication Data

Shimko, Keith L., 1962–
    Images and arms control : perceptions of the Soviet Union in the
    Reagan administration / Keith L. Shimko.
        p.      cm.
    Includes bibliographical references (p.     ) and index.
    ISBN 0-472-10284-2 (alk. paper)
    1. Nuclear arms control—United States—Decision making.
2. Soviet Union—Foreign relations—1985–   3. Soviet Union—Foreign
relations—1975–1985.   4. United States—Foreign relations—Soviet
Union.   5. Soviet Union—Foreign relations—United States.
6. Reagan, Ronald.   I. Title.
JX1974.7.S4718   1991
327.1′74—dc20                                              91-30714
                                                                CIP

## Acknowledgments

As is the case with many academics, this, my first book, grows out of my doctoral research. As a result, my debts are to all of those people who supported me through the process that led to this point. Indirectly, there are those who made life enjoyable during my studies—family and friends who provided support for, and needed distractions from, academic pursuits. My parents were always supportive, never dwelling on the fact that their twenty-five-year-old son was still "in school" and without a "real" job. I was also fortunate to have many friends at Indiana University who made my time in Bloomington fun—whether it was rooting on the Hoosiers, nights at Crazy Horse, or simply hanging out in Woodburn Hall, they made life bearable. They know who they are, and I thank them all.

Intellectually and academically, my debts begin with Stanley Michalak and others at Franklin and Marshall College who sparked my interest in international relations and foreign policy, urging me to pursue further study. I am grateful for the financial assistance I received during my studies from the Department of Political Science and the Graduate School at Indiana University. Additional support was provided by the Institute for Humane Studies in the form of Claude R. Lambe Fellowships. I am indebted to the members of my doctoral committee, who helped me with this project as well as in many other ways, particularly John Lovell and Dina Spechler. Thanks also to Beth Turner for all her help in preparing the manuscript for publication. My greatest debt is to Harvey Starr. I cannot count the number of times I stuck my head into his office to ask if he had "a minute." Even though the minute usually turned into a half hour or more, his door was always open. Whether I wanted to flesh out a new problem, try a new idea, or simply bolster a sometimes fragile graduate student ego, I never left disappointed. Though all these people deserve credit for many of the positive elements of the present study, the shortcomings are my own responsibility.

# Contents

CHAPTER 1

# Introduction

It is a truism that people act on the basis of their perceptions of reality. Since all decisions are ultimately made by individuals, acting alone or in concert, cognitive variables are important elements in explanations for all purposive human behavior. As John Steinbruner argues:

> There is no one who would seriously contest that the brain is the ultimate locus of decision making . . . whenever we speak of such things as organizational processes, political bargaining, and rational calculation, we tacitly know that in the final analysis the phenomena involved are based on human mental operations. (1974, 91)

While virtually no one denies the importance of psychological variables, there are those who question the utility of research that focuses on them. No less a figure than Hans Morgenthau has argued that attempts to explain and study foreign policy in terms of the beliefs and motivations of decision makers are "futile" (1967, 5–6). This is not because he thought psychological factors are unimportant; on the contrary, by defining his own central variable—power—as the "*psychological relationship* between those who exercise it and those over whom it is exercised," Morgenthau recognized the centrality of perceptual variables (1967, 27, italics added). According to Morgenthau, the problem is that psychological variables cannot be observed directly and are, therefore, unknowable. The logic is impeccable, though not consistently applied, since "power" cannot be directly observed and measured, yet this does not prevent Morgenthau from studying international relations in terms of power.

If this criticism of psychological approaches to the study of foreign policy (and any other form of decision making) is taken to its logical conclusion, much social scientific and historical research would have to be abandoned because many of the key variables are "unknowable" in the sense that they are not directly observable—for example, utility, political legitimacy, relative deprivation, oppression, and even public opinion. All of these variables are inferred from things that can be observed, such as domestic unrest and people's responses to questions. It is impossible to study and understand complex social phenomena if one is restricted to variables that can be observed directly. It is hard to imagine a satisfactory explanation of any historical event without reference to the thoughts, beliefs, needs, desires, and motivations of people—none of which can be observed directly.

Recognizing the importance of cognitive variables, students of foreign policy have often turned to them in search of explanations for state behavior (or, more precisely, the decisions and behavior of political leaders). Whether it be "operational codes," "belief systems," "worldviews," "definitions of the situation," "misperceptions," or "mirror images," the psychological milieu of decision makers has always occupied a central place in foreign policy analysis. The present study is in this tradition, drawing upon existing theory and research, and, I hope, contributing to it. The purpose of this study is to explore the nature of the relationship between one cognitive variable—images of the enemy—and policy preferences. The substantive focus is images of the Soviet Union and their impact on the policy preferences of prominent decision makers in the Reagan administration in the area of strategic arms policy. The question examined is that posed by Richard Herrmann: "Do views of the Soviet Union determine the policy choices of American leaders?" (1986, 841). I am not trying to establish the validity or accuracy of the decision makers' images; this would open a can of methodological and epistemological worms that is best left sealed for the moment. I ask only how X's image influences his or her policy choices, not whether X's beliefs were correct.

I am not attempting to "prove" or "disprove" any particular theoretical perspective; I am not engaged in strict hypothesis testing. Although such an approach has its place in theory building, explicit hypothesis testing is not the only route to knowledge, nor is it always appropriate. The overall strategy for investigation in this study is twofold. On the one hand, I want to examine what existing theory has to tell us about the relationship between images and policy preferences: why, how, and under what circumstances should we expect a connection. Having done this, I want to see whether the cases under consideration are consistent with the expectations generated by existing theory. In this sense, I am engaging in a loose form of hypothesis testing—an "expectation" is an imprecise form of hypothesis. On the other hand, I want to use the present study to identify shortcomings in existing theory, suggesting revisions and refinements. Bjorn Christiansen elaborates on the two strategies of research that are enmeshed in this study.

> The interplay between theory and empiricism may vary . . . we may stress the empirical side and let the theory grow out of the material, or we can let the theory be the string and let our empirical material serve exclusively for the testing of predictions derived from special hypotheses . . . the empirical-inductive method will come into play at the initial

exploratory phase of the investigation of a particular phenomenon. The hypothetical-deductive method, on the other hand, will only be applicable when a particular theory begins to take shape and we gradually approach a theoretical structure. (1959, 7)

The study of images and other cognitive variables is not uncharted territory; it is an exaggeration to claim, as does Deborah Larson, that "the use of cognitive theories to explain foreign policy-making is in its infancy" (1985, 62). There is a body of research and theory that serves as a basis for this project. But we have not yet reached a stage of having a fully developed theory from which we can derive a series of specific, testable hypotheses (Larson 1985, 62). We are at an intermediate stage of theory development.

## Research Questions

### Theoretical Focus

This volume builds upon a well-established body of theory and research in the study of foreign policy decision making—operational code analysis.[1] An actor's operational code has been conceptualized as a cluster of beliefs and attitudes, instrumental and philosophical, that influences behavior (George 1979; Holsti 1970 and 1977b). An operational code is a collection of cognitive variables, each of which is susceptible to investigation. Instead of focusing on the operational code of one individual (e.g., Holsti 1970; Starr 1984; Walker 1977), this project concentrates on one element of the operational code for a number of individuals. While it would be ideal to examine the full operational code of each subject, there are a number of obstacles to such an approach. First, when we consider the large number of beliefs that constitute an individual's operational code, studying them all for several individuals is a formidable task indeed. Manageability requires that either the number of subjects or number of variables be reduced (this is, of course, the classic dilemma of balancing the number of cases with the number of variables). Second, the operational code contains a number of very abstract, philosophical beliefs, such as the nature of political conflict. The most satisfying operational code analyses have been performed for individuals who produced a rich body of writing about international affairs (e.g., Kissinger and Dulles). My subjects have not done so. I will be sensitive to other operational code beliefs that

---

1. Strictly speaking, the operational code is not a theory, but rather "a guideline for describing some of the political beliefs of policymakers . . . a descriptive set of analytical categories" (Cottam 1986, 17, 12). Operational code beliefs take on theoretical significance only when combined with theories of cognition that postulate a certain relationship between beliefs and behavior.

might stand out, since they may help in the understanding of the influence of enemy images, but I am not constructing an elaborate method designed to identify these beliefs.

Accepting the practical need to limit the number of independent variables, we must determine which element(s) of the operational code should be singled out. Two criteria come to mind: first, it should be a central or "core" element of the operational code; and second, the writings and statements of the subjects should be sufficient to allow fruitful investigation. The operational code literature has focused on two philosophical beliefs—the nature of political conflict and the image of the opponent. Drawing the distinction between central and peripheral components, Alexander George classifies the "image of the enemy" as one of the core elements of the operational code (1979, 100). Jerel Rosati agrees, arguing that "the image of the opponent or adversary serves as the foundation for understanding an actor's belief system about the larger international environment" (1984, 187 n. 11).

The centrality of the enemy image has been accepted even by those who have not worked within an operational code framework. Robert Osgood observes that "American postwar foreign policy has been defined . . . largely by the nation's response to its perception of the Soviet threat" (1981, 1).[2] Daniel Yergin's 1977 account of the triumph of the "Riga axioms" over the "Yalta axioms" in the immediate postwar period is basically the story of a more malevolent image of the Soviet Union replacing the more benign image that had prevailed during World War II. Political leaders have also cited the enemy image as a key determinant of policy: Kissinger's distinction between revolutionary and status quo states presents two different enemy images, each carrying different policy responses. Thus, it appears the image of the enemy has been accepted as a key element of an individual's operational code, if not the most important component.

The second criterion is more practical than theoretical—the availability of data. The image of the enemy meets this criterion as well. While we might search in vain through congressional testimony or press conferences for a decision maker's comments on the underlying nature of political conflict, images of the enemy, explicit and implicit, are likely to be more abundant. A secretary of defense will probably have more opportunities to speculate about why the Soviets did this or that, rather than why nations go to war in the abstract. Certainly we might be able to "tease out" beliefs on esoteric issues from statements on concrete matters, but the less explicit the comments, the more likely we are to draw invalid inferences.

---

2. Osgood's wording is awkward, since it does not make sense to say that the United States has *responded to* its perception of the Soviet threat; more accurately, we can say that the United States has responded to the Soviet Union on the basis of its perception of the Soviet threat.

Having chosen images of the enemy as the independent variable, what is to be explained? Many operational code analyses have generally attempted to draw connections between beliefs and behavior (e.g., Holsti 1970; Rosati 1982, 1984 and 1987; Starr 1984). In these cases, behavior has been conceptualized as national or administration policy, which is why operational codes analyses have dealt mainly with figures who dominated the policy process. The focus of this study is slightly different: the *policy preferences* of the key decision makers, not national or administration policy, will be the dependent variable (though in some cases, particularly with respect to the president, the distinction may be difficult to make). The focus on policy preferences is justified because if images have an influence on national policy, it is through their impact on the policy positions of prominent decision makers who make up the policy-making "menu" from which national or administration policy is ultimately derived. Those who have done work within the operational code tradition agree that policy preferences may be the most useful point of reference. Holsti observes that "it is not very fruitful to assume direct linkages between beliefs and behavior, because the role beliefs play in policy-making is more subtle and less direct" (1976, 54). George agrees, suggesting that behavior not be the focus because "the influence of an actor's beliefs is likely to be more weighty in determining his policy preferences" (1979, 100).

In thinking about the relationship between images and national policy, it is useful to conceive of a two-step process involving separate conversion processes: first, the conversion of images into policy preferences at the individual level; and second, the process of formulating policy from the various proposals. This study examines the first conversion process: How do images held by decision makers influence their formulation and/or choice of policy options? Why do certain beliefs predispose an individual to favor some policies and oppose others? What are the important intervening or antecedent variables that might increase or decrease the significance of images? This study does not systematically examine the second conversion process, in which these competing policy preferences are aggregated or translated into national policy.

## Substantive Focus

Once the theoretical concerns have been specified, the major decisions involve the substantive focus: What area of policy should be emphasized? What decision makers should we examine? This project focuses on U.S. arms control policy during the eight years of the Reagan administration. The individuals selected are President Reagan, Secretary of State George Shultz, Secretary of Defense Caspar Weinberger, Richard Perle, and Richard Burt.

The selection of arms control policy is guided by what I view as a basic rule of research: exploration of the relationship between two variables should begin by studying those areas, situations, and issues where one would reasonably expect to find some relationship. The early stages of research and theory building should begin with the "easy cases"; the hard ones come later. If no relationship is found under conditions where common sense would lead us to expect one, the long-term value of the research program is called into question. If a relationship is discovered, the utility of the research program has been established. There are, of course, no hard and fast rules for deciding which policy areas meet this requirement; one has to rely on existing theory, common sense, and informed intuition. Of the possible policy areas we could have selected to explore the relationship between images of the Soviet Union and policy preferences, it is difficult to think of one more appropriate than arms control. If images of the Soviet Union are not significant variables in this area, one must wonder whether they would be important in any area.

I have chosen the Reagan administration for a variety of reasons. Most commentators have been struck by the extremely negative portrayal of the Soviet Union voiced by Reagan throughout his political career and early in his administration. Not since the height of the cold war had the Soviet Union been described as an evil empire or cited as the locus of evil in the modern world. Seyom Brown writes, "the Soviets are assumed by the Reaganites to be truly impressed by little in international relations other than who has the military capability and the will to use it" (Osgood 1981, 30). And Leroy Miller argues that "the Reagan administration has considered the Soviet Union a morally questionable, militarily menacing giant on the brink of economic and political collapse" (1987, 987).

Despite talk about the views of "the Reaganites" and *the* Reagan administration, little systematic work has been done except for two studies of Reagan (Glad 1983; Hermann 1983). Virtually all the material on the Reagan administration is impressionistic and journalistic, which is fine and very useful as far as it goes (in fact, the present study would have been impossible without it). But given the general impression of an administration divided by acrimonious policy debates, it is surprising that differing images within the administration have not received more systematic attention. It is not that disagreements about the nature of the Soviet Union have gone unrecognized: Strobe Talbott, whose work sparked my interest in using this case to explore the influence of enemy images, realized the underlying divisions.

> The Reagan administration had the look of a coalition government. Haig, Eagleburger, and Burt were the leaders of one faction . . . those who believed it was possible for the U.S. to make agreements with the Soviets that were in the interests of America and the West . . . At the other end of the spectrum were the Pentagon civilians . . . and they

tended to the view that the U.S. could not ultimately count on its allies and should not really do business with the Soviet Union. (1985, 14)

Several questions flow from Talbott's observation. What was it about the first faction's image of the Soviet Union that made it more willing to conclude agreements? Why did the second group think that the United States "should not really do business with the Soviet Union'? To what extent were the administration's debates over arms control shaped by disagreements about the nature of the Soviet Union and its foreign policy? How and why do images influence policy preferences at the level of the individual decision maker? This study addresses these questions.

In terms of theory building, there are benefits to be derived from looking at several decision makers. One of the traditional criticisms of case studies focusing on psychological variables is that "individual studies are not always easily compared and, as a result, are less cumulative than they might otherwise be" (Holsti 1976, 50). How do we increase the utility of such studies? Holsti talks about "the importance for knowledge cumulation of comparing the belief systems of two or more leaders in a given situation" (1976, 51). By selecting individuals from the same administration, operating in the same international environment and domestic political context and dealing with the same issues, we are able to "control" for a number of variables that would complicate a study that stretched across administrations. Unlike natural scientists, social scientists cannot experimentally manipulate variables. The best we can do is control variables through a careful selection of cases. Of course, it is never possible to control for all variables that might affect the relationship being examined; selecting a group of contemporaneous policymakers is one way to control for as many variables as possible.

Why have I chosen Reagan, Weinberger, Shultz, Burt, and Perle? First, by all accounts, they were the key players within the administration in the area of arms control policy. Second, an initial reading of secondary sources suggested that their policy disagreements were based, at least in part, on different beliefs about the Soviet Union's motives, capabilities, and behavior. Third, there appeared to be enough information in terms of statements while they served in the Reagan administration in order for us to usefully study their images and policy preferences. Thus, there are convincing practical and theoretical reasons for the selection of these five individuals.

In terms of policy debates, we first need to look at disagreements about the overall utility of arms control and negotiations with the Soviet Union. This will allow us to place more specific policy debates within the broader framework of the decision makers' general arms control orientations. In terms of concrete policy debates, we will examine the four issues that dominated arms control discussions during the Reagan years. Two of these were legacies from the Carter administration—the scheduled deployment of new intermediate range nuclear missiles (INF) in Europe and negotiations dictated by the 1979 "dual track" decision, and the future of the SALT II agreement. The two other issues were products of the Reagan administration: the Strategic Arms Reduction Talks (START) and the Strategic Defense Initiative (SDI), particularly the latter's relationship to the former. There were disagreements within the Reagan administration on all of these issues. We want to see whether and how these divisions reflected different images of the Soviet Union.

## Organization of the Study

This study is divided into three sections. The first deals with questions of theory and method: How do we conceptualize national and enemy images? What insights can we gather from existing theory about the relationship between images and policy preferences? How do we go about operationalizing images and determining the decision makers' beliefs about the Soviet Union? How do we know if these images were important in shaping policy preferences? The second section is devoted to presenting my research on the images. The third section examines the debates within the administration on the five arms control issues and, in each case, attempts to determine whether and how the decision makers' images of the Soviet Union influenced their orientation toward arms control, in general, and their policy choices on specific issues. Finally, the study ends with a conclusion and summary that draw the empirical and theoretical material together to answer the key question: What do we know about the relationship between images and policy preferences that we did not know before?

# Part 1
# Theory and Method

CHAPTER 2

# Conceptualizing National and Enemy Images

If we paused for a moment to consider how our behavior in the course of a given day was shaped by the images we hold of various features of our environment, we would realize that it is no exaggeration to say that "we live by organized images" (Pettman 1975, 205). As newborn children, our world must appear as a chaotic mass of stimuli without meaning. Young children must be restrained from crawling in front of cars because they have yet to acquire an image of cars as potentially dangerous objects. Eventually, children learn from their parents that cars can be harmful to one's health; if they choose not to believe this, experience will soon validate the lesson. As a result of socialization and experience, people slowly build up images that combine to form their psychological milieu, their subjective world. As Pettman observes, "out of infantile chaos we derive ordered constructs, and a sense of order itself, which we then reimpose upon events" (1975, 205). It is through this process of "reimposing" images that they exert an influence on our behavior.

Images can be conceptualized as mental pictures composed of our accumulated knowledge, that is, beliefs and attitudes regarding our surroundings. They are intellectual constructs that bring order to our world. We possess images of everything—inanimate objects, ourselves, other individuals, social groups, and even situations. For example, consider the expectations and feelings evoked by two very different situations: walking alone down a dark, inner-city street late at night, and strolling down Fifth Avenue during the busy Christmas shopping season. Our socialization tells us that the first situation is to be avoided at all costs, whereas many of us will go out of our way to place ourselves in the second situation. Even if we have never had anything bad happen to us on dark, inner-city streets, we have all learned that they are potentially dangerous. Because of the images that we cling to, many people would walk many blocks out of their way to travel on crowded, well-lit streets. It may or may not be safer to walk on Fifth Avenue, but this is immaterial because our actions are shaped by what we believe to be true (Boulding 1956, 5–6).

Since images are mental constructs developed through socialization and experience, they can be altered in response to new information. As Burgess

11

explains, "an image is a dynamic concept: that is, images are subject to redefinition as a result of the operation of interactive and feedback processes" (1968, 7). Our images of certain objects may be different tomorrow, and the changes in these images may produce important behavioral modifications. Thus, characterizing images as significant and fairly stable mental artifacts that help determine our actions does not imply that they are constant and immutable.

## National Images

Just as we all possess images of various features of our immediate environment, we also have images of our more remote international environment. Some individuals may have international images that are more fully developed or complex than others, but anyone who thinks about international affairs has international images. Drawing from Burgess, we can use the term *strategic image* to refer to "the organized representation of important features of the foreign policy environment as articulated by authoritative decision makers" (1968, 4). Individuals can have strategic images of the "nature" or "essence" of international relations in general, ranging from chaotic and conflictual to orderly and cooperative. Marxists and realists would certainly have different images of the dynamics of world politics. Individuals can also have images of international phenomena, such as John F. Kennedy's (and Barbara Tuchman's) image of war as a result of miscalculation and the loss of control. Kennedy's behavior during the Cuban missile crisis provides a concrete example of how a decision maker's image of war can affect his or her policy choices. Individuals also have images of other key actors in international politics, such as multinational corporations (beneficial or destructive) and international organizations (ineffectual or helpful). Perhaps most important, decision makers possess images of nations, including their own country, allies, and enemies.

While national images are only one component of an actor's belief system, they are generally regarded as central or "master" beliefs. Because of this consensus concerning the importance of national images, many scholars have attempted to define the concept, with very similar results. In their study of bargaining in international crises, Snyder and Diesing define a national image as "a set of beliefs about the nature and characteristic behavior of some bargainer" (1977, 286). According to Robert Jervis, "a decision maker's image of another actor can be defined as those beliefs about the other that affect his predictions of how the other will behave under various circumstances" (1970, 5). But perhaps the most basic and general definition is provided by William Scott: "conceived of within the framework of cognitive theories, an image of a nation (or of any other object) constitutes the totality of attributes that a person recognizes (or imagines) when he contemplates that nation" (1965, 72). These definitions are adequate as a point of departure, but greater differentiation and specificity are needed if we are to develop a research project around the concept of national images in general, or enemy images in particular.

According to Scott, there are three components of national images: the cognitive component is a person's subjective knowledge about a nation; the affective component is his or her like or dislike, approval or disapproval, or level of hostility toward a nation; and the behavioral component consists of a person's action tendencies toward a nation. Using this definition, Scott argues that "beliefs about nations . . . and notions of what ought to be done in relation to them are probably closely intertwined in the typical image structure . . . certain response repertoires appear to follow almost directly from the image content" (1965, 72, 83).

It should be obvious that this common conceptualization of national images is a little troublesome for our purposes. There are no great methodological or conceptual problems, but it is awkward to define images as containing an action component. To view behavioral tendencies as part of an individual's national image is tantamount to defining one of our variables (enemy images) as including the other (policy preferences). Remembering that definitions, per se, are neither correct nor incorrect but simply more or less useful, it seems to make more sense to work with a definition of national images that does not include an actor's behavioral predispositions. This reconceptualization of national images leaves us with only two components, the cognitive and evaluative. Of these two, this study is designed to tap the decision maker's cognitive image, his or her image content, not the intensity of dislike or hostility displayed toward the opponent. We are interested in the actor's beliefs about the enemy, not his or her emotional reaction toward it. And instead of viewing image content and behavioral tendencies as "intertwined within an image structure," as Scott does, they are defined as separate variables.

Just as the concept of national images has been broken down into distinct analytical categories, the cognitive component has also been divided in order to provide a scheme for systematic investigation. Recall that we defined an image as the "totality of attributes" an observer thinks of when contemplating an object. The number of possible attributes that constitute a "totality" is large indeed. But for foreign policy research we are interested in those attributes that can be expected to be significant for the formulation and evaluation of foreign policy options. The secretary of state might think of "good literature" and "bad food" when thinking about country X, but it would take a real stretch of the imagination to consider these attitudes relevant for foreign policy.

What are the important facets of the national image for a foreign policy decision maker? Most of the scholars who have studied national images have selected essentially the same image components, with minor variations for particular research questions. Snyder and Diesing identify six key components: ultimate aims, specific aims, the opponent's preference function, unity of the government, bargaining style, and probable strategy (1977, 308). Ole Holsti argues that the cognitive portion of the image involves "beliefs about the goals, strategies, tactics, sources of motivation, [and] approaches to political calculation" (1977b, 61). And Richard Cottam singles out motivation, capability, decisional style, locus of decision making, and the interaction of domestic forces (1977, 64). Within each of these components, different researchers define categories quite differently, but there seems to be general agreement about what is important.

Drawing upon the work of Snyder and Diesing, Holsti, and Cottam, I suggest that it is useful to think in terms of a series of questions one would ask a person in order to determine his or her image of a nation (in this study, these questions will be "asked" and "answered" only indirectly through an examination of public statements). First, what are the opponent's goals and objectives in foreign affairs? What is its foreign policy designed to achieve? Second, why does the opponent pursue these goals? What motivates it? Third, how will the opponent respond to one's own nation's policies? Fourth, what are the opponent's capabilities? How powerful is it? Fifth, how does the opponent arrive at decisions? Sixth, how does the opponent view one's own nation? Answers to these questions should provide a reasonably complete picture of someone's enemy image.

## Delineating Image Content

The process of delineating the content of an individual's image of a nation begins with posing the questions listed previously and developing categories that correspond to potential answers. What we then have are typologies of national objectives, motivation, capabilities, and so forth, that can be used to classify and compare decision makers' perceptions. Scholars have been doing this for a long time. For example, the international relations literature is replete with attempts to develop typologies of states according to their foreign policy goals and objectives. Perhaps the most basic and commonly employed typology is Hans Morgenthau's distinction between imperialist and status quo states (1967, 36–68). While this particular distinction strikes me as too restrictive, it is useful to develop such schemes because they facilitate systematic investigation and comparisons. The problem with efforts to construct typologies is that there is no logical limit to the number of categories they can contain; while the simple imperialist/status quo dichotomy seems excessively crude, organized study is not aided by an endless proliferation of classifications. For a typology to be usefully employed it must be manageable, reasonably inclusive, analytically significant, and empirically valid. That is, it should (1) allow for the classification of most individuals, (2) revolve around theoretically important distinctions, and (3) conform to the way in which most people really think about the issues involved (this last criterion is particularly important for typologies of perceptions).

## Intentions, Goals, and Objectives

If we asked decision makers to identify the most important thing one can know about an opponent's foreign policy, its ultimate objectives would probably be at the top of the desired knowledge list. It is often the case that debates among decision makers about how to respond to an adversary's moves revolve, consciously or not, around disagreements about the reasons why these moves were taken in the first place. Thus, reconstructing an individual's image of an opponent should begin with attempts to determine his or her perceptions of its ultimate objectives. The typology of foreign policy goals used in this study is a composite of those employed by Morgenthau (1967), Cottam (1977), Snyder and Diesing (1977) and Holsti (1977b). Each category in the typology is designed to capture a significant perspective of the "directional thrust" of Soviet foreign policy that can be found in the statements of public officials as well as scholarly treatments of Soviet policy.

If we think in terms of a spectrum of foreign policy aims, it is possible to conceive of an extreme where a nation seeks the unlimited expansion of its influence, the destruction of rival power centers, and the achievement of a hegemonial international position. The perception that an opponent desires unlimited expansion is often accompanied by the belief that it is following a coherent master plan in "a conspiratorial quest to conquer the world" (Pranger 1979, 8). In the case of the Soviet Union, this plan is often seen as including not only direct military expansion but also an attempt to achieve influence by fostering revolutions abroad. But it is not the means of expansion that leads to the classification of a nation as *unlimitedly expansionist* or *destructionist*, rather its ultimate objectives lead to such a classification. The demands and actions of nations perceived in this manner are viewed as illegitimate and unreasonable because they are not motivated by defensive considerations or justifiable fears. The possible impact of a decision maker's perception of an opponent as unlimitedly expansionist is fairly obvious: it is difficult to find areas of common interest and possible compromise with an enemy perceived as relentless in its expansion. How can one reach agreements with an enemy bent on one's destruction? The perception that the enemy is unlimitedly expansionist makes it unlikely that a "limited adversarial" relationship can be established (Larson 1985, 331).

Moving along our foreign policy aims spectrum, it is possible to imagine a nation whose goals, while still expansionist, are substantially more modest than those of a destructionist state. The objectives of what we might label a *revisionist* or *limitedly expansionist* state involve the extension of influence, but not a radical transformation of the existing power distribution or the elimination of major rival power centers. A revisionist state seeks to improve its position vis-à-vis other states but does not aim toward the achievement of a hegemonial position; it desires greater influence, not world domination. A state whose goals are seen as revisionist is often viewed as taking advantage of opportunities for expansion as they arise, not relentlessly following some blueprint for world conquest (Jervis 1976, 61). The objectives of a limitedly expansionist state may even be seen as "legitimate" and "reasonable" in the sense that it is "normal" for states to seek greater influence in an anarchic environment.

While the differences between revisionist and destructionist states may seem only a matter of degree, they are potentially crucial in determining how to deal with an opponent. A limited adversarial relationship is possible with a nation that is not thought to be pursuing one's own destruction; there will probably be more perceived areas of common interests with an opponent who accepts one's existence. An example of how a shift of perceptions regarding the enemy's goals can influence an individual's policy proposals can be seen in the case of Henry Kissinger. His belief that the Soviets had abandoned their revolutionary goals in the wake of the Cuban missile crisis led him to develop the rationale for a policy of détente (Stoessinger 1976, 80–81). And it is no coincidence that many of the harshest critics of détente were those who did not share Kissinger's perception of altered Soviet objectives.

Moving still further along our aims spectrum, we can identify a more conservative orientation that can be described as *status quo* or *defensive*. A nation's foreign policy can be classified as status quo if it "envinces a deep concern that conflicts be settled without violence, seeks to do no more than maintain the relative influence it already exerts in world affairs, and makes no moves to undermine the prevailing actor system" (Cottam 1977, 99). A status quo power is concerned with defending its present international position. This perspective is probably exemplified by George Kennan, who argues that the Soviet Union has changed radically since the days of Stalin and is now ruled by a group of conservative men beset by internal problems and already over-extended in the international arena (Kennan 1977). The perception of one's adversary as essentially status quo does not entail a belief that the status quo is morally just, only that the opponent is "motivated by preservation rather than by aggrandizement" (Holsti 1977b, 95). One can think of many ways in which decision makers who see a status quo opponent might differ in their policy proposals from those who see an expansionist opponent. Robert Jervis provides one example by noting that "if the adversary is mainly seeking security, increased arms may give it confidence to be reasonable . . . . The USSR is [according to this perspective] more tractable when it has enough strength to feel secure" (1976, 80). Finally, one can imagine a foreign policy that aims toward neither expansion nor preservation but rather accepts international trends and developments that result in a decrease in its influence. Such a foreign policy can be labeled *acquiescent* (Cottam 1977, 100). While it is unlikely that such an orientation would be associated with an enemy, it is not inconceivable. For example, it might be argued that internal and external challenges to the enemy's regime are so great that it has no option but to adopt a policy of accommodation and acquiescence. This is an image of an opponent in decline, unable to expand or even defend its position. In response, it might be proposed that the opponent no longer be viewed as an enemy or that new pressures should be applied so that the adversary can be disposed of once and for all or so that gains can be made at its expense.

Since this study focuses on strategic arms policy, it is necessary to construct a separate typology of the opponent's objectives in this specific policy area. The key distinction is whether the Soviets are pursuing *superiority* or are willing to settle for *parity* in nuclear capabilities. Superiority is defined as the ability to launch a disarming first strike. There are a number of possible ramifications of differing perceptions of this on arms control policy. We would expect, for example, a decision maker who believes that the Soviets are attempting to achieve nuclear superiority to be skeptical about the wisdom of reaching arms limitation or reduction agreements. After all, it will be argued, if the Soviets want to achieve superiority and have agreed to sign an agreement, they must think the treaty advances this goal. This being the case, what could the United States possibly gain? This does not mean that the decision maker would never favor an agreement (he or she may be convinced that the Soviets are mistaken in their belief that the treaty serves their interests), only that he or she will be more skeptical than someone who thinks the Soviets have accepted parity.

## Motivations and Sources of Goals and Objectives

In examining a decision maker's image of the opponent, it is important to consider not only his or her perceptions of its objectives, but also his or her beliefs about *why* the enemy pursues these goals. If the adversary desires a complete transformation of the international system, why does it want this? To borrow Kennan's famous phrase, what are the sources of the enemy's conduct? When we are discussing why an actor behaves in a certain way, we are dealing with his or her motivation. Richard Cottam, who provides the best treatment of this subject, defines foreign policy motivation as "that compound of factors which predispose a government and people to move in a decisional

direction in foreign affairs" (1977, 31). The expression "motivational compound" is used to emphasize that all but the most simplistic of images will
contain a number of factors that are seen as shaping the opponent's behavior.

The decision maker's perception of the enemy's motivational compound
is potentially significant in at least two respects. First, if an individual perceives the opponent's motivational compound as composed of factors that are
relatively enduring, he or she is unlikely to hold out much hope of any
dramatic change in its foreign policy in the near future. Someone who views
transitory factors as playing a more significant role is going to see more
opportunities for change. Second, the perception of motivating forces will
also influence a decision maker's confidence in the ability of external forces
(such as his or her own country's policies) to modify the opponent's goals. If
an individual traces the opponent's behavior to dispositional forces (i.e.,
inherent in the nature of the enemy's regime or society), he or she will
probably be unlikely to propose and support policies designed to accommodate the adversary. Jervis explains that "if the other's hostility is seen as rooted
in autonomous drives, there is no reason to examine one's own policies to see
if they may be self-defeating. There is no need to make special efforts to
demonstrate your willingness to reach settlements" (1976, 351).

It is probably best to begin surveying the possible perceived sources of
motivation by employing the distinction between dispositional and situational
forces. Perhaps the most frequently cited dispositional source of Soviet foreign policy is *ideology*. According to this view, Soviet behavior is doctrinally
inspired by the writings of Marx, Lenin, and Stalin. This ideology supposedly
contains an imperative for expansion and world revolution that guides Soviet
foreign policy. The quintessential expression of this is probably John Foster
Dulles's contention that we could learn all we needed to know about Soviet
foreign policy simply by reading Stalin's *Problems of Leninism*: "this work of
Stalin's has become to the Communist Party what Hitler's *Mein Kampf* was to
the Nazi Party. It spells out the creed and purposes of Soviet Communism and
its plans and methods for achieving world domination" (in Hoopes 1973, 64).
A somewhat related perspective sees Soviet policy as flowing logically from
the "needs" of a totalitarian/authoritarian regime. Such regimes, for one
reason or another (e.g., the need to divert attention from internal repression),
are by their very nature expansionist. What we might label the *logic of
totalitarianism* perspective was succinctly expressed by Richard Nixon: "the
Soviet Union is an inherently aggressive power because its totalitarian system
cannot survive without expansion" (in Hoffmann 1988, 36). According to the
logic of totalitarianism perspective, it is not communism per se that prompts
expansion, but rather the totalitarian nature of contemporary communist
states. Someone like Nixon might argue that communist states are necessarily
totalitarian because of certain tenets of Marxism-Leninism, but a scheme of

foreign policy motivation should not be based on this assumption: we want to allow for the classification of individuals who do not view communist ideology and totalitarianism as necessarily intertwined.

In addition to the features of the regime, we can cite *culture, geography,* and *history* as important dispositional motivating forces. The most familiar attempt to provide a cultural explanation for an enemy's foreign policy is Nazi Germany, where many believed that German culture was intrinsically chauvinistic, aggressive, and militaristic. With regard to geography, one need not accept a crude form of geopolitical determinism to see it as important in the explanation of a nation's foreign policy: geography may only be a contributing or facilitating factor. Christer Jonsson, for example, suggests that the "land-locked" Soviet Union and insular, "seaward-looking" United States may be prone to expansionism partly because of their geographical positions (1984, 35). When we cite history as an important source of a nation's behavior we can mean anything from the belief that its foreign policy is determined in a metaphysical sense by immutable historical laws to the notion that the "lessons of history" weigh heavily on decision makers' minds (Jonsson 1984, 32). Generally, a reference to the historical determinants of foreign policy implies that the nation is "pursuing goals that have traditionally been associated with that nation, irrespective of the regime, leadership, or specific circumstances" (Holsti 1977b, 98). The belief that Soviet leaders continue the traditional quest for a warm water port is a good example of this mode of analysis.

As was the case with regime type and ideology, it is possible that cultural, geographical, and historical forces might be so tightly enmeshed in an individual's image structure that it may be impossible to identify them separately. For example, it might be argued that the Soviet Union's geographical position has made it vulnerable to invasions, which in turn have created a suspicious and paranoid culture that continues to shape Soviet foreign policy. All three forces are seen as reinforcing each other according to this view, and it is difficult to say which is most important.

Another internal determinant of a nation's foreign policy is the demands and pressures of powerful segments of that society that have *vested interests* in pursuing certain goals. It is possible to identify many groups that could be influential, such as foreign affairs bureaucracies, the military, powerful socioeconomic interests, and so on. We are all familiar with attempts to explain U.S. foreign policy by referring to the clout of the military-industrial complex, the national security bureaucracy, or some "power elite." It is possible to locate analogous interests within Soviet society. The pressures of groups such as the military might be perceived as particularly important in guiding the development and procurement of strategic weapons systems.

A final internal source of motivation involves the human dimension of foreign policy. According to this perspective, the other nation's behavior is largely a function of the motives, aspirations, needs, or desires of a powerful leader or group of leaders. While, strictly speaking, *leadership characteristics* are dispositional factors, they differ from those discussed previously in that they are usually not as enduring: countries change their leaders more often than they change their culture, political system, or ideology. Given this study's focus on the Reagan administration, this might be a key perceptual variable in view of the changes in Soviet leadership during the 1980s.

Under the general rubric of external or situational sources of motivation we can distinguish between what Holsti calls *power politics* and *external pressures* (1977b, 98–99). The power politics perspective, as the appellation suggests, is most closely associated with traditional, realist explanations of state behavior. According to this point of view, one's opponent is motivated by the same systemic imperatives and incentives that motivate every nation in an anarchic, competitive, and inherently insecure international environment. The desire to expand influence in order to enhance one's security is the "natural" objective of all states, regardless of regime type, ideology, or culture. An external pressures (or action-reaction) explanation differs in that the adversary's behavior is seen as a response to specific threats and actions of other states. This is the perspective that informs most of the revisionist accounts of Soviet behavior in the cold war. As Pranger explains, "in this view, the Soviet Union's expansion and consolidation of its socialist revolution is an understandable response to the expansion by the United States" (1979, 7). For both of these variants on the situational sources of motivation, the emphasis is on the reactive (or preemptive) nature of the opponent's foreign policy, whereas dispositional explanations tend to stress its initiatory character.

## Capabilities

As Ralph White notes, fear of another actor is the result of a perception that he or she has hostile intentions toward you as well as the capability to inflict harm. Hostility without power or vice versa is not a cause for concern because "if either is zero, the product is zero" (White 1984, 336). The relationship between intentions and capabilities is also pointed out by Scott: "the perception of a nation as strong or weak can probably be expected to interact with the judgement of its intentions (benevolent or malevolent) in determining the action component of the image" (1965, 74). Thus, the perception of capabilities forms one-third of what we might consider the hard core of an individual's enemy image: intentions, motivation, and capabilities.

Fortunately, it is easier to construct categories for perceptions of capabilities than was the case for objectives and motivation. We are concerned primarily with how decision makers view the capabilities of their opponent vis-à-vis their own country; that is, we are interested in perceptions of relative military capabilities. The logical categories to employ for this are *superiority*, *parity*, or *inferiority*: the opponent is either stronger, just as strong, or weaker than one's own country. Certainly there can be gradations with the first and last classifications, but measuring such subtle differences in perceptions strikes me as an extremely difficult and tenuous enterprise. The simple trichotomy is a good place to start.

When dealing with perceptions of relative military capabilities, it is not only the general evaluation that is significant, but also perceptions about specific components of military power. Of course it would be possible to identify a host of areas that are potentially important in shaping a decision maker's preferences in strategic policy, such as conventional hardware, personnel, the quality of weapons, or theater nuclear forces. For example, much of the debate surrounding the ratification of the INF treaty and future START agreements focuses on the need to pursue parallel reductions (asymmetrical) in conventional forces because the Soviets were thought to enjoy an advantage. Many would oppose deep reductions in strategic weapons in the face of continued conventional imbalances. Thus, it may be important to gauge a decision maker's perception of relative military capabilities in both the *nuclear* and *conventional* spheres.

## Decision Processes

In addition to the core image components of intentions, motivation, and capabilities, there are a number of other potentially significant beliefs for shaping an individual's policy choices. The policymaker's perception of how the opponent arrives at its policies or decisions is one such belief. There are at least three decision processes that might be perceived (corresponding to Graham Allison's models of foreign policy decision making) (Allison 1971; Holsti 1977b, 100–101). First, the *rational actor* perspective provides a portrait of the opponent as a unitary, monolithic actor whose decisions are carefully considered in terms of whether they advance its foreign policy goals. Second, a *bureaucratic politics* model sees decisions as the result of competition and compromise among the influential segments of the political elite, particularly governmental organizations, pursuing their own interests in the decision process. Third, an *organizational process* approach views behavior as the result of bureaucracies involved in the formulation and implementation of policy following standard operating procedures (SOPs).

In his study of images of Soviet arms control compliance, Gary Guertner (1988) provides an excellent example of how perceptions of decision-making style can influence preferences in the area of strategic arms policy. A policymaker who does not perceive the importance of bureaucratic processes and SOPs will probably see violations of past treaties as deliberate attempts to achieve unwarranted advantages: a rational actor perspective implies that all actions are taken in order to help achieve some national objective. On the other hand, someone who realizes that political leaders cannot control all the actions of governmental organizations may not be as quick to charge deliberate cheating; violations may be the result of bureaucratic inertia and SOPs that are contrary to the desires of political leaders. This variation in the perception of deliberate cheating, which derives from different views of the opponent's decision processes, can be expected to influence the decision maker's faith in future agreements.

If an individual views another nation as hostile and also believes that its actions are the result of a unified, rational decision process, then potentially threatening behavior will be seen as purposely threatening. Thus, a decision maker's perception of the Soviet Union's decision process may be crucial to understanding his or her evaluation of the threat posed by its strategic arsenal; and the perception of the level of threat can shape an individual's policy choices on a wide range of issues, from the necessity for an arms buildup to the wisdom of arms control negotiations to the stance that should be adopted once talks commence.

## Strategy and Tactics

Bargaining, negotiations, and deterrence are all international processes that have, at their core, expectations on the part of the actors concerning how other actors will behave in response to various policies. If actor A wants to achieve an objective, and if the attainment of the desired goal is dependent on the behavior of B, then A's policy choices must revolve around his or her perceptions of B's strategies. Thus, a key component of a decision maker's enemy image is his or her perceptions of how the opponent will respond to his or her own nation's policies. Generically speaking, the crucial expectations are the enemy's anticipated reactions to policies of firmness and accommodation.

There are two primary expectations about the opponent's response to policies of firmness: the enemy will *back down* or it will *adopt its own hard-line* policies (i.e., reciprocate; see Holsti 1977b, 100–101). Let me illustrate the importance of these expectations by imagining a debate over the wisdom of an arms buildup to meet the threat posed by the opponent's recent buildup. There will probably be one group of policymakers arguing that a buildup is the only way to induce the enemy to abandon its policies and adopt a more conciliatory approach to arms negotiations: the demonstration of firmness will lead the opponent to back down. Another group will probably counter that a buildup will be seen as threatening, and therefore, the adversary will only accelerate its buildup in response. As a result of their expectations, the first group would likely favor a buildup and the second would oppose it. Expectations about the opponent's response to policies of accommodation are analogous to those discussed previously. Some individuals may anticipate that the adversary will *reciprocate moderation*. Others, of course, will argue that the enemy will interpret conciliatory policies as a sign of weakness and *exploit the situation* for its own advantage. Those who expect reciprocity will probably see conciliatory policies as the only way to ease tensions between the two countries, whereas individuals who expect the enemy to take advantage of such policies would contend that they will worsen the conflict by encouraging the opponent to push harder (notice that these different perspectives are at the center of the debate between spiral and deterrence theorists).

Another key perception in any adversarial relationship involves the actor's beliefs about the trustworthiness of its opponent. While it is not logically necessary that opponents are seen as untrustworthy, the insecurity inherent in an anarchic state system tends to instill a sense of suspicion about the statements and actions of others. While the general perception of the enemy's trustworthiness can be expected to influence all facets of a decision maker's policy preferences, in the area of strategic arms policy the focus is on whether the Soviets can be trusted to abide by the terms of treaties. It is possible to distinguish at least three different viewpoints of treaty compliance. According to the first school of thought, the Soviets have abided and will continue to *abide by* the terms of arms *agreements*. The second perspective portrays the Soviet Union as abiding by the letter of treaties (*technical obedience*) but consistently taking advantage of loopholes and ambiguities to pursue policies contrary to the spirit of the agreements. Finally, others argue that "the Soviets cannot be trusted, have *cheated* in the past, and plan to do so in the future. Arms control is a one-way street [that lulls] Americans into a false sense of security" (Guertner 1988, 36).

## The Metaperspective

Thus far we have been dealing with perceptions of various features of the opponent's motives, intentions, and behavior; that is, what the enemy is, what it does, and why it does what it does. The so-called metaperspective involves a decision maker's perception of what his or her opponent *thinks*. While it is sometimes awkward to discuss "perceptions of perceptions," these are potentially key variables in conflicting relations. The most important part of the metaperspective is the decision maker's perception of how his or her opponent sees his or her country.

Let us use the following scenario to demonstrate how differences among decision makers' metaperspectives might lead to debates over policy. Imagine that there are two U.S. political leaders, US#1 and US#2, both of whom believe that U.S. policies are purely defensive. The two differ, however, in terms of how they think the Soviets view U.S. policy. US#1 thinks that the Soviets also see U.S. policy as defensive, whereas US#2 believes that the Soviets see the United States as hostile and threatening. Suppose that, within this perceptual environment, the Soviets embark upon an arms buildup, which they claim is necessary to counter the U.S. threat. US#1 will see the Soviet Union's justification as propaganda designed to excuse its own provocative policies. US#2, while not happy with the Soviet buildup, will probably see it as the result of an exaggerated Soviet fear of the United States. For US#1, the Soviet buildup is an immediate cause for concern and must be dealt with firmly, whereas US#2 will probably be less alarmed and might warn against actions that will increase Soviet paranoia. Different perceptions of Soviet perceptions lead to conflicting interpretations of Soviet actions, and these interpretations influence a decision maker's choices of policy responses. Thus, in examining a decision maker's image of the enemy, it is important to know whether he or she thinks the opponent sees his or her nation as expansionist and threatening or defensive and harmless.

In addition to the opponent's perceptions of one's nation, we might also want to consider a decision maker's beliefs about the enemy's view of certain international phenomena—for example, the inevitability of war or conflict. Given this study's emphasis on strategic arms policy, I want to focus on the decision maker's perceptions of the opponent's views of the inevitability and "winnability" of nuclear war. Again, it is possible to imagine a host of policy disagreements stemming from such perceptions. Let us revive the hypothetical decision makers US#1 and US#2. Assume that US#1 shares Richard Pipes's belief (1982) that the Soviets think they can "fight, win, survive, and recover" from a nuclear war, whereas US#2 sees the Soviets as accepting the viability and desirability of mutual deterrence and adhering to the view that such a war would be unwinnable. We can probably expect US#1 to paint a more ominous picture of Soviet missiles that are, potentially, first-strike weapons than would US#2. And because US#1 does not believe that the Soviets accept mutual deterrence, he or she will probably see a greater likelihood of nuclear war. Given these divergent perceptions, we can probably expect US#1 to see a greater need for some form of strategic defense than US#2.

## Conclusion

An individual's enemy image is, in reality, a collection of perceptions about the opponent. There is no such thing as *the* enemy image, but rather a range of possible images. How many different images are there? If we confined ourselves to the perceptual options discussed in this chapter and attempted to calculate the number of potential combinations, we would end up with more than a hundred. Luckily, the situation is not as chaotic as this might seem: researchers have observed a tendency for certain core perceptions to accompany others, for example, the belief that the opponent is ideologically motivated often coincides with the perception of unlimited expansionist goals. And it is difficult to imagine how other combinations could occur, for example, an ideologically motivated, unlimitedly expansionist state that will reciprocate accommodative policies. (Table 2.1. summarizes those beliefs that tend to appear together in hard and moderate enemy images.) Exactly why certain perceptions tend to coincide is a matter of debate, but some scholars have postulated that personality characteristics or cognitive styles might play a role in shaping an individual's general outlook and, therefore, his or her images of specific actors (see Rokeach 1960).

Recognizing the empirical tendency for certain perceptions to appear in groups, many scholars have attempted to devise overall enemy image types reflecting these perceptual constellations (from which the information in table 2.1 is drawn). Social psychologists, however, are quick to point out that, because the human mind does not operate according to the rules of formal logic, contradictory and inconsistent beliefs can coexist within an image structure. As a result, no constructive purpose is served by creating our own

**TABLE 2.1.　Enemy Images**

|  | Hard-line Images | Moderate/Soft Images |
|---|---|---|
| Goals/objectives | Unlimited expansion | Limited expansion/status quo |
| Policy motivation | Ideology | Defense/security (paranoia) |
|  | Logic of totalitarianism | External pressures/threats |
|  | Vested interests (military) | Power politics |
|  |  | Vested interests |
|  |  | Ideology |
|  |  | Leadership traits |
| Strategy/tactics | Back down only to firmness | Reciprocate firmness |
|  | Exploit restraint | Reciprocate restraint |
|  | Untrustworthy | Trustworthy (qualified) |
|  | Violates agreements/exploits loopholes | Abides by agreements |
| Decision style | Rational/unified actor | Pluralistic/bureaucratic |
| Metaperspective | "Knows" U.S. is not a threat | Sees possible U.S. threat |
|  | Rejects mutual deterrence | Accepts mutual deterrence |
|  | Sees nuclear war as winnable | Sees nuclear war as unwinnable |

*Sources*: Cottam 1977, 31–53; Dallin and Lapidus 1987, 199–202; Herrmann 1985; Jervis 1976, 58–84; Pranger 1979; Snyder and Diesing 1977, 202.

scheme of image types at this point. But the ideal types developed by others suggest the sort of images we might look for among our subjects.

Once we have determined the key components of a national image, we must examine how and why this image exerts an influence on the decision maker's policy preferences. This chapter accomplished the first task, the next chapter addresses the second.

CHAPTER 3

# Theory

Any study of the role of beliefs and attitudes in decision making benefits from the work of cognitive or social psychologists, who describe their discipline broadly as the study of individual behavior in social contexts (Secord and Blackman 1964, 1). Their work is crucial to understanding the significance of images because they "'black box' the mind and scrutinize the regularities in human performance which the individual feeds out as various social stimuli are fed in" (Pettman 1975, 200). We are primarily interested in those theories that provide insights into the way people perceive, analyze, and utilize information about their environment; that is, cognitive theories that fall under the general rubric of the "information-processing paradigm" (Jonsson 1982, 3). Since this study focuses on the relationship between beliefs and behavioral predispositions, theories that highlight the role and significance of attitudes in the cognitive process are most relevant.

The interdisciplinary traffic that has characterized political science during the past few decades has been a useful development, but not one free of dangers. The transfer of knowledge from one discipline to another would be fairly unproblematic if there were an established body of theory and research that had been experimentally verified and widely accepted within the parent discipline. Unfortunately, this is not the case in cognitive psychology. Theoretical controversies, competing explanations, and empirical confusion are the norm within the field; basic concepts are inadequately defined, fundamental insights are disputed, and test results are routinely questioned. There is no evidence that much has changed since John Steinbruner characterized cognitive psychology as "an intensely researched, but loosely ordered field, rich in promising leads, unintegrated experimental results, partial theories, and a great many unresolved arguments" (1974, 91).

In this study, no attempt is made to lift theories out of cognitive psychology and apply them rigidly to the case in question. Nor is any effort made to lay out and test contending theories. Even within the confines of carefully controlled behavior labs, using relatively simple scenarios and manipulating key variables, cognitive psychologists have found it difficult to test their theories. It would be unrealistic and presumptuous to claim to do so here. Instead, I want to draw upon a range of theories and approaches, contending and complimentary, in order to gather insights into the relationship between an individual's beliefs about another country and his or her policy preferences. That is, I plan to follow some of the "promising leads" and use some of the "partial theories" Steinbruner speaks of to explore the role of national images in foreign policy decision making.

### Images as Independent Variables

Even those who have not explicitly employed cognitive theories of attitude change and stability have often been struck by the tendency for people to sustain their beliefs in the face of contradictory evidence. In her study of the use of information and intelligence by U.S. decision makers prior to the Japanese attack on Pearl Harbor, Roberta Wohlstetter concludes that "apparently human beings have a stubborn attachment to old beliefs and an equally stubborn resistance to new material that will upset them" (1962, 393). It is because attitudes and beliefs persist over time that they are potentially important for understanding an individual's behavior. If beliefs were constantly changing in response to new information, they would simply be reflections of environmental stimuli and, therefore, not significant explanatory variables. It is through an understanding of the mechanisms of attitude maintenance that we can see how an individual's beliefs about another nation can exert some systematic influence on his or her policy preferences.

The most fully developed attitude theories that are helpful in accounting for attitude stability are those classified as "balance" theories, alternatively labeled "dissonance," "congruity," "consistency," and "homeostatic" theories. According to Tannenbaum and Gengel, "generally, these [balance] models contend that the introduction of inconsistency in a set of cognitive relationships sets up mechanisms which operate, directly or indirectly, to restore consistency" (1986, 303). Theoretical debates tend to revolve around exactly *why* and *how* this occurs, but all balance theorists agree that it happens.

The most influential balance theory is probably Leon Festinger's theory of cognitive dissonance. Festinger begins by noting that an individual's belief system is composed of cognitive elements, which he defines as "any knowledge, opinion, or belief about the environment, about one's self, or about one's behavior" (1957, 3). These cognitive elements are related to each other in one of three ways: they are either consonant, dissonant, or irrelevant. Two elements are "in a dissonant relation if, considering the two alone, the obverse of one element would follow from the other . . . [that is,] X and Y are dissonant if not X would follow from Y" (13). The presence of dissonance between two or more elements produces "psychological discomfort" that "will motivate the person to try to reduce dissonance and achieve consonance" (3).

According to Festinger, "cognitive dissonance can be seen as an antecedent condition which leads to activity oriented toward dissonance reduction, just as hunger leads to activity toward hunger reduction" (3).

Balance theorists such as Festinger argue that individuals confronted with information that contradicts their beliefs will experience discomfort because people prefer their cognitions to "make sense" or "fit" (Pettman 1975, 209). Faced with such conflicts of cognitions, the individual is driven to resolve them in some way. At first blush the remedy would appear obvious: if presented with evidence that smoking is dangerous, for example, the individual should change his or her beliefs about the wisdom of smoking; if a cruel person behaves with compassion, one should change one's image of that person. But we all know that people do not always react like this: images, attitudes, and opinions often persist despite apparently disconfirming evidence. This is possible because the alteration of preexisting beliefs is the only way to restore cognitive balance.

Let me briefly illustrate some of the mechanisms that can be employed to deal with cognitively threatening information. Assume that person X has a best friend, Y, who he or she thinks is honest and trustworthy. Suppose further that X is told by a third friend that Y was seen stealing from the store where the three work. In this case, X's knowledge of Y's actions is inconsistent with his or her image of Y. As a result, X experiences psychological discomfort that he or she must resolve. One way to resolve the conflict is for X to revise his or her image of Y. But this is not the only, or even the most likely, option. For example, X could also reject the information by arguing that his or her informant must be mistaken or lying. Even if this is not possible, X could preserve his or her image by convincing himself or herself that extenuating circumstances must have "forced" Y to do something against his or her will. Some of the mental devices that people will employ to reduce or avoid dissonance may seem a bit "irrational," but balance theory "does not rest upon the assumption that man is a rational animal, but rather it suggests that man is a rational*izing* animal" (Aronson 1968, 6).

Thus far I have identified two key components of balance theories: first, it is argued that people find psychological inconsistencies intolerable and are motivated toward cognitive balance; and second, there are many ways to maintain and restore balance. The next question is obvious: Do people demonstrate a preference for certain modes of balance maintenance over others? Not all balance theorists address this issue per se, but "psychologists are generally agreed that the basic structure of attitudes, once established, is very resistant to change" (Steinbruner 1974, 102). That is, instead of adjusting beliefs and attitudes to fit new information, people display a bias toward manipulating information to fit their beliefs.

The issue of attitude stability is complex because some types of attitudes are more resistant to change than others. It is theorized that "central" or "core" beliefs will be more durable than peripheral beliefs. The centrality of a given belief is determined by its place within an individual's cognitive structure: if many other cognitive elements are dependent on a particular belief, it is assumed to be more central than those that are relatively independent. Core beliefs are more resistant to change because altering them would set off a cognitive chain-reaction resulting in a major restructuring of a person's belief system (see Jervis 1976, 297; Pilisuk 1968). It is assumed that people would rather not overhaul their belief systems very often. As Larson observes, "it is simpler and requires less mental effort to assume that one's fundamental beliefs are correct" (1985, 41).

These basic insights concerning the stability of beliefs and attitudes are important for this study because, as I pointed out in the last chapter, national images are collections of beliefs about the nature and characteristic behavior of other countries. I also noted that a decision maker's image of his or her country's primary adversary is a core element of his or her foreign policy belief system. Therefore, enemy images are prime candidates for cognitive variables that will exhibit substantial stability over time. This stability will be achieved through a variety of mechanisms involving the perception, interpretation, and recall of information. And the manner in which individuals deal with information will inevitably influence their behavioral predispositions. Understanding the impact of images requires a fuller appreciation of their role in the processing of information, and it is to this that I now turn.

## Images and Perception

Basic discussions of the role of images often begin by describing them as "lenses" or "filters" through which individuals receive information. Of course the primary purpose of filters is to keep out undesirable material. Within the framework of cognitive theories, "undesirable" elements are bits of information that contradict existing beliefs. An individual's first line of defense in the protection of his or her images is the exclusion of inconsistent information. The idea that individuals will avoid or censor belief-discrepant information has been a staple of balance theories since their inception. As Festinger predicts, "when dissonance is present . . . the person will actively avoid situations and information which would likely increase dissonance" (1957, 3).

There is no denying that the selective-exposure hypothesis has a certain commonsense appeal. Everyone can cite examples of biased perception. In our own work, for example, we have all probably been frustrated by students who enter lectures with preconceptions about their professor's political views and leave with their beliefs confirmed. If asked how they came to this conclusion, the students would be able to cite some material from class that substantiated their beliefs; but they probably "missed" the information that contradicted those beliefs. As a foreign policy example, we can point to the failure of U.S. policymakers to recognize evidence of a Sino-Soviet split in the late 1950s and early 1960s because the schism was inconsistent with their image of communism as a monolithic international movement. Accepting evidence of divisions within the Communist bloc would have required significant revisions of foreign policy belief systems; therefore, such information was not perceived. It is relatively easy to think of many cases that support Rapoport's observation that "without falsifying a single fact, entirely contradictory descriptions can and are given of persons, situations, social orders, etc., by selecting (often unconsciously) only features which support preconceived notions" (1960, 258).

There is more than one type of selective exposure. The examples of students screening out information about their professors and U.S. policymakers failing to recognize evidence of a Sino-Soviet split illustrate a passive form of censorship based on expectations. The students "expected" a certain type of professor and U.S. policymakers "expected" unity among communist nations and were therefore "on the lookout" for, and more sensitive to, information that supported these expectations. No conscious choice was made to ignore or reject the contradictory information; preexisting images simply predisposed them to notice certain clues over others. Again, we can look to Wohlstetter's Pearl Harbor study for an excellent case of passive selective exposure.

> What these examples illustrate is . . . the very human tendency to pay attention to the signals that support current expectations about enemy behavior. If no one is *listening for* signals of an attack . . . then it is very difficult for the signals to be *heard*. (1962, 392, italics added)

Individuals can also consciously choose to expose themselves to belief-supporting information while avoiding belief-discrepant information. In the realm of foreign policy, an image of an untrustworthy opponent who consistently violates treaties may prompt a decision maker to engage in a more extensive and careful search for evidence of current violations than would an image of an enemy who abides by agreements. Thus, on an anecdotal level at least, it does seem as though people will search for information that substantiates their views, not evidence that subverts them. There are, however, limits to an individual's ability to filter out uncomfortable information. Even in cases where the decision maker is forced to examine inconsistent information, he or she can still screen it out by rejecting it as false (Boulding 1956, 8–9). One common way to dismiss inconsistent information is to question the credibility of the source: the person must have some incentive to distort the information. Since it is almost always possible to contrive some ulterior motive for the informant, belief-discrepant information is easily rejected as unreliable or purposely deceptive. Indeed, this form of selective exposure might be particularly important in adversarial relations, where the source of information is often the enemy itself.

It has been stressed that the selective-exposure hypothesis has strong "intuitive" and "anecdotal" appeal because the empirical evidence is mixed, to say the least. Social psychologists are divided on whether the prediction is confirmed by experimental evidence. Illustrating this lack of consensus, in a volume on consistency theories, one author concludes that "the current evidence concerning interest in supporting and discrepant information warrants the conclusion that people tend to seek out supporting information and avoid discrepant information" (Mills 1968, 775); but only eleven pages later, another researcher argues that "there is no empirical evidence indicating a general preference for supportive information over nonsupportive information, regardless of whether the test was conducted under neutral, high-dissonance, or low-confidence conditions" (Sears 1968, 786).

## Images and Interpretation

Although selective exposure is a potentially powerful image defense mechanism, decision makers are not always able to exercise complete control over the information to which they are exposed. Nor is it possible to dismiss inconsistent information in all cases. Once these methods of belief-defense have failed, individuals can resort to biased interpretations of information to protect their beliefs. This is possible because social stimuli involve actions taken by actors whose intentions can never be known or established beyond a shadow of a doubt. There is inevitably some element of uncertainty in social interactions, and it is always possible to offer more than one plausible interpretation of information. Most of us have probably witnessed this problem firsthand in debates where one side offers evidence it thinks is compelling support for its argument only to have the opposition "twist" the information to support its position. The problem is that people "know" more than they see because information is processed through a lens of accumulated attitudes, beliefs, and opinions that give it meaning. The same information processed through different lenses comes out with different meanings. The same actions are interpreted differently depending on the observer's preexisting beliefs. This bias is also reflected in the way people interpret the behavior of friends and enemies: if a friend does something nice for us, we assume that this reflects their kind nature; but if an enemy does that same thing, we wonder what they "have up their sleeve." We can identify similar tendencies in international politics. If an adversary follows policies that are in your country's interests, it is often assumed that they were a response to external pressures or a lack of capabilities; but if the opponent's policies are aggressive, they are assumed to reflect its natural tendencies, not any response to external threats. The reverse usually occurs when explaining one's own country's policies: conciliatory behavior is seen as a reflection of your nation's peaceful nature, whereas aggressive policies are "forced" by external challenges. Almost any action of one's own country or another country can be interpreted is such a way as to be consistent with the observer's image. The quintessential example of interpretational bias is, of course, John Foster Dulles, who "consistently reinterpreted both truculent and conciliatory messages from the Soviet Union so as to make them fit into an unchanging image of an aggressive, implacably hostile, and dynamic Russia" (Deutsch and Merritt 1965, 146).

As with selective exposure, biased interpretations can be traced largely to the expectations generated by images. On a personal level, we expect stingy people to be cheap, enemies to be unfriendly, and friends to be nice. If the behavior of these people is open to several plausible explanations and if one of these is compatible with our expectations, the supporting interpretation will be accepted. As Jervis explains, "if an actor expects a phenomenon to appear, he is likely to perceive ambiguous stimuli as being that phenomenon. When one is sure that an object will be present, it takes very little information, or information that bears little resemblance to the object, to convince one that one is seeing it" (1976, 153).

## Images and Memory

The final stage in the processing of information is memory and recall. Just as it was argued that an individual's beliefs influence his or her perception and interpretation of information, it is also hypothesized that people tend to remember belief-consistent information better than belief-discrepant information. The selective-memory hypothesis, like the selective-exposure hypothesis, has strong commonsense and theoretical appeal, but it has also produced confusing experimental findings. According to Zanna and Olson, "the results from studies testing the selective-learning hypothesis . . . can perhaps best be described as 'unambiguously inconclusive'. . . . attempts to demonstrate an effect of attitude on memory have resulted in inconsistent and contradictory findings" (1982, 77). Perhaps because it is so easy to gather anecdotal evidence for selective memory, there is still widespread support for the hypothesis among social psychologists. It does seem to be true that people find it easy to recall the bad things done by people they dislike, while they are less quick to remember bad things done by people they like. The uncomfortable information has not been forgotten, but it does not come immediately to mind.

But how do we reconcile the intuitive and theoretical attractiveness of the selective-memory hypothesis with the disappointing test results? The answer might be found in recent research that distinguishes between two different types of learning, "forced" and "incidental." An example of forced learning is university instruction: students are under pressure to learn and recall belief-discrepant information because of the fear of punishment in the form of poor exam grades. In the past, experiments were often conducted in settings where the subjects knew, or had good reason to suspect, that they would be tested. Selective memory does not operate under these conditions. In most real-world situations, there is no omnipresent pressure to remember belief-discrepant information. The latest experiments show that "the attitude-memory relation was supported only when task instructions did not force the subject to pay close attention to the content of the material per se" (Zanna and Olson 1982, 79). Since foreign policy decision makers operate under conditions that do not require them to retrieve belief-discrepant information, we can expect them to repress such information in favor of belief-consistent information.

### Images and Policy Preferences

Once we have accepted the idea that beliefs influence the way in which people process information, it does not take any great theoretical leap to conclude that these beliefs also influence behavioral predispositions. This jump is made simply by assuming that people decide how to act on the basis of the information, or "knowledge," available to them. But how exactly do national images influence policy preferences? In what sense do they "shape" and "guide" policy choices? The most satisfying attempt to address these questions is provided by Alexander George.

> The actor's operational code beliefs introduce two types of predispositions, not determinants, into his decision making: (a) diagnostic propensities, which extend or restrict the scope of search and evaluation and influence his diagnosis of the situation in certain directions; and (b) choice propensities, which lead him to favor certain types of action alternatives over others. (1979, 103)

It is easier to illustrate how images create these propensities if we view the individual's decision making process as a series of analytically distinct, though empirically intertwined, stages; the analysis of the situation, the formulation and evaluation of policy options, and the choice of policy.

### Analysis and Evaluation

The analysis stage corresponds roughly to what others have classified as the decision maker's "definition of the situation," in which he or she "seek[s] out a description of the problem and put[s] it into perspective" (Brady 1978, 175). Even at this early stage there can be significant disagreements among decision makers because of their selective attention to facts. Virtually all foreign policy situations are complex in the sense that there are many potentially important factors that deserve the policymaker's consideration. By focusing on certain aspects of complicated situations while ignoring others, actors can arrive at very different descriptions of what is happening. For example, suppose we are dealing with a decision maker's description of the balance of power between his or her country and an adversary. An individual who adheres to a very threatening image of the opponent might tend to focus on those measures of military strength in which the enemy enjoys a substantial advantage, while decision makers with more benign images may emphasize those areas where the opponent is at a disadvantage and, in doing so, arrive at a very different description of the military balance. Thus, looking at the same "facts," decision makers may arrive at different descriptions because of image-induced selective attention. Certainly these varying descriptions will lead to different policy recommendations.

The diagnostic propensities of images are likely to be most evident at the stage where decision makers put the situation "into perspective." It is at this point where appraisals are made concerning the level of threat posed by developments in adversarial relations. Because the situation itself rarely provides enough information to make such judgments, the decision maker must draw upon his or her knowledge of similar situations and the key actors involved. Perhaps the classic example of different evaluations based on incompatible enemy images is the debate surrounding the response to Hitler's rearmament program and territorial demands in the 1930s. On the one hand, there were those who urged the Western nations to stand firm because they viewed Hitler's actions as specific manifestations of more generally expansionist aims: conceding to Germany's demands and permitting rearmament would only lead to greater demands and future aggression. On the other hand, those who saw Hitler as pursuing limited and justifiable territorial revisions argued that the long-term danger of meeting these demands was minimal; in fact, the real danger lay in a frustrated and aggrieved Germany. The Soviet invasion of Afghanistan provides a more recent example. Knowledge of the invasion was not sufficient to evaluate the threat posed to U.S. interests. The invasion's significance was judged by placing it in a broader image of Soviet objectives. The Committee on the Present Danger was more alarmed than George Kennan, because its members viewed the invasion within the framework of a more menacing image of the Soviet Union than did Kennan.

Once the situation has been described and analyzed, the decision maker must make policy recommendations. Burgess notes that "because policymaking is future oriented, [recommended] courses of action are to a large extent determined by the policymaker's subjective calculations of future configurations and their relation to postulated goals" (1968, 7). The process of formulating policies and evaluating those advanced by others inevitably involves making predictions about the consequences of following alternative policies. Since the outcomes of foreign policy situations are rarely determined unilaterally, an integral part of the decision maker's "subjective calculation of future configurations" is his or her estimation of how other key actors will react to various policies. Thus, perceptions of the other actors' strategies and tactics contained in national images are important for evaluating policy options because they create expectations about the behavior of others that are essential for predicting the results of proposed policies.

### Policy Choice

It is through their impact on the decision maker's description and analysis of foreign policy situations as well as his or her estimates of the consequences of policies that images introduce what George calls "choice propensities." National images, of course, are not the only components of a decision maker's belief system that shape policy choice, nor are cognitive variables the only ones that influence policy preferences. Because images are only one part of the decision-making calculus, it is impossible to argue that they determine policy choice in any simple sense, hence the emphasis on "propensities."

These choice propensities can be thought of in positive and negative terms. Images exercise a positive influence in the sense that they lead a decision maker to expect a favorable result from a certain range of options. In a negative sense, images might generate predictions about the consequences of certain policies that would immediately rule them out of serious consideration. Thus, images may be important contributory variables in the formulation and selection of policies, and they may even be sufficient variables when it comes to ruling out others (I will say more about "negative predictions" in the next chapter).

The insight that images may be important for explaining why decision makers are favorably disposed to some policies while others are rejected outright also implies that we cannot expect images to dictate the specifics of policy preferences. Let me illustrate this point by examining the relationship between prejudice and discrimination, which has long puzzled social psychologists. One of the main problems researchers have faced in establishing a link between the two is that there are many ways to discriminate and display hostility. Therefore, people with identical attitudes and beliefs about a minority group may exhibit different overt behaviors. But showing that people with the same beliefs behave differently does not disprove the existence of a systematic relationship between beliefs and behavior. Knowing that someone is prejudiced may allow us to predict discriminatory behavior, but not the exact form this behavior will take. We can think of analogous examples in foreign policy. For instance, it might be that an individual's image of the Soviet Union will predispose him or her to oppose arms control and, therefore, to favor negotiating positions that are "nonnegotiable." But a knowledge of the decision maker's image will not be sufficient to predict the exact contents of his or her preferred negotiating stance.

A slightly different dilemma is highlighted by distinguishing single actions (microbehavior) from general behavioral trends (macrobehavior). Researchers studying the attitude-behavior relationship are often perplexed by those cases where people take actions that are clearly at odds with their beliefs. Again, the prejudice-discrimination relationship is commonly used to illustrate the problem. Icek Ajzen points out that an accurate "assessment of discrimination requires consideration of a wide range of behaviors with respect to the minority group . . . , failure to obtain strong relations between prejudice and discrimination has typically been due to the use of only one or two particular actions as measures" (1982, 9). The observation that prejudiced people treat minority co-workers with respect does not disprove the existence of a relationship between beliefs and behavior. There may be pressures in the workplace that overwhelm tendencies toward hostile treatment that dominate in other contexts. Similarly, policy choices in one or two instances that contradict the decision maker's enemy image do not establish the irrelevance of images. One needs to look at a series of decisions to discover what pattern emerges. Paraphrasing Ajzen and Fishbein: while knowledge of a decision maker's enemy image can tell us little as to whether he will favor a particular policy, it can tell us something about his overall policy predispositions (1980, 18).

## Individual Variations

Still another problem that must be confronted when examining the relationship between an individual's beliefs and their behavior involves those factors that can strengthen or weaken the impact of beliefs. Since we have already observed that images influence decision making through their role in information processing, we must recognize that other variables that influence this process may increase or diminish the significance of preexisting beliefs. Mark Snyder (1982) argues that much of the confusion and disappointment in studies of the attitude-behavior relationship stem from a failure to realize that there is no theoretical or empirical reason to expect a strong correspondence in each and every case; in fact, there are compelling reasons to expect otherwise. Current research suggests that the relationship between beliefs and behavior may vary depending upon a number of idiosyncratic factors. That is, the impact of images on policy preferences may be greater for some individuals than for others.

Even though balance theorists usually argue that the drive toward consistency is universal, there is a recognition that individuals differ both in terms of their tolerance for inconsistencies as well their preferred method of restoring consistency. For this reason, "it has been suggested that the predictive accuracy of theories of consistency might be improved by taking into account personality variables that are widely considered to be important determinants of cognitive and social behavior" (Glass 1968, 615). Unfortunately, not much progress has been made in this direction, and it is not hard to understand why. When we consider the diversity of personality variables that are potentially significant, their relationship to tolerance for inconsistencies, and their impact on an individual's preferences for various modes of consistency maintenance, the complexity is almost mind-boggling. If we add to this the methodological and empirical problems of operationalizing personality variables, the difficulties seem insurmountable. Still, there have been a number of attempts to explore the impact of other idiosyncratic variables on the cognitive process that contribute to our understanding of the image-policy preference relationship.

The influence of dogmatic personality traits has received substantial attention. Based on the pioneering work of Rokeach (1960), the hypothesis is that:

> authoritarian and dogmatic persons . . . seek to structure situations in cognitively consistent and simple ways. Furthermore, inconsistent stimuli should be rejected, distorted, ignored, or denied. By contrast, equalitarian or low dogmatic individuals should be more able to tolerate cognitive inconsistency. (Miller and Rokeach 1969, 625)

In general, these predictions have been confirmed. In their study of the relationship between dogmatism and memory, Klieck and Wheaton found that "high dogmatic subjects recalled more information that supported their own side of the issue than opposing information, whereas low dogmatic subjects showed no bias in recall" (in Zanna and Olson 1982, 81). Relating this to the present study, we might expect highly dogmatic individuals to exhibit more stable and simplistic images. In addition, we can anticipate a stronger relationship between images and policy preferences because dogmatic individuals are less likely to include belief-discrepant information in their decision making.

Still others have pointed to differences in cognitive style to explain variations in the image-behavior relationship. In her study of the development of cold war belief systems, Deborah Larson argues that intellectuals who engage in thoughtful self-reflection are particularly disturbed by cognitive inconsistencies. According to Larson, Dean Acheson was an "introspective intellectual" possessing a coherent and complex worldview who was "bothered" by inconsistencies among his beliefs, as well as between his beliefs and behavior. "Practical politicians," on the other hand, are not bothered by "gaping" inconsistencies. In fact, the behavior of some individuals was so contrary to the expectations of orthodox attitude theories that Larson doubts that such theories are applicable at all in some cases. (Larson 1985, 49–50, 339–42)

## Images as Dependent Variables

The bulk of this chapter has dealt with the influence of images *on* policy preferences. Logically, however, this does not exhaust the possibilities concerning the nature of the relationship between the two variables. Images as independent variables in decision making have been stressed because "traditional thinking about the direction of causality in attitude theory has assumed that attitudes cause behavior" (Triandis 1971, 6). Over the years, a number of scholars have questioned this theoretical asymmetry in cognitive psychology by suggesting that the causal arrow points in the opposite direction. After all, as Abelson wryly observes, "we are all very well trained and very good at finding reasons for what we do, but not very good at doing what we find reasons for" (1972, 25). As a result of this new work, some of the key elements of traditional approaches have come under intense scrutiny.

The primary assault on the core assumption of dominant attitude theories has been launched by advocates of "self-perception theory." According to Daryl Bem, one of the theory's major proponents, "the crux of the self-perception interpretation . . . is that the individual's own behavior will be used by him as a source of evidence for his beliefs and attitudes to the extent that the contingencies for reinforcement for engaging in the behavior are subtle or less discriminable" (1978, 228). That is, people "give meaning" to their behavior by constructing attitudes and beliefs that are consistent with it. People do not carefully deduce their behavioral predispositions from their beliefs but rather "infer" their beliefs from their behavior. Self-perception theorists are usually careful to use "infer" and "explain" in quotation marks, because they do not mean to imply that people are aware of what they are doing. Instead, it is assumed that there is a subconscious process of rationalization geared toward providing individuals with intellectual justifications for their actions.

Once we have become accustomed to the apparently counterintuitive idea that behavior causes beliefs, it is not difficult to think of cases that lend it some validity. For example, when representatives of interest groups argue in favor of legislation that will benefit their constituents, they will almost always argue that it will also help the wider public. While these arguments are easily dismissed as self-serving rationalizations, it is probably the case that they are genuinely believed by those who make them. People tend to convince themselves that policies that benefit them will help everyone. On the surface it might seem like such people are motivated by a concern for the general welfare, and they may actually think that they are, but their support for the legislation is dictated by self-interest. As Jervis notes, people often develop beliefs that serve "the important function of permitting them to act with clear consciences" (1980, 98).

Applied to this study, self-perception theory would predict that "statesmen first set their policies toward another state and then develop the image that supports and *would have led* to such a policy" (Jervis 1980, 95, italics added). For example, it is plausible to argue that people who serve as secretary of defense are subject to institutional pressures to support policies that necessitate increases in defense expenditures. But because these pressures are often subtle, the individual does not see himself or herself as having been "forced" into supporting these policies. In order to justify these policy preferences, the secretary will develop a foreign policy belief system that provides intellectual support for them. A key component of this belief system might be an image of an aggressive and relentlessly expansionist adversary. In public statements (and in his or her own mind), it will seem as though this image has led to certain policy choices; in fact, the cognitive dynamics were reversed. (The problems for empirical research posed by this approach are obvious.)

Needless to say, the self-perception approach introduces a number of theoretical "wrenches" into this study, one of which is reflected in Larson's question: "if beliefs are epiphenomena of behavior, does this mean that a person's attitudes, thoughts, or opinions are readily separable from a scientific explanation of his actions?" (1985, 45). Since self-perception theorists have never argued that behavior causes beliefs for all individuals at all times, the answer is "it depends." Referring to her distinction between introspective intellectuals and practical politicians, Larson argues that self-perception accurately describes the cognitive modus operandi of the latter group. Practical politicians are neither ideologues nor "systematizers of ideas" and are capable of entertaining a variety of inconsistent beliefs at the same time, none of them firmly held. Such a hodgepodge of beliefs cannot possibly provide a clear blueprint for behavior. Lacking clear cognitive guidelines, the influence of external or situational forces increases. Once policy preferences are established as a result of these forces, the decision maker draws upon his or her pool of beliefs, choosing those that are consistent with his or her policy choices at any given moment. Thus, a study of the relationship between images and policy preferences should be sensitive to the possibility that the causal arrow may point in any direction, depending on the individual in question.

We must be aware not only of differences among individuals, but also differences for the same individual over time: beliefs that are the result of a policy choice at one time may exercise an independent influence on policy preferences later on. Once a person adopts a policy position and constructs a belief system supportive of this position, he or she may develop an attachment to these beliefs that will carry over into other decisions and situations. Using the example of the secretary of defense whose image of the enemy was devised to support policy preferences induced by bureaucratic pressures, we can imagine a situation where this image becomes so firmly entrenched during his or her tenure in office that it would persist after the original pressures were no longer operative. Researchers have labeled this the "foot-in-the-door" phenomenon. Thus, self-perception theory may provide a more accurate description of the relationship between images and policy preferences for one period, while traditional attitude theory may be more relevant in another.

## Summary and Conclusions

In this chapter, I have examined the theoretical linkages between a decision maker's national images and his or her policy preferences. The basic argument is that images can be either a cause or consequence of policy choice. The hypothesis that images are important explanatory variables is drawn from traditional attitude theories in cognitive psychology. This view rests upon the assumption that images are relatively coherent and durable collections of beliefs that shape an individual's policy preferences through their impact on his or her perception, interpretation, and recall of policy-relevant information. Because preexisting beliefs affect the processing of information, they also influence the decision maker's description and analysis of foreign policy situations, as well as his or her evaluations of policy options. The diagnostic and evaluative implications of images lead to predispositions to support some policies and oppose others. More recent attitude theories suggest that images are more accurately viewed as post-hoc intellectual constructs designed to justify policies (both to the decision maker and others) that were "chosen" for other reasons. While often portrayed as "archrivals," these approaches are actually complementary, and both contribute to our understanding of the relationship between images and policy preferences.

# CHAPTER 4

# Method

How do we know what a person believes? How do we determine the content of a person's belief system? Problems of definition and measurement are an integral part of any research enterprise, but the difficulties are often thought to be particularly acute in the realm of beliefs and attitudes. The crux of the problem is that we can never observe and measure an individual's beliefs directly; they must be inferred from indicators that can be observed. Generally speaking, there are two primary indicators, behavior (or behavioral predispositions) and/or communications (written and oral). Within the framework of this study, behavior would be an inappropriate indicator whose use would result in an empirical tautology. There is no choice but to rely on communications. Lacking direct access to the subjects, which may not even be desirable, this communication consists of written and oral statements. Whenever beliefs and attitudes are inferred, whether it be through content analysis, personal interviews, or questionnaires, there are a number of issues that must be addressed, even if they are not resolved to everyone's satisfaction. One set of issues involves the mechanical "nuts and bolts" of definition procedures; the other set concerns questions of validity and reliability.

Inference from communications requires some form of content analysis: the question is not whether or not to use content analysis, but rather which techniques are most practical and theoretically useful. As Carney observes, "content analysis is the technique to use if the task is to assess someone's image of reality" (1972, 195). The options are occasionally presented as either qualitative or quantitative analysis; in fact, there is no incompatibility between the two, and this study uses them in conjunction because "it is by moving back and forth between these approaches that the investigator is most likely to gain insight into the meaning of data" (Holsti 1969, 11). Quantitative analysis, which is more appropriately described as systematic analysis, entails the construction and application of an explicit coding scheme that promotes analytical clarity and empirical rigor while facilitating efforts at replication and extension. Qualitative analysis involves a more impressionistic, interpretive, and nuanced evaluation of the subject's statements.

Several decisions need to be made in any systematic content analysis. First, what materials will be included in the study—what statements are going to be used as the basis for inference. Second, how are the categories of content to be defined—what coding scheme will be employed? Third, what are the recording and context units? Finally, what system of enumeration will be used—how will the data be presented? (See Holsti 1969, 94–126; Johnson and Joslyn 1986, 207–9; Nachmias and Nachmias 1981, 261–64.)

## Data Sources

As a basis for inference, this study uses the subjects' publicly available statements that contain information about their beliefs concerning the Soviet Union. The systematic coding is applied to all public statements made during the subjects' tenure in the Reagan administration for which printed transcripts are obtainable. In the case of President Reagan, these documents are conveniently collected in the *Weekly Compilation of Presidential Documents* (which are eventually bound as part of the *Public Papers of the Presidents* series). Included are all Reagan's speeches, interviews, press conferences, and so on. For George Shultz and Richard Burt, the primary sources are transcripts of congressional testimony and statements included in the *Department of State Bulletin*. Congressional transcripts are also the main source for Caspar Weinberger and Richard Perle, but there are also scattered journal and op-ed pieces as well as news show transcripts (e.g., "Face the Nation"). There are some statements that are attributed to the subjects that were not actually made by them and probably not even read by them. Examples of such "phony communication" are the written responses to questions submitted by congressmen and foreign journalists; these are not included. The rule of thumb employed is that the subjects actually had to *say* what is attributed to them (e.g., speeches and interviews) or there must be a reasonable expectation that they read the statement and approved of it (e.g., prepared testimony and journal articles). Also excluded are multiple appearances of "canned speeches," which applies mainly to Reagan's campaign speeches that were repeated verbatim up to five times per day preceding elections; in these cases, only the first delivery of the speech is coded. Statements from before and after the subjects' service in the administration are used when relevant and available, but they are not included in the systematic coding.

## The Coding Scheme and Content Categories

The most important step in any systematic content analysis is the construction of the coding scheme and delineation of the content categories; as Bernard Berelson observes, "content analysis stands or falls by its categories . . . a content analysis can be no better than its system of categories" (1952, 147). There are two key issues. First, the categories must be theoretically useful. In the present study, exploring the relationship between images and policy preferences, this means that the content categories must center on those aspects of the enemy image that one would reasonably expect to be related in some systematic manner to policy preferences. Second, the categories employed must be exhaustive and mutually exclusive, which ensures that each recording unit will fall into one and only one category (i.e., will not be coded more than once).

As I noted in chapter 2, a decision maker's image of another actor "includes beliefs about the goals, strategies, tactics, sources of motivation, approaches to calculation and other characteristics" of that actor (Holsti 1977b, 61). The coding scheme used in this study is a modified version of Ole Holsti's (1977b) detailed scheme of operational code categories, which has been revised in order to clarify certain categories and to add aspects of the image that might be particularly relevant in the area of strategic arms policy.

The scheme (presented in outline form, below) should be viewed as a series of "questions" that one "asks" the subject indirectly through the documents. After each of the categories (IA, IB, etc.) there is an explanation of what is coded in that category, except where the meaning is obvious. The categories and coding rules have been developed deductively and inductively in interaction with the documents; as a result, the coding rules are more fully developed for those beliefs that appeared frequently in the subjects' statements (the reader will notice that the coding scheme draws heavily on the material in chap. 3).

    I. What are the Soviet Union's general foreign policy goals?
        A. *Unlimitedly expansionist/destructionist.* The Soviet Union aims toward a radical transformation of the international system involving the elimination of competing centers of power. This is frequently expressed in terms of the Soviets seeking world domination, global hegemony, or the creation of a "one-world Communist state." The perception that the Soviets are following a well-thought-out master plan is also sometimes implied.
        B. *Limitedly expansionist/revisionist.* According to this view the Soviets are seen as expansionist (as in IA) but their goals are more limited in that they do not seek a radical transformation of the system or the destruction of the United States as a major power center and rival.
        C. *Expansionist/unspecified.* This is coded when the author expresses the view that the Soviet Union is expansionist, but it is unclear from the statement how extensive these expansionist tendencies are. It is not possible to distinguish between IA and IB.

    D. *Status quo/defensive.* The Soviet Union is thought to be primarily concerned with the maintenance of its current position and holding on to what it has, not with further expansion and aggrandizement. This may represent either satisfaction with the current state of affairs or fear of a pending erosion of its position.

    E. *Acquiescent/accommodating.* The Soviet Union is perceived as willing to make geopolitical accommodations that entail a diminution of its current status.

    F. *Other/mixed.*

II. What are the Soviet Union's nuclear objectives?

    A. *Superiority.* The Soviets are perceived as striving for the ability to launch a disarming first strike against the United States. Coded either when this is specified or if the author states that "superiority" is the goal. (Code only when the reference is specifically to *nuclear* objectives, not when the author refers vaguely to a desire for military superiority.)

    B. *Parity.* The Soviets are not seeking the ability to launch a first strike. Code if the author states that parity is the goal, or mutual vulnerability is the Soviet goal.

    C. *Inferiority.* (Almost certainly not needed.)

    D. *Other/mixed.*

III. What are the relative nuclear capabilities of the Soviet Union?

    A. *Superior.* The Soviet Union has a disarming first-strike capability. (Coded when this view is expressed or when the term *superiority* is actually used.)

    B. *Imbalances/advantages.* The Soviets are perceived to enjoy overall imbalances in various important measures of nuclear strength or advantages in particularly significant categories of weapons. (Statements about an existing "window of vulnerability" are coded in this category. Also code when there are references to the need to "restore" or "regain" the nuclear or strategic balance.)

    C. *Parity.* The Soviets are seen as "roughly equal" with the United States in overall nuclear capabilities. (Also coded if the author states that the nuclear balance is "stable.")

    D. *Inferior.*

    E. *Other/mixed.* The author offers a description of the nuclear balance that is either confused or does not fit into one the preceding categories.

IV. What are the relative capabilities of the Soviet Union in INF?

    A. *Superior.* Coded when the term *superiority* is used to describe

the balance of INF forces or when the Soviets are portrayed as having a "monopoly" on this class of weapons.
   B. *Advantages/imbalances*
   C. *Parity*. See IIIC.
   D. *Inferior*.
   E. *Other/mixed*.
V. What are the Soviet Union's relative conventional capabilities?
   A. *Superior*. Coded when the term *superiority* is actually employed or when the portrait presented is one of Soviet advantages in many types of important weapons systems that are not offset by U.S.-NATO advantages in other types of weapons systems.
   B. *Parity*. The Soviet and U.S.-NATO balance of forces is roughly equal. Also coded when the author portrays a situation in which Soviet advantages are compensated for by U.S. advantages or when the conventional balance is described as "stable."
   C. *Inferior*.
   D. *Other/mixed*. Coded when the author is clearly expressing beliefs about the conventional balance but it is unclear precisely what the subject is saying. For example, if it is stated that the Soviets enjoy "numerical superiority" while the United States has a "technological edge," but it is not clear if the U.S. edge offsets Soviet advantages.
VI. What motivates Soviet foreign policy?
   A. *Ideology*. Soviet foreign policy is perceived as doctrinally inspired by the works of Marx, Lenin, and Stalin either directly (e.g., the Soviets want world domination because that is what Marx prescribed) or indirectly (e.g., ideology colors the way in which Soviet leaders perceive the world).
   B. *Logic of totalitarianism*. Soviet policy is seen as the logical or "necessary" outgrowth of a totalitarian or authoritarian political system.
   C. *Culture*. Elements of the Soviet/Russian political culture shape Soviet policy.
   D. *Geography*. Features of Soviet terrain influence foreign policy goals (e.g., the land-locked position of the Soviet Union creates tendencies toward expansion).
   E. *History*. The Soviet Union is seen as following goals that have been followed throughout Soviet history and that would be pursued regardless of the type of regime.
   F. *Vested interests*. Soviet policy is designed to serve the needs and interests of powerful segments of Soviet society, such as

the military-industrial complex or more general "state interests."

G. *Personalities*. Soviet foreign policy is shaped by the desires, needs, motivations, or views of its present leader or group of leaders.

H. *Power politics*. Soviet policy is shaped by the same systemic forces as any great power operating in an international system characterized by anarchy and insecurity.

I. *External challenges*. Soviet policy is motivated by specific external threats and challenges (or perceived threats and challenges); its policy is reactive, not initiatory. (Code only if the threat or pressures are discussed in somewhat concrete terms, not when vague references to "suspicions" are mentioned.)

J. *Other/mixed*.

VII. What is the Soviet decision process?

A. *Rational Actor*. Decisions are made by a central leader or group of leaders who have no major conflicts on policy issues. Decisions are carefully calculated to meet predetermined foreign policy objectives. This is not coded when the author simply speaks about the Soviet Union as if it were a unified actor (e.g., the Soviets placed troops there because . . . ), but only when the subject is clearly commenting on the Soviet decision-making structure.

B. *Bureaucratic politics*. Decisions are portrayed as the result of bargaining and compromise between various bureaucratic and institutional interests and factions in the government. Decision making is not dominated by a single leader or unified group.

C. *Organizational process*. Decisions are seen as the result of following standard operating procedures within the context of government organizations.

D. *Other/mixed*. Any description of decision making that does not classify as A, B, or C. In particular, statements about the presence of factional struggles and policy disagreements not related to bureaucratic interests. Also includes discussions of "collective" decision-making processes.

VIII. How do the Soviets respond to policies of "firmness"?

A. *Back down*. A belief that, "by pursuing policies of firmness or boldness, one will cause the opponent to back down, to concede important points, or even abandon major foreign policy undertakings" (Holsti 1977b, 101). Also a belief that the Soviets only "respect" strength and determination.

B. *Reciprocate*. The Soviets have and can be expected to meet firm policies with hard-line policies of their own. They will not concede points but will respond in kind.

    C. *Other/mixed*.

IX. How do the Soviets respond to policies of restraint and accommodation?

    A. *Exploit/take advantage*. "According to this view, if one makes a concession or a conciliatory gesture, the [Soviet Union] will seize the opportunity to register a gain, will interpret it as a sign of weakness, or will otherwise make an effort to put it to his advantage" (Holsti 1977b, 100).

    B. *Reciprocate*. The Soviets will match one's restraint and accommodation.

    C. *Other/mixed*

X. What is the Soviet record of treaty compliance?

    A. *Violates/cheats*. The Soviets have violated treaties in the past and can be expected to continue to do so.

    B. *Technical obedience*. The Soviets abide by the letter of agreements but routinely take actions that violate their spirit. They can be expected to take advantage of loopholes and ambiguities.

    C. *Abide*. The Soviets abide by the terms and spirit of agreements.

    D. *Other/mixed*.

XI. What is the Soviet view of nuclear war?

    A. *Winnable*. The Soviets (a la Richard Pipes) believe that a nuclear war can be fought and won. The Soviets reject the assumption of mutual assured destruction.

    B. *Not winnable*. The Soviets do not view a nuclear war as winnable; they accept the premise of mutual assured destruction.

    C. *Other/mixed*.

XII. How do the Soviets view the United States?

    A. *Aggressive/threatening*. The Soviets (perhaps wrongly) view the United States as a threat to their security.

    B. *Peaceful/defensive*. The Soviets "know" that the United States is peaceful and poses no threat to their security.

    C. *Other/mixed*. Coded particularly when the subject talks about "mutual suspicions," "hostility," and "Soviet paranoia."

## Recording and Context Units

Once we have decided the content to be examined or inferred and the categories into which it will be divided and classified, we must determine what the recording and context units will be. By recording unit I mean "the smallest body of content in which the appearance of reference will be counted," and the context unit "is the largest body of content that may be examined in characterizing a recording unit" (Nachmias and Nachmias 1981, 261). According to Krippendorff, "most content analyses use one or more of five different ways of delineating and identifying these units: syntactical units, referential units, physical units, propositional units, and thematic units" (1980, 60–61). Similarly, Holsti proposes five possible units: single words or symbols, themes, characters, grammatical units, or items (1969, 116–17). And Johnson and Joslyn suggest that the researcher may want to code (1) each word, (2) each theme, (3) each character or actor, (4) each sentence, or (5) each paragraph (1986, 208).

When using content analytic techniques to study images, there appears to be general agreement that the "theme" is the preferable recording unit. Holsti advises that "for many purposes the theme . . . is the most useful unit of content analysis. It is almost indispensable in research on propaganda, values, attitudes, beliefs, and the like" (1969, 116). Nachmias and Nachmias make the same point, observing that "themes are most frequently employed in the study of propaganda, images, and values" (1987, 262).

The theme has major benefits and shortcomings as a recording unit. The major problem is the difficulty of providing a general definition. Coding each paragraph or sentence is relatively straightforward because they are easy to distinguish. But themes are a lot like pornography: they are easy to spot once you see them, but it is very difficult to establish clear guidelines for identifying them. Nonetheless, Carney makes a valiant attempt: "By themes is meant a conceptual entity; an incident, thought process, or viewpoint which can be seen as a coherent whole" (1972, 159). It is because themes are defined as conceptual rather than grammatical entities that they are better suited to the study of belief systems: people think in terms of themes, not paragraphs and sentences. But this conceptual strength is also a mechanical weakness because, as Krippendorff explains, "thematic units require a deep understanding of the sources of language with all the shades and nuances of meaning and content. While it is easy for the reader to recognize them, it is generally difficult to identify them reliably" (1980, 63). Along the same lines, Carney notes that "using themes as counting units often enables ingenious analyses, producing very dramatic findings . . . , the trouble is, however, that they are not clear-cut, self-evident wholes as words are . . . . Consequently, there tend to be problems of reliability in coding them" (1972, 159).

Let us take an example: the actor's beliefs about the Soviet Union's decision-making structure. If the subject believes that decisions are the result of bureaucratic bargaining and compromise, he or she may reveal this in one sentence: "the Soviet decision to deploy fewer SS-20s was the result of a compromise between the military and civilian economic interests." This would be coded as an appearance of the theme that Soviet decision making is bureaucratic. Alternately, the subject may go on for paragraphs detailing the internal struggle. This lengthy description would also be coded as one appearance of the same theme. Thus, themes may be contained in phrases, sentences, paragraphs, or even entire documents.

In this study, we are interested in what beliefs are expressed and how often they are conveyed. In order to do this it is best to code each distinct appearance of a theme. That is, the theme will serve not only as the recording unit but also as the context unit. If, for example, the document was adopted as the context unit, any theme would only be coded once per document, regardless of how often it appeared. By using the theme as the context unit, themes will be coded each time they appear. As an illustration, let us assume we are coding an instance of Richard Perle's congressional testimony. In his opening statement, he voices his opinion that the Soviets are superior to the United States in nuclear capabilities. This would be coded under IIIA in the coding list. Suppose that, in his testimony, Perle offers this evaluation again in response to three different questions. If the document were the context unit, we would still only have one coding for the theme of nuclear superiority; if the theme is the context unit, we would have a total of four codings for nuclear superiority.

There are at least two problems that are immediately apparent. The first concerns the notion of "distinct appearances" of a theme. How does the coder make the distinction? No clear rule can be offered; there is an element of judgment involved. The rule of thumb is that some other idea or issue must be raised or discussed (though not necessarily regarding the image of the Soviet Union) separating the themes in order for them to be considered distinct and recorded separately. For example, three consecutive paragraphs detailing Soviet treaty violations would be considered one appearance of the theme that the Soviets violate treaties. If those paragraphs are separated by discussions of other issues, there would be three codings of the theme. A second problem concerns documents where the same issues are raised repeatedly, and specific references are actually elaborations of the same theme. This was a problem mainly for congressional testimony designed to address only one issue, particularly Soviet treaty violations. If every appearance of the theme is recorded, there would be hundreds of codings for the same theme in one document. This could inflate the apparent significance of this belief. In these few cases an arbitrary limit of five codings was set.

Once the data are gathered, how will they be presented? The most commonly used methods of presentation or enumeration in content analysis research are appearance systems, frequency systems, and measures of intensity. Several studies of enemy images have adopted different techniques than those employed in this study. The most common has been evaluative assertion analysis, which uses an intensity system of enumeration to measure an actor's image along several scales such as friendship-hostility, satisfaction-frustration, good-bad, and so on (see Starr 1984). The reason I avoid this frequently used technique is that the image components that I am interested in are not usefully defined in scalar terms. This study employs a simple appearance system in which the results of the content analysis will be displayed in terms of the absolute frequency with which various themes appeared in the coded documents.

### Data Validity

After the data have been gathered and presented, we must deal with questions concerning the validity of inferences based on this data, that is, we must consider whether we are measuring what we claim to be measuring. As Carmines explains, "the fundamental question with regard to measurement inference is how validly and reliably these indicators represent the unobserved theoretical construct. In other words, do the measured indicators provide an accurate, consistent, and repeatable representation of their unmeasured theoretical constructs" (1986, 23)? Let us begin with the issue of validity. The first set of validity problems stems from the limitations of the data base, which, in our case, involves only publicly available statements. Use of internal memos, documents, and letters (which also have potential validity problems) is not yet possible. In and of itself this is not a severe problem. The validity of our inferences is called into question on this account only if private communications present a different picture than public ones, that is, if the data used contain systematic bias. While the problem is unavoidable at this point, it does not deal a fatal blow. Fortunately for this study, if not for the conduct of U.S. foreign policy, the Reagan administration was not known for its ability to keep squabbles and policy differences out of the public eye. It is unlikely that the individuals being examined conveyed one image of the Soviet Union in public and a radically different image behind the cloak of government secrecy. This does not mean that there were no pressures for the subjects to alter their views slightly in public, and these pressures will be discussed as the results are presented, but the problems do not seem to be debilitating.

The problems associated with relying on public statements revolve around the distinction between "representational" (or "expressive") and "instrumental" communication. The statements of policymakers are not always designed to convey their true beliefs but might also be "intended to persuade, justify, threaten, cajole, manipulate, evoke sympathy and support, or otherwise influence the intended audience" (Holsti 1976, 43). For example, the secretary of defense might project an extremely negative and menacing image of the opponent when testifying before appropriations committees in order to create an intellectual climate amenable to increased defense expenditures. The secretary of state, on the other hand, might present a more moderate image in order to sell an arms control treaty to the foreign relations committee. In neither case can we assume that their statements accurately reflect their beliefs, nor can we assume that statements that serve instrumental purposes do not represent genuine beliefs. There is no easy way to distinguish instrumental from representational communication. Identifying the "audience" and trying to infer the "intended purpose" of statements, as Larson suggests (1988, 248–50), is a deceptively simple solution that raises all sorts of problems. When the president gives a speech, for example, how do we know the intended audience? The immediate audience? The American people? U.S. allies? The Soviets? Taking every important statement, determining the audience, and trying to uncover the indented purpose would result in an endless and tedious morass. It would raise a second and third set of validity and reliability problems because of one's *inferences* about the audience as well as the intended purpose.

Yet another problem involves authorship of statements. If an actor's statements are written by someone else, the inferences based on these are more suspect than those based on self-authored statements. For Shultz, Weinberger, Perle, and Burt this is not a major problem because the overwhelming majority of the evidence is congressional testimony (and news conferences for Shultz) that include lengthy question and answer periods. Obviously, in these cases, the individuals "authored" their own responses. In Reagan's case, there is also a sizable body of press conferences and interviews involving spontaneous responses. Prepared speeches do not seem to pose much of a problem. Although Reagan did not write his own speeches, he was actively involved in the process of drafting and rewriting them. As Mandelbaum and Talbott observe, "what he cared about were speeches. . . . He worked at fine-tuning his speeches with an enthusiasm that he rarely devoted to other duties" (1984, 129). How much of this "fine-tuning" involved content as opposed to delivery technique is questionable, but it does not seem unreasonable to assume that he would not have agreed to a speech that was at great variance with his beliefs. (It is also important that I found no significant difference between the content of his spontaneous responses and his prepared statements.)

In conclusion, it should be recognized that we can never be absolutely certain that we are measuring beliefs accurately. No useful purpose is served by avoiding this unpleasant fact. When final push comes to final shove, there is almost always some persuasive reason for systematic bias in the evidence that casts doubt on its validity: as A. J. P. Taylor laments, "all sources are suspect" for one reason or another. As social scientists, the best we can do is take steps that increase our confidence in the validity of our data and to recognize the significance of whatever residual doubts remain. Ultimately, there is no substitute for informed judgment based on one's knowledge of the material, the individuals, and the circumstances surrounding the statements.

## Data Reliability

Reliability refers to whether or not another researcher, examining the same material and following the same coding rules, would arrive at the same results. It is useful to make the initial distinction between internal and external reliability. Internal reliability is a problem when several coders are involved in a project; this is not a problem for this study because I coded all the documents. External reliability becomes an issue when another researcher attempts to replicate the study or extend it by applying the same coding rules to other subjects. I have been able to conduct a reliability check by having two graduate students code a sample of documents after familiarizing themselves with the coding scheme and rules.

Before the results of the reliability tests are discussed, I must admit that the selection of themes as recording units is likely to create problems of reliability. It should be recognized that any content analysis beyond the simple counting of words will pose problems because "there is no such thing as the 'content' of document, 'content' that is independent of the person examining the document. The same document can mean wholly different things to different users. 'Content' is produced by the interaction between the reader and the document" (Carney 1972, 197). The use of themes increases the problems "because of the long chains of cognitive operations [sometimes] involved in the identification of thematic units" (Krippendorff 1980, 64). This problem is tackled by making the coding rules and categories as explicit as possible. But even the clearest coding scheme cannot overcome obtuse and ambiguous documents.

The nature of thematic content analysis is such that two types of reliability check are needed. In a "document" check, the coders are asked to apply the coding scheme to an entire document, reporting which themes appear and how often. While this allows us to see if different people arrive at the same overall picture, there are two shortcomings to this approach. First, it is a poor check of noncoding; technically, every passage that is not coded should be counted as an agreement, but this would skew the results because even a fifty-page document has only a dozen or so themes. Second, the document check does not tell us if coders who identify the same themes were extracting them from the same statements. To compensate for these weaknesses, a "passage" check is also performed in which the coders were given selected portions of documents (a few sentences or a paragraph) in order to see if identical passages are coded that same way.

The results of the document check are contained in table 4.1. Each of the

**TABLE 4.1. Results of Document Coding Check**

| Category | Coder 1 | 2 | 3 |
|---|---|---|---|
| Soviet foreign policy goals | | | |
|   Unlimitedly expansionist | 1 | 1 | 1 |
|   Limitedly expansionist | 0 | 0 | 0 |
|   Expansionist (unspecified) | 12 | 16 | 16 |
|   Status quo/defensive | 0 | 0 | 0 |
|   Acquiescent/conciliatory | 0 | 0 | 0 |
|   Other/mixed | 0 | 0 | 0 |
| Soviet nuclear objectives | | | |
|   Superiority | 3 | 1 | 2 |
|   Parity | 0 | 0 | 0 |
|   Other/mixed | 0 | 2 | 0 |
| Soviet nuclear capabilities | | | |
|   Superior | 5 | 3 | 4 |
|   Advantages/imbalances | 9 | 8 | 7 |
|   Parity | 0 | 0 | 0 |
|   Inferior | 0 | 0 | 0 |
|   Other/mixed | 4 | 2 | 2 |
| Soviet conventional capabilities | | | |
|   Superior | 2 | 3 | 3 |
|   Parity | 0 | 0 | 0 |
|   Inferior | 0 | 0 | 0 |
|   Other/mixed | 1 | 2 | 2 |
| Soviet policy motivation | | | |
|   Ideology | 3 | 3 | 3 |
|   Logic of totalitarianism | 0 | 1 | 0 |
|   Culture | 0 | 0 | 0 |
|   Geography | 0 | 0 | 0 |
|   History | 2 | 1 | 1 |
|   Vested interests | 2 | 2 | 2 |
|   Idiosyncracies/personalities | 0 | 0 | 0 |
|   Power politics | 0 | 0 | 0 |
|   External challenges | 0 | 0 | 0 |
|   Other/mixed | 0 | 0 | 0 |
| Soviet decisional process | | | |
|   Rational actor | 2 | 1 | 1 |
|   Bureaucratic politics | 0 | 0 | 0 |
|   Organizational process | 0 | 0 | 0 |
|   Other/mixed | 0 | 0 | 0 |
| Soviet response to firmness | | | |
|   Back down | 10 | 9 | 8 |
|   Reciprocate | 0 | 0 | 0 |
|   Other/mixed | 0 | 1 | 0 |
| Soviet response to restraint | | | |
|   Reciprocate | 0 | 0 | 0 |

(*continued*)

**TABLE 4.1.** (*Continued*)

| Category | Coder 1 | Coder 2 | Coder 3 |
|---|---|---|---|
| Exploit | 4 | 4 | 4 |
| Other/mixed | 0 | 0 | 0 |
| Soviet treaty record | | | |
| Violates/cheats | 17 | 18 | 14 |
| Technical obedience | 0 | 1 | 1 |
| Abides | 0 | 0 | 0 |
| Other/mixed | 1 | 0 | 1 |
| Soviet view of nuclear war | | | |
| Winnable | 2 | 1 | 1 |
| Not winnable | 0 | 0 | 0 |
| Other/mixed | 0 | 0 | 0 |
| Soviet view of United States | | | |
| Peaceful | 0 | 0 | 0 |
| Aggressive | 0 | 0 | 0 |
| Other/mixed | 0 | 0 | 0 |

three coders (myself and two others) were given sixteen documents of varying length—long congressional testimony to short news conferences—and asked to code them according to the previously presented scheme. The two coders were given about an hour of instruction and three practice documents (which are not included in results in table 4.1). The results of the document check were good—there is only a slight difference in the number of times certain themes were recorded, which probably stems from difficulties involved in identifying "distinct" themes as opposed to continuations of themes expressed earlier in the same document.

For the "passage check," each coder was given forty-three paragraphs taken from different documents, each containing one or no themes. In twenty-nine cases all three coders recorded the same theme, and in the remaining fourteen cases two were in agreement (there were no instances of all three coders disagreeing). Unlike the document check, there is a precise measure of intercoder reliability applicable to the passage check—the composite reliability coefficient (Holsti 1969, 137; Larson 1988, 244), which can be calculated using the following formula:

$$\text{Composite Reliability} = \frac{N\,(A)}{1 + [(N - 1)\,(A)]},$$

where $N$ = the number of judges, and $A$ = the average proportion of agreement. The average proportion of agreement for our check was .89 (i.e., 1.0 in

29 cases and .66 in the other 14). With three judges, this yields a composite reliability coefficient of .96, which is very high indeed.

## Identifying Policy Preferences

In thinking about the concept of policy preferences, it is useful to distinguish between ideal and advocated preferences. Ideal policy preferences are those policies the decision maker would most like to see implemented. They are his or her preferences before any compromises have been made. Advocated preferences, on the other hand, are those proposals that the individual actually advances in policy debates. For a variety of reasons, ideal preferences may never be voiced, even within the administration. An individual may, for example, preemptively compromise his or her ideal preferences, realizing that they have no reasonable chance of being adopted and not wanting to expend any political capital on their behalf in a futile struggle. It may not even be possible to identify a decision maker's ideal preferences, and we cannot assume that the ideal and advocated preferences are identical. The advocated preference (or policy recommendation, which may be a more accurate label) will usually be more easily and reliably identified.

Let us take an example to illustrate these points. Suppose that individual X believes that arms control is a complete waste of time and energy that, in the long run, damages the nation's security. We would expect X to advocate that arms control be completely abandoned in favor of a military buildup. At the same time, however, X knows that, for a variety of reasons (e.g., domestic political pressures), the administration must pursue arms negotiations. Recognizing this, X does not even consider proposing an outright renunciation of arms control but rather puts forward a negotiating position that seems reasonable and is politically acceptable but that actually hinders progress. Complete rejection of arms control is X's ideal preference, the nonnegotiable position is his advocated preference. This study focuses on the latter, since it is probably unrealistic to attempt to identify the former.

How do we find out what the policy preferences of the individuals in question are? In some sense, this is both easier and harder than identifying subjects' beliefs about the Soviet Union. It is easier in that the question of where people stand on certain issues is addressed more explicitly, both by the individuals themselves and people writing about the administration. More journalists were concerned with finding out what Shultz's position on INF was than were worried about determining his perceptions of Soviet policy motivation. But determining policy preferences is also more difficult, because the individuals are agents and representatives of an administration that (usually) has specific policy positions that they often feel obligated to support in public. This is probably not the case when it comes to images of the Soviet Union—it is unlikely that there is an administration "line" that officials must abide by (except, perhaps, when they are asked directly whether they agree with a particular statement made by the president). Because there is pressure to express support for administration policies that might differ from their preferences, we cannot rely exclusively on the decision makers' public statements. We must place a greater reliance on secondary sources of information about the nature of internal policy debates. Luckily, in the accounts of Reagan administration policy struggles, there seems to be very little disagreement about the nature of these debates, the content of competing policy preferences, and the lines of battle in the area of strategic arms policy.

## Linking Images and Policy Preferences

The most difficult methodological and analytical problem of this study is found at its core: How do we establish an empirical link between images and policy preferences? How do we show that images are (or are not) significant explanatory variables? Alexander George's insights are particularly helpful for resolving some of the key issues. George identifies two procedures that can be used to probe the explanatory power of beliefs.

> The first is the procedure of establishing "congruence" (or consistency) between the content of beliefs and the content of decisions. The second is the procedure of tracing in some detail the steps in the process by means of which given operational code beliefs influence the assessment of incoming information, help shape the individual's definition of the situation, and influence his identification and evaluation of options. (1979, 105)

As is usually the case in research whenever there is more than one way to proceed, the selection of one option over another involves serious trade-offs. George explains that the two approaches are differentiated partly on the basis of how much data they require: "the congruence approach requires much less information than the process-tracing approach" (George 1979, 105). When approaches have different information requirements, the researcher must consider the manageability of each approach as well as the availability of data. On both of these accounts, the congruence approach is preferable for the present study.

This project focuses on five individuals over a number of years, examining the debates among them on several issues. A strategy of process tracing for each individual over a series of decisions would prove unmanageable. A process-tracing approach would necessitate restricting the study by either eliminating subjects and/or looking at only one or two decisions. But if we narrow the focus, we lose the benefits derived from studying a variety of individuals and decisions. Furthermore, because of the recency of the issues examined and the lack of access to internal documents, we would not even have the information needed for a process-tracing approach (Larson 1985 provides an example of the process-tracing approach that relies heavily on personal papers and archival material). Thus, manageability and restricted access to information leads to the adoption of a congruence approach. George describes this approach:

> Having first established the subject's beliefs on the basis of relevant behavioral data . . . the investigator considers whether the subject's policy preferences and decisions are consistent with those beliefs . . . [and] the determination of consistency is made deductively. From the actor's operational code beliefs, the investigator deduces what implications they have for decision. If the characteristics of the decision are consistent with the actor's beliefs, there is at least a presumption that the beliefs may have played a causal role in this particular instance of decision making. (1979, 106)

In the same vein, Sjoblom proposes what he labels an "explanatory approach" that involves:

> some sort of predictions . . . in the following form: belief B is only consistent with option A (or a range of options A1 - N), and if the actor's belief system contains belief B, we predict that he will choose option A (or one of the options in the range). This may be a rather strong prediction . . . [as a result] it can be necessary to use weaker alternatives (e.g., the belief B is inconsistent with option C, so we may predict option C will not be chosen or probably will not be chosen). (1982, 68)

These approaches are essentially the same; the only difference is the emphasis Sjoblom places on noncongruent, negative predictions that might emerge from image analysis. This is consistent with my previous contention that images introduce both positive and negative policy predispositions. Furthermore, Sjoblom's stress on "ranges of options" implicitly recognizes that images do not unilaterally determine the details of policy preferences in every case.

The concepts of negative predictions and option ranges are related. Since any image is consistent with more than one policy preference, it may be very difficult to specify (in advance) the full range of options that are consistent with any given image. This makes specific, a priori, deductive predictions problematic. In terms of positive predictions, the best we may be able to accomplish is the identification of the broad guidelines within which the subject's policy preference should fall. In terms of negative predictions, it may be easier to identify specific policy options that will not be seriously entertained by someone holding a particular image. That is, an image may be neither sufficient nor necessary for a decision maker to support a policy, but it may be sufficient for him or her to reject alternative policies.

Having opted for a congruence approach, one must be cognizant of its limitations. The major shortcoming is the problem of establishing causal connections. Showing that certain policies are consistent with a given set of beliefs does not prove the causal importance of those beliefs. The obvious question is whether the relationship is genuine or spurious. It may be that another, antecedent variable explains why the individual adopted a given image and policy preference—psychological and personality variables may be placed in this category. One might also postulate role pressures as the key to explaining images and preferences. The basic problem is, of course, one of coping with plausible alternative explanations.

Although the nature of social scientific research precludes any conclusive resolution of this problem, we are not helpless. A careful selection of cases allows us to "control" for certain variables and thereby rule out some alternative explanations. Some alternatives may be ruled out by the particulars of a given case. "Confidence that the consistency between beliefs and actions is of causal significance is enhanced if it is encountered repeatedly in a sequence of interrelated decisions taken by an actor over a period of time" (George 1979, 107). One can support a case for the causal significance of beliefs by showing that belief system changes preceded changes in policy preferences. None of these solutions is without its problems; for example, changes in beliefs and preferences may be so closely temporally intertwined that firm conclusions are not possible. Obviously, there are limits to what can be done with competing explanations.

As in the case of data validity, the best one can do is take steps that increase confidence in our conclusions. Cases must be chosen strategically. The consistency between beliefs and policy preferences must be examined carefully. Alternative explanations should be evaluated on the basis of the evidence at hand. Hopefully, one will end up with a study that increases our understanding of the foreign policy decision-making process by providing a theoretically consistent and empirically plausible account of the issues under investigation. The identification of problems, however, does not require the abandonment of an approach or line of inquiry, but it does demand both a recognition of limitations and caution in drawing conclusions.

# Part 2
# Images

CHAPTER 5

# The Hard Line According to Richard Perle
# and Caspar Weinberger

The Soviet Union is, in George Orwell's words, a place "where yesterday's weather can be changed by decree," a totalitarian state that has failed in virtually every respect except ownership of the means of destruction. It tolerates no freedom, no dissent at home, and where it casts its shadow there is neither liberty nor joy. . . . God knows what decisions might be made in the totalitarian structure of the Soviet Union.
—Richard Perle (U.S. Cong. 1985c, 315, 351)

Tonight, one out of four countries around the globe is at war. In virtually every case, there is a mask on the face of war. In virtually every case, behind the mask is the Soviet Union and those who do its bidding.
—Caspar Weinberger (1986a, 258)

By virtually all accounts, the leading figures of the Reagan administration's hard-line faction on arms control policy were the Pentagon civilians, particularly Secretary of Defense Caspar Weinberger and Assistant Secretary of Defense for International Security Policy Richard Perle. Of the two, Perle's appointment was the least surprising. A Democrat who served on the staff of Senator Henry Jackson (D-Washington) throughout most of the 1970s, Perle developed a reputation as a fierce critic of détente in all of its manifestations, saving his harshest criticisms for U.S. arms control policy as embodied in the SALT process. In the mid 1970s, he joined with other conservative Democrats to form the Committee on the Present Danger, an organization dedicated to opposing détente. Perle was a veteran of the battles over SALT I and the Anti-Ballistic Missile (ABM) Treaty and was a key figure in the nonratification of SALT II. Because of his pessimistic assessment of Soviet-U.S. relations and his occasionally Machiavellian political tactics, Perle earned the nickname "the Prince of Darkness" (a description that reportedly did not bother him). For the same reasons he also earned a position in the Reagan administration. Given his bureaucratic skills, knowledge of arms control, and the absence of any high-level strategic thinkers in the Reagan administration,

Perle quickly exerted influence far beyond his formal station. According to one account, "Perle ended up having more impact in arms control than any other official in the U.S. government" (Talbott 1985, 17).

The appointment of Caspar Weinberger was more of a leap into the unknown; the absence of a long track record of foreign policy views meant that he was something of a mystery. His fiscal conservatism was renowned as a result of his budget cutting as Director of the Office of Management and Budget (OMB) during the Nixon administration, earning him the nickname "Cap the Knife." Conservatives, however, were concerned that Weinberger might actually be a moderate Republican whose budget-cutting zeal was not matched by an enthusiastic embrace of the conservative foreign policy agenda. In 1972, for example, Weinberger warned that "the identification of a threat to security does not automatically require an expenditure in the defense budget to neutralize it . . . [because] the nation's resources being limited, it is necessary to consider what is being given up to meet the threat" (U.S. Cong. 1985j, 569). To many, these were not the words of an ideal candidate to preside over the largest peacetime military buildup in U.S. history. But these skeptics would soon learn that they had nothing to fear. As several caustic wits observed, "Cap the Knife" turned into "Cap the Shovel."

### Perle and Weinberger View the Soviet Union

Foreign Policy Objectives

In a 1979 article ominously entitled "Echoes of the 1930s," Perle argued that "anyone who has studied the interwar period and reads today's newspapers tends to experience an uneasy sense of déjà vu" (Perle 1979, 11). The similarity stemmed from "the sense that many institutions of government in the United States and among our North Atlantic allies are inadequately inoculated against the disease of appeasement that swept through Europe forty years ago" (11). This analogy between the 1930s and the 1970s and 1980s was a recurring theme in Perle's statements. On the issue of increased technology transfers to the Soviet Union during the 1970s, for example, Perle argued:

> I think if anyone had suggested in 1941 or 1942 that the United States should share its military technology with Germany under Hitler, that proposal would certainly have been regarded as preposterous, just as I think it is preposterous now to permit the Soviets to acquire military technology, given the state of the relationship between the United States and the Soviet Union. (U.S. Cong. 1985n, 109)

Perle was quick to point out that the analogy was not perfect; the Soviet Union's foreign policy was not "a latter-day version of German policies," and

Brezhnev was not "another Hitler." Still, Perle's sense of danger would not have been so strong, nor the dangers of appeasement so great, if he did not see some significant similarities between the goals of Nazi Germany and those of the Soviet Union.

The extent and nature of these similarities are unclear; it is not possible to infer exactly what he thought the ultimate objectives of Soviet policy were (see table 5.1). Whether this lack of clarity reflects uncertain beliefs or the absence of opportunities to discuss his views, we cannot know. There is no question that he viewed the Soviet Union as an expansionist power. In Perle's view, the invasion of Afghanistan was "part of a larger picture of Soviet aggressiveness" (U.S. Cong. 1981a, 9). He argued that a strengthening of NATO's southern flank and a U.S. presence in the Middle East were essential because "there is nothing that the Soviets would welcome more than a vacuum through which they could pass unimpeded" (U.S. Cong. 1985b, 25). Using a colorful metaphor, he described the Soviet Union as "a hotel burglar [who] goes down a corridor trying all doors until he finds an open door and in he goes" (U.S. Cong. 1985a, 42).

The important question is not whether Perle saw the Soviets as expansionist, but how expansionist he thought they were. If the Soviets seek global hegemony, there would be few, if any, areas of common interest. Though there is not enough evidence on this point to draw firm conclusions, a few statements by Perle point toward a perception of more expansive aims: "as the people of Hungary, Czechoslovakia, Angola, Afghanistan, and Poland know . . . the Soviets are willing to put into practice, whenever given the opportunity, their long-held doctrinal commitment to spread throughout the world a

**TABLE 5.1.  Soviet Foreign Policy Objectives**

|                          | Perle | Weinberger |
| ------------------------ | ----- | ---------- |
| Unlimitedly expansionist | 1     | 11         |
| Limitedly expansionist   | 0     | 0          |
| Expansionist/unspecified | 20    | 168        |
| Status quo               | 0     | 0          |
| Acquiescent              | 0     | 0          |
| Other/mixed              | 0     | 8          |

*Note*: Tables 5.1 through 5.13 present the results of the content analysis described in chap. 4. The numbers represent the frequency with which the themes appeared in the statements of Perle and Weinberger during their service in the Reagan administration. For Perle, there was a total of 66 documents; for Weinberger, there were 105 documents (in both cases primarily congressional testimony). A complete listing of documents appears in the bibliography.

communist system, led and responsive to Moscow" (U.S. Cong. 1985c, 311). Whether this was hyperbole or not is debatable.

In Weinberger's case, one also finds a tendency to equate the predicament of the United States in the 1970s and 1980s with that of the West in the 1930s. Asked about his repeated references to time "running out" on the United States, Weinberger explained:

> . . . when I say I don't know how much more time we will have, I am frankly thinking of a situation like the one faced in 1938 and 1939. There was an apparent huge buildup on one side and a lack of awareness on the part of governments and in the minds of many in Europe as to what was necessary to respond to that. . . . I am haunted by the fact that as this gap opens, you have to do something to close it. There is a big gap now in too many areas. (U.S. Cong. 1982e, 304)

He warned that "if it is not careful, the democratic West might one day find itself in the same dangerously weak position that the allies were in when Germany attacked in 1939. But it might not have the time to recover as it did in World War II" (Weinberger 1987, 12–13).

Like Perle, Weinberger obviously saw the Soviet Union as an expansionist power; accordingly, the goal of U.S. policy was to "bring a halt to the further expansion and consolidation of the Soviet empire" (U.S. Cong. 1982h, 21–22). These expansionist tendencies were most evident in the Middle East and the Third World, where "the Soviets fish in troubled waters with great frequency and regularity" (U.S. Cong. 1984c, 6). In particular, "the Soviets have targeted the less industrialized countries as a region for the expansion of their empire" (U.S. Cong. 1983e, 164). Of course, that area of the Third World that troubled the administration most was Latin America, where Weinberger argued that "the purpose [of Soviet involvement] is . . . to attack the United States in this way, their incremental way . . . knowing that as they got closer that would mean that we would have to . . . pull ourselves out of Europe, and out of Japan and Korea, which would serve Soviet purposes very well globally" (CBS News, 1983a).

Whereas the extent of Soviet expansionist goals was somewhat unclear in Perle's statements, there is no such ambiguity in Weinberger's case. He adhered to the classic cold war view that the Soviet Union's objectives were unlimited (see table 5.1). Worried about the thaw in U.S.-Soviet relations during Reagan's second term, Weinberger cautioned that "we must not allow impatience to dominate common sense, nor can we allow our well-planned and steady rebuilding of America's defenses to be overcome by a childlike hope for détente with a country whose sole aim is, and always has been, world domination" (Weinberger 1986b, 295). Analyzing the course of U.S.-Soviet relations over the past few decades, Weinberger maintained that:

. . . the most important elements of our relations with the Soviet Union have been constant or have changed very slowly over the postwar years . . . the ambition of Soviet leaders to extend the sway of Marxism, Leninism . . . [is] supported by enormous military force. The 1977 Brezhnev constitution reiterates that it is Soviet Russia's aim, indeed its duty, to spread the communist system to all countries of the world. And this long-held doctrine of Soviet domination is backed up with the full force of the Red Army. (U.S. Cong. 1985a, 46)

This evaluation of Soviet policy objectives was constant throughout Weinberger's tenure in office (and beyond); if anything, his views became more strident, even after Gorbachev's rise to power. In 1987, shortly before leaving the administration, Weinberger was still convinced that "everything they are doing, all that we are seeing, intelligence reports and everything else, indicate very clearly to us that they continue to try to secure their basic overall strategic goal which is and always has been world domination" (U.S. Cong. 1987b, 176).

## Policy Motivation

Why did the Soviet Union pursue these objectives? That is, what forces motivated Soviet foreign policy? In the case of Perle, what is most interesting is the virtual absence of any discussion of Soviet policy motivation (see table 5.2). This was somewhat surprising, given my initial expectations that Perle and other administration officials would stress the ideological basis of Soviet policy. I was not able to locate a single instance where Perle discussed Marxism-Leninism in relation to Soviet foreign policy; in fact, I cannot recall any use of the term *Marxist-Leninist* in any of his statements about the Soviet Union. And although Perle routinely described the Soviet Union as a total-

**TABLE 5.2. Soviet Policy Motivation**

|  | Perle | Weinberger |
|---|---|---|
| Ideology | 1 | 3 |
| Logic of totalitarianism | 0 | 0 |
| Culture | 1 | 0 |
| Geography | 1 | 3 |
| History | 1 | 0 |
| Vested interests | 0 | 1 |
| Personalities | 0 | 1 |
| Power politics | 0 | 0 |
| External threats | 0 | 0 |
| Other/mixed | 2 | 9 |

itarian or authoritarian state, he did not argue that an expansionist foreign policy was the necessary outcome of such a regime. Nor did he discuss personalities, culture, or external threats as possible sources of Soviet behavior. Of course, this does not signify the absence of beliefs about these issues; it simply means that we cannot draw inferences with any confidence.

One gets a more complete, if not altogether clear, picture from Weinberger (see table 5.2). In his case, the Soviet Union was frequently described as a Marxist-Leninist state, a description often made in the context of discussions about Soviet foreign policy, even if he did not *explicitly* say that ideology drove policy. The strictness of the coding rules in this respect leads to an underestimation of the importance of ideology (if we rely only on the quantitative analysis). For example, in the previously quoted statement about the 1977 Brezhnev constitution, Weinberger spoke of the Soviet desire to "extend the sway of Marxism-Leninism" and the "doctrine of Soviet domination." He did not explicitly say that Marxist ideology necessarily led to a doctrine of Soviet domination, but there is no doubt that this is what he was implying. Speaking generally about Soviet policy toward the Third World, Weinberger argued that "they do not promote free trade or open economies or personal freedom . . . [because] economic prosperity and freedom are the *enemies of their ideology*" (U.S. Cong. 1986d, 54; italics added). Again, the implication seems clear.

In addition to ideology, Weinberger cited economic and geographic sources of Soviet expansion. He observed that "the Soviets are very active in the Mideast. They are going to become an energy-importing nation before too much longer. An obvious area for them to proceed is down through Afghanistan, Iran, and Iraq toward the oilfields" (U.S. Cong. 1982d, 258). (The majority of the statements coded as "other/mixed" in table 5.2 are statements of this variety). Elsewhere, he discussed the Soviet desire for a warm water port as another factor encouraging Soviet expansion into the Mideast (U.S. Cong. 1985f, 3558).

Perhaps even more interesting and significant is Weinberger's view of which forces *did not* influence Soviet goals. Given the change in Soviet leadership during the previous eight years, the most relevant of these nonfactors is personalities. Weinberger contended that "the Soviets have had a basically conservative military doctrine . . . but the people in charge of the Kremlin are quite old . . . and they are possibly going to change and change doctrines. If they did, we would have more to worry about" (U.S. Cong. 1982e, 290). At first blush this indicates a belief that leadership change can bring policy change; but if we look closer at Weinberger's views, we see that only the means were subject to alteration, not the ends (also note that he did not suggest the possibility of a change in direction that would leave the United States with less to worry about). When questioned about the impact of Gorbachev, Weinberger responded that "regardless of who is the general secretary of the Soviet Union and how young he is, or how healthy he is, or how well he dresses . . . their policy remains the same: to acquire an increasing amount of military strength each year" (U.S. Cong. 1987g, 8). After leaving the administration, Weinberger continued to speak of "the fundamental and unchanging nature of the Soviet system" in which "no general secretary will be allowed to alter in any fundamental way the never-changing Soviet goal of world domination" (Weinberger 1988, 701).

Also significant is Weinberger's belief that external challenges and threats, particularly from the United States, could not be the motivating force behind Soviet policy and weapons procurement. Typical was his claim that "they do not need a new intercontinental bomber to defend the Soviet Union, and it is not being produced because of a fear of the United States. It is being produced in keeping with their plan to secure worldwide military superiority and domination" (U.S. Cong. 1982g, 214). Similarly, "the Soviets do not need an aircraft carrier to defend the Soviet Union . . . they do not need the increased number of divisions to defend the Soviet Union . . . they do not need all the additional fighters and bomber aircraft and all the armored fighting vehicles and all the ICBMs . . . to defend the Soviet Union" (U.S. Cong. 1982f, 8). One begins to wonder what the Soviets did need to defend the Soviet Union.

## Nuclear Doctrine

For this study, I am particularly interested in the subjects' perceptions of the Soviet Union's nuclear strategy. The key distinction in this regard is whether the Soviets are seen as being satisfied with nuclear parity or whether they desire superiority. On this point, Perle's and Weinberger's views are identical (see table 5.3). According to Perle, the Soviets "desire military superiority at all levels conventional, strategic, and theater nuclear. They wish to control escalation by maintaining a clear margin of superiority at all points along the spectrum of potential conflict" (U.S. Cong. 1982a, 4370). In Perle's lexicon, superiority entailed the ability to launch a first strike against the United States that would inflict considerable damage to U.S. forces while retaining suffi-

TABLE 5.3.  Soviet Nuclear Objectives

|  | Perle | Weinberger |
|---|---|---|
| Superiority | 9 | 15 |
| Parity | 0 | 0 |
| Other/mixed | 0 | 1 |

cient Soviet forces to deter a U.S. counterstrike. Nowhere did he suggest that the Soviets would be willing to settle for strategic parity. Precisely what the Soviets planned to do with this first-strike capability was a little fuzzy, but Perle did not expect a nuclear attack out of the blue, stressing instead the possibilities for coercion and intimidation. The following exchange provides some insights.

> *Senator Warner*: Would you surmise from the direction in which they are going with their modernization program that indeed their goal is coercion and intimidation?
>
> *Mr. Perle*: I know of no other way to interpret the emphasis they have placed in the forces they have chosen to acquire.
>
> *Senator Warner*: It seems to me that a conclusive case can be made that this is the direction in which they are moving toward an aggressive strategic posture.
>
> *Mr. Perle*: I agree with that. (U.S. Cong. 1983e, 2435)

Weinberger voiced similar concerns, arguing that the Soviets' "tremendous activity, their continued modernization, their working on different types of missiles to replace those before they deploy the first set, is an indication of a clear desire for attempted superiority" (U.S. Cong. 1981r, 4; see table 5.3). Furthermore, "the Soviet desire for overwhelming superiority and acceptable risks of U.S. retaliation are theories that they have followed for many years and, I believe, continue to follow" (U.S. Cong. 1981i, 7).

Consistent with Perle's perception of a Soviet quest for nuclear superiority was his belief that the Soviets did not accept the doctrine of mutual assured destruction (table 5.4). Stated bluntly, "they have constructed forces capable of attacking and destroying our ability to respond because I do not think they believe in mutual destruction" (U.S. Cong. 1985k, 149). As evidence that the Soviets did not "believe in mutual destruction," Perle pointed to their civil defense program, which he thought "could lead Soviet decision makers to conclude that the level of destruction we could inflict in retaliation . . . could be kept within manageable proportions" (U.S. Cong. 1982g, 4919). And in the area of arms control, the Soviets "were not prepared to

**TABLE 5.4.  Soviet View of Nuclear War**

|              | Perle | Weinberger |
|--------------|-------|------------|
| Winnable     | 5     | 25         |
| Not winnable | 0     | 1          |
| Other/mixed  | 1     | 3          |

accept agreements that would have left each side with a relatively invulnerable deterrent" (U.S. Cong. 1981d, 111).

The perception of Soviet nonacceptance of mutual assured destruction was, if anything, even more pronounced in Weinberger's analysis of Soviet objectives (see table 5.4). According to Weinberger:

> . . . from the beginning, Soviet nuclear doctrine has been fundamentally different from U.S. doctrine in that it sees nuclear conflict as merely a more destructive form of conventional conflict. Put another way, Soviet doctrine has always asserted the possibility of fighting and winning a nuclear war. (U.S. Cong. 1982p, 14)

Typical of those who shared this view, Weinberger cited the Soviet Union's experience in World War II to suggest a greater willingness, on its part, to accept the destruction that would accompany any nuclear exchange: "there is now a possibility that the Soviet Union, who took 25 to 30 million casualties in the last war, may begin to perceive that they could indeed continue to exist as a country and ultimately prevail, should they make the first strike" (U.S. Cong. 1983e, 226). Like Perle, he argued that the Soviet force structure, Soviet moves toward improved defensive systems, and Soviet civil defense plans all "indicate that the Soviets are beginning to believe that they could fight and win a nuclear exchange and emerge with what they might call manageable losses" (U.S. Cong. 1982i, 43–44). In the wake of some rather loose talk on the part of several administration officials about limited nuclear war and its consequences, Weinberger was asked about the "winnability" of a nuclear war.

> *Senator Cranston*: . . . can anyone win a real nuclear war, surviving with enough of one's civilization left to consider it a victory?
> *Secretary Weinberger*: . . . I do feel confident that the Soviets must believe they can, and that they are developing techniques, specifically refiring capability, which clearly indicates that belief. (U.S. Cong. 1981r, 26)
> *Senator Pell*: Mr. Secretary, in your view do you think that either the Soviet Union or the United States considers a nuclear war winnable?
> *Secretary Weinberger*: I have seen nothing to indicate that the Soviets do not believe this. It appears that they think that they can win, that they can prevail. The rhetoric shifts from week to week. But when you look at the arsenal that has been amassed on a perfectly steady basis over 21 years, none of it really defensive in character, I have to conclude that is the assumption which underlies all of their thinking. (16)

Relative Military Capabilities

Perle and Weinberger perceived the Soviets to be superior in virtually all
categories of military capabilities (see tables 5.5 and 5.6). For our purposes,
however, the most important issue is: How successful had the Soviets been in
achieving their objective of nuclear (particularly strategic) superiority? Perle
consistently expressed the view that the Soviets enjoyed substantial "advan-
tages/imbalances" in nuclear weapons (table 5.6). He did not argue that
"rough parity" existed between the powers, a phrase he employed only for the
purpose of ridicule. According to Perle, "by every one of the measures which
in 1969 gave us preponderance, today the Soviets have preponderance: in
numbers of ICBMs, number of SLBMs, throw-weight, and so down the line"
(U.S. Cong. 1981b, 32). Only in the number of warheads did he perceive a
U.S. advantage. But did the Soviet Union have a usable (i.e., disarming) first-
strike capability? Perle offered a somewhat evasive evaluation: "the Soviets
have in much of their ICBM force the capacity to destroy most of the hardened
silos in which our ICBMs are based . . . they have a partial first strike
capability" (U.S. Cong. 1984b, 48). Asked if he would trade the U.S. arsenal
for the Soviet, Perle responded that "if my purpose were a strategic force with
a first-strike potential and with the power to coerce and intimidate, then I
would much rather have the Soviet force . . . in an offensive mode, it beats
our strategic force hands down" (U.S. Cong. 1983a, 44). When the nuclear

**TABLE 5.5.  Soviet Military Capabilities
(Conventional)**

|              | Perle | Weinberger |
|--------------|-------|------------|
| Superior     | 26    | 49         |
| Parity       | 0     | 0          |
| Inferior     | 0     | 0          |
| Other/mixed  | 1     | 14         |

**TABLE 5.6.  Soviet Military Capabilities (Nuclear)**

|                      | Perle | | Weinberger | |
|----------------------|-----------|-----|-----------|-----|
|                      | Strategic | INF | Strategic | INF |
| Superior             | 10        | 6   | 19        | 1   |
| Advantage/imbalances | 46        | 20  | 180       | 16  |
| Parity               | 0         | 0   | 0         | 0   |
| Inferior             | 0         | 0   | 0         | 0   |
| Other/mixed          | 6         | 0   | 9         | 0   |

freeze was being debated in Congress, Perle was asked again which arsenal he would prefer: "if you freeze us now, I would rather have the Soviets' strategic force" (U.S. Cong. 1984h, 55). He was the only administration official to give such a response. Thus, in Perle's view, the Soviets enjoyed significant strategic advantages, and if they had not yet reached their goal of a first-strike capability, they were very close.

In general, it appears that Weinberger shared Perle's evaluation that the Soviets enjoyed significant advantages. Like Perle, he rejected the idea that a rough parity existed between the two countries, flatly asserting that "there isn't a rough equivalence or parity" (U.S. Cong. 1985f, 3556). If the situation was not one of parity, how did Weinberger describe it? After his confirmation hearings, Weinberger set as one of the administration's key goals the need "to redress the *inferior* position that we now occupy" (U.S. Cong. 1981b, 553; italics added). But explicit references to "inferiority" or "superiority" were the exception; more common were vaguer references to the need to "restore" or "regain" a sufficient nuclear deterrent, which implied that such a deterrent was not in place as of the early 1980s. According to Weinberger:

> What we are trying to do is catch up to a point . . . where we have a degree of strength that will deter Soviet aggression because they know that if they launch some kind of first strike against us, the cost will be higher than they can bear because of our ability to retaliate. We are trying to regain that kind of strength. (U.S. Cong. 1981l, 275)

Thus, the administration's strategic modernization program was designed "to *get us back* to a degree of nuclear strength that we need to have an effective deterrent" (U.S. Cong. 1982i, 41; italics added).

Rarely was Weinberger pressed on exactly what he meant by his constant calls to "regain" and "restore" the U.S. nuclear deterrent. On one occasion, however, he was directly asked by Senator Quayle (R-Indiana) whether "it would be your opinion that we are not in a position of strength and adequate deterrence now." Weinberger's response was straightforward: "Sadly, I have to agree that we are not, no" (U.S. Cong. 1982a, 31). Despite his evaluation that the United States did not have an adequate deterrent, he "would not for a moment exchange anything [with the Soviets] because we have an immense edge in technology" (U.S. Cong. 1982i, 41). But apparently this technological advantage was not sufficient to secure an adequate deterrent.

Examined more closely, some confusion emerges from Weinberger's statements. On several occasions, for example, he defended the administration's buildup on the grounds that the United States was facing the "prospect" of Soviet superiority (U.S. Cong. 1981c, 553); at other times he agreed with President Reagan's evaluation by arguing that "they do have a definite margin of superiority" (U.S. Cong. 1982i, 62). Furthermore, he described the "window of vulnerability" as "the period that *will occur* if we do nothing to improve our strategic strength" (U.S. Cong. 1981n, 4; italics added). Elsewhere, however, he said the administration was closing the window of vulnerability. But how is it possible to close a window that has yet to be opened? The general impression one gets is of someone who believed that the Soviets were "ahead" in some sense and chose his words to paint a very menacing picture, but who was not exactly clear about the precise extent, nature, or implications of these imbalances.

One intriguing aspect of both Perle's and Weinberger's evaluations of Soviet capabilities is the apparent shift that occurred sometime in 1984 (see table 5.7). All references to Soviet strategic superiority appeared in 1984 or earlier. In addition, the emphasis on Soviet advantages/imbalances decreased dramatically. This diminished stress given to Soviet superiority and advantages, however, was not accompanied by any statements indicating the onset of strategic parity. Why the shift? It may be that the administration's modernization had persuaded them that the United States was genuinely closing the gap. A more cynical explanation would stress the utility of claiming that the Soviets were superior; that is, Perle and Weinberger exaggerated Soviet advantages in order to create support for a military buildup or as an excuse for delaying arms control. (After all, how could the United States "negotiate" from strength if it was inferior?) Once they stopped claiming that the Soviets were superior, Perle and Weinberger picked up on another theme that provided an excuse for not signing agreements—the Soviets could not be trusted.

### Strategy and Trustworthiness

Yet another similarity between Perle and Weinberger was their expectation of how the Soviet Union would react to U.S. policies (see tables 5.8 and 5.9). Referring back to Perle's parallels between the 1930s and 1970s and 1980s, one of his recurring messages was the folly of believing that unilateral restraint or negotiated settlements could somehow alter the adversary's goals. The West's restraint in building up its military power in the 1930s did not slow

**TABLE 5.7.  Soviet Nuclear Capabilities**

|  | Perle | | Weinberger | |
|---|---|---|---|---|
|  | 1981–84 | 1985–87 | 1981–84 | 1985–87 |
| Superior | 10 | 0 | 19 | 0 |
| Imbalances/advantages | 36 | 10 | 150 | 30 |
| Parity | 0 | 0 | 0 | 0 |

German rearmament. In Perle's view, the 1970s were years of U.S. restraint; strategic modernization was minimal and few new weapons systems were acquired. The Soviets used this period not merely to "catch up" with the United States, but to achieve strategic advantages consistent with their goal of superiority. On the wisdom of relying on negotiated settlements to restrain one's adversary, Perle pointed to the failure of limited concessions to satisfy Nazi Germany. Similarly, the SALT treaties did not inhibit the Soviet quest for superiority. According to Perle, the Soviets could not be expected to reciprocate U.S. restraint; they exploited it. The Soviets did not alter their policies to abide by agreements, they negotiated treaties that conformed to their objectives.

The same basic themes are found in Weinberger's statements. Generically speaking, he argued that "the Soviet Union is not impressed by self-restraint, which we have tried, but by determination" (U.S. Cong. 1983g, 101). It is "only strength . . . which impresses the Soviet Union" (Weinberger 1987, 13). Drawing on recent experience, he concluded:

> . . . we have tried this business of slowing down, unilaterally hoping that, either because of economic problems, or because we set a good example, the Soviets would follow suit . . . Unfortunately, there is no indication that ever happened in the 1970s and there is not the slightest suggestion that it will happen now. (U.S. Cong. 1985j, 524)

Weinberger also doubted whether negotiated settlements had been, or would be, effective mechanisms for modifying Soviet behavior because "they

**TABLE 5.8. Soviet Response to Policies of Firmness**

|             | Perle | Weinberger |
|-------------|-------|------------|
| Back down   | 21    | 99         |
| Reciprocate | 0     | 0          |
| Other/mixed | 0     | 1          |

**TABLE 5.9. Soviet Response to Restraint**

|             | Perle | Weinberger |
|-------------|-------|------------|
| Reciprocate | 0     | 0          |
| Exploit     | 22    | 46         |
| Other/mixed | 0     | 0          |

sign treaties which fit with their plans" (U.S. Cong. 1986g, 710). Only through the demonstration of U.S. will and strength could the United States hope to induce Soviet concessions or inhibit further expansion of the Soviet empire; in the absence of U.S. power, Soviet policy became "more obnoxious" (U.S. Cong. 1983g, 114).

Perle's pessimistic assessment of Soviet behavior was expressed most consistently and constantly in his evaluation of Soviet trustworthiness (table 5.10). Perle argued that the Soviets had violated every major treaty they signed with the United States—SALT I, SALT II, the ABM Treaty, treaties on chemical and biological warfare, the Helsinki Accords, and so on. This cheating took two forms: first, a scrupulous adherence to the technical requirements of agreements while taking advantage of gray areas in order to achieve advantages inconsistent with the spirit of the treaties; and second, outright violations of "central treaty provisions" (Perle 1987e, 177). According to Perle, "while [the United States] regards the spirit of agreements as a guide to their implementation, the Soviets do not; they care nothing for the spirit of it, and while it suits their purpose, little more for the letter" (U.S. Cong. 1984b, 7). The loopholes and ambiguities that fostered circumvention were "in almost every instance . . . the result of Soviet unwillingness to agree to precision" (U.S. Cong. 1985a, 29). And when the loopholes were not big enough, "the Soviets will violate agreements when they find it in their interest to do so and they will do so for even relatively modest improvements basic to their security" (U.S. Cong. 1985a, 6). The fact that Soviet violations usually added little, if anything, to overall Soviet military capabilities was taken as evidence of a complete lack of respect for agreements: if the Soviets were not constrained by even the most modest provisions, how could they be expected to abide by truly significant agreements that reduce Soviet military power?

We find a similar, if somewhat less nuanced, view of Soviet treaty compliance in Weinberger's case (see table 5.10). By "less nuanced" I mean that the concept of "technical obedience" (i.e., compliance with the letter but

TABLE 5.10.  Soviet Treaty Record

|  | Perle | Weinberger |
|---|---|---|
| Violates/cheats | 76 | 52 |
| Technical obedience | 45 | 3 |
| Abides | 3[a] | 3[a] |
| Other/mixed | 0 | 9 |

[a]Instances when Perle and Weinberger were asked about very specific compliance issues. They admitted that the Soviets were abiding by particular provisions of agreements.

not the spirit of agreements) was not prominent in his analysis. The options in Weinberger's mind appear to have been either adherence or violation, and there was no question on which side of the fence the Soviets fell. As Weinberger saw it, "there is a long history of Soviet violations" (U.S. Cong. 1986d, 102). This was true in the case of SALT II (which they were "violating every day"), the ABM Treaty (which they "have violated and continue to violate with impunity"), and biological and chemical weapons conventions (CBS News 1986b; U.S. Cong. 1984e, 229). Stated simply, "if they want to violate something, they will violate it" (US Cong. 1986g, 672). As a result, "you can't trust [the Soviets] unless you have *absolute* verification" (CBS News 1986b; italics added).

As was the case with Perle's and Weinberger's evaluation of Soviet nuclear capabilities, one finds a shift in emphasis over time. In Perle's case, there was suspicion about Soviet trustworthiness throughout his tenure in office, but after 1984 there was a shift from emphasizing technical obedience to stressing outright violations (see table 5.11). For Weinberger, there was an even more unusual and dramatic shift: prior to 1984 he did not display much concern about the Soviet treaty record at all, but, beginning in 1984, this became one of the most prominent aspects of his statements about the Soviet Union (see table 5.11). It is probably no coincidence that the first administration report on Soviet treaty violations was released in January, 1984, which is the precise point at which these shifts took place.

This shift is interesting when considered along with Perle and Weinberger's changing evaluation of Soviet nuclear capabilities, particularly in Weinberger's case. If the claims of Soviet strategic superiority were merely rationales or excuses to delay arms control during Reagan's first term, what would happen when the gap had been closed? This would seem to open the door for serious "negotiations from strength." But even then, how could the United States sign an agreement with a country that had no respect for treaties? Thus, there is the possibility that this newfound concern for Soviet treaty violations was more than a sudden realization of Soviet untrustworthiness.

**TABLE 5.11.  Soviet Treaty Record (Breakdown)**

|  | Perle | | Weinberger | |
|---|---|---|---|---|
|  | 1981–83 | 1984–87 | 1981–83 | 1984–87 |
| Violates | 7 | 69 | 4 | 48 |
| Technical obedience | 21 | 23 | 2 | 1 |
| Abides | 3 | 0 | 2 | 1 |
| Other/mixed | 0 | 2 | 6 | 3 |

## Soviet Decision Structure

Perle's discussion of Soviet treaty violations highlights another key aspect of his image—the perception of a highly rational, centralized, and unified decision-making structure (see table 5.12). Whenever weapon systems were acquired or treaty provisions violated, these decisions were portrayed as carefully calculated attempts to further some strategic objective. The existence of treaty loopholes and ambiguities was not simply the result of inherently vague language or complex issues; it was a conscious attempt by Soviet leaders to circumvent the intentions of the treaty. For example, Perle argued that "the Soviets deliberated during the conduct of the [SALT I] negotiations on whether what later turned out to be loopholes were wide enough for them to draw various programs through" (U.S. Cong. 1984d, 16). Concerning loopholes that permitted the SS-19 missile program, "the Soviets knew they were building that loophole into the treaty" (U.S. Cong. 1984d, 25). This rational actor portrait appears in other areas as well. Discussing the Soviet civil defense effort, Perle confessed that "I know of no way to explain the Soviet investment except in terms of a perception on their part that it strengthens their position" (U.S. Cong. 1982g, 4927). Finally, when asked about alternative explanations for the growth and structure of the Soviet strategic force, Perle argued, "if you ask the chiefs whether it is likely that the Soviets would expand their forces . . . without some military objective, they would be inclined to my view that the Soviets do not do that, that they develop plans and stick to them" (U.S. Cong. 1985h, 94).

Nowhere is there any indication that Perle saw other forces at work. The idea that programs like civil defense might be driven by parochial bureaucratic interests did not occur to him. An explanation for Soviet reliance on ICBMs, which stressed the impact of a military psychology that traditionally emphasized land power, is not entertained. There was not a single reference to the existence of factional or bureaucratic interests or any divisions within the leadership. Even when Perle recognized that treaty violations were militarily insignificant, he still argued that they were the result of Soviet *perceptions* that they would result in some strategic advantage. He did not argue that such

TABLE 5.12.   Soviet Decision Style

|                         | Perle | Weinberger |
|-------------------------|-------|------------|
| Rational actor          | 10    | 9          |
| Bureaucratic politics   | 0     | 1          |
| Organizational process  | 0     | 0          |
| Other/mixed             | 1     | 2          |

actions and policies must be treated *as if* they were the result of careful and deliberate decisions to achieve advantages; he repeatedly stated that he could think of no other possible explanation.

For Weinberger, there were a few isolated references that departed from the perception of a unified and rational Soviet decision-making structure. For example, concerning the prospects for arms control, he argued that "there are elements within the Soviet Union now that recognize that an arms limitation of a meaningful character would be in the interests of both sides" (U.S. Cong. 1981a, 31). He also suggested that "there was some internal argument" within the Soviet leadership about an invasion of Poland in 1980 (U.S. Cong. 1982, 286). Despite the occasional recognition of factions and policy debates, Weinberger did not offer any sustained analysis of their implications; such observations were the exception, not the rule (see table 5.12). More common was his portrait of the Soviets as "very good chess players in every sense . . . they are very methodical, and it is easier for them to follow a fixed policy because they have considerably more tenure in their higher officials and they have no real constraints by public opinion" (U.S. Cong. 1983b, 123). The absence of public opinion and the highly centralized nature of Soviet decision making were among Weinberger's most consistent themes. He argued that "the society they have enables them to decide, four, five, or six men in the Kremlin, that they want military superiority" and "they can make a decision tomorrow to increase their defense spending by 50, 60, 70 percent just on the determination of two or three people in the Kremlin" (U.S. Cong. 1985c, 53; U.S. Cong. 1987g, 95).

## Soviet Perceptions of the United States

Unfortunately, public officials are seldom asked about how they think Soviet leaders see the United States. This is because the questioners probably share the assumption that the Soviets view us pretty much as we view ourselves. Weinberger and Perle were no different in this respect. On those few occasions when Perle and Weinberger were asked about Soviet perceptions of the United States, particularly the administration's military buildup, it was evident that their already menacing image of the Soviet Union was combined with a belief that the Soviets should not, and did not, view the United States as a threat (table 5.13). Discussing the situation in Europe, Perle argued that "they can be quite confident in the Kremlin that the United States is not going to launch an aggressive war against them. . . . We can have no such confidence" (U.S. Cong. 1983b, 18). On several occasions Perle was questioned about the Soviet perception of the Reagan administration's strategic modernization program. Bearing in mind the 1980 Republican platform's pledge to regain military superiority, the administration's plans to build the MX missile, the D-5 Trident II missile, and the Pershing II (all highly accurate missiles with hard-target kill capabilities), and Reagan's commitment to a defensive system, could the Soviets possibly think that the United States was moving toward a first-strike capability? Perle was asked this question several times, but he never gave the argument any credence. The following response is indicative of his typical reaction.

> Implicit in your formulation is the notion that the Soviets believe that the United States has or will have the capability . . . as well as the will to launch a first-strike . . . I do not happen to believe that . . . the Soviets have some history to go on here. In the period in which the United States possessed a nuclear monopoly, when it would have been easy to threaten and intimidate the Soviet Union, we did not do so. (U.S. Cong. 1985m, 121)

In my discussion of Weinberger's view of Soviet policy motivation I touched upon his beliefs about Soviet perceptions of the United States. He rejected the idea that the Soviet military buildup was a response to any U.S. threat; but he went one step further by denying that it is motivated by a fear of the United States, no matter how unreasonable (see table 5.13). In one particularly revealing interview, Weinberger was pressed on the same issue as was Perle—whether it was possible that the Soviets might look at the U.S. buildup and conclude that our intentions were somewhat less than benign. Not surprisingly, the answer was no: "they know perfectly well that we will never launch a first strike" (NBC News 1983). A disbelieving Marvin Kalb pursued the matter further: "Mr. Secretary, but you understand how the Soviet Union could think, in its own strategic planning, that the United States, and this administration particularly, is seeking a first strike?" Weinberger would not concede the point: "No, I don't see any way in which they could believe that" (NBC News 1983). Speaking more generally about the Soviet military buildup of the last two decades, Weinberger concluded, "what has been happening with the Soviet Union is not the building of careful Soviet defenses

TABLE 5.13.  Soviet View of the United States

|  | Perle | Weinberger |
| --- | --- | --- |
| Aggressive/threat | 0 | 0 |
| Peaceful/no threat | 4 | 4 |
| Other/mixed | 1 | 2 |

brought on by a siege mentality caused by a rapacious West, but simple ability [sic] to carry out the doctrine of world domination" (U.S. Cong. 1984e, 129).

## Image Summary

The image that emerges from an examination of Perle's and Weinberger's statements is simple and consistent, both internally and over time (with two exceptions, already noted). According to both, the Soviet Union was an expansionist power, perhaps with unlimited ambitions. It sought military superiority at all levels, including nuclear weapons. The Soviets had either achieved superiority or were very close to doing so (at least before 1984). The Soviet leadership did not accept the assumptions underlying mutual assured destruction (MAD); it believed that under certain circumstances a nuclear conflict could be fought and won. The Soviets violated both the letter and spirit of agreements whenever they believed it was in their interests to do so. Soviet actions, from treaty violations to weapons procurement to civil defense programs, were carefully planned to further Soviet strategic objectives. Soviet actions could not be explained by any rational fear because the United States had not, did not, and would not use its nuclear force to intimidate, and the Soviets were well aware of this.

One is immediately struck by the similarities between Perle's and Weinberger's images of the Soviet Union and the "inherent bad faith model" and diabolical enemy image presented, respectively, by Ole Holsti (1962) and Ralph White (1968 and 1984). With the possible exception of Perle's lack of emphasis on ideology in Soviet policy and the addition of nuclear terminology not used in the 1950s, their images of the Soviet Union are virtual carbon copies of Dulles's. In their "reconsideration" of the inherent bad faith model, Stuart and Starr observe that "the concept was almost sui generis because it was inextricably tied to the character of John Foster Dulles. Virtually all other American foreign policy makers have been consigned to a vague category which might be called 'not inherent bad faith'" (1981–82, 2). Not so for Richard Perle and Caspar Weinberger.

# CHAPTER 6

## Moderates in the Midst?

*Senator Humphrey*: . . . do you think it is wise to submit the security of the United States and the West to a treaty whose cosignatory is a nation conducting criminal activities [in Afghanistan] against a largely defenseless people?
*Secretary Shultz*: Come off it, Senator.

—(U.S. Cong. 1985d, 3554)

We should not allow ourselves . . . if something positive happens somewhere to get carried away with euphoria. Nor, given our strength and the Soviet interest in working with a strong country like the United States, should we go into paroxysms of despair either.
—George Shultz (U.S. Cong. 1985c, 55)

After Ronald Reagan was elected president in 1980 and speculation turned to the likely composition of his cabinet, most assumed that George Shultz, a friend of Reagan's from California, would get the nod as secretary of state. There were, however, problems with Shultz. Despite his conservative credentials, "some of the more militant Reaganites doubted that he had firm enough views of the world situation. There were, they felt, too many soft sides to his character" (Gwertzman 1983, 13). Many on the Republican party's right wing, such as Senator Jesse Helms (R-North Carolina), feared that Shultz was really a pragmatic and moderate establishment Republican whose views were insufficiently strident. Shultz's service as secretary of the treasury under Nixon, which involved meetings with top Soviet leaders regarding the economic aspects of détente, did not exactly reassure his more conservative critics, for whom any association with détente was suspect. Conservative supporters could point out that Shultz was a founding member of the Committee on the Present Danger, but this did not carry much weight because he was clearly not one of the committee's guiding forces or more vocal members. Given these liabilities, Reagan opted for Alexander Haig, a former supreme commander of NATO and Nixon's chief of staff, whose anticommunist credentials could not be questioned, even though some conservatives grumbled about his ties to Henry Kissinger.

While many thought Shultz was not enough of a hard-liner, there were some who saw little difference between him and other administration officials. Robert Dallek, claiming that the Reagan administration "lack[ed] intellectual range," thought that "Reagan's State Department does not trail far behind his defense officials in taking a hard anticommunist line . . . former Secretary of State Alexander Haig and his successor George Shultz are vigorous advocates of standing up to the Soviets" (1984, 135). Dallek concluded that "he [Shultz] is less moderate than he is given credit for" (137). As if it were not enough to be simultaneously too hard-line and too moderate, there were still others who criticized Shultz for having no foreign policy "line" at all. One commentator labeled Shultz "the nowhere man," quoting an administration source as saying, "he doesn't stand for anything . . . this is a guy who has never thought about the really big issues of global politics . . . he doesn't have much knowledge, no views" (Kondracke 1983, 19). In short, there was no consensus on Shultz's foreign policy views.

When Shultz took over the controls at State he found a staff upon whom he would rely heavily. Foremost among them, particularly in the area of arms control, was Richard Burt. A "defense intellectual" who previously served as a national security correspondent for the *New York Times*, Burt had earned a reputation as a pragmatic conservative and a critic of SALT II. But his criticisms of the treaty were less vehement than those of Perle and various members of the Committee on the Present Danger; he simply argued that, on balance, the treaty favored the Soviet Union (see Burt 1978). Burt did not place his criticisms of SALT II within any sweeping denunciation of the arms control process, though there were features of the political dynamics at work in SALT that troubled him. All of this made him acceptable to conservatives, even if he never garnered their enthusiastic support. Haig, however, was impressed by Burt and urged that he be placed in charge of the Bureau of Politico-Military Affairs, commonly referred to as the State Department's "mini-Pentagon." Reagan complied with Haig's wishes. By the time Shultz entered the picture, Burt was already well-established in the State Department and deeply embroiled in the administration's arms control battles.

The relationship that developed between Shultz and Burt resembles that of Perle and Weinberger in several respects. Neither Shultz nor Weinberger had much experience in foreign policy matters when he entered office. Nor did they have a broad knowledge or deep understanding of nuclear issues, strategy, and weapons systems. But both proved to be quick studies, mastering the necessary details of nuclear arms and arms control in short order. Each also relied on his more knowledgeable and experienced subordinate; Burt for Shultz and Perle for Weinberger. Although their roles were similar, differences were to be found in the advice Burt and Perle offered their superiors.

## Shultz and Burt View the Soviet Union

### Foreign Policy Objectives

Despite his reputation as the administration's moderate, there was no expectation that Shultz would view the Soviet Union as peaceful and nonaggressive. *Moderate*, after all, is a relative term, and the basis of comparison was people like Perle. Not surprisingly, Shultz concurred with the image of an expansionist Soviet Union willing to use force directly and indirectly to increase its influence around the globe (see table 6.1). According to Shultz:

> The Soviet Union does not share our vision of a peaceful international order and it seems prepared, all too often, to impose its vision by the use of force. In the past twenty years the Soviet Union has continued a relentless military buildup, nuclear and conventional, surpassing any legitimate need for self-defense. (*DSB*, September, 1985, 27)[1]

The belief that Soviet military capabilities greatly exceeded any possible defensive requirements, which hints at offensive designs, was expressed by all of the individuals in this study, and Shultz was no exception: "their naval and ground forces are well beyond the maximum conceivably necessary for defense" (*DSB*, October, 1983, 30). It was the growing Soviet ability to project force as a result of improved naval forces and increased airlift capabilities that Shultz found worrisome because "it has given them the ability to intervene when they perceive areas of opportunity" (U.S. Cong. 1983a, 573). "The demonstrated willingness of the Soviet Union to use that strength, ruthlessly and without compunction," made these developments all the more dangerous in Shultz's eyes (*DSB*, December, 1982, 13–14).

Burt echoed Shultz's concerns about Soviet "expansionism," "adventurism," and "meddling" (see table 6.1). Burt observed that "we would all prefer a Soviet Union that didn't threaten our interests, that didn't use military force. We would all like a Soviet Union that shared in our values" (U.S. Cong. 1984e, 7). Obviously Burt thought that the Soviet Union did threaten our interests, did use military force, and did not share our values. Like Shultz, Burt was disturbed by the growth of Soviet forces because "the emergence of the Soviet Union as a global military power has enabled the Soviet leadership to pursue a forward strategy" (U.S. Cong. 1985a, 317). These newfound capabilities not only increased *possibilities* for a more aggressive Soviet strat-

---

1. The quotes from Shultz and Burt, except where otherwise noted, are from congressional testimony, which is cited in the same manner as for Perle and Weinberger, or the Department of State Bulletin, which is cited as: (*DSB*, month, year, page).

egy, they actually brought about a "concomitant increase in Moscow's *willingness* to use force in international relations" (U.S. Cong. 1983, 4; italics added). According to Burt:

> Soviet global influence has expanded as the direct result of the growth in Soviet forces . . . they now have the capability and the will to project power around the globe and intervene in the affairs of other nations—and they have done so: by direct military actions in Afghanistan, by overt threats in Poland, by proxy in the Middle East, Central America, and Southeast Asia, and by propaganda in Western Europe. (U.S. Cong. 1982b, 38)

Asked about possible changes in Soviet policy accompanying Andropov's rise to power in 1983, Burt answered, "we see no indication to date that the Soviet practice of neoimperialism, an assertive foreign policy backed up mainly by the growth of military power, is in any way going to be changed or evolve" (U.S. Cong. 1983a, 4).

While Burt saw no evidence of any change in the Soviet policy of "neoimperialism," he did not see many signs of success either, noting that "in the past five years the Soviets have not added to the list of clients they acquired in the 1970s" (U.S. Cong. 1985a, 333). What accounted for the apparent failure of Soviet efforts at expansion? Burt explained, "this is due, no doubt, to a combination of economic constraints, leadership uncertainties, as well as renewed U.S. strength" (U.S. Cong. 1985a, 333). Shultz was similarly impressed by the absence of Soviet gains: "before President Reagan took office, they seemed to be moving in here, there, and elsewhere all the time. Since his arrival the picture has been different" (*DSB*, December, 1982, 36). Shultz did not see any reason to believe this lack of success indicated any fundamental change in Soviet objectives, since he maintained that "the Soviet Union and its proxies are [still] using military force in the most brutal man-

TABLE 6.1.  Soviet Foreign Policy Objectives

|  | Shultz | Burt |
|---|---|---|
| Unlimitedly expansionist/destructionist | 0 | 0 |
| Limitedly expansionist/revisionist | 0 | 0 |
| Expansionist/unspecified | 239 | 29 |
| Defensive/status quo | 0 | 0 |
| Other/mixed | 6 | 3 |

*Note*: Tables 6.1 to 6.11 provide the results of the content analysis performed using the procedure outlined in chap. 4. The total number of documents was 151 for Shultz and 30 for Burt. The documents are listed in the bibliography.

ner to expand and maintain their control" (*DSB*, April, 1987, 5). Shultz did not really provide an explanation for this lack of success, but the subtle implication was that U.S. strength was the key. Burt, however, was the only administration official to cite reasons other than U.S. policy as a critical factor.

In some respects, these warnings of Soviet expansionism are similar to those voiced by Weinberger and Perle. In the cases of Shultz and Burt, however, the finding that is potentially most significant centers around what they did not say. The coding of their statements did not reveal a single reference to Soviet policy being unlimitedly expansionist. There was no mention of a Soviet quest for world "domination," "revolution," "hegemony," or a "one-world communist state." There was nothing about the Soviet Union desiring the elimination of the United States, the destruction of democracy and capitalism, or the ultimate triumph of communism. Although Shultz spoke generally about the "lessons of the 1930s—that appeasement of an aggressor only invites aggression and increases the danger of war," one does not find the consistent and repeated attempts to draw parallels between the 1930s and the 1970s and 1980s that were found for Perle and Weinberger (1985, 718). Agreements and interactions with the Soviet Union were not portrayed as comparable to dealings with Nazi Germany. While caution should be exercised in drawing conclusions from the absence of statements, the comparison with others is striking. And one would think that if Shultz and Burt viewed Soviet goals in more expansive terms they would have said so at least a few times. The absence of any statements about unlimited Soviet goals suggests that Shultz and Burt perceived Soviet aims as less robust than did Weinberger or Perle (or Reagan, as we shall see in the next chapter).

## Policy Motivation

Shultz's view of the forces that shaped Soviet foreign policy was the most nuanced and complex set of beliefs of the five individuals included in this study (see table 6.2). Shultz agreed that ideology was a central factor: "so long as the Soviet system is driven by ideology and national ambition . . . true friendship and cooperation will remain out of reach" (1985a, 706). He thought "the Soviets' interventionist policies in the Third World [were] the result of ideology combined with new capabilit[ies]" (*DSB*, December, 1984, 3) "There is," he claimed, "a sense in which one of the attributes of Marxism is its desire to subvert and overthrow other governments" (*DSB*, September, 1983, 48).

Unlike Weinberger and Reagan, however, Shultz's view of the role of ideology was subtle. Shultz observed that, while "we can debate how fully Soviet leaders follow [their] ideology," there is no doubt ideology "helps shape a political culture that does not accommodate well to compromise or truly positive relations with opponents" (*DSB*, December, 1984, 1). The belief that ideology is important because of its role in shaping Soviet political culture and influencing the outlook of Soviet leaders is a fairly sophisticated theme that one does not find in the analyses of other administration officials. Furthermore, Shultz's discussions of the ideological basis of Soviet policy were always tempered by including other forces that combined with ideology to shape Soviet behavior. For example, he claimed that "the Soviet Union is driven not only by Russian history and Soviet state interests, but also by what remains of its revolutionary ideology to spread its system by force" (*DSB*, April, 1984, 18). It follows that Soviet policy is "driven" not only by ideology, but also by Russian history and Soviet state interests. By consistently incorporating other key variables into his analysis of Soviet motivation, Shultz routinely downplayed the significance of ideology.

There were times when Shultz sounded more like Kissinger than a typical Reaganite, offering an essentially realist, power politics view of the roots of the superpower rivalry. In a 1988 speech, as President Reagan was speaking enthusiastically about the dawn of a new era, Shultz was cautioning:

> I find it difficult to believe that our relations with the Soviet Union will ever be "normal" in the sense that we have normal relations with most other countries. There are only two superpowers . . . . It seems unlikely that the U.S.-Soviet relationship will ever lose what has always been and is today a strongly wary and at times adversarial element. (*DSB*, April, 1988, 41)

Shultz was clearly suggesting that a significant part of the explanation of the U.S.-Soviet conflict could be found in the simple fact that the two countries were the dominant powers in the world. That is, the distribution of power and the competition for influence and security all but dictated some level of hostility and suspicion. This was basically a classic realpolitik view of the

**TABLE 6.2.  Soviet Policy Motivation**

|                          | Shultz | Burt |
| ------------------------ | ------ | ---- |
| Ideology                 | 8      | 0    |
| Logic of totalitarianism | 1      | 0    |
| History                  | 3      | 2    |
| Culture                  | 1      | 0    |
| Idiosyncratic            | 3      | 2    |
| Vested interests         | 1      | 0    |
| External challenges      | 2      | 1    |
| Power politics           | 1      | 0    |
| Other/mixed              | 8      | 0    |

cold war as the inevitable result of the search for security in an anarchic, and therefore insecure, international system.

Shultz also accepted, with qualifications, the thesis that the Soviet Union's historical experience contributed to its current behavior. He observed, "it has been argued that Soviet behavior is partly motivated by historical insecurity, that they suffer from an endemic paranoia stemming from centuries of war and foreign invasion" (*DSB*, December, 1984, 1). Though Shultz found this explanation "inadequate" for certain aspects of Soviet policy, such as involvement in third world conflicts, he did not reject these insecurities as either irrelevant or nonexistent. Attempting to account for the Soviet investment in ABM research and other types of defense, for example, Shultz speculated that "the Soviets having been invaded a few times, perhaps understandably have a greater orientation than we toward defense" (U.S. Cong. 1987a, 391). This is a far cry from the explanation offered by others in the administration. Even though Shultz was willing to entertain many explanations for Soviet behavior, he did not combine these into a single, fine-tuned view of "the sources of Soviet conduct." Still, Shultz displayed a level of complexity and sensitivity to alternative explanations that had no parallel among the other officials in this study.

In contrast to Shultz, there is very little in Burt's statements about the motivations for Soviet policy. Other than one or two brief references to Soviet "paranoia" and the insecurity created through a history of invasions, one finds almost no clues about Burt's views concerning the sources of Soviet behavior. In this sense, Burt resembles Perle more than Shultz; there are no references to the ideological underpinnings of Soviet policy or anything else. Given the relatively small number of documents for Burt (even fewer than for Perle) it is wise to avoid drawing any firm conclusions regarding Burt's beliefs about the forces that shape Soviet behavior.

## Nuclear Objectives and Doctrine

Burt and Shultz did not discuss the Soviet Union's ultimate nuclear objectives or nuclear doctrine at any length. What is available, however, suggests much less menacing views than those expressed by Perle and Weinberger (see table 6.3). Only on a few occasions did Shultz hint that the Soviets were striving for

**TABLE 6.3. Soviet Nuclear Objectives**

|             | Shultz | Burt |
| ----------- | ------ | ---- |
| Superiority | 1      | 0    |
| Parity      | 0      | 0    |
| Other/mixed | 2      | 1    |

nuclear superiority (coded as other/mixed because they are so vague). He warned, for example, that "the Soviets must know that in the absence of equitable and verifiable agreements we will proceed with defense programs that will deny them superiority" (*DSB*, December, 1984, 3). "Only if they see no possibility of achieving superiority," he predicted, "will they agree to real arms reductions based on equality" (U.S. Cong. 1983i, 110). According to Shultz, the Soviet nuclear buildup "showed no signs of abating, even after the achievement of strategic parity" (*DSB*, April, 1988, 39). Furthermore, "Soviet military doctrine stresses war fighting and survival in a nuclear environment [and] the importance of numerical superiority" (*DSB*, January, 1987, 32). Strictly speaking, Shultz did not come right out and say that the Soviet objective was nuclear superiority (as Perle did), but this was the gist of these statements. In Burt's case, the references are even more unclear. The closest Burt ever came to attributing a desire for nuclear superiority to the Soviets was his claim that "Soviet goals are now seen to go well beyond any measure of equality" (U.S. Cong. 1982b, 35). Such statements are clearly not in the same league as the warnings by Perle and Weinberger about the Soviet drive for a disarming first-strike capability.

Yet another contrast with the Pentagon civilians was the absence of references to a Soviet belief that a nuclear war could be "fought and won" (see table 6.4). Although Shultz made a few references to Soviet "war-fighting strategy," it does not necessarily follow that the Soviets believed a nuclear war was winnable. After all, the United States itself had been moving toward a war-fighting strategy, but no administration official argued that the United States believed it could win a nuclear war. And although Shultz saw Soviet forces as "designed for preemption," this also does not entail a belief in the winnability of nuclear war. Shultz did note that "strategic doctrine *in the West* has ultimately relied for decades on the balance of terror," but the context does not allow any conclusion about whether he thought this was also true in the East (1985, 703; italics added). On Soviet plans to launch a first strike, Shultz was, to say the least, equivocal. Responding to questions about the first-strike potential of the MX missile, Shultz denied that it was intended for such a purpose, but he did argue that the MX "makes it less possible for the Soviets to, if they contemplate, and I am not saying they are contemplating,

**TABLE 6.4.  Soviet Nuclear Doctrine**

|              | Shultz | Burt |
|--------------|--------|------|
| Winnable     | 0      | 0    |
| Not winnable | 0      | 0    |
| Other/mixed  | 3      | 3    |

but if somebody is contemplating a first strike against the United States" (U.S. Cong. 1985g, 58). Shultz did, however, worry about the prospects for coercion: "without arguing the question of whether the Soviets are prepared to launch a nuclear first strike . . . a critical imbalance in strategic capabilities could make them bolder in a regional conflict or major crisis" (U.S. Cong. 1983i, 109).

Burt also emphasized the Soviet adoption of a war-fighting strategy, but only with regard to the European theater: "the Soviet Union in training, in doctrine, and in the structure of its forces, is prepared to fight a nuclear war in Europe." Burt immediately added that he was "not suggesting that the Soviets intend to provoke a war. But if it comes, the Soviets are ready to escalate rapidly to the nuclear level" (*DSB*, November, 1981, 56). Burt asked rhetorically, "how, then, is the alliance to respond to Soviet behavior? By mirroring it? By adopting a war-fighting strategy?" (*DSB*, February, 1982, 44). The unprovided answer, of course, is that the alliance already had a war-fighting nuclear strategy that contemplated the first use of nuclear weapons. Still, he claimed that "it is the Soviet Union which is developing [the] ability to fight and win a nuclear war in Europe" (U.S. Cong. 1982b, 36). What is significant is Burt's focus on the European theater; he never argued that the Soviets believed they could fight and win a strategic nuclear conflict. Burt was also hesitant about whether the Soviets would strike the United States first (which is an integral part of the "fight and win" scenario). He would only say, "I am not going to comment on the likelihood of a Soviet first strike or the likelihood of Soviet surprise attack, but as cautious, conservative military planners, we can't rule out that contingency" (U.S. Cong. 1982b, 43). Again, one cannot fail to see the differences between this and the ominous warnings of Perle and Weinberger, particularly the latter. Moreover, Burt pointed out that "the Soviet Union has had a terrible experience with war, this is a country that has lost between 12 and 20 million people in World War II. I do not think the Soviets are looking for war" (57).

## Relative Military Capabilities

Like everyone else in the administration, Burt and Shultz recognized Soviet superiority in conventional forces, at least in a quantitative sense, though Shultz warned that "it is possible to overrate the ability of Soviet conventional forces around the world" (U.S. Cong. 1987c, 845; see tables 6.5 and 6.6). Their discussion of the nuclear balance was more interesting. The Pentagon civilians were convinced, at least during Reagan's first term, that the Soviets had either achieved nuclear superiority or were getting very close (their characterizations of the nuclear balance oscillated between evaluations of Soviet superiority and Soviet advantages/imbalances). At no time did either

Perle or Weinberger speak in terms of nuclear parity. Neither Burt nor Shultz assessed the U.S. predicament in similarly alarming terms. In their case, one finds some inconsistencies, but the fluctuations are between statements about Soviet advantages and others indicating the existence of strategic parity (there is, however, agreement about Soviet superiority in intermediate range nuclear forces; see table 6.6).

Burt frequently described the nuclear balance in terms that Perle and Weinberger avoided and even ridiculed (table 6.6). During the administration's first year, Burt claimed, "the Soviet Union has achieved *parity* in intercontinental range forces" (*DSB*, October, 1982, 55; italics added). The use of "parity" was no fluke or slip of the tongue; Burt would use this term repeatedly throughout his tenure in the State Department. In 1983, as other key officials (including the president) were speaking of the Soviet Union's "margin of superiority," Burt explained that the INF deployment in Europe "reflects a considered response to a widely felt European need for an evolutionary adjustment to NATO's capabilities to account for the onset of strategic parity" (U.S. Cong. 1982a, 36). Burt deemed the missiles necessary because "shifts in the military balance and the emergence of U.S.-Soviet strategic parity . . . have raised anew issues of American reliability" (*DSB*, March, 1983, 51). And, as of 1985, Burt remarked that "we find ourselves running hard to maintain strategic nuclear parity with the Soviet Union" (U.S. Cong. 1985a, 317). Thus, Burt often contradicted other Reagan officials who saw the Soviets as superior to the United States.

TABLE 6.5.  Soviet Military Capabilities (Conventional)

|  | Shultz | Burt |
|---|---|---|
| Superior | 12 | 5 |
| Parity | 0 | 0 |
| Inferior | 0 | 0 |
| Other/mixed | 5 | 1 |

TABLE 6.6.  Soviet Nuclear Capabilities

|  | Schultz | | Burt | |
|---|---|---|---|---|
|  | Strategic | INF | Strategic | INF |
| Superior | 0 | 3 | 0 | 9 |
| Advantage/imbalance | 10 | 4 | 10 | 1 |
| Parity/balance | 4 | 0 | 6 | 0 |
| Other/mixed | 9 | 0 | 6 | 1 |

Burt, however, not only contradicted others, but himself as well. At times he identified important areas of Soviet advantage, potentially at odds with his description of strategic parity. He occasionally spoke of the administration's efforts to "restore the balance" of strategic forces (e.g., U.S. Cong. 1982a, 6 and 1984b, 13). Using a rather nebulous characterization, which no other Reagan official employed, Burt argued that "in the past twenty years, the Soviets have moved from inferiority, to parity, to what Senator Nunn has called 'parity-plus'" (U.S. Cong. 1985a, 317). He opposed the nuclear freeze because "under present circumstances [it] would only legitimize Soviet nuclear advantages" (U.S. Cong. 1983c, 7). A freeze would have perpetuated "US inferiority in several categories" of the nuclear balance, particularly large, MIRVed, and highly accurate ICBMs (e.g., SS-17s, SS-18s, and SS-19s) (U.S. Cong. 1983c, 20). Burt even went further in one instance.

> . . . it is possible, given their capabilities to attack a large fraction of our land-based forces, that if we were to attempt to retaliate in kind, launch a retaliatory strike against [Soviet] land-based forces, that [the Soviet Union] would still have sufficient land-based forces surviving to then attack again. (U.S. Cong. 1982e, 33)

Such a scenario embodies the basic logic of the window of vulnerability argument. The inconsistencies between these statements and those about strategic parity are striking. Still, it is significant that Burt never said that Soviet forces were superior to U.S. forces, and on only one occasion did Burt convey the idea of a window of vulnerability, though he avoided using the phrase. Furthermore, Burt consistently stressed that Soviet advantages existed in *some areas*, implying offsetting U.S. advantages in others.

In Shultz's case, the picture is even less clear (see table 6.6). He apparently agreed with Perle's view that the Soviets possessed "great advantage in destructive power" (i.e., throw-weight) and talked about the need to "redress existing imbalances" in strategic forces (*DSB*, April, 1988, 6 and June, 1984, 29). But Shultz went well beyond vague references to "restoring the balance"; he frequently came very close to describing Soviet capabilities in a manner that indicated a disarming first-strike capability. For example, he saw "a Soviet advantage in heavy, accurate ICBMs with multiple warheads that could threaten the survival of the land-based portion of U.S. forces" (*DSB*, February, 1986, 2). He claimed that Soviet ICBMs were "capable of destroying virtually the entire land-based portion of our retaliatory forces" (*DSB*, December, 1985, 22). Shultz was usually very careful to qualify his statements by adding "almost," "virtually," and "could." And he spoke about the dangers to the "land-based portion of our retaliatory forces," suggesting that other weapons of retaliation would remain. A few times, however, Shultz presented a truly menacing portrait of Soviet capabilities: "the Soviet Union has acquired the capability to put at risk the fixed, land-based missiles of the United States . . . with only a fraction of the force, leaving many warheads to deter retaliation" (*DSB*, December, 1985, 23). It would be difficult to find a better explanation of the window of vulnerability.

Elsewhere Shultz provided less pessimistic assessments of the situation. Testifying shortly after Reagan's comments about the Soviet Union's "definite margin of superiority," Shultz was asked, "do you think that either side can attain and maintain superiority over the other?" He replied, "well, there are categories of weapons in which the Soviet Union now has a distinct advantage. I suppose there are some in which we do. So superiority/inferiority is difficult to judge" (U.S. Cong. 1982a, 171). By 1984, Shultz was claiming that "we have restored the strategic balance," and in 1985 he referred to "the present conditions of nuclear balance" (*DSB*, October, 1984, 20 and May, 1985, 27). But it is difficult to know what to make of such statements. Why did the United States need to "redress" nuclear imbalances when the balance had already been "restored'? What was the nature of the nuclear balance if the Soviets nearly possessed a disarming first-strike capability?

### Strategy and Trustworthiness

On one issue, at least, Shultz and Burt appeared to be in step with their counterparts in the Pentagon: their expectations of how the Soviet Union would respond to U.S. restraint and resolve. The Soviets, they argued, tended to exploit U.S. restraint and back down only in the face of strength and determination (see tables 6.7 and 6.8). According to Shultz, during the 1970s,

**TABLE 6.7. Soviet Response to U.S. Firmness**

|  | Shultz | Burt |
|---|---|---|
| Back down | 24 | 21 |
| Reciprocate | 0 | 0 |
| Other/mixed | 2 | 2 |

**TABLE 6.8. Soviet Response to U.S. Restraint**

|  | Shultz | Burt |
|---|---|---|
| Exploit | 19 | 9 |
| Reciprocate | 1 | 0 |
| Other/mixed | 0 | 0 |

while "the United States was beset by economic difficulties, neglecting its own defenses, and hesitant about its role in the world, the Soviets exploited these conditions." In response to U.S. timidity, "they relentlessly continued to build up militarily, [and] they and their clients moved more boldly in the geopolitical arena" (Shultz 1985, 706). Soviet behavior during the 1970s and throughout its history "shows that when the Soviets have perceived weakness . . . they have seized the opportunity to gain an advantage" (*DSB*, December, 1984, 3). Because of "Moscow's history of taking advantage of any weakness," Shultz claimed, "one thing we have learned over the years is that the Soviets respect strength and firmness" (U.S. Cong 1985d, 3527). Reciprocated restraint and accommodation are unreasonable expectations since "their code of behavior has not included categories for voluntary self-restraint." In addition to stressing the virtue of strength, Shultz warned that "strength alone will never achieve a durable peace" between the United States and the Soviet Union (*DSB*, December, 1984, 2).

Like Shultz, Burt pointed to the Soviet Union's policies during détente to illustrate a propensity to take advantage of U.S. restraint. The Soviet military buildup, begun in the 1960s, "continued through a period when the West pursued policies of détente, when the United States cut back on its military budgets, and when NATO undertook virtually no nuclear modernization" (*DSB*, November, 1981, 58). "Unilateral restraint," he argued, "did not produce Soviet restraint. On the contrary, the Soviet Union implemented expansionist policies in far regions of the world, and carried out the most intensive conventional and nuclear military buildup in peacetime history" (U.S. Cong. 1983c, 6). All of this led Burt to "agree with [former Secretary of Defense] Harold Brown's observation about U.S.-Soviet arms competition: 'when we build, the Soviet Union builds; and when we don't build, the Soviet Union still builds'" (U.S. Cong. 1983g, 28). Burt predicted that "East-West relations will only improve if the Soviet Union is convinced of the determination, unity, and staying power of the West" (U.S. Cong. 1985d, 3). And Burt, like everyone else in the Reagan administration, consistently asserted that the Soviets would negotiate seriously (i.e., make concessions to the U.S. position) only if given the "incentive" to do so, otherwise no Soviet accommodations would be forthcoming. Thus, "without visible and continuing support for our modernization effort, the Soviets would have little incentive to negotiate seriously" (U.S. Cong. 1982a, 37).

What would happen after the West displayed the requisite strength and managed to secure an arms treaty with the Soviet Union? Prior to 1984, the year that began with the release of a report detailing Soviet treaty violations, Shultz did not seem at all concerned with Soviet compliance (see table 6.9). Even after the report was made public, he expressed concern in the mildest terms. Several months after the report was issued, Shultz was asked about its contents and the potential impact on future negotiations. He characterized the report as follows:

> There was a report made by the President to Congress last January [1984], I believe it was and seven instances were picked out, and they illustrate various kinds of problems connected with arms control agreements with the Soviet Union . . . you have to watch vague things in treaties that mean different things to different people. (*DSB*, November, 1984, 33)

At a news conference, Shultz was questioned about the administration's charges of Soviet violations. A correspondent characterized the report as claiming the Soviets were "violating more or less every treaty they have entered with the United States." Shultz rejected this conclusion. While admitting there were instances of violations, Shultz quickly added, "that's a far cry from the way you phrased it of saying that they violate every agreement they ever make. I don't think that's a fair statement about them or anyone's characterization of them" (*DSB*, September, 1984, 6). Actually, it was a very accurate description of Perle's and Weinberger's portrait of the Soviet record.

While Shultz recognized individual violations, once even speaking of a "pattern" of violations, he was very circumspect in his analysis of Soviet actions. He referred, for example, to "the Soviet practice of stretching their implementation of agreements to the *edge* of violation and *sometimes* beyond" (*DSB*, December 1985, 21; italics added). Regarding Soviet compliance with SALT II, Shultz pointed out that "the Soviet Union has taken lots of actions to stay within the SALT limits" (U.S. Cong. 1986g, 321). "Both sides," he argued, "have shown considerable restraint in this regard" (U.S. Cong. 1988a, 92). Although he conceded that "the Soviet record of compliance with treaties is far from perfect," Shultz also noted, "the Soviet pattern of behavior is *not* one of wholesale violations of arms control treaties" (U.S. Cong. 1988d, 9 and 1988a, 27). While such a statement might have stemmed from the need to "sell" the INF Treaty to skeptical senators, it was in line with Shultz's previous comments.

TABLE 6.9.  Soviet Treaty Compliance

|                     | Shultz |         |      |
| ------------------- | ------- | ------- | ---- |
|                     | 1982–83 | 1984–88 | Burt |
| Violate             | 0       | 40      | 5    |
| Technical obedience | 0       | 2       | 2    |
| Abide               | 0       | 1       | 0    |
| Other/mixed         | 1       | 11      | 2    |

For Burt, one finds only a few scattered references to Soviet violations (table 6.9). He expressed "real doubts over whether the Soviet Union is adhering to the threshold ban of 150 kilotons" (U.S. Cong. 1984d, 17). Burt displayed concerns about Soviet violations of the Helsinki agreements, and he was certain that chemical and biological weapons conventions had been violated in Afghanistan by the Soviet Union and in Southeast Asia by its allies. He agreed that "the Soviet Union has violated aspects of SALT II without any question of a doubt" (U.S. Cong. 1985a, 341). Burt also warned of Soviet actions that went against the spirit of agreements, even if the letter was being followed: "there is not simply the difficulty of outright Soviet violations . . . while you might argue the Soviets have not technically violated the submarine conversions aspect of the treaty [SALT II], they are certainly undermining or circumventing it" (U.S. Cong. 1985a, 341). Taken as whole, however, one is impressed by the relative lack of accusations of violations. Burt refrained from making broad generalizations about Soviet "cheating." Burt did not dwell on the issue either, even after the administration's report was released. Furthermore, he rarely raised the subject of his own accord; the majority of his comments were in response to pointed questions, which differed from Perle and Weinberger, who seldom missed an opportunity to raise the issue.

## Soviet Decision Style

An examination of Shultz's and Burt's analyses of Soviet foreign policy does not provide many insights into their views of how the Soviet decision-making process works; relevant comments were few and far between, and they were often unrelated to foreign policy decision making (table 6.10). In Burt's case, what few statements are available suggest a departure from the perception of a highly unified, centralized, and rational decision structure. The most prominent theme in Burt's comments was ignorance about what goes on behind Kremlin walls: "there are so many things we don't know about how the Soviet Union makes decisions" (U.S. Cong. 1984b, 22). Burt speculated that "they seem to still take decisions in a collegial fashion as a collective leadership . . . [though] certain individuals in that leadership seem to have a great deal of influence" (U.S. Cong. 1984e, 5–6). In general, however, Burt lamented the

**TABLE 6.10. Soviet Decision Structure**

|                          | Shultz | Burt |
| ------------------------ | ------ | ---- |
| Rational actor           | 0      | 0    |
| Bureaucratic politics    | 0      | 1    |
| Organizational process   | 0      | 0    |
| Other/mixed              | 4      | 3    |

fact that "we get very little detail on how or why they make decisions" (U.S. Cong. 1984e, 5). Though similar caveats were occasionally offered by Perle and Weinberger, they nonetheless went on to portray Soviet decisions as resulting from a unified and rational process; Burt did not. Asked about the behind-the-scenes maneuverings in Moscow on policy issues and leadership questions, Burt replied, "I wish we knew enough about Soviet bureaucratic politics to be able to engage in the sort of analysis you would like. We don't. There are very few Strobe Talbotts in Moscow" (U.S. Cong. 1983a, 15). Presumably, knowledge of these bureaucratic struggles would have yielded important information for understanding Soviet actions. The potential influence of bureaucratic forces was mentioned again with respect to domestic reforms in the Soviet Union, when Burt warned of "bureaucratic barriers that would impede any effort at far-reaching and meaningful reform" (U.S. Cong. 1983a, 16). Burt did not extend this discussion to the realm of foreign policy. Thus, what little evidence there is does not indicate that Burt saw the Soviet Union as a monolithic rational actor; in fact, the limited evidence points in other directions.

Despite the fact that we have more material for Shultz than for Burt, there is less information about Shultz's view of Soviet decision making. Like Burt, Shultz occasionally pointed to the difficulties of speculating about why and how the Soviets made any particular decision. He noted, for example, "we may never know what decision-making process the Soviet leadership went through before deciding to deploy the SS-20" (U.S. Cong. 1988a, 15). There were a few very superficial comments about Gorbachev replacing various leaders with people more sympathetic to his agenda, which vaguely implied the existence of policy disputes within the top leadership. None of this, however, was very concrete. And more in line with a rational actor model, Shultz pointed to "the Soviet Union's great advantages: continuity, patience, the ability to fashion a long-term strategy and stick to it" (U.S. Cong. 1985a, 6). In general, no clear picture emerges. One does not, however, get the same impression from Shultz's comments as from Perle's and Weinberger's. There was no talk of "three or four" people in the Kremlin making all the decisions. Every action was not presented as a carefully calculated component of overall strategic design. Loopholes and ambiguities were not portrayed as cynical treaty implants designed to facilitate future circumvention. The rational actor orientation did not dominate and permeate the analysis of Shultz or Burt.

## Soviet Perceptions of the United States

There was literally no direct evidence concerning Shultz's and Burt's views of how Soviet leaders perceive the United States (see table 6.11). There are only the slightest indications that Burt and Shultz did not share the assumption that Soviets leaders "knew" the United States to be peaceful and nonthreatening. Burt's occasional references to Soviet "paranoia" suggested that the Soviets were fearful of someone, but he did not specify whether these were fears of the United States. When Burt was asked about the first-strike potential of the forces envisaged in the administration's strategic modernization plan, he did not respond, as did Perle, that the Soviets could not possibly think we would attack them; Burt simply argued that the proposed systems would not enable the United States to launch a disarming strike (U.S. Cong. 1983e, 33).

Shultz's comments are similarly vague. He did argue that, in order to improve relations with the Soviet Union "we must persuade the Soviets . . . that we have no aggressive intentions" (*DSB*, November, 1984, 3). Was Shultz saying that the Soviets did believe the United States had aggressive intentions? It is not clear. Shultz occasionally talked about the "suspicions" between the two countries that generated hostility and mistrust, thus implying the existence of Soviet suspicions of the United States (e.g., *DSB*, April, 1988, 41). Following the November, 1985, summit meeting in Geneva, Shultz was asked what he learned as a result of his encounters with Gorbachev. "I learned," he said, "that his view of the United States is very different from how I believe the United States is" (*DSB*, January, 1986, 28). Unfortunately, he did not elaborate on precisely what he meant. Even though these are sketchy comments, they at least hint at some sensitivity to the different perspective and perceptions of the Soviet Union, even if they are not sufficient to permit firm conclusions; but when these comments are combined with the absence of claims that the Soviets "knew" the United States presented no threat, we have a potentially significant departure from a classic hard-line enemy image.

## Image Summary

Because Shultz and Burt felt politically vulnerable from the conservative wing of the Republican party, some have suggested that their public rhetoric was more hard-line than their actual beliefs. We do not currently have access to the

TABLE 6.11.  Soviet View
of the United States

|  | Shultz | Burt |
| --- | --- | --- |
| Defensive/peaceful | 0 | 0 |
| Threatening/aggressive | 0 | 0 |
| Other/mixed | 1 | 0 |

material needed to prove this. But despite pressures to adopt the more hard-line view that prevailed in certain segments of the Reagan administration, Shultz and Burt still conveyed a more consistently moderate image of the Soviet Union, often contradicting Perle, Weinberger, and even Reagan on key issues. Although it would be easy to do so, one must avoid exaggerating the differences. Shultz and Burt were hard-liners in the broader sense of the term: they saw the Soviet Union as an aggressive and expansionist power that threatened its neighbors and U.S. interests around the globe; they were worried about the growth of Soviet military power and suspicious of Soviet plans for this new power; and they viewed U.S. strength and resolve as necessary for inducing Soviet restraint, fearing that weakness or unilateral restraint would be an invitation for Soviet advances. Recalling the explication of the beliefs typically associated with hard-line and moderate enemy images (chap. 2), we can see that Burt and Shultz combined elements of both. Even though there are some inconsistencies, the combinations of beliefs we find for Burt and Shultz are not confusing or chaotic; they form a type of enemy image that is quite consistent and fairly common.

In his survey of images of the Soviet Union held by segments of the "attentive public," Richard Herrmann (1985) identifies three competing models, each based on a different set of assumptions about the nature and sources of Soviet foreign policy behavior. He labels these images "communist expansionism," "realpolitik expansionism," and "realpolitik defensive." As Herrmann recognized, his three models are roughly analogous to Gamson and Modigliani's (1971) "destructionist," "expansionist," and "consolidationist" enemy images. Herrmann's communist expansionist model is similar to the inherent-bad-faith model and diabolical enemy image discussed in relation to Perle and Weinberger. This image does not seem appropriate for describing the views of Shultz and Burt; the realpolitik expansionist model seems more applicable. The primary differences between the two images are that the realpolitik expansionist model places less emphasis on ideology as the motivating force behind Soviet policy; it insists that the military balance between the two powers is stable, or at least not dangerously out of balance; and it sees Soviet leaders as accepting the basic principles of mutual deterrence (Herrmann 1985, 378–79). While no individual can be expected to align completely with any ideal type of image, the realpolitik model provides the better representation of Shultz's and Burt's beliefs. In addition to offering different analyses of Soviet behavior, each model leads to different policy prescriptions, which will be our focus when we turn to the issue debates within the administration.

CHAPTER 7

# Reagan and the Soviets

*Mr. Wallace*: . . . I think that the problem we've had during the whole four and a half years of the Reagan administration is still there. Different officials speak with different voices.
*Mr. Kalb*: They speak with different voices, and on policy towards the Soviet Union, I think you're absolutely right. The differences really reflect the road map of the president's own feelings about the Soviet Union, and they are not crystal clear.

—"Meet the Press," May 19, 1985

The day Ronald Reagan entered the White House was not a bright one for advocates of arms control and improved relations with the Soviet Union. For years Reagan had preached against the follies of arms control, détente, and U.S. military restraint. In the eyes of many, Reagan remained committed to a classic, almost caricatured, cold war image of the Soviet Union as an ideologically inspired power bent on the triumph of communism on a global scale. In a 1962 speech, for example, Reagan characterized Soviet communism as "a single worldwide force dedicated to the destruction of our free enterprise system and the creation of a world Socialist State" (Edwards 1987, 549). Reagan portrayed the cold war as a moral "struggle between right and wrong and good and evil," a battle in which accommodation itself was a form of immorality (*CPD* 1983, 364).[1] Critics feared, and supporters hoped, that such an apocalyptic view would leave little room for compromise, restraint, or agreements of any sort. Furthermore, this image appeared to be deeply ingrained, an indelible part of Reagan's belief system. There was little evidence that his views had changed. Betty Glad observed that "what one sees from Reagan's statements on world affairs from 1965 to only 1982 is the static quality of his views. Adopting a perspective very similar to that of John Foster Dulles in the 1950s, Reagan has not changed" (1983, 67). To make matters even worse, Reagan displayed little knowledge or interest in foreign affairs,

---

1. All quotations attributed to Reagan, except where otherwise noted, are from the *Weekly Compilation of Presidential Documents*. Quotes will be cited as follows: (*CPD* year, page).

so it was difficult to see what could induce any change in his beliefs or the policies that were expected to flow from them. The situation seemed bleak.

Initially, Reagan did little to ease his critics' fears. It was in his first press conference that he made the famous observation that the Soviets "have openly and publicly declared that the only morality they recognize is what will further their cause, meaning that they reserve unto themselves the right to commit any crime, to lie, to cheat, in order to attain that" (*CPD* 1981, 57). Not since the days of John Foster Dulles had such harsh rhetoric been heard. Even more ominous was the tendency for Reagan and his advisers to wax nostalgic about the days of U.S. military superiority. In a 1980 interview with Lou Cannon, Reagan asked, "Since when has it been wrong for America to be first in military strength? How is military superiority dangerous?" (Cannon 1980). It was assumed that arms control would occupy a very low place on the administration's priority list. As late as 1984 Robert Dallek would confidently predict that "it seems unlikely that the Reagan administration will desist from [its] approach and try to reach meaningful arms control agreements with Moscow" (1984, 161). It looked like it was going to be a very long four years, perhaps eight.

At the same time Reagan was being portrayed as an ideological cold warrior, someone who would set the United States on a course of intensified confrontation with the Soviet Union, there was also a perception of Reagan as the consummate politician, capable of bending in whichever direction the winds of public opinion blew. Reagan's tenure as governor of California was filled with examples of his taking actions that contradicted his firmly expressed beliefs (see Dallek 1984). And there were a few early indications that, as president, Reagan the politician might triumph over Reagan the ideologue, such as his lifting of Carter's grain embargo. Despite these few hopeful signs, nobody predicted the changes in U.S.-Soviet relations witnessed during Reagan's second term. Who would have anticipated that arms control would move up from the far back burner to become a consuming passion of Reagan's last few years? Any changes in policy will be discussed in later chapters; in this chapter, I will examine his image and see whether there were any significant changes and, if so, when they took place.

## Reagan Views the Soviet Union

### Foreign Policy Objectives

One of the central themes of Reagan's presidential campaigns and his first few years in office was the failure of the United States to keep pace with the Soviet military buildup of the 1970s. The "Vietnam syndrome" and the naïveté of détente, he argued, caused the United States to let down its guard, just as the traumatic experiences of World War I and the hope for peace had rendered the West unable and unwilling to meet the Nazi challenge in the 1930s. Like Perle and Weinberger, Reagan often looked to the 1930s for lessons about the 1970s and 1980s. Implicit in such historical analogies are images of actors whose similarities make the comparisons relevant for contemporary decision makers. According to Reagan:

> One of the great tragedies of this century was that it was only after the balance of power was allowed to erode and a ruthless adversary, Adolf Hitler, deliberately weighed the risks and decided to strike that the importance of a strong defense was realized too late. . . . For those of us who lived through that nightmare, it's a mistake that America and the free world must never make again. (*CPD* 1983, 258)

The parallels for the Western powers involved the loss of will and the consequent erosion of the military power needed to deter aggression; for the Soviet Union and Germany the similarities involved their military buildups and expansionism. Reagan maintained that, during the 1970s, "the Soviet Union [was] engaged in the greatest military buildup in the history of man, and it cannot be described as necessary for their [sic] defense. It is plainly a buildup that is offensive in nature" (*CPD* 1981, 711). This description of the Soviet buildup as "the largest in the history of man" became routine.

The danger of Soviet expansionism was the most clearly and consistently articulated element of Reagan's image (see table 7.1). He referred to the Soviet Union as "an empire whose territorial ambition has sparked a wasteful arms race" (*CPD* 1982, 986), and he spoke of its "relentless drive to conquer more lands" (*CPD* 1984, 1031). Not surprisingly, the most frequently discussed aspect of Soviet expansionism was with regard to Central America, where "Nicaragua is just a pawn in the Soviet grand strategy of expansion"

**TABLE 7.1. Soviet Policy Objectives**

|  | 1981 | 1982 | 1983 | 1984 | 1985 | 1986 | 1987 | 1988 |
|---|---|---|---|---|---|---|---|---|
| Unlimitedly expansionist | 2 | 4 | 4 | 0 | 3 | 6 | 1 | 0 |
| Limitedly expansionist | 0 | 0 | 0 | 0 | 0 | 0 | 0 | 0 |
| Unspecified expansionist | 12 | 24 | 44 | 25 | 27 | 31 | 31 | 19 |
| Defensive status quo | 0 | 0 | 0 | 0 | 0 | 0 | 0 | 0 |
| Acquiescent/accommodating | 0 | 0 | 0 | 0 | 0 | 0 | 0 | 0 |
| Other/mixed | 0 | 1 | 0 | 2 | 2 | 2 | 3 | 2 |

*Note*: Tables 7.1 through 7.11 present the results of the content analysis according to the rules laid out in chap. 4. The counts represent the frequency with which the different themes appear in the coded documents. All the documents were taken from the *Weekly Compilation of Presidential Documents*. There were a total of 403 documents that contained at least one theme.

and "the Nicaraguan communists are no more and no less than agents of Soviet expansionism" (*CPD* 1985, 687, 755). Particularly interesting was Reagan's perception of how Soviet policy in Central America fit into the larger scheme of things.

> A key Soviet objective has long been to turn Central America into a beachhead for subversion. [By tying us down] into this hemisphere, by penetrating our vital sea lanes, and crippling our ability to meet our commitments worldwide, the Soviets will find it much easier to intimidate other nations and expand their empire. (*CPD* 1985, 389)

What was the Soviet grand strategy? What were the ultimate objectives of Soviet policy? Reagan left little doubt about the answers to these questions: "I know of no leader of the Soviet Union since the revolution, and including the present leadership, that has not repeated . . . their determination that their goal must be the promotion of world revolution and a one-world communist state" (*CPD* 1981, 57). Elaborating on his commentary about the immorality of Soviet policy, he argued that "the only morality they recognize is that which will further their cause, which is world revolution" (*CPD* 1983, 362). And well into his second term, after some commentators had already perceived a shift in tone and policy, Reagan was still claiming that "the Soviet Union is expansionist. They have a belief that their purpose must be to bring about world revolution to a one-world communist state" (*CPD* 1986, 666). Worst of all, "they have declared that the United States is the final enemy" (*CPD* 1985, 1061).

At the same time Reagan was identifying global expansion and domination as the goal of Soviet foreign policy, he was also arguing that Soviet adventurism had ceased, or at least ceased to be effective, since he entered office: "The Soviet Union, which has been expanding over the years vastly in their [sic] territory and the people under its control . . . hasn't expanded into an extra square inch since we've been here" (*CPD* 1982, 1229). As of 1986, "not one square inch of territory has been lost" (*CPD* 1986, 286). By 1987, Reagan still boasted that "in the past six years, not a single inch of territory has fallen to communist aggression" (*CPD* 1987, 31). Why had the Soviet empire not grown under Reagan's watch? Clearly it was not for lack of effort because "while talking about reforms at home, the Soviet Union has stepped up its efforts to impose a failed system on others" (*CPD* 1987, 968). Shortly before welcoming Gorbachev to Washington in December, 1987, Reagan continued to claim that "even as their economy flags, the Soviets spend billions to maintain and impose Communist rule abroad" (*CPD* 1987, 1394).

But if the Soviets had "stepped up their efforts," why did they fail to extend their influence? Though not explicitly stated, the obvious implication was that the administration's policies were responsible for thwarting Soviet expansionism: "in the last half of the 1970s, we were not deterring . . . today we are" (*CPD* 1984, 491). Thus, Reagan's analysis of Soviet behavior was similar to Perle's and Weinberger's in that it contained the classic attributional bias elaborated by Jervis.

> When the [enemy's] behavior is undesired, the actor is likely to see it as derived from internal sources rather than as being a response to his own actions. . . . [But] when the [enemy] behaves in accord with the actor's desires, he will overestimate the degree to which his policies are responsible for the outcome. (Jervis 1976, 343)

As the rhetoric between the superpowers eased during Reagan's second term, the president was occasionally asked about his apparently softening views of the Soviet Union. He usually resisted any suggestion that his views had mellowed: "I haven't changed from the time I made a speech about the evil empire" (*CPD* 1987, 1425). Despite these protests, it is clear that in some respects his views did shift slightly, though it would be easy to exaggerate the magnitude of these changes. The most obvious modification concerned the issue of ultimate foreign policy objectives. Throughout his presidency, one of Reagan's favorite observations was that Soviet leaders themselves had openly declared their objective of world domination; this was their stated goal, he argued, not his opinion. Toward the end of 1987, however, Reagan would alter his familiar statement when asked about Gorbachev.

> He is also the first Russian leader who has never reiterated before the grand national Communist congress that the Soviets are pledged to world expansion a one-world Communist state. That has been the stated goal of previous leaders. He has said no such thing. (*CPD* 1987, 1405)

It is difficult to know exactly what to make of such statements. Notice that Reagan did not argue that the Soviets had abandoned their goal of world domination; he only said that Gorbachev never publicly repeated what past leaders had said (as a result, this statement is coded as "other/mixed" in table 7.1). Reagan also cautioned, "as to whether it was an oversight or he didn't think it was necessary or not, I don't know" (*CPD* 1988, 468). Furthermore, even this modest change did not occur until the very end of 1987, only weeks after Reagan spoke of continued Soviet efforts to "impose a failed system" on others. Nonetheless, it does represent a potentially significant change.

## Policy Motivation

As one might expect, given Reagan's emphasis on the Soviet drive for global domination, ideology played an important part in his perception of the forces behind Soviet policy (see table 7.2). Virtually every statement about Soviet global ambitions was accompanied by claims that these impulses were the logical outcome of Soviet ideology. According to Reagan, "that religion of theirs, which is Marxis[m]-Leninism, *requires* them to support and bring about a one-world Communist state. And they've never denied that" (*CPD* 1982, 62; italics added). The 1979 Soviet invasion of Afghanistan was "further proof that they are following an expansionist policy that is based on the Marxian doctrine, and the Marxist-Leninist doctrine, that communism must [be] a one-world that it must be a one-world communist state" (*CPD* 1986, 796). And while Reagan never cited any specific works or passages to substantiate his claims, he was apparently convinced that "Marx said that . . . the only [way communism] would succeed is when the whole world is that way" (*CPD* 1986, 666). When Soviet journalists asked Reagan where he had read this in the works of Marx, the president was at a loss.

> Oh my, I don't think I could recall and specify here and there. But I'm old enough to have had a great interest in the Soviet Union, and I know that in the things I studied in college, when I was getting my own degree in economics and sociology, that the declarations of Karl Marx, for example, that Karl Marx said your system, communism, could only succeed when the whole world had become communist. And so, the goal had to be the one-world communist state. (*CPD* 1988, 688)

Obviously, when Reagan talked about the role of ideology, he did not follow Shultz's subtle analysis that ideology influenced policy because of its influence on the way Soviet leaders see the world; Reagan's view of the role of ideology was similar to Weinberger's in suggesting a slavish Soviet adherence to the supposed dictates of Marxism-Leninism.

Although there is no question about the overwhelming importance of

TABLE 7.2.  Soviet Policy Motivation

|                    | 1981–84 | 1985–88 |
|--------------------|---------|---------|
| Ideology           | 11      | 2       |
| History            | 0       | 0       |
| Geography          | 0       | 0       |
| Personalities      | 0       | 6       |
| Culture            | 0       | 0       |
| Vested interests   | 0       | 0       |
| External challenges| 1       | 2       |
| Power politics     | 0       | 0       |
| Other/mixed        | 2       | 1       |

ideology in Reagan's image, one does find occasional references to other forces and alternative explanations, particularly Soviet fears of the West. While "there is no question that the Soviet Union has made it plain that they are embarked on an expansionist program," Reagan observed, "you have to wonder if this is not based on their fear and suspicion that the rest of us in the world mean them harm" (*CPD* 1985, 1003). In a 1983 interview, Reagan argued that "they are the ones that seek [expansion], whether it's out of paranoia on their part and believe me, everyone's an enemy, and so they have to be aggressive or whether it's the Marxist-Leninist theory" (*CPD* 1983, 1741). On another occasion, he talked about "their worldwide aggression, their denial of human rights, whatever it's based on whether it is a concern that they are threatened by the Western world or whether it is just a determination to pursue the Marxist-Leninist theory of world domination" (*CPD* 1982, 696). And during a 1982 interview, Reagan was asked, "Do you think, as some people do, that they're primarily a sort of defensive, fearful country . . . or do you think they still have an appetite for other people's territory?" Somewhat surprisingly, Reagan responded, "Well, I think there's a combination of both. At least they talk a great deal about their fear that the world is going to close in on them" (*CPD* 1982, 62). In all these instances Reagan went on to stress the impact of ideology, but his responses displayed at least some doubt and a greater willingness to entertain other ideas, which is something we did not find for Perle or Weinberger.

When I examined Reagan's perception of Soviet foreign policy goals, I saw a very slight shift, toward the end of his presidency, away from the notion that global domination was the primary Soviet objective. Concerning policy motivation, we see a decreased emphasis on ideology as the source of Soviet behavior beginning in 1985 and an increase in references to personality factors (see table 7.2). It is certainly no coincidence that Gorbachev came to power in 1985 and the first meeting between the two heads of state took place in November of that year. Prior to 1985, there was nothing in my analysis of Reagan's views that suggested that leadership changes could result in significant policy change. If anything, he stressed the immutability of Soviet objectives derived from ideology: "all of us need to be better informed about the *unchanging* realities of the Soviet system. We are in a long-term twilight struggle with an implacable foe of freedom" (*CPD* 1985, 865, italics added). He cautioned that "we cannot assume that their ideology and purpose will change; this implies *enduring* competition" (*CPD* 1985, 1426, italics added).

Even though there was a decreased emphasis on ideology and increasing references to changes flowing from the emergence of Gorbachev, it was only a slight and very vague shift. Reagan would talk generally about Gorbachev being "different" from past leaders, more straightforward, sincere, and serious about reforming the Soviet Union. In the realm of foreign policy, Reagan stressed two things: first, unlike past Soviet leaders, Gorbachev was willing to pursue real reductions in nuclear arms; and second, Gorbachev supposedly did not repeat the pledge to spread communism throughout the world. During the last year of his presidency, for example, Reagan was asked about his changing views of the Soviet Union and whether he no longer thought it was an evil empire. He responded:

> My views haven't changed. But you must remember that the Soviet leaders, when I first came into office, kept dying. And there was little chance to work with [them] on some of the things I thought should be straightened out. Now there is a new leader, and he does seem to want to make some changes in their system. I have always wanted to take up the matter of human rights, and there has been some improvement in that. Regional conflicts—and we see them now—this leader wanting to get out of Afghanistan. So, I think progress could be made. (*CPD* 1988, 336)

Although it is difficult to identify precisely what changes Reagan thought Gorbachev had in mind and why the new Soviet leader was not committed to the Marxist-Leninist injunction to pursue global revolution, Reagan's comments about the "unchanging" Soviet system virtually disappeared by 1986–87. They would soon be replaced by thoughts of "a new era in history, a time of lasting change in the Soviet Union" (*CPD* 1988, 735).

### Nuclear Objectives and Doctrine

When Reagan spoke of the Soviet military buildup of the 1960s and 1970s as the largest in history, he left little doubt about the purpose of this buildup—military superiority over the United States and the geopolitical advantages this would bring. "When we took office in 1981, the Soviet Union had been engaged for 20 years in the most massive military buildup in history. Clearly, their goal was not to catch us, but to surpass us" (*CPD* 1984, 491; see table 7.3, [the numbers in the table are small because Reagan usually referred to "military superiority" in general, which is not coded for "nuclear superiority"

**TABLE 7.3.  Soviet Nuclear Objectives**

|             | Reagan |
|-------------|--------|
| Superiority | 2      |
| Parity      | 0      |
| Other/mixed | 0      |

specifically]). According to Reagan, "year in and year out, at the expense of its own people, the Soviet leadership has been making a relentless effort to gain military superiority over the United States" (*CPD* 1986, 287).

This quest for military superiority was in both the conventional and nuclear areas. Reagan observed that "it was assumed that the treaties [SALT I and ABM] were based on acceptance of parity on offensive weapons systems, but the Soviets have continued to race for superiority" (*CPD* 1985, 901). In terms of strategic weapons, "the Soviet Union is acquiring what can only be considered an offensive force. They have continued to build far more intercontinental ballistic missiles than they could possibly need simply to deter an attack" (*CPD* 1983, 440).

If the Soviets were pursuing nuclear superiority, what precisely did they plan to do with this capability? Did the Soviet Union's desire for superiority entail a rejection of the doctrine of mutual assured destruction? On these issues there were two strands of thought evident in my analysis of Reagan's views (see table 7.4). On the one hand, Reagan argued that the Soviets did not accept the idea that security is enhanced if both sides are vulnerable: "It was assumed [in SALT I and the ABM treaty] the Soviets would accept the innocent notion that being mutually vulnerable to attack was a common interest. They haven't" (*CPD* 1985, 901). But did Soviet leaders think that they could wage and win a nuclear conflict? In Reagan's view:

> . . . everything that has been said, everything in their manuals, indicates that, unlike us, the Soviet Union believes that a nuclear war is possible. And they believe it is winnable, which means that you could achieve enough superiority that your opponent wouldn't have a retaliatory strike capability. (*CPD* 1981, 957)

"The Soviet Union," he claimed, "does not share our view of what constitutes a stable nuclear balance. It has chosen instead to build nuclear forces clearly designed to strike first and disarm their [*sic*] adversary" (*CPD* 1985, 606). Such statements could easily have come out the mouth of Perle or Weinberger.

On the other hand, one finds statements that paint a very different picture

**TABLE 7.4. Soviet Nuclear Doctrine**

|              | Reagan |
| ------------ | ------ |
| Winnable     | 2      |
| Not winnable | 0      |
| Other/mixed  | 3      |

of Soviet leaders and their intentions. When he was not portraying Soviet leaders as ruthlessly planning to carry out or threaten a nuclear attack, Reagan described them as anxious to avoid a nuclear conflict because they were aware of the dangers and certain devastation that would ensue. He believed that "the Soviet people and their leaders understand the importance of preventing war" (*CPD* 1982, 622). And he claimed to have:

> . . . no doubt that the Soviet people and, yes, Soviet leaders have an overriding interest in preventing the use of nuclear weapons. The Soviet Union within the memory of its leaders has known the devastation of total conventional war and know that a nuclear war would be even more calamitous. (*CPD* 1982, 584)

The last part of this statement is particularly telling. Recall that Weinberger had pointed to the Soviet experience in World War II as evidence that Soviet leaders might be willing to incur the damage of a nuclear war; Reagan pointed to the same experience as evidence of Soviet hesitancy to accept such devastation again. While it might be possible to reconcile these apparently contradictory trends in Reagan's thought, there is no evidence that he recognized or resolved them.

## Military Capabilities

Reagan rode into the White House denouncing his predecessors for "unilateral disarmament" and naive self-restraint that, he argued, had opened a "window of vulnerability" in strategic weapons as well as worsened the conventional gap between the superpowers. Claims about Soviet conventional superiority were uncontroversial; his comments about Soviet strategic capabilities were less widely accepted. Nonetheless, Reagan left no doubt about his conviction that the Soviets had surpassed the United States in nuclear capabilities (see tables 7.5 and 7.6). Despite the emphasis placed on nuclear issues during his

**TABLE 7.5.  Soviet Military Capabilities (Conventional)**

|             | Reagan |
|-------------|--------|
| Superior    | 17     |
| Parity      | 0      |
| Inferior    | 0      |
| Other/mixed | 1      |

campaign, however, Reagan was not particularly knowledgeable or interested in the arcane details of nuclear weapons; even his most ardent supporters recognized that he had only a rudimentary understanding of nuclear issues.

Worse than his failure to grasp details was Reagan's apparent ignorance of some basic facts. His claim that ballistic missiles could be recalled is, by now, a familiar bit of Reagan lore. Although Reagan has convincingly argued that he was misquoted and misinterpreted in this particular instance, there are other cases where even he admitted his ignorance. For example, during his 1984 debate with Democratic challenger Walter Mondale, the president was asked about the practicality of his administration's initial START proposal, which stressed large cuts in ICBMs while minimizing and delaying cuts in bombers and cruise missiles. Reagan remembered that "the Soviet Union, *to our surprise* and not just mine made it plain when we brought this up that they placed, they thought, a greater reliance on land-based missiles" (*CPD* 1984, 1599; italics added). One wonders who else was really "surprised" by this little tidbit of information. Because of this lack of knowledge, Reagan's evaluation of the Soviet Union's nuclear capabilities was, to put it mildly, confusing.

In March, 1982, Reagan described the predicament of the United States in alarming terms: "the truth of the matter is that on balance, the Soviet Union does have a definite margin of superiority, enough so that there is a risk and there is what I have called . . . a 'window of vulnerability'" (*CPD* 1982, 399). Notice that Reagan did not elaborate on the precise nature of this risk. Even with the administration's strategic modernization program, this "dangerous window of vulnerability" would not be closed "until the mid-eighties" (*CPD* 1982, 150). The nuclear freeze was anathema because it "would leave in place dangerous inequalities in the nuclear balance" and would freeze "the Soviet Union into a position of superiority" (*CPD* 1982, 1013, 715).

It is amazing how seldom Reagan was really pressed on what he meant by the "window of vulnerability" and Soviet "superiority." Did this mean that the Soviets possessed a disarming first strike capability? In an April, 1982,

**TABLE 7.6.  Soviet Military Capabilities (Nuclear)**

|  | Strategic | INF |
|---|---|---|
| Superiority | 7 | 11 |
| Advantages/imbalances | 28 | 5 |
| Parity | 0 | 1 |
| Other/mixed | 6 | 0 |

press conference, the president was challenged (the exchange appears in its correct and unedited entirety):

> *Q*. Do you think that they have a first-strike capability against the United States?
> *The President*. I think that at the moment, on the strategic intercontinental ballistic missile program and our triad, I think that we do. Those who say that, well, we have something of a deterrent now, yes, I think so, too.
> *Q*. But do they have a first-strike capability, Mr. President? Can they strike us with impunity?
> *The President*. I think I spoke of that the other night, that, yes, we would have surviving missiles in our submarines, airborne of those planes that were airborne at the time of an attack. Their missiles are aimed at our silos, our ballistic missiles, land-based missiles. But would our retaliation result in further devastation of the United States? So, I think I made it clear look, I'll tell you something; let me give you the answer. Tomorrow, in Georgetown, Secretary Haig is going to be making a speech on this entire subject of nuclear deterrents and the nuclear power, so I recommend that you. (*CPD* 1982, 429)

Obviously, Reagan had trouble dealing with these questions once he was forced to move beyond the level of phrases and simple characterizations. As Garry Wills observes, "Reagan liked the phrase 'window of vulnerability,' though he was never able to explain the arguments' stages" (1987, 337). And there is no evidence that his views became any clearer. In 1984, for example, he judged that "for the first time in a number of years, [the United States] has enough deterrent capability [so] that the Soviet Union, I don't think, would decide that it would be in their [*sic*] interest to take any action" (*CPD* 1984, 920). Despite this, "a nuclear freeze would prevent the *restoration* of a stable nuclear balance" (*CPD* 1984, 493; italics added). But if the United States had an adequate deterrent, why was the balance unstable? As of 1985, the Soviet Union continued to "have such a superiority" even though "we think that we have enough of a deterrent . . . that retaliation would be more than anyone would want to accept" (*CPD* 1985, 401, 1106). When Reagan was asked about the adequacy of the American deterrent by Soviet reporters, he explained, "Somebody might say that with the sense of that we have sufficient for a deterrent [sic], that, in other words, we would have enough to make it uncomfortable if someone attacked us. But, no, your arsenal does outnumber ours by a great number" (*CPD* 1985, 1347). But eight months earlier Reagan contended that "they don't have enough of a margin today—to tempt them into a first strike" (*CPD* 1985, 170). One searches in vain for an explanation of what this "superiority" entailed if the United States had a sufficient deterrent. In 1986, Reagan still claimed that "we're still playing catchup, and this imbalance is a threat to world peace" (*CPD* 1986, 1243). The only change one finds is after 1986, when references to the "window of vulnerability," Soviet "imbalances," and superiority disappeared. But these statements were not replaced by more reassuring assessments of the nuclear balance (see table 7.7); Reagan simply ceased to comment on this issue.

Just as there were contradictory strands of thought in Reagan's evaluation of Soviet nuclear doctrine, there were similar, even more glaring, inconsistencies in his view of Soviet nuclear capabilities. Reagan could argue that the nuclear balance was unstable, necessitating a buildup to "restore" the U.S. strategic deterrent, at the same time he thought the United States possessed a survivable retaliatory strike. As was the case with Soviet nuclear doctrine, there is no evidence that Reagan ever resolved or even recognized the contradictions.

## Strategy and Trustworthiness

There was no confusion in Reagan's expectations of how the Soviets would respond to U.S. policies (see table 7.8). According to Reagan, "history has shown what works and what doesn't work. Unilateral restraint and good will do not produce similar reactions from the Soviet Union" (*CPD* 1983, 1406–7). "The Soviets," he argued, "have seen our restraint only as an opportunity to gain the advantage" (*CPD* 1985, 366). Policies based on the expectation of reciprocated restraint were, in Reagan's view, hopelessly naive. As a result, "our foreign policy must be rooted in realism, not naïveté and self-delusion . . . [but] a recognition of what the Soviet empire is all about . . . . They respect only strength and resolve in dealings with other nations" (*CPD* 1982, 78).

Like everyone else in his administration, Reagan pointed to Soviet behavior during the 1970s to support and illustrate his views. During the 1970s, "the Soviet response to our unilateral restraint was to accelerate its military buildup, to foment revolution in the developing world, to invade neighboring Afghanistan, and to support the repression in Poland" (*CPD* 1983, 24). It was

**TABLE 7.7. Soviet Nuclear Capabilities (Strategic)**

|                      | 1981 | 1982 | 1983 | 1984 | 1985 | 1986 | 1987 | 1988 |
|----------------------|------|------|------|------|------|------|------|------|
| Superiority          | 0    | 3    | 2    | 0    | 1    | 1    | 0    | 0    |
| Advantages/imbalances| 3    | 9    | 8    | 2    | 3    | 3    | 0    | 0    |
| Parity               | 0    | 0    | 0    | 0    | 0    | 0    | 0    | 0    |
| Other/mixed          | 1    | 0    | 1    | 2    | 2    | 0    | 0    | 0    |

during the period of détente that "too many of our leaders [he never specifies who] saw the Soviets as mirror images of themselves. If we would simply disarm, the Soviets would do likewise" (*CPD* 1983, 265). In reality, Reagan argued, détente was "one-way restraint that was never returned by the other side . . . while past American leaders hesitated or naively hoped for the best, the Soviet Union was left free to pile up new nuclear arsenals" (*CPD* 1983, 1190).

This perspective carried over into Reagan's analysis of Soviet negotiating behavior. Early in his administration, the president observed that "unless we demonstrate the will to rebuild our strength and restore the military balance, the Soviets, since they're so far ahead, will have little incentive to negotiate with us" (*CPD* 1982, 1058). Because of his administration's policies, "the Soviets . . . found out that they [were] facing a belated U.S. modernization program. . . . I think that is the *only* reason they came to the table to discuss arms reduction" (*CPD* 1983, 1720; italics added). These themes would reappear consistently throughout Reagan's presidency. In this component of his image there was no change; statements made in the final year of his administration could just as easily have been made on day one.

> . . . the Soviets get down to serious negotiation only after they are convinced that their counterparts are determined to stand firm. . . . The least indication of weakened resolve on our part would lead the Soviets to stop the serious bargaining, stall diplomatic progress, and attempt to exploit this perceived weaknesses. (*CPD* 1988, 504)

How could the Soviets be expected to behave once they have reached an agreement with the United States? Reagan's skepticism about Soviet trustworthiness was evident in repeated references to the Soviets' willingness to "lie" and "cheat" to achieve their objectives. This did not bode well for arms control because of "the overwhelming evidence of Soviet violations of international treaties" (*CPD* 1983, 109; see table 7.9). "Evidence abounds," he contended, "that we cannot simply assume that agreements negotiated with

**TABLE 7.8.  Soviet Response to U.S. Policy**

|              | U.S. Firmness | U.S. Restraint |
| ------------ | ------------- | -------------- |
| Back down    | 68            | —              |
| Reciprocate  | 1             | 0              |
| Exploit      | —             | 58             |
| Other/mixed  | 1             | 0              |

the Soviet Union will be fulfilled" (*CPD* 1983, 1352). Reagan's beliefs on this topic are similar to Weinberger's in two respects. First, Reagan's worries were expressed in terms of outright violations, with virtually no emphasis given to the possibility of Soviet technical obedience (abiding by the letter but violating the spirit of agreements). Second, there is a dramatic increase in his expressions of concern during his second term, particularly in 1986–87 (see table 7.9). It is almost certainly no coincidence that 1986 was the year Reagan decided to abandon his policy of abiding by the terms of SALT II. It was also during this period when Reagan began to argue that the strategic defense initiative (SDI) was necessary, even with dramatic arms reductions, because of the possibility of Soviet cheating (i.e., SDI as an "insurance policy"). This one aspect of Reagan's image is the only one that appears to become more hard-line during his second term. Only one month before the signing of the INF treaty, for example, Reagan quipped, "it is said for them arms agreements are like diets: the second day is always the best, because that's when you broke them" (*CPD* 1987, 1333).

## Soviet Decision Structure

Reagan's view of the Soviet decision-making structure was slightly different than that of others in his administration (see table 7.10). In particular, it differed from Perle's and Weinberger's images of a highly unified, monolithic, and always rational decision style. Reagan claimed that "Soviet policy is really determined by a dozen or so individuals in the Politburo . . . it is a collective government" (*CPD* 1985, 286). While this is similar to Weinberger's observation that "three or four" people in the Kremlin determine policy, Reagan placed greater stress on the possible disagreements among Soviet leaders: "I think that there comes a time when since they sort of rule by committee, the Politburo, that there isn't a consensus there on the course they should be taking" (*CPD* 1984, 815). And in the case of Gorbachev, "I think it is evident that he is running into opposition, that there are those who want to cling to what are more Stalinist policies" (*CPD* 1988, 652). Thus, Reagan differed slightly in this respect from the classic, hard-line enemy image.

**TABLE 7.9. Soviet Treaty Record**

|                     | 1981 | 1982 | 1983 | 1984 | 1985 | 1986 | 1987 | 1988 |
|---------------------|------|------|------|------|------|------|------|------|
| Violates            | 0    | 4    | 3    | 2    | 7    | 20   | 10   | 5    |
| Technical obedience | 0    | 0    | 1    | 0    | 0    | 0    | 0    | 0    |
| Abides              | 0    | 0    | 1    | 0    | 0    | 0    | 0    | 0    |
| Other/mixed         | 0    | 0    | 4    | 2    | 0    | 1    | 1    | 0    |

Reagan's explanation of the Soviet decision to break off arms talks in 1983 offers some insights into both his perceptions of Soviet decision making and his overall cognitive style. Immediately following the walkout, Reagan was asked why the Soviets had left the talks, given his claims that U.S. firmness would lead the Soviets to negotiate. Several times Reagan offered the same answer:

> . . . there is an article I could call to your attention in the *Economist* called "May Hibernation." It was an idea that hadn't occurred to me, but I think it makes a great deal of sense: that they are not deviously planning something or having a great plan going forward. The author of this article said that they don't have any answers right now, so they've just hunkered down and they're hibernating. (*CPD* 1984, 813)

The problem, he said, was that "we're so accustomed to viewing the Soviets as engaged in various kinds of machinations and so forth" when the reality might be that "the silence is because they don't know what to say right now" (*CPD* 1984, 833). By 1987, however, Reagan had apparently forgotten about the *Economist* article, claiming "the Soviets did walk out of the arms talks. It was part of [a] sophisticated ploy to [influence] public opinion here and in Europe" (*CPD* 1987, 223). This incident illustrates what many have observed; the impressionable nature of Reagan's belief system. He demonstrated a tendency to accept the most recent idea or piece of information that caught his eye, even if it was not consistent with other things he had said.[2]

### Soviet Perceptions of the United States

Contradictions and tensions surfaced again in Reagan's view of how the Soviets perceived the United States (see table 7.11). On the one hand, there were times when he seemed to agree with Weinberger and Perle's assessment that the Soviets did not see the United States as a threat.

> . . . it is the West that has to feel that the Soviet Union is at war with us on the basis of their [*sic*] great military buildup. I don't think they can point to anything from our side that indicates that . . . If we had aggressive intent wouldn't we have acted when we could have done so easily? I

---

2. There are other instances of this impressionability. For example, when Reagan claimed that racial discrimination no longer existed in South Africa in 1982. It was soon discovered that he had recently read an article in *Commentary* to the effect that progress had been made in eliminating some racial barriers in South Africa. Reagan's staff quickly corrected his views (Gelb 1985, 104).

**TABLE 7.10.  Soviet Decision Structure**

|  | Reagan |
|---|---|
| Rational actor | 1 |
| Bureaucratic politics | 0 |
| Organizational process | 0 |
| Other/mixed | 7 |

**TABLE 7.11.  Soviet View of the United States**

|  | Reagan |
|---|---|
| Defensive/peaceful | 2 |
| Threat/aggressive | 0 |
| Other/mixed | 19 |

think that's the greatest guarantee that it isn't the West that threatens the world with war. (*CPD* 1982, 696)

Reagan was confident that "Soviet leaders *know full well* there is no political constituency in the United States or anywhere in the West for aggressive military action against them" (*CPD* 1983, 267; italics added). Furthermore, he believed that "Mr. Gorbachev *knows* the depth of my commitment to peace" (*CPD* 1986, 838; italics added). All of this is consistent with a classic, hard-line enemy image: the aggressive enemy is aware of our peaceful intentions.

The confusion emerges when we consider Reagan's view that the cold war was sustained by "paranoia," "hostility," and "suspicions" that "keep our two countries . . . at odds with each other" (*CPD* 1985, 1318). "I think there is a great *mutual* suspicion between the two countries," Reagan observed, even if "ours is more justified than theirs" (*CPD* 1985, 288; italics added). "Mutual," of course, implies that the Soviets entertain suspicions of the United States. Indeed, one of Reagan's goals in his first meeting with Gorbachev was to "try [to] eliminate some of the[se] *mutual* suspicions" (*CPD* 1985, 557; italics added). Even though Reagan warned the United States to "beware the temptation . . . to simply call the arms race a giant misunderstanding," he assured it that "if we can reduce the suspicions between our two countries, the reduction of arms will easily follow" (*CPD* 1983, 364; *CPD* 1985, 1318). Reagan recognized that "the Soviet Union tends to be distrustful and suspicious that things presented to them are perhaps concealing some ulterior motive" (*CPD* 1985, 1360). Asked about how he planned to lessen superpower tensions, Reagan responded, "I intend to do everything I can to persuade them of our peaceful intentions" (*CPD* 1983, 362). But if Soviet leaders "know full well" that the United States posed no threat, why do they have to be "persuaded"?

### Image Summary

Distilling the essence of Reagan's views about the Soviet Union is no easy task. Listening to and reading Reagan's speeches and press conferences are like observing two different people, Reagan the pessimist and Reagan the optimist. Reagan the optimist believed that the superpower conflict was based on misguided suspicions that could be bridged if only he could persuade the Soviets of U.S. peaceful intentions; Reagan the pessimist described the cold war as the inevitable outcome of conflicting ideologies and inherently antagonistic forms of government. Reagan the optimist believed that the United States had sufficient power to safeguard it from attack; Reagan the pessimist saw his country as vulnerable to the arsenal of an evil empire. Reagan the optimist saw the forces of evil and totalitarianism on their way to the dustbin of history; Reagan the pessimist saw a need for constant and eternal vigilance against these same menacing forces. Reagan the optimist thought Soviet leaders were aware of the dangers of nuclear war; Reagan the pessimist believed these same leaders were cynically and cruelly planning to wage and win a nuclear war. It seems as though, in Ronald Reagan, the gloomy ideologue was constantly wrestling with the lofty idealist, and one was never quite sure who was winning. In this respect, it can be argued, Reagan embodied the contradictions present in the U.S. foreign affairs psyche.

Hendrick Smith has observed that "Shultz's world is painted in grays; Weinberger's in blacks and whites" (1988, 582). If we wanted to continue the Smith metaphor, we might say that Reagan's world was painted in a hodgepodge that could combine to make black, white, or almost any shade of gray. This brings us back to Marvin Kalb's remarks about the "road map" of the president's mind. There are times when Reagan sounded like Perle or Weinberger, and others when he reminded us of Shultz or Burt. But the impression one gets is not like the infamous Vance/Brzezinski speeches for Carter, where it seemed as though paragraphs had been mechanically cut and pasted together. One senses that Reagan actually believed what he said, even if it contradicted something he had said days or moments before. This indicates a genuine confusion in beliefs and opinions.

This is not to say that Reagan's image was complete and utter chaos: there were elements of consistency and ordered change. There was consistency in Reagan's belief that the Soviet Union was an expansionist power, his doubts about Soviet trustworthiness, and his view that U.S. strength and determination were prerequisites for Soviet accommodation. His view of ultimate Soviet foreign policy objectives underwent some revision in terms of the global nature of Soviet expansion, but this was very modest and occurred very late. Related to this slightly altered perception of Soviet foreign policy goals, Reagan became convinced that new leadership in Moscow brought with it real changes in Soviet foreign and domestic policy, even if he was not very explicit about the nature and extent of these changes. His protests notwithstanding, on these two points Reagan did alter his views.

In addition to these elements of consistency, change, and confusion, one is also struck by the superficial nature of his beliefs. This came out most vividly whenever Reagan was pressed to explain his views in greater depth and when he was questioned about apparent inconsistencies. From where in the works of Marx and Lenin did the imperative of global domination emerge? How was the Soviet Union superior in strategic weapons if the United States had the ability to respond with a damaging retaliatory strike? Did the Soviet Union actually fear the United States and the administration's strategic buildup? Did the Soviets believe they could fight and win a nuclear war or did they know that both powers would be devastated by any nuclear exchange? Once Reagan moved beyond the level of generalities, it became clear that his beliefs were not based on a firm foundation of knowledge and supporting assumptions.

In part these apparent conflicts among some of his beliefs about the Soviet Union might reflect keen political instincts and clever posturing. Reagan may have been responding to the mood of the public. After all, he was the only elected official included in this study. He was the only one who needed to have his finger on the pulse of public opinion. A politician who was consistently negative about the prospects for negotiated agreements with the Soviet Union would probably not appeal to the majority of the people. Despite deep-seated suspicions about the Soviet Union and communism, most U.S. citizens want to believe in the possibility of agreement and compromise. Just as preaching "gloom and doom" on domestic policy issues does not get a politician very far, such a strategy does not get much mileage on foreign policy issues. As an astute politician, Reagan must have been aware of this at some level. This does not entail a cynical and conscious manipulation of rhetoric, but perhaps more of a gut-level or instinctive political acumen. Unfortunately, it is hard to tell where political tactics end and genuine cognitive confusion begins.

The confusion and superficiality of several components of Reagan's image are to be expected, given the manner in which he acquired his beliefs about the Soviet Union. Although I do not systematically try to identify the sources of images, it is interesting to note that most accounts (e.g., Edwards 1987; Gelb 1985; Wills 1987) point to Reagan's early experiences with communists in the Screen Actors Guild during the 1940s as the crucial formative phase. Reagan himself recognized the impact of his Hollywood days, pointing out that "I had some experience with communists—not of the Soviet kind, but domestic, in our own country, some years ago when I was president of a labor union there" (*CPD* 1983, 1582). Asked about his knowledge of the Soviet Union and Soviet negotiating behavior, the President responded:

> I know that it sounds kind of foolish maybe to link Hollywood, and experience there, to the world situation, and yet, the tactics seemed to be pretty much the same. . . . It was a communist attempt to gain control of the motion picture industry, because at that time the Hollywood motion picture industry provided the film for 75 percent of the playing time in all the theaters of the world. It was a great propaganda device, if someone wanted to use it for that, that's ever been known. (*CPD* 1981, 1197)

Leslie Gelb observes that "the President's ideas about the world situation flow from his life, from personal history rather than study" (1985, 24). If this is true, the most relevant life experiences in terms of Reagan's views of the Soviet Union were his dealing with communists (or perceived communists) in Hollywood. As a result, he developed a general suspicion and dislike of anything considered communist, including the Soviet Union. But his beliefs about the Soviet Union did not emerge from any careful consideration of Soviet history, ideology, or policies; his image was simply a generalized reaction to the Soviet Union as a communist phenomenon. Since his views about the Soviet Union were extrapolations from these experiences, we would not expect a very well-grounded image of the Soviet Union. Furthermore, we might expect changes in his image to be set in motion by a new set of personal experiences, such as his meetings with Gorbachev.

# Part 3
# Policy Debates

# CHAPTER 8

# The Utility or Futility of Arms Control?

Meaningful negotiation in any area presumes a degree of common interest among the parties involved. If the actors' interests are diametrically opposed, it will be impossible to find any common ground upon which an agreement can be based. As Snyder and Diesing conclude in their study of international crisis bargaining:

> . . . the necessary condition for bargaining to occur is the coexistence of conflicting and common interests. . . . Bargaining occurs only if the common interest in reaching an agreement is strong enough and/or the conflicting interests weak enough to create a "bargaining range," a range of conceivable settlements that both parties would prefer to no settlement. (1977, 476)

Given the cognitive focus of this study, it is more appropriate to argue that bargaining requires a *perception* of conflicting and common interests if there is to be any hope of success, which Snyder and Diesing recognized: "it is not necessary that such a range 'objectively' exist; it is sufficient that parties perceive one" (476). This is important because arms control is a particular form of bargaining—i.e., formal negotiations designed to regulate (i.e., reduce, limit, restructure) weapons systems. If either party to arms control negotiations perceives the other's objectives to be completely contradictory to its own, it is hard to see how an agreement can be achieved. Only if both sides believe that their common interests outweigh their conflicts will the negotiations lead anywhere. This is why images are potentially essential for understanding a decision maker's assessment of the utility of arms control. Since images contain beliefs about the opponent's foreign policy goals and, at least for this study, nuclear objectives and strategy, they are crucial for defining the "bargaining range." Without phrasing it in such explicit terms, this is what many of Reagan's critics feared, that the bargaining range would be very small indeed, if not totally nonexistent. As Talbott observed, "the Reagan administration deemed Soviet-American diplomacy suspect almost by definition, since even on the chilliest terms, diplomacy presumes that a degree of civilized discussion and behavior is possible" (1985, 48). How, critics wondered, could any agreement be reached if the Soviet Union was viewed as a militarily superior and ideologically motivated enemy determined to conquer the globe and, if necessary, prepared to launch thousands of nuclear weapons at the United States in a first strike? How does one bargain with an adversary who seeks your destruction?

## The Agnostics

The "rap" on the Reagan administration as it entered office was that, beneath a facade of concern for the shortcomings of the SALT treaties and the frequently expressed desire to achieve "real" arms control, there was a fundamental hostility to arms control of any sort. The chief culprit, according to this analysis, was Richard Perle, who many feared would use his considerable intellectual and political skills to prevent any progress in arms control. Perle's sincerity was repeatedly called into question by skeptical congressman and journalists. He usually replied by claiming to support "real" arms control, not the "cosmetic" limitations that resulted from the SALT negotiations. In one especially revealing exchange, Perle explained, "it seems to me that agnosticism on the utility of arms control is not a bad position to take. It depends on the proposals, and it depends on the agreements. So I am neither for nor against arms control" (U.S. Cong. 1981b, 31). In one sense, Perle's self-description is probably accurate, but in arms control, as in religion, there are shades of agnosticism. Perle's arms control agnosticism was analogous to the religious agnostic who rejects all the trappings of traditional religion, does not pray or attend church, and who argues against the follies of religion at every opportunity, but who still holds out the abstract possibility that there may be a higher being. That is, he was about as close as one can come to arms control atheism without actually being an atheist. Although Weinberger was not as articulate in describing his position, it was indistinguishable from Perle's.

Perle's and Weinberger's agnosticism about arms control stemmed partly from their belief that the dynamics of negotiation inevitably favored the Soviet Union because of the nature of its society and political system. As a "closed" and "regimented" society with a totalitarian-authoritarian political system, the Soviet Union enjoyed advantages that the United States, as an open society, did not. As Perle argued, Soviet leaders "do not have a public opinion to satisfy, they do not have a press that is sometimes critical of them, they do not have to face reelection, and they do not have a critical, politically independent voice at home" (U.S. Cong. 1981b, 36). Without these political pressures, the Soviets are better able to set objectives, implement plans, and carry them out over the long term. In a passage reminiscent of Tocqueville's famous observation about the deficiencies of democracies in foreign affairs, Perle elaborated on the relative political weaknesses of democracies.

> Arms control can be, in my judgment a great benefit to the United States . . . provided it meets certain criteria. Here I think we get to the crux of the problem. . . . If I may say so, it is easier for democracies to abandon [their] fundamental purposes than it is for totalitarian systems because we have a public opinion with which we have to be concerned, we have a press that is often critical, to which we feel bound to respond, and we have elections at regular intervals.
>
> Under the pressure of electoral politics the temptation is to conclude agreements because it is a sign of statesmanship, and they are regarded as a sign of success that a more hopeful world, a more stable world and peaceful world can be created through the mechanism of bilateral agreement.
>
> The pressure on democratic governments to produce agreements is far greater than the pressure on our negotiating partners. As a result, we find ourselves at every turn negotiating with obvious disadvantages of the political asymmetries that apply to us. (U.S. Cong. 1984g, 271–72)

It would be difficult to imagine a more concise explication of the diplomatic shortcomings that supposedly accrue to the United States as a result of its political system. (Notice that while Perle began by talking about the criteria for the success of arms control, he only gave reasons for its destined failure.) The problem, however, went beyond differences in political institutions and mechanisms for decision making. Perle would not have lamented the impact of public opinion if it pushed in the direction of greater firmness and resolve in dealings with the Soviet Union. Perle was not worried about the *existence* of public pressures, but rather the *type* of pressures exerted.

Moreover, it is not only the impact of public opinion on negotiations that troubled Perle, but also the impact of negotiations on public opinion. While public opinion tended to promote unwise accommodation, the talks themselves induce a decreased sense of threat, thereby eroding public support for policies needed to counter the threat. Perle referred to this phenomena as the "psychology of negotiation" and the "psychology of moderation," which "ha[ve] tended to lead us to expect moderation [from the Soviet Union] when moderation turned out not to be the case" (U.S. Cong. 1984b, 274). It was as if public opinion and negotiation fed off each other to weaken the nation's resolve. This was not a problem for Soviet leaders for two reasons: first, they were not really influenced by public opinion; and second, they were more able to manipulate the perception of threat.

The potential dangers are found not only during the course of negotiations, but also in the aftermath of "successful" talks. The following exchanges illustrate Perle's perspective on the dangers of concluding arms treaties.

> *Senator Thurmond*: Mr. Perle what, in your opinion is the most serious pitfall in an arms control reduction agreement with the Soviets?
> *Mr. Perle*: I think it is the false sense that we can protect the security of this nation and our allies through arms control. (U.S. Cong. 1985a, 31)

> *Mr. Perle*: . . . past experience has shown that the diminution in the sense of threat that follows arms control will make it very difficult to obtain the funds for protective measures.
> *Senator Bingham*: If you take that argument to its logical conclusion, then your view would be that whatever actions we might take to diminish the perception of threat are counterproductive to our nation's security. Is that correct?
> *Mr. Perle*: I would not take it to that conclusion. (U.S. Cong. 1984e, 3546)

Perle did not explain why he would not reach that logical conclusion. Weinberger expressed similar fears. Even in the absence of negotiations and agreements, Weinberger had his doubts about the intestinal fortitude of democratic societies. "As you know from the study of history," he informed a congressional committee, "it has been hard to persuade democratic states over the centuries that it is essential to make sacrifices and substantial investments in the preservation of their freedom and security" (U.S. Cong. 1981o, 51). Soviet defense officials presumably do not have the same worries because "they don't suffer from the kinds of restraints of the type that constrain the United States and other free world budgets" (U.S. Cong. 1982g, 225). Unlike U.S. leaders, "they don't care what they do to their civilian economy because they don't have the kind of system in which anybody has to worry about public opinion" (U.S. Cong. 1985d, 78).

In Weinberger's view, the normal hesitancy of democratic societies to do what they must to defend themselves was exacerbated during arms control negotiations. Asked about his position on arms control, Weinberger responded, "I have no problem with arms control talks, I have a great problem with the effect arms control might have on public opinion if they [the talks] appear to make progress" (U.S. Cong. 1982e, 292). Apparently his experiences as secretary of defense did not change his views: shortly before leaving office in the fall of 1987, Weinberger warned once again that "it is essential to maintain public support. This is difficult to do in a democratic society that basically doesn't like defense spending and never has" (U.S. Cong. 1987b,

448). One wonders what role the Reagan administration's arms control efforts played in reinforcing his beliefs.

In addition to the negotiating advantages enjoyed by the Soviets, the closed nature of Soviet society and the centralization of decision making facilitated the violation of treaties by allowing a degree of secrecy impossible in the United States. According to Perle, "a great deal of what we want to know about Soviet behavior is easy for them to verify about our own, since it is published, it is widely discussed, things that are difficult for us to learn about Soviet programs are freely conveyed in hearings like this" (U.S. Cong. 1984i, 85). "I don't believe that our structure of government is capable of violations," Perle contended, because "it would mean at least dozens of people knowingly violating a treaty to which the United States was a party. . . . I think at all levels of society people would simply refuse to issue orders necessary to implement a violation" (U.S. Cong. 1984i, 65). Presumably, the structure of the Soviet government posed no such obstacles.

## Common Interests?

The political asymmetries between the two powers were not, in and of themselves, the crucial issue; they were dangerous because the country that enjoyed the advantages had certain objectives. If the Soviet Union desired the same ends as the United States, its diplomatic advantages would not have been any great cause for concern. The real problem was that the negotiating advantages were combined with profoundly hostile and threatening objectives. Perle and Weinberger perceived Soviet objectives in a manner that all but precluded the identification of common interests. Whether they were aware of it or not, the result was a zero-sum analysis of the strategic relationship in which anything that advanced Soviet goals was, by definition, contrary to U.S. interests. Such a view left little room for reasonable compromise.

At the level of overall policy goals, we have Weinberger's unchanging characterization of the Soviet Union as an ideologically inspired power pursuing global hegemony, the worldwide triumph of communism, and the elimination of liberal democracy and capitalism. If the superpower conflict is seen in these terms, it becomes a struggle for survival, not simply a competition for influence and security. It is the ultimate zero-sum "game." Larson explains that an "image of the Soviet Union as bent on world revolution and relentlessly expanding into all vacuums remove[s] the possibility of establishing a 'limited adversary' relationship with the Soviets" (1985, 331). Exactly how this translates into a position on arms control is uncertain, but clearly it does not lay the intellectual foundation for thinking of U.S.-Soviet relations in the framework of common interests and mutually beneficial agreements.

The SALT process that incurred the wrath of Perle and Weinberger was an attempt to institutionalize a nuclear balance in which each side possessed an invulnerable retaliatory force sufficient to deter the other side from launching a first strike. SALT's architects hoped that the result would be mutual security based on mutual vulnerability. The success of SALT, however, depended on both sides believing that this was a desirable state of affairs. In was on this key point that the most effective critics of SALT focused: many simply did not believe that the Soviet Union accepted the strategic premises that guided the U.S. approach to SALT. According to these critics, the Soviets were not willing to settle for nuclear parity during the 1970s but continued to race for superiority. Perle and Weinberger agreed with this basic criticism; indeed, Perle was one of its major proponents. Whereas supporters of SALT assumed that the Soviet Union and the United States had essentially compatible goals on nuclear issues, Perle and Weinberger believed that the two countries approached nuclear questions from irreconcilably different perspectives.

This perceived conflict of goals and strategies is the critical element for understanding Perle's and Weinberger's skepticism about the utility of arms control. The dilemma is clear: if the Soviet Union's goals were what Perle and Weinberger perceived them to be, how could any agreement be reached that would be acceptable to both parties? If the Soviets were seeking nuclear superiority, and if they wanted to acquire the ability to fight and win a nuclear war, these goals could only be achieved at the expense of U.S. security. Conversely, if the United States sought nuclear parity and invulnerable retaliatory forces, this could only be achieved at the expense of Soviet goals. As a result, it is virtually impossible to see how U.S. and Soviet goals could be enhanced simultaneously.

Not surprisingly, one finds very few references to "common interests" or "mutually beneficial" agreements in Perle's and Weinberger's discussions of arms control. Indeed, since they spent most of their time detailing the shortcomings and follies of arms control, there is relatively little information about what they thought could be achieved. On a few occasions, however, they did identify what "real" and "meaningful" arms control would entail. After listening to Perle elaborate on the problems of arms control, one member of Congress was prompted to ask, "is there any point in negotiating with them?" Perle responded, "it is incumbent upon us to prepare to enter an agreement, when an agreement can be negotiated that diminishes the threat we face and genuinely reduces the military threat the Soviet Union poses" (U.S. Cong. 1982a, 69). And testifying before another committee, Perle explained that "the test of any agreement ought to be whether it diminishes the threat Soviet forces pose to the United States" (U.S. Cong. 1982b, 56). These statements are indicative of the way Perle thought about "real" arms control: it was a one-way street. There was never any discussion of what the Soviets had to gain from arms control. Arms control was defined in terms of what the United States stood to gain, not what both powers could achieve.

Similarly, Weinberger spoke of "real" arms control as if it were something the Soviets would accept only if they had no real option. In his opinion, "the Soviets will respond seriously to proposals for meaningful and equitable reductions only if they have a real need to do so" (U.S. Cong. 1981r, 5). Speculating on the chances for a START agreement, Weinberger observed, "I think the Soviets want to have an agreement on reductions. They need one" (U.S. Cong. 1987e, 292). In the same vein, Perle argued that "the Soviets have no reason to come to an agreement unless they conclude that the alternative to an agreement is a worsening of their security or, alternatively, an improvement in our security" (U.S. Cong. 1983a, 13). Even though the language used was subtle, the impression one gets is that the Soviets would accept "real" arms control only as a last resort; it is as if the Soviets had to be forced into doing something that was contrary to their interests. All of this is consistent with Perle's and Weinberger's perceptions of Soviet objectives and strategy: "real" arms control required the Soviets to accept agreements that were inconsistent with their supposed goal of strategic superiority.

The fundamental conceptual shift in the nature of arms control entailed by Perle's and Weinberger's views about the Soviet Union cannot be underestimated. If the two countries are seen as sharing the goals of stability, parity, and mutual security, arms control is a matter of finding ways to codify these underlying common interests. If the Soviets are seen as aiming to upset the balance, achieve superiority, and place U.S. forces at risk, "real" arms control requires the Soviets to abandon their objectives and strategy.

## Toward "Real" Arms Control?

It is easy to show that Perle and Weinberger were skeptical about the utility of arms control; they repeatedly admitted as much. Their harsher critics charged that Perle and Weinberger were not merely skeptical of arms control, but dead set against it. As Brownstein and Easton observed, "skeptics argue[d] that Perle puts forward proposals so unbalanced as to make Soviet acceptance impossible . . . [and] once arms control has proven a dead end, this analysis of Perle's views continues, the U.S. can engage in a massive buildup that the Soviets cannot match" (1983, 500). These fears were not without foundation, since Perle seemed to go a step beyond mere skepticism on a number of occasions. Regarding the possibilities for arms control, for example, Perle warned that "we have to do it with our eyes open, in a realistic sense of its limitations and its futility" (U.S. Cong. 1985a, 34). *Futile* is not a word usually employed to describe a process one supports or expects to succeed. Nonetheless, Perle and Weinberger insisted that they supported real and meaningful arms control, emphasizing that they held the process to a higher standard than supporters of traditional arms control.

Establishing Perle's and Weinberger's skepticism is no problem. Demonstrating that their negotiating proposals were asymmetrical and unbalanced will also be a relatively easy task. Can we, however, show that the critics were right, that Perle and Weinberger cynically crafted proposals designed to thwart arms control altogether? The simple answer is no. Does this mean that we must take their expressions of sincerity at face value? Again, the simple answer is no. Based on what we know about Perle's and Weinberger's view of the Soviet Union, Soviet foreign policy, and the dynamics of superpower negotiations, we can make an informed, albeit inconclusive, judgment about their sincerity. That is, we can reach a tentative conclusion about whether they actually intended their proposals to advance or halt arms control.

Consistent with his criteria for successful arms control, Perle argued that "it is not in our interest to sign agreements that do not entail a *significant* improvement in the military balance" (Brownstein and Easton 1983, 500). We can safely assume that Perle and Weinberger believed their proposals would bring about such an improvement. But this only addresses the "what" of meaningful arms control, not the "how." Ultimately, the question of whether Perle and Weinberger intended their proposals to move the arms control process forward or thwart it depends on whether they expected these proposals to lead to an agreement. When we look at Perle's and Weinberger's image of the Soviet Union on the one hand and their definition of meaningful arms control on the other, a number of nagging questions come to mind, raising doubts about their sincerity.

To begin with, if the Soviets were prepared to violate the SALT treaties for the most minor of strategic advantages, why would they accept a treaty that shifted the military balance "significantly" in the direction of the United States? If the Soviets were, to use Weinberger's words, "very good chess players," why would they accept a treaty that radically altered their relative capabilities? If, as Perle warned, "we have to recognize that no arms control agreement is going to halt the Soviet investment in nuclear forces" (U.S. Cong. 1984g, 275), how could he think that his proposals would stand a chance? The key issue was recognized by Perle himself.

> The question of deep reductions entails the question of how far are the Soviets willing in the context of a negotiated agreement to relinquish what I believe the evidence shows to have been a driving objective of their strategic program for the last decade or more. That is, the acquisition of a preponderance of strategic nuclear weapons. It is a terribly important question whether they are in fact prepared to relinquish that objective. (U.S. Cong. 1981b, 31–32)

Indeed, this was a terribly important question, one that Perle and Weinberger had to answer if they wanted to argue convincingly that their proposals really could (as opposed to should) serve as the basis for an agreement. How and why would the Soviets give up what had been their "driving objective" for more than a decade? Perle and Weinberger never provided a persuasive answer to this question. In fact, examining their analysis of Soviet objectives and the superpower relationship, it is difficult to see how they could have anticipated agreements along the lines they proposed. This is not to say that these questions could not be answered. Two possibilities come immediately to mind. First, one could argue that the Soviet Union's internal problems, particularly its economic weaknesses, might provide the needed impetus for abandoning grandiose strategic objectives. Second, one could predict that a U.S. military buildup designed to deny the Soviets their quest for superiority might convince them of the futility of this goal. If these two alternatives are combined, the result could be a very persuasive explanation of why the Soviets might accept treaties that prevented the establishment of Soviet superiority.

While others in the administration, particularly the president himself, gave a lot of weight to the possible strategic ramifications of Soviet economic problems, Perle and Weinberger did not. Certainly they were cognizant of the sorry state of the Soviet economy, but it was not a matter they dwelled on. It was usually only in response to very pointed questions that Perle or Weinberger considered the potential military consequences of the Soviet economic crisis, and then only in very subdued terms. On one occasion, for example, Perle was asked about an article by the director of the Arms Control and Disarmament Agency, Eugene Rostow, that stressed the economic dilemmas faced by Soviet leaders and how these might work to the advantage of the United States. Perle's response was interesting.

> I rather suspect that when he referred to economic pressure he was referring to the depressed state of the Soviet economy and the difficulty it is sometimes assumed they will have in sustaining an arms race . . . whether the Soviets can sustain that buildup will depend on whether one can make a plausible case that it is going to produce a significant military advantage. If we fail to respond, that buildup will indeed produce a significant advantage. . . . If, on the other hand, we maintain our strategic deterrent, the Soviet expenditure in the long run will be futile. In that context, one would hope that they would recognize the advantage to them, as well as to us, of entering into serious arms control. (U.S. Cong. 1982k, 13)

For Perle, this was very cautious and hesitant language. His use of words like *assumed*, *in the long run*, and *one would hope* was uncharacteristic for someone who was usually very sure of his analysis. Weinberger made a few vague references to the Soviets "needing" an arms reduction treaty, but he was not very explicit about what he meant. Perle and Weinberger never argued that a change of Soviet goals and strategy was imminent because of their economic problems. Nor did they claim, as Reagan did, that the Soviet Union had just about reached the limits of its ability to produce more military hardware through squeezing the civilian sector.

Closely related to the economic argument is the possibility that a U.S. buildup might provide the needed incentive for the Soviets to abandon their pursuit of strategic superiority. This would be consistent with the basic peace-through-strength logic that permeated the Reagan administration. Perle, for example, argued that "to the extent to which they become persuaded that this administration means to redress the military balance, they may find arms control alternatives to competition more appealing." Perle routinely qualified this type of statement with "may" and "might," as if he was not convinced that even a U.S. buildup would be sufficient. Weinberger made the same general points: "an enhanced strategic posture offers our best hope of negotiating a meaningful arms agreement with the Soviet Union" (U.S. Cong. 1981, 12). A similar theme appears in repeated statements that the administration's buildup was the only reason the Soviets came (and later returned) to the negotiating table.

Although this modernization-as-an-incentive-for-real-reductions argument has a certain surface plausibility, it seems somehow inadequate in the context of my overall analysis of Perle's and Weinberger's views. A number of questions remain. For example, why would a few years of U.S. strategic modernization induce the Soviets to abandon a goal they had been pursuing with an almost single-minded obsession for more than a decade? Why wouldn't the Soviets simply sit back and wait for the natural hesitancy of democratic societies to kick in and derail the modernization program?

This last question speaks to the final issue that Perle and Weinberger failed to address; the problem of political asymmetries. One of the cornerstones of their criticism of SALT was the detrimental impact of the interaction of public opinion and negotiations on the U.S. position and the absence of similar pressures on the Soviets. Arms control, however, always requires negotiations, whether the goal is limitations or genuine or deep reductions. In claiming to support real arms reductions, Perle and Weinberger never explained why the unfavorable political dynamics that perverted the SALT process would not also affect negotiations aimed at reductions. Why wouldn't the Soviets prove as adept at manipulating the weaknesses of U.S. democracy as they had been in the past? Indeed, one suspects that the goal of dramatic reductions would only increase the public's reluctance to support the expensive weapons systems that Perle and Weinberger claimed were necessary to force the Soviets into reductions. Furthermore, would not the problem be particularly acute if, in the words of Weinberger, the talks "appeared to make progress"?

While it would be inaccurate to say that Perle and Weinberger presented no explanation of why the Soviets would accept the kind of reductions they advocated, one is struck by the difference between their elaborate explanation of why arms control had failed and their fuzzy explanation of why "real" arms control could succeed. Perle and Weinberger's analysis of why arms control had not served U.S. interests was based on the perception of political asymmetries and a fundamental conflict of superpower objectives. The problem was that they devoted little attention to how political asymmetries and strategic conflicts could be overcome in order to reach the kind of agreements they claimed to favor.

### The Believers

Continuing the religious analogy introduced by Perle's self-description as an arms control agnostic, we might classify Burt and Shultz as arms control believers, even if they were not devout in their faith. By all accounts, Burt and Shultz were the leading figures in the Reagan administration favoring arms control, consistently searching for ways to move negotiations forward. Of course, "leading figures" entails a judgment about their relative position; whether they would have emerged as the key proponents of arms control in a different cast of characters is open to speculation. After all, as one Soviet diplomat observed, this was an administration where the *doves* were members of the Committee on the Present Danger. In the case of Perle and Weinberger, it was easy to understand why they were less than anxious to pursue arms control: their image of the Soviet Union and analysis of the negotiating dynamics did not hold out much hope for favorable agreements; on the contrary, the expectation was that the results would be harmful. Burt and Shultz are a little harder to get a firm handle on. While it is clear they did not accept the pessimistic assessment of Perle and Weinberger, it is less clear exactly what Burt and Shultz believed could be accomplished.

### SALT and Its Legacy

The debate over arms control in the early 1980s was largely an extension of the disagreements over the SALT process and furor over SALT II. Perle, Weinberger, and Reagan came into office as firm opponents of SALT II; one searches in vain for any kind words from them about the treaty. The same cannot be said of Burt. Certainly he could not be included among the ranks of SALT II's enthusiastic supporters, if there were any, but neither was he a harsh critic. In fact, reading Burt's analysis of the "scope and limits of SALT" (1978), it is difficult to tell whether he favored or opposed the treaty, a problem that would not be encountered in an analysis of Perle's views. On the one hand, Burt thought it was "difficult to escape the conclusion that, during the treaty, a shift in the strategic nuclear balance will in fact occur" (1978, 760). On the other hand, he cautioned that "whether the asymmetries that could arise under the treaty are significant is a difficult question to answer" (1978, 761). Although the shifting balance might, "at least on paper," give the Soviet Union the ability to knock out the land-based portion of the U.S. triad, Burt was more concerned about the political consequences that would flow from the perception of Soviet strategic advantages. Unlike Perle and Weinberger, Burt was not preoccupied with the military options such imbalances would afford the Soviets; he was worried about the more ambiguous political ramifications, particularly with respect to the Atlantic alliance (Perle had raised the same concerns).

Despite these apparently severe problems, Burt claimed that "this does not mean that the SALT [II] agreement now nearing completion must be judged as a failure. . . . It provides for lower overall launcher numbers, it limits Soviet MIRVed ICBMs, and it permits the deployment of American ALCMs aboard bombers" (1978, 768). The difference in tone between Burt's and Perle's comments is striking. Whereas Perle argued that the SALT process itself was responsible for the strategic predicament of the United States, both directly through limitations on strategic modernization and indirectly by instilling a diminished perception of threat, Burt located the problem elsewhere. According to Burt, "the shifting overall balance as well as the more specific problem of Minuteman vulnerability are not really the product of arms control negotiations. Instead, they are the result of *earlier* Soviet and American weapons procurement decisions that have inevitably been reflected in the outcome of negotiations" (1978, 767; italics added). Burt lamented the fact that "an agreement . . . that should be viewed as an accommodation to reality is now widely being considered an accommodation to the Soviet Union" (1978, 770).

Though Burt's position on SALT II was somewhat equivocal, he did warn that "if the SALT process itself is not put under scrutiny, superpower arms control may not survive" (1978, 770). Burt suggested some changes at the beginning of the Carter administration: "future strategic arms control efforts will have to embrace a wider category of weapons . . . [and] be better directed towards controlling qualitative developments" (Burt 1976, 17). SALT II, in Burt's opinion, did not accomplish this. But more important than Burt's specific recommendations is the general manner in which he analyzed and criticized SALT. There were no sweeping denunciations of the entire process. The flaws in the SALT II treaty were not portrayed as the logical outcome of an inherently biased negotiating process. Burt viewed the patient as sick, not terminally ill.

## Democratic Dilemmas

One of the key reasons for Perle's and Weinberger's arms control agnosticism was their analysis of the diplomatic deficiencies of democratic states in dealing with adversaries with highly centralized political systems. Burt and Shultz were not oblivious to these problems. Shultz, for example, spoke of:

> . . . the Soviet Union's great advantages: continuity, patience, the ability to fashion a long-term strategy and stick to it. . . . The democracies, in contrast, have long had difficulty maintaining the same consistency, coherence, discipline, and sense of strategy . . . free societies are often impatient. Western attitudes have fluctuated between extremes of gloom and pessimism on the one hand and susceptibility to a Soviet smile on the other. (U.S. Cong. 1985a, 6)

Continuing to emphasize the problems of coherence and consistency, Shultz observed, "we have tended too often to focus on either increasing our strength or on pursuing a course of negotiations. We have found it difficult to pursue both simultaneously" (*DSB*, December, 1984, 2). Burt identified similar problems.

> Most important, [a successful] strategy requires patience. This is perhaps the hardest quality for a democracy to practice in the conduct of foreign affairs. Many of our problems in dealing with the Soviet Union over the course of the past 20 years have been self-generated. There has been a tendency for the public, the congress, and policymakers to swing between unwarranted euphoria and undue pessimism. (U.S. Cong. 1982a, 350)

Though this seems very similar to the analysis of Perle and Weinberger, there are important differences. First, Perle and Weinberger never warned about the dangers of "undue pessimism"; the whole thrust of their analysis was the tendency toward excessive optimism and naïveté. Shultz and Burt stressed the problem of *consistency*, devoting attention to the dangers of excessive confrontation and unwise compromise; Perle and Weinberger were only concerned with the latter. Second, Perle and Weinberger argued that the process of negotiation per se was an (if not the) important cause of unrealistic optimism; Burt and Shultz did not attach the same causal significance to negotiations. In fact, Shultz claimed, "we do not agree with the view that negotiated outcomes can only sap our strength or lead to an outcome in which we will be the loser" (*DSB*, December, 1984, 4). This seems to be a direct criticism of the Perle and Weinberger thesis. Thus, while Shultz and Burt did recognize that democracies have problems in diplomacy, they did not portray them as debilitating.

### Common Interests

The second element of Perle's and Weinberger's arms control agnosticism was their perception of Soviet foreign policy and nuclear goals. Both believed that the Soviets approached nuclear strategy from a fundamentally different perspective than the United States, making it difficult to envision agreements that would be acceptable to both countries. Perle and Weinberger put forward a very clear and consistent image of Soviet goals and doctrine: the Soviets wanted strategic superiority in line with a doctrine stressing the fightability and winnability of nuclear war. Burt and Shultz did not make these claims. Given that this view of the Soviet Union was almost an article of faith in conservative foreign policy circles, this was a significant omission. The problem, however, is that Burt and Shultz did not present any coherent alternative perspective. Burt and Shultz did not argue that the Soviets wanted strategic superiority, but they also did not say the Soviets would settle for parity. Burt and Shultz did not attribute to the Soviets a belief that a nuclear war could be fought and won, but they also did not say the Soviets accepted the tenets of mutual assured destruction. Shultz and Burt never spelled out exactly what they thought the Soviets wanted.

It is difficult to say whether this lack of clarity reflected genuine uncertainty. This seems to be a reasonable assumption for Shultz, since he had no background in thinking about nuclear weapons and strategy prior to becoming secretary of state. Burt, however, was very familiar with both the technical and conceptual issues surrounding the arms race. Is it possible that he did not have a clear view of Soviet goals and doctrine? It is not inconceivable. Although Burt was well informed about nuclear issues, his areas of expertise were Western Europe and the alliance; he was not, and never claimed to be, an expert on Soviet politics and strategic thought (though one does not have to be an expert to have firm beliefs about these issues). A related possibility is that Burt viewed questions of goals, doctrine, and motivation as irrelevant, or at least of secondary importance, in comparison to capabilities.

A final possibility is that Burt did have beliefs about Soviet goals and doctrine but simply did not express them very explicitly. We might look for some clues in Burt's analysis of SALT II. As I have noted, when Burt looked at the treaty, he was concerned that it would permit a shift in the strategic balance. He was not, however, worried that the Soviets would actually contemplate or threaten an attack, even if they had the ability, "on paper," to implement one. Burt even resurrected Harold Brown's characterization of a Soviet first strike as a "cosmic roll of the dice," a phrase the former Defense Secretary used to indicate his skepticism of the entire scenario. Instead, Burt was troubled by the potential for Soviet exploitation of the perceptions of a shifting balance. His paramount concern was the impact in Europe, where these perceptions might increase doubts about the reliability of the U.S. commitment.

What does this critique of SALT II tell us about Burt's view of the Soviet Union's approach to nuclear weapons? Strictly speaking, nothing. But in suggesting what the United States had to worry about, Burt was making implicit assumptions about what the Soviets were up to, or at least not up to. Burt apparently did not think the Soviets would launch a first strike, even if they had the technical ability to carry one out. He did think the Soviets would exploit emerging strategic imbalances to further their political goals. Burt did not claim that the Soviets were determined to acquire a disarming first-strike capability, nor did he say the Soviets wanted parity; but he did argue that the Soviets would exploit a situation in which they had certain advantages. (Whether he thought the Soviets were merely opportunistic or carefully planning this state of affairs is uncertain).

While none of this provides conclusive evidence, it does suggest a different view of the Soviet Union than that offered by Perle and Weinberger. It was an analysis that went beyond a focus on capabilities to a consideration of what the Soviets would do with their new capabilities. Burt presented a picture of the Soviet Union reaping benefits from perceptions of a shifting balance, not a Soviet Union trying to radically disturb the underlying stability of mutual vulnerability. It was a picture of a Soviet Union willing to exploit doubts about the credibility of the U.S. strategic deterrent, not a Soviet Union prepared to launch a nuclear attack on the assumption that it could win the ensuing conflict. Perle's and Weinberger's Soviet Union was out to undermine the structure of mutual deterrence by denying the United States a credible deterrent; Burt's Soviet Union might have an interest in a basically stable nuclear balance, even if it tries to achieve advantages on the outer limits of that balance.

It is no surprise, then, that Burt described the purpose of arms control in different terms than his Pentagon counterparts. Whereas Perle and Weinberger emphasized the reduction of the Soviet threat to U.S. forces, never recognizing any threat in the opposite direction, Burt stressed more balanced criteria. According to Burt:

> Our arms control efforts, like our modernization program, are a means
> to the same objective: protecting the security of the United States, our

allies, and furthering international stability. . . . We want agreements that will result in substantial reductions of the nuclear arsenal of both sides, insure equality of forces, and promote strategic stability. (U.S. Cong. 1982e, 8)

"What we are trying to achieve in both our START and INF negotiations [is] not just reductions alone," Burt explained, "we are focusing on those aspects of the balance which are the more destabilizing forces of *the two sides*" (U.S. Cong. 1983c, 20; italics added). There are two key differences between this and Perle's and Weinberger's goals for arms control. First, Perle and Weinberger would have been loath to even suggest that the United States possessed destabilizing weapons, since all U.S. forces were obviously intended for defense, not offense, which the Soviets knew full well. Second, when Burt talked about the goals of arms control, one is not left wondering what benefits the Soviets would derive from it.

Regardless of which of these admittedly speculative explanations one accepts as the more accurate account for Burt's lack of clarity, the basic point is the same: Burt did not approach arms control with an assumption that the United States and the Soviet Union had irreconcilable nuclear goals and strategies. Certainly he did not see complete compatibility. Because the two sides' approaches did not overlap perfectly, arms control was not an easy task. Even if the Soviets had an interest in basic stability, they also had an interest in preserving certain imbalances that could be exploited. Though these advantages would not allow the Soviets to carry out a disarming first strike with any confidence, they were definitely undesirable from the U.S. standpoint. The Soviets would not give up these advantages without an incentive to do so: "it is essential to keep this point in mind—that our ability to negotiate reductions with the Soviet Union depends on their perception of our willingness to maintain a military balance" (U.S. Cong. 1982e, 8). While this emphasis on the need to demonstrate U.S. strength and resolve sounds very much like Perle and Weinberger, there is an important distinction. In Perle's and Weinberger's analysis, meaningful arms control required that the Soviet Union abandon what had supposedly been its "driving objective" for more than a decade (i.e., a disarming first-strike capability), Burt's analysis did not lead to this conclusion.

In some senses, Shultz presents a more interesting case than Burt. Although Shultz had little background in U.S.-Soviet relations, and even less in strategic issues, he was not devoid of relevant experience. After all, one does not enter office as a blank slate and earn Henry Kissinger's glowing endorsement: "if I could choose one American to whom I would entrust the nation's fate, it would be George Shultz" (Gwertzman 1983, 14). This was heady praise for a man who had no real foreign policy expertise. Certainly Shultz's portrait of U.S.-Soviet relations was often vague. He thought there was a Soviet threat, but he was not very clear about the nature of the threat. He was troubled by the growth of Soviet strategic power, even if he was not sure of the reasons for, or implications of, the Soviet buildup. He offered no coherent view of Soviet nuclear goals and doctrine; there are not even enough clues to engage in a little detective work. Nonetheless, Shultz was committed to the pursuit of arms control. Why?

Shultz's image of the Soviet Union provides only part of the explanation for his support of arms control efforts. The most we can say is that his image was a permissive factor: there was nothing about his image that precluded the identification of common interests between the United States and the Soviet Union. Simply on the basis of his image of the Soviet Union, we would not anticipate opposition to arms control, but we would also not predict that Shultz would be the administration's leading arms control advocate. That is, the pursuit of arms control was consistent with his image, but not the necessary result of it. To understand Shultz's approach to arms control, we need to look at other factors in his intellectual and professional background. Perhaps most important is his academic and professional interest in economics, particularly his specialization in labor management and dispute mediation. Gwertzman explains:

> [Shultz's] involvement in economics helps him to transpose to his new field the kind of discipline and way of ordering things that he learned in his economic activities . . . for instance, his stints as a labor management mediator during his academic career . . . convinced him that every issue can be seen from various vantage points. Almost every view of the problem proves to have some merit, he says, if you study it carefully enough, and what you must do is listen and try to figure out ways to "move the situation along." (1983, 15)

One of the more striking aspects of Shultz's comments about U.S.-Soviet relations is how much they sound like they were lifted out of a textbook on resolving and mediating conflicts. "The condition for successful negotiations exists," he observed, "when both sides stand to gain from an agreement or stand to lose from the absence of an agreement" (*DSB*, December, 1984, 3). With regard to the superpower relationship, "we know that any agreement you make with a strong partner such as the Soviet Union . . . will not only have to serve your interests, but also their interests" (4). He cautioned that "we have to accept the fact that our respective goals may be incompatible, making agreements impossible to reach" (3). The problem of nuclear weapons, however, was not one of those irreconcilable issues because "the United States and the Soviet Union have a profound and overriding common interest in the avoidance of nuclear war" (*DSB*, June, 1984, 28). "In the thermonuclear age," Shultz argued, "there is a common interest in survival; therefore, both sides have an incentive to moderate the rivalry and seek ways to control nuclear weapons and reduce the risks of war" (1985, 706). Thus, even though Shultz did not have a very well-developed view of what the Soviets wanted to accomplish in the area of nuclear weapons, he did see a basic common interest that could serve as a basis to "move the situation along." This may not seem like much, but it is more than Perle and Weinberger ever conceded.

### The Dreamer?

In examining Reagan's image of the Soviet Union, I noted that it seemed to embody many of the contradictions and tensions found in the U.S. foreign affairs psyche. In this sense, Reagan was a wonderful reflection of the society that chose him to lead it. Perhaps nowhere were the implications of these tensions more evident than in the realm of U.S.-Soviet relations in general, and arms control in particular, an area in which Reagan confounded some of his most ardent supporters and surprised some of his more virulent critics. Reagan was simultaneously a harsh critic of arms control and a firm supporter of arms control goals so lofty that the SALT supporters he once called naive were left aghast.

Reagan's hostility to the SALT process and treaties was well known. Throughout his 1976 and 1980 campaigns he made all the standard arguments against SALT I and II: the United States was lulled into complacency by détente, it was unduly restricted by the SALT treaties, and the Soviet Union raced ahead at an alarming rate. Reagan was convinced that the United States stood still during the 1960s and 1970s, which he described as a period of "unilateral disarmament." One of his favorite stories involved a cartoon portraying a Soviet general's reaction to the Reagan defense buildup: "I liked the arms race better when we were the only ones in it," the general informed a colleague (see *CPD* 1982, 1322). The notion that there was no arms "race" at all was a perennial theme. As a result, Reagan could claim in all sincerity that his administration "put into place the *first* realistic buildup of our strategic forces *in over twenty years*" (*CPD* 1982, 60; italics added). But U.S. restraint and Soviet expansion were not the only problems with the SALT treaties. Reagan also criticized them for failing to actually reduce nuclear weapons, demeaning them as so-called arms control. As Reagan explained shortly after entering office, "the SALT [II] treaty . . . permits a continued buildup on both sides of strategic nuclear weapons but, in the main thing [*sic*], authorizes an immediate increase in large numbers of Soviet warheads" (*CPD* 1981, 57). Even though his denunciations of SALT were often quite harsh, Reagan maintained that he was not opposed to arms control per se, but rather favored "genuine arms control."

## Knowing the Enemy

Like Perle and Weinberger, Reagan blamed the failure of SALT to achieve real arms control on the inability (or unwillingness) of U.S. leaders during the 1970s to grasp the nature of the Soviet threat. He argued that détente and SALT had been guided by the naive assumption that the Soviets were just like us. Reagan would have none of this. He believed "in talking with some knowledge of the other fellow's aims and what his tactics are and what you are going to do" (*CPD* 1981, 1198). The implication was that his predecessors did not have his knowledge.

What were the "other fellow's" aims? Reagan believed that Soviet leaders were committed to the supposed Marxist-Leninist injunction to spread communism to the entire world. In pursuing this objective, he thought the Soviets wanted military superiority over the West. Furthermore, the Soviet Union "does not share our view of what constitutes a stable nuclear balance"; they believed that a nuclear war could be fought and won, a doctrine Reagan claimed to have read about in Soviet military journals (*CPD* 1985, 606). On the basis of this information, we would probably surmise that Reagan would be led to agree with Perle and Weinberger on the futility of arms control. In fact, however, he was generally upbeat about the prospects for genuine arms control. Certainly, he became more enthusiastic later in his presidency, but even early on he never exhibited the same pessimism and despair as Perle and Weinberger. In the case of Burt and Shultz, cautious optimism was understandable because they did not perceive the fundamental conflict of nuclear goals and strategy. Reagan did, however, perceive such a conflict, and in many instances portrayed the Soviet threat in more alarming terms than either Perle or Weinberger, particularly with respect to the Soviet drive for global domination. Still, Reagan remained optimistic about the possibilities for arms control. Why?

## Political and Economic Asymmetries

Although Reagan shared Perle's and Weinberger's view of the conflict of objectives the United States and the Soviet Union, he presented a very different analysis of the political asymmetries. In reading Weinberger's and Perle's discussions of the relative political strengths of the United States and the Soviet Union, one is never quite sure which side would eventually prevail; indeed, it often seemed as though they believed the Soviet Union had the upper hand. For Reagan, there was no doubt about who would ultimately emerge victorious—the West. But Reagan's discussion of the political and economic asymmetries operated on a different level. Perle and Weinberger stressed differences in political institutions, the role of public opinion, and the degree of political centralization between the United States and the Soviet Union. In each of these areas the Soviets enjoyed the advantage. Reagan's analysis, however, dealt with political asymmetries in a broader context, emphasizing underlying economic strengths and weaknesses and differences in the political legitimacy of the Soviet regime versus liberal democracies. On these counts, Reagan found the Soviet Union wanting and the West fundamentally healthy. It is Reagan's view of the basic weaknesses of the Soviet economy and political system that provides the key to understanding how he could be hopeful about arms control despite the fundamental conflict in goals and objectives between the two superpowers.

On the U.S. side of the conflict, Reagan never expressed concerns about the impact of public opinion on arms control negotiations or vice versa. This is not to say that he possessed a well-developed view of the negotiating advantages afforded by democratic institutions, but clearly he was not preoccupied with the supposedly crippling effects of public opinion. While there were occasional complaints about congressional actions or popular protests that "undermined" the U.S. negotiating position, there were no Tocquevillian warnings about the inherent shortcomings of democratic institutions. At the same time Perle was lamenting the tendency for public opinion to push democratic governments into unwise accommodations, Reagan was bragging that "day by day democracy is proving itself a not-all-too-fragile flower" (*CPD* 1982, 743). As Weinberger warned about the problem of sustaining public support for defense spending in the wake of arms control treaties, Reagan brushed aside such concerns. He was asked with regard to the INF treaty whether "the American people, as a result, might perceive communism as less of threat than it should." Reagan responded confidently, "I have more faith in the American people than that . . . we're a pretty independent people . . . and I think the American people are aware of the shortcomings of communism . . . so, I don't fear that the American people would do that" (*CPD* 1987, 1405). Apparently, his secretary of defense did not have as much faith.

On the Soviet side of the equation, Reagan consistently portrayed the Soviet Union as a fundamentally weak society, occasionally speaking as if it were on the verge of collapse. In the eyes of some, this was inconsistent with his view of the Soviet Union as a menacingly expansionist and powerful adversary, but there is no necessary contradiction. Perhaps it was Reagan himself who provided the most succinct summary of his image of the Soviet Union: "It's spilling over with military hardware. The Soviets have not built a society; they've built an arsenal" (*CPD* 1981, 812). Despite (and partly because of) its successes in acquiring military power, "the Soviet empire is faltering because its rigid centralized control has destroyed incentives for innovation, efficiency, and individual achievement" (*CPD* 1982, 582). When asked what he learned about the Soviet Union during his first eighteen months in office, Reagan responded, "I don't think they've changed their habits. . . . I think, however, that they're in a more desperate situation than I had assumed they were economically" (*CPD* 1982, 402). These economic problems, he argued, would ultimately "undermine the foundation of Soviet society" (*CPD* 1982, 582).

Because of the Soviet emphasis on military production, "they've got their people on a starvation diet as far as consumer products are concerned" (*CPD* 1981, 957). When these economic shortcomings are combined with political oppression, the result was public disillusionment and a desire for change: "I just can't believe that a system such as this can continue to hold its people and other people in subjugation, and that someday, the people are not going to say, hey, there's a better way to do things" (*CPD* 1985, 279). The unpopularity of the regime that presided over this mess was such that "the Soviet Union would remain a one-party nation even if an opposition party was permitted, because everyone would vote for the opposition" (*CPD* 1982, 743). All of this confirmed Reagan's belief that "Communism is an aberration. It's not a normal way of living for human beings" (*CPD* 1981, 520).

Of more immediate consequence for U.S. foreign policy and arms control was Reagan's belief that the Soviet Union had just about reached the limit in terms of its ability to devote resources to the military. "Since they have already strained their economy to the limit," Reagan observed, "they are not really able to adequately provide for their people with consumer goods and food, because everything is devoted to their military buildup" (*CPD* 1982, 59). Because of this economic crunch, "I doubt if they could expand their military production anyplace beyond where it is right now" (*CPD* 1984, 754). "We know," Reagan claimed, "that they are pretty much at the maximum of output and have been for some time" (*CPD* 1984, 754). Thus, Reagan was convinced that, despite the Soviet leadership's ability to channel resources into the military sector, there were very real political and economic obstacles in the way of any further Soviet military buildup.

Perle and Weinberger never provided a clear explanation of why they favored arms control, "real" or otherwise, with an adversary whose objectives were so at odds with those of the United States. Perle and Weinberger gave only a vague outline of why the Soviets would accept the sort of reductions they proposed. This is why Reagan's view of Soviet economic weaknesses and the resulting limits on the growth of Soviet forces is so important. In Reagan's mind, these problems were so serious that the Soviets would eventually have to accept the types of agreements he wanted. And this process would be speeded up if these internal pressures were combined with the external pressure of a U.S. arms buildup. According to Reagan, "no American president must ever sit across the negotiating table from someone dedicated to the destruction of our way of life unless our military strength is such that the other side has a darned good reason to negotiate a reduction of weapons" (*CPD* 1982, 299). Reagan apparently thought that the impending U.S. buildup and the inability of the Soviets to increase their military output provided that "darned good reason."

More than anyone else in the administration, Reagan pointed to the U.S. buildup as an attempt to deny the Soviets their goal of superiority, thereby inducing them to abandon this goal. Since the Soviets had reached the limits of their military productivity, "they know they can't match us if there is such a[n arms] race, which means that the only alternative for them is to watch us catch up or to sit down at the table and work out something in which they don't have to run the risk of someone being superior to them" (*CPD* 1984, 754). "I think we can sit down," he argued, "and maybe have some realistic negotiations because of what we can threaten them with" (*CPD* 1981, 957). The Soviets could be expected to agree to reductions "because they have an awareness that we're determined not to allow them to have superiority over us" (*CPD* 1985, 169). In the final analysis, "they know our capacity industrially, and they can't match it" (*CPD* 1981, 957).

Reagan's image of a menacing but basically weak Soviet Union does not inevitably lead to support for arms control. In fact, it is consistent with a policy of opposition to arms control, based on the logic that an arms race will hasten the Soviet Union's slide into the dustbin of history. Alternatively, this image could also lead to support for arms control because it presents the possibility of gaining genuine Soviet concessions. How do we explain Reagan's selection of the second path? Of course, a purely political argument would suffice: Reagan pursued arms control because his domestic and international publics demanded it. Certainly this is part of the reason, but it is not the complete explanation. The public clamor for arms control did not demand that Reagan go as far as he eventually did.

## Common Interests

There was more to Reagan's position on arms control than his belief that the threat of an arms race would force the Soviets into genuine arms reductions. While this was a coherent and plausible scenario, it does not really account for Reagan's references to "common interests" and "mutually advantageous agreements." On many occasions, Reagan argued that the reductions he proposed "would be in their interest as well as ours" (*CPD* 1983, 76). "We should always remember," he told one audience, "that we do have common interests and foremost among them is the avoidance of war and reducing the level of arms" (*CPD* 1984, 41). Reagan explained that real arms control was possible because "we do, of course, have much common ground on which to negotiate" (*CPD* 1985, 366). Unlike Perle and Weinberger, Reagan was willing to talk about U.S.-Soviet relations in the context of common interests. But this raises a number of questions. For example, if genuine reductions were in the interests of both countries, why did the United States have to threaten the Soviets with a debilitating arms race to get them to negotiate seriously? And if the Soviets wanted world domination, military superiority, and the capability to fight and win a nuclear war, in what sense would real reductions be in the interests of both countries?

To understand how Reagan could perceive "much common ground" with an adversary whose goals he perceived to be so contradictory to those of the United States, it is necessary to distinguish between two uses of the concept of "interests." On the one hand, interests can be used in the context of the goals an actor is pursuing at any time, in which case, anything that advances these goals is in that actor's interests. Alternatively, interests can be defined in a broader, more "objective" sense that transcends an actor's current goals. When Reagan talked about genuine reductions being in the interest of the Soviet Union, he did not mean that they would advance the Soviet goals of military superiority and a nuclear war–winning capability. If this were the case, the reductions would certainly not have been in the interests of the United States. Whether he was aware of it or not, Reagan frequently used interests in the second sense—"real" national interests divorced from a regime's operational goals. Reagan's analysis of U.S.-Soviet relations appeared to be influenced not only by his perception of Soviet foreign policy and nuclear objectives, but also by a more basic belief in the existence of harmony of interests between peoples and nations, even though these interests were not always embodied in the policies of particular governments. This would be consistent with Reagan's attachment to a free-market economic philosophy, which also flows from classical liberal assumptions about an underlying harmony of interests.

While establishing the presence of such a belief would require a full operational code study, there are two aspects of Reagan's analysis of U.S.-Soviet relations that indicate a belief in a harmony of interests. The first was discussed in my examination of Reagan's perception of how the Soviets viewed the United States. Scattered among statements about the Soviets being aware of the peaceful intentions of the United States, Reagan frequently referred to the "suspicions" and "mistrust" that propelled the arms race. The emphasis on "suspicions" suggested that the conflict was largely illusory, based on misunderstandings and misperceptions that could be cleared up through summitry and personal meetings. "I believe," Reagan explained, "that people's problems can be solved when people talk to each other" (*CPD* 1982, 585). Whenever he was asked about what he hoped to accomplish in his meetings with Gorbachev, Reagan spoke of "persuading" the Soviet leader of the peaceful intentions of the United States or convincing him that SDI was a purely defensive weapon, assuming that if he could educate Gorbachev on these points, their disagreements would cease. Reagan argued that "if we reduce these suspicions between the two countries, the reduction of arms will easily follow" (*CPD* 1985, 1318). Arms control, then, became an exercise in dispelling unwarranted suspicions, not a process of reconciling conflicting superpower objectives.

Reagan's belief in a harmony of interests is even more apparent in his insistence on differentiating between the Soviet people and the Soviet government: "it is important to begin by distinguishing the people inside the Soviet Union from the government that rules them. Certainly we have no quarrel with the people, far from it" (*CPD* 1986, 837). This distinction, which is a classic element of liberal thought about international relations (see Waltz 1959, 98), is significant in light of Reagan's belief that "the people" of the United States and the Soviet Union share the same essential values, goals, and desires, even though they are not always reflected by their governments (of course, it was exclusively the Soviet government that was assumed not to reflect the desires of its people). "I think that the people of all countries have something in common," Reagan observed; as a result, "I doubt that the people have ever started a war" (*CPD* 1981, 708). At an even more basic level, "I believe with all my heart that if a generation of young people throughout the world could get to know each other, they would never make war upon each other" (*CPD* 1986, 839). An Enlightenment liberal could not have said it any better. The difficulty was getting governments to follow the will of the people. Early in his administration, the president was asked about the contents of a series of letters he sent to Brezhnev. Reagan said that "because the people of all countries have a great many things in common . . . I have suggested [to Brezhnev] that maybe we might sit down sometime and see what the people really want" (*CPD* 1981, 709). Presumably, if governments reflected what "the people really wanted," the superpower conflict could be eased, perhaps even eliminated; after all, have "the people" ever started a cold war?

It is always difficult to say how this type of general belief about the nature of political conflict will influence policy preferences on any specific issue. In Reagan's case, it seems as though his belief in the existence of a basic harmony of interests and values, his faith in the value of reason and persuasion, and his conviction that knowledge and correct information could overcome conflicts and "suspicions" all served to counteract the very pessimistic implications of his view of the Soviet threat. There is no evidence that Perle and Weinberger, whose views about the Soviet threat Reagan largely shared, had any similar beliefs to offset the gloomy implications of their images of the Soviet Union.

## Summary and Conclusions

I began this chapter by explaining why we would expect images to play an important role in shaping a decision maker's assessment of the arms control process. The key point was that images contain beliefs about the opponent's goals and objectives, which are crucial for defining the degree of common interests. The perception of common interests was assumed to be a prerequisite for a favorable evaluation of arms control efforts. And, indeed, in each case we found that the decision maker's image of the Soviet Union was important for understanding individual approaches to arms control. But the complete story is more complicated. In no case did we find that the decision maker's image was sufficient for understanding his evaluation of the utility of arms control. For each individual there were other factors that either reinforced or mitigated the tendencies introduced by their beliefs about the Soviet Union.

In the case of Perle and Weinberger, their image of the Soviet Union's nuclear goals and doctrine instilled a skepticism about the prospects for reaching agreements that were in the interests of the United States. It was almost as if any agreement that would be acceptable to the Soviets would be automatically suspect. The perception of conflicting goals, however, does not necessarily rule out the possibility of advantageous agreements; it does require that the adversary either abandon its objectives or be willing to sign treaties that contradict them. Perle and Weinberger failed to provide a well-developed and consistent account of why the Soviets would do either. The pessimistic tendencies introduced by this image of the Soviet Union were exacerbated by a view of the negotiating process in which the Soviets enjoyed all the advantages. These advantages stemmed not only from characteristics of the Soviet system (e.g., a high degree of political centralization), but also from the weaknesses of democratic societies. Thus, it was a combination of their image of the Soviet Union and their assessment of the political capacities of the United States that led Perle and Weinberger to their arms control agnosticism.

Burt and Shultz presented problems in that the explanatory significance of their images is less obvious than for Perle and Weinberger. This is because their beliefs about the Soviet Union's nuclear goals and objectives were ambiguous. As a result, it was hard to say to what extent they perceived common ground between the two countries. In Burt's case we were restricted to a negative conclusion—he did not perceive a complete incompatibility a la Perle and Weinberger—but we were unable to say anything else with confidence. Shultz was clear in identifying at least one common interest: both the

United States and the Soviet Union shared a desire to avoid war and reduce the risks of war. This perception of a basic common interest was reinforced by a more general faith in the efficacy and value of negotiations as a way to manage and ameliorate disputes. The result was support for arms control and a belief that something worthwhile could be achieved, even if Shultz was not very clear about exactly what could be accomplished.

Without a doubt, Reagan presented the most interesting case. Perhaps this is because his beliefs about the Soviet Union and international politics in general appeared to pull him in opposite directions. On the one hand, his perception of the Soviet Union as an unlimitedly expansionist power determined to achieve military superiority over the United States was not exactly conducive to an optimistic evaluation of the arms control process. On the other hand, his view of the Soviet Union as a weak society, economically and politically, created a perception of great opportunities for the United States. When all this was placed within the framework of a more fundamental belief in the existence of common desires, interests, and values that transcended immediate conflicts between governments, the result was a basis for hope and optimism despite recurring bouts of pessimism.

# CHAPTER 9

# The INF Debate

As the Reagan administration entered office promising to sweep away the old regime, it inherited several unresolved issues from the Carter years. The most pressing of these issues was the forthcoming deployment of U.S. intermediate range nuclear missiles in Europe. The planned deployment originated in European concerns over intermediate range missiles deployed by the Soviet Union in the late 1970s. Of particular concern were the Soviet SS-20s, mobile missiles carrying three warheads with a range of approximately 4,500 km. With this range, the SS-20s could strike most NATO targets, even when launched from Soviet territory. The problem for the NATO allies was that they lacked weapons with similar capabilities, leading many to fear that a serious gap had opened in the potential ladder of escalation, thereby endangering NATO's flexible response strategy.

In response to these developments, in December, 1979, NATO unanimously decided to accept a new contingent of U.S. missiles. The gap in NATO's capabilities was to be filled with a combination of 464 Tomahawk ground-launched cruise missiles (GLCMs) and 108 Pershing II ballistic missiles, both highly accurate, single-warhead weapons. These new systems would give NATO the ability to strike targets in the western part of the Soviet Union, with the Pershing IIs being able to accomplish this in about five to six minutes. In a strict military sense, the new missiles were intended to offset the Soviet SS-20s, filling in the gaps in NATO's flexible response capabilities, but the value of the missiles went beyond these narrow military considerations. More generally, the new deployments would provide a visible reaffirmation of the U.S. commitment to the defense of Europe.

Recognizing the widespread unease about the prospect of new U.S. nuclear weapons on the continent, NATO called on the United States to negotiate with the Soviet Union, the goal being a reduction in the number of missiles to be deployed beginning in 1983. The decision to proceed with plans for the new missiles while simultaneously pursuing negotiations was dubbed the "dual track." The Europeans hoped that the talks would result in equal ceilings for U.S. and Soviet forces; the expectation was not that the need for the missiles would be eliminated entirely, since the broader political imperatives for deployment would remain. When the negotiations began in October,

1980, the U.S. position embodied these expectations. The Carter administration proposed equal levels of forces, counting the Pershing IIs and GLCMs against Soviet SS-20s, SS-4s, and SS-5s (the latter two being older missiles with ranges between 2,000 and 4,000 km.). Not much was accomplished before Reagan's landslide victory over Carter in November, 1980. The talks were put on hold awaiting the new administration, and no one knew exactly what to expect.

### The First Round, 1981–83: To Talk or Not to Talk

A number of Reagan's foreign policy advisers had doubts about the wisdom of the initial dual-track decision, as did many others on both sides of the Atlantic. Skeptics pointed out that the targets for the new missiles could easily be covered by U.S. strategic forces, making the Pershing IIs and GLCMs militarily redundant. This view was shared by such diverse figures as Richard Perle, Paul Nitze, and Paul Warnke. The deployment was seen as an excessively expensive and potentially divisive salve intended to calm the nerves of jittery European leaders. Despite these reservations, most thought that the United States could not renege on its commitment, and Reagan's declaration of support for the dual track following his meetings with Margaret Thatcher in February, 1981, settled the issue. With the deployment issue behind them, Reagan's advisers turned to the next key questions: first, when would talks with the Soviet Union be resumed; and second, what would be the U.S. negotiating position?

There is relatively little information about the debate surrounding the first issue. What is available indicates that Perle and Weinberger were in no hurry to resume INF negotiations; in fact, they made several attempts to delay the resumption of the talks. In what became a constant refrain on arms control issues, Perle warned of the dangers of being pressured, rushed, and stampeded into any agreement. He proposed an administration study assessing the Soviet threat to NATO in preparation for the negotiations. Weinberger carried these suggestions into administration meetings. In addition to this stalling tactic, Weinberger and Perle cited the crackdown on Solidarity in Poland as a reason to delay the resumption of negotiations. Pressure to begin negotiations came from European allies, Congress, and the State Department, where the key figures were Secretary of State Haig and Undersecretary of State Lawrence Eagleburger. As was typical, Reagan left the debate to subordinates, so he was not intimately involved in the discussions at this stage. Furthermore, the March, 1981, assassination attempt left the president indisposed during much of the debate. Haig eventually appealed to Reagan, who authorized Haig to commit the United States to the resumption of talks by the end of

1981. The announcement was made in May at a meeting of NATO representatives. The really rough issues still lay ahead.

## The Zero Options

By the time the debate over the U.S. position was in full swing, Burt had been confirmed and taken his position in the State Department. The battle over INF centered on the competing approaches offered by Burt and Perle. After losing his bid to postpone the talks, Perle was faced with the problem of devising a negotiating position. He responded with the so-called zero option. The basic logic of the zero option was that the United States would forego the deployment of its Pershing IIs and GLCMs in exchange for the elimination of Soviet INF. The debate was complicated by the existence of several zero option proposals within the Reagan administration (Risse-Kappen 1988, 83). Actually, there were more than two zero options.

Perle's zero option contained the central trade-off that characterized all the zero options—an exchange of Pershing IIs and GLCMs for Soviet SS-20s, SS-4s, and SS-5s. Perle's formulation, however, went well beyond the basics of the zero option. Perle proposed that the Soviets eliminate not only their SS-20s, SS-4s, and SS-5s, but also their SS-12s and SS-22s (Barrett 1983, 313). The SS-12s and SS-22s were short-range intermediate forces (SRINF) with ranges between 500 and 1,000 km. That is, Perle went further than the zero option in long-range intermediate forces (LRINF). Perle's logic for including SRINF was flawless: although these systems had shorter ranges, if they were deployed in forward bases in Eastern Europe, it would be possible to cover most of the targets originally taken by Soviet LRINF. Perle did not stop there. Not only would all LRINF and SRINF in Europe have to be eliminated, but those stationed in Asia would also have to go. Again his logic was impeccable: since these weapons were mobile, it would do no good to eliminate them geographically, since they could be redeployed from Asia to Europe in the event of a crisis. Perle's version of the zero option was a combination of a "double zero option" (LRINF and SRINF) and a "global zero option" (abolition worldwide). Thus, the Soviets were being asked to give up five complete weapons systems in which they had a substantial investment in return for 572 as yet undeployed U.S. missiles. As was the case with Perle's attempts to delay the talks, Weinberger immediately and enthusiastically embraced Perle's recommendations, as he would continue to do throughout the next six years.

Others in the administration, particularly Haig, Burt, and Eagleburger, were alarmed. Although the zero option put forward by Perle and supported by Weinberger was simple, dramatic, and perfectly consistent, it was also feared to be completely unrealistic. Haig argued that such a position was a complete nonstarter: "the fatal flaw with the zero option as a basis for negotiation is that it was nonnegotiable" (Haig 1984, 229), with "zero" describing its chances for success as well. This was an opinion shared by many outside the administration as well. Especially troublesome was the suspicion that its nonnegotiability was the very feature which made the zero option attractive to Perle and Weinberger. Walter Slocombe speculated that "there's a school of thought in this administration that hopes the proposal is so brilliant that the Soviets will never accept it and that rather than advancing negotiations, it will stop them" (Talbott 1985, 80). Given the uncertainties about whether the Europeans would actually accept the new missiles, no reasonably astute political observer could have anticipated Soviet acceptance of the zero option prior to the deployments. Presumably, that was the whole point.

Burt and Haig countered with a different version of the zero option that they viewed as more negotiable, more palatable to European allies, and more in line with the December, 1979, decision. Their so-called zero plus closely resembled the position the Carter administration adopted in the preliminary round of talks. While keeping the eventual goal of complete elimination of LRINF, the zero plus called for reductions in current Soviet deployments and future U.S. deployments to equal levels, with the precise figures being left to the negotiations. In addition to moving away from the strict goal of zero, the State Department's plan did not require the elimination of SRINF. Burt and Haig argued that such a demand was unrealistic and unintended by the December, 1979, decision. The question of global limits remained. With an absolute zero requirement, global elimination seemed logical. But if the two countries agreed to, say, an equal ceiling of 600 warheads, would the Soviets be required to divide their allotment between Asia and Europe? State's position on global limits at this point in the debate is unclear.

Realizing that Burt and Haig were favoring an alternative to his zero option, Perle devised a fallback position in the event that zero plus became the basis of the administration's strategy. In this case he argued that any agreement had to include a ban on refires, that is, stored missiles that could be used to reload the launchers after a first-round attack. Again, the logic of Perle's position was undeniable: if the Soviets could keep an inventory of missiles, they could easily circumvent the treaty. The practical problem was that an inventory ban would require incredibly intrusive on-site inspection of production and storage facilities. One can only imagine what type of verification procedures would have been required to satisfy Perle of Soviet compliance (see Talbott 1985, 288–90). Thus, in the event that his zero option was not adopted by the administration, Perle wanted to amend the zero plus in such a way as to make it less negotiable.

In the eyes of most, the zero plus was clearly the more negotiable, flexible, and realistic of the two options. Still, it is important not to exaggerate the differences in this respect. In the short term, neither proposal was likely to produce any agreement. Both demanded asymmetrical reductions and neither addressed Soviet concerns about other forward-based U.S. systems (e.g., bombers) or British and French nuclear forces. But the main obstacle to an agreement was the political situation in Europe. As long as there was any possibility that the Germans, Dutch, and Italians might refuse to accept the missiles, the Soviets were unlikely to sign any treaty that either legitimized the presence of new U.S. missiles or restricted Soviet deployments. The Soviets had little to gain by accepting a treaty before NATO had displayed the will to go forward with the deployments. As a result, the Soviet negotiating position from 1981 through 1983 was, if anything, even more extreme and inflexible than the original U.S. position.

Perhaps more important for our purposes than the overall negotiability of the two options were their structure and content. With regard to U.S. concessions, Perle and Weinberger advanced a minimalist position; that is, they wanted to restrict as much as possible the number of U.S. weapons systems that would be limited. Bombers, air-launched cruise missiles, and other forward-based systems, for example, were not included, even though these were all weapons systems the United States could use to circumvent an INF agreement. In this respect, Haig and Burt agreed with Perle and Weinberger. When it came to the Soviet side, however, Perle and Weinberger adopted a maximalist position in the sense that they wanted to include the widest possible range of systems. This is where Burt and Haig broke ranks. While this type of minimalist/maximalist position is probably typical, and even wise, in early phases of negotiations, Perle and Weinberger adopted a position that was extreme even in the context of the Reagan administration. While some, such as Paul Nitze, supported the zero option as an *initial* negotiating position, Weinberger and Perle consistently opposed any attempts to move away from their goal of absolute, global zero. In a sense the zero option was not a negotiating position at all, but rather an ultimatum.

The desire for asymmetrical reductions, shared by all in the administration, was to be expected, given the common perception of Soviet advantages in this class of weapons. But the demand for asymmetrical reductions is not the only interesting feature of the Perle-Weinberger zero option. One is also struck by how carefully the zero option was crafted to account for every possible means by which the Soviets could violate the spirit and letter of any potential agreement. The insistence on "global zero" was designed to prevent the redeployment of Soviet missiles to Europe, thereby circumventing regional sublimits. The inclusion of SRINF was intended to prevent an increase in these systems that could accomplish the same tasks as the longer range systems. The proposed ban on refires and missile inventories would preclude a quick "breakout" of an INF treaty. Thus, Perle's formulation of the zero option appears to have been driven not only by his perception of dramatic Soviet advantages, but even more so by his belief that the Soviets could (and probably would) attempt to violate an agreement. Indeed, Perle's eventual criticism of the INF treaty signed in 1987, which was his original "global double zero," was not that it required insufficient Soviet concessions, but rather that it provided too many loopholes ("open invitations") for Soviet cheating. Later, Perle argued that the Soviets had already circumvented the INF treaty by replacing all the eliminated INF missiles with new SS-25s, strategic range missiles that can be aimed at closer European targets.

All of the infighting over the U.S. position on INF initially took place without the involvement of the president. Throughout the early part of his first term, Reagan was preoccupied by his domestic agenda, particularly his push for tax and budget cuts. The administration, however, had committed itself to begin talks by the end of 1981. The internal debate showed no signs of resolving itself; as a result, the outstanding issues had to be dealt with at the top. At a November 12 meeting of the National Security Council (NSC) on the impending talks, the battle lines were clearly drawn: Weinberger made the case for Perle's zero option while Haig pushed for the zero plus (Burt and Perle were not present at NSC meetings) (Talbott 1985, 72–74). Perle had cleverly managed to gain the support of the Joint Chiefs, but their enthusiasm for the plan was, to say the least, tepid. The absolute zero option had several things going for it in the struggle for Reagan's support. First, it was simple and easy to understand; there were no complicated trade-offs or sublimits to worry about or explain. Second, it contained an apparently reasonable demand for equality in weapons, if not equality in reductions. Third, it was a bold political initiative that could help capture the moral high ground. By all accounts, these are the primary reasons Reagan was drawn to Perle's proposal. But, as would become routine in the Reagan administration, the president compromised between the two options by accepting the goal of zero without including Soviet SRINF. In a November 18 speech, the President announced the administration's global zero-option proposal (*CPD* 1981, 1062–67).

## A Walk in the Woods

The INF negotiations continued in Geneva throughout the first half of 1982 without much progress. The U.S. negotiator, Paul Nitze, was growing impatient with the lack of movement; he did not accept the assignment in order to preside over some dead-end, public relations spectacle. Nitze originally lent his support to the zero option, but, unlike Perle and Weinberger, he did not see zero LRINF as the immutable goal of the talks. Despite orders from Washington to stick to the zero option, Nitze embarked upon a series of talks with his Soviet counterpart, Yuli Kvitsinsky, to see if some headway could be made in the face of the stubbornness demonstrated by both Moscow and Washington. In July, 1982, Nitze approached Kvitsinsky with a rough proposal. He suggested that each side be limited to 75 LRINF launchers in Europe. In the Soviet case, this translated into 75 SS-20 missiles, or a total of 225 warheads (i.e., three per missile). In Asia, the Soviets would be allowed 90 SS-20s, roughly the level of current deployments. Older SS-4s and SS-5s were to be completely eliminated, which the Soviets were probably planning to do in any case because of their age. In exchange for these reductions, the United States would abandon the Pershing IIs altogether, deploying only 75 GLCM launchers, each of which carried 4 single-warhead cruise missiles, resulting in a total deployment of 300 warheads. To many, the "walk in the woods" proposal was a good deal; the United States would end up with 75 more LRINF warheads *in Europe* than the Soviets, and the Soviets would not have to worry about the Pershing IIs. With the negotiators in Geneva having accomplished their job, the action now shifted back to Washington and Moscow. (For accounts of this episode, see Jensen 1988, 199–200; NAS 1985, 215–16; Newhouse 1989, 355–56; and Talbott 1985, 92–115).

Unfortunately for Nitze and his scheme, "the 'walk in the woods' formula was worked out at a time when the unilateralist arms control opponents like Richard Perle dominated in Washington" (Risse-Kappen 1988, 100). Part of the reason for the dominance of this faction was the political vacuum at the State Department in the summer of 1982. Secretary Haig had resigned in June for a variety of reasons. During his first year in office, Shultz did not devote much of his energy to East-West issues, preferring to focus his attention in other areas, particularly the Middle East. And since even Shultz recognized his own lack of knowledge concerning nuclear issues, he especially avoided arms control matters (see Gwertzman 1983, 28–30). Another ear potentially sympathetic to the Nitze formula in the administration was Burt. Unfortunately, Burt became embroiled in a battle on Capitol Hill, where Senate conservatives were trying to block his recent nomination to become Assistant Secretary of State for European Affairs. Still, Nitze did discuss his plan with Burt and Shultz. Shultz was apparently neither enthusiastic about the plan nor strongly opposed to it (it is difficult to tell why). Burt, who was initially skeptical and cautious, eventually decided to oppose Nitze.

Nitze knew better than to expect support from the Pentagon civilians. After all, his plan backtracked from the goal of zero INF, it rejected the quest for global parity, and it proposed the abandonment of the Pershing IIs. The expected opposition quickly emerged. When Perle first got wind of what was afoot in Geneva, he immediately turned his attention to the plan's drawbacks and weaknesses. As he became aware of the details, Perle's opposition did not diminish. His misgivings were eventually summarized in a memo to Weinberger that constituted an assault on the plan from virtually every angle. The tone of the memo was described as "violent" (Newhouse 1989, 357). Many of the points raised were to be expected—the plan retreated from the goal of zero and it legitimized global inequality in the Soviets' favor through its Asian sublimit. Other objections were more surprising, and perhaps even disingenuous. For example, Perle expressed concern that the abandonment of the Pershing IIs might create political problems for West German Chancellor Helmut Kohl, who had supported deployment in the face of substantial domestic opposition (Perle displayed no similar sensitivity for Helmut Schmidt's plight the previous year when Burt and Haig used the same arguments in favor of zero plus). Furthermore, when Kohl learned of the "walk in the woods" plan later in 1982, he indicated that he would have supported it; in fact, he tried to revive the proposal as the deployment date approached (Risse-Kappen 1988, 81).

Weinberger's reaction to the Nitze proposal is interesting and potentially important for understanding how his beliefs influenced his policy preferences. He was initially informed about the plan at an NSC meeting in early August— before Perle was aware of the details. Weinberger apparently did not voice any opposition at this meeting (nor did he express support). As Newhouse observes, "Weinberger did not take a position at first" (1989, 356). He did, however, tell the others present at the meeting that he would have to consult with advisers at Defense, which obviously meant Richard Perle. Once Perle's objections became known to Weinberger, he quickly adopted Perle's position in its entirety. And at the September 13 NSC meeting, scheduled to make a final decision on the plan, Weinberger "delivered a withering attack on the Nitze initiative, following closely the script Perle had prepared for him" (Talbott 1985, 144). In the course of two or three weeks, Weinberger had gone from no clear position to launching a devastating critique of the "walk in the woods" formula. The only change in this period was Weinberger's new awareness of Perle's views.

Reagan was apprehensive about the Nitze deal at first, but he did not reject it outright; it appears that he could have been persuaded to go along. Reagan's doubts centered on Nitze's proposal to abandon the Pershing IIs. All accounts of the president's thinking about nuclear issues refer to his preoccupation with the distinction between "fast fliers" and "slow fliers." In Reagan's mind, the former were undesirable, at least in Soviet hands, because they were destabilizing (his own modernization program, however, included several "fast fliers"). Reagan recognized that the Nitze plan would have required the United States to give up all of its fast fliers, leaving NATO to rely solely on GLCMs, which were slow fliers. The Soviets, on the other hand, would retain a large number of SS-20 ballistic missiles, which were fast fliers. Reagan wondered whether this trade-off was a good deal. He wanted to know what the Joint Chiefs thought about the swap (see Jensen 1988, 200; New-house 1989, 356; Talbott 1985, 132, 136).

The military had never been fully convinced of the military need for the Pershing IIs; they were seen primarily as political, not military, necessities. In response to the White House's queries, the Joint Chiefs produced an equivocal paper. While hesitant to give up a weapon system, they concluded that the Pershing IIs were not essential and could be traded away, if the Soviets offered appropriate concessions. Though this was not exactly a ringing endorsement of the Nitze proposal, it certainly was not the outright rejection being urged by their civilian superiors. The paper, which was not to the liking of Perle and Weinberger, was "intercepted" before it reached the president's desk.

Reagan entered the crucial September 13 meeting skeptical of Nitze's plan, but not firmly opposed. The opposition, however, enjoyed the upper hand at the meeting. "The State Department didn't work up a coherent position because it was leaderless; Shultz had just arrived and understood nothing of what had occurred" (Newhouse 1989, 356). General Vessey, chairman of the Joint Chiefs, remained on the sidelines, content to allow Nitze to make the case against the military need for the Pershing IIs. Weinberger argued forcefully against the plan. Still concerned about the inequalities in slow and fast fliers, the president decided to stay with the original zero option. It is important to note, however, that Reagan was willing to at least entertain the prospect of an agreement that departed from a goal of zero; he did not react reflexively against the idea of a compromise.

## Away from Zero

When reading accounts of foreign policy decision making in the Reagan administration, one is struck by the fact that policy issues were seldom viewed as settled. Losses and victories were seen as temporary. Thus, despite Reagan's decision to stick with the zero option, advocates of greater flexibility did not give up. There were reasons for optimism. First, as I have noted, Reagan did not seem to be set in his support of the zero option. Second, political pressures at home and in Europe were pushing in the direction of the zero plus. Third, and perhaps most important, people such as Burt, Nitze, and Eagleburger saw the new Secretary of State as a potential ally who might be able to take up the battle against Perle and Weinberger without an abrasive personality like Haig's getting in the way.

Burt's opposition to the "walk in the woods" proposal did not signal any newfound enthusiasm for the zero option. Shortly after that issue had been laid to rest, Burt began to consider alternatives. In the fall of 1982, he devised a proposal calling for each side to limit its intermediate range forces to 300 warheads. The difference between this plan and the failed Nitze effort was that

Burt wanted the Pershing IIs included in the 300-warhead limit, and he wanted it to apply globally. (Talbott 1985, 155–57). Burt spent the next several months trying to gain the support of others, including Shultz. Meanwhile, the Geneva negotiations had degenerated into an exchange of hollow rhetoric and endless charges of bad faith. As 1982 turned to 1983, the deadline for the deployment was fast approaching. Demonstrations in Europe and the United States grew. The Soviets offered a barrage of new proposals (containing very few meaningful concessions), and the Europeans, particularly the West Germans, began to clamor for a change in the U.S. position (in the late fall of 1982 the Europeans became aware of the scuttled "walk in the woods" deal; they were not pleased that it had been rejected without consultation). Reagan himself was becoming concerned about the continued lack of progress; according to Talbott, "he was worried about 'getting too dug in on zero'" (1985, 171). Shultz, who was becoming a firm supporter of a more flexible U.S. position, suggested that the administration move toward Burt's 300-warhead plan. Perle and Weinberger continued to oppose any give on the zero option. Reagan, however, decided that the time had come to move away from zero. Although administration spokesmen denied that Reagan's move was determined by political pressures and protests, it is difficult to identify a more persuasive explanation.

In a February, 1983, speech, the president declared that "we're negotiating in good faith in Geneva, and ours is not a take it or leave it proposal. . . . Ambassador Nitze has been instructed to explore . . . every proposed solution" (CPD 1983, 267–68). To Perle and Weinberger, of course, the zero option was exactly that, a take it or leave it proposition. Furthermore, Reagan insisted that "the only basis on which a fair agreement can be reached is that of equality of rights and limits between the United States and the Soviet Union" (267). This was beginning to sound more and more like the zero plus. Although even these concessions were too much for Perle and Weinberger, others in the administration and Europe wanted Reagan to go even further and offer an "interim solution," a concrete proposal. In discussions leading up to the presentation of a new U.S. position, Perle and Weinberger refused to budge. Burt argued that in order to guarantee European acceptance of the missiles, which he thought was essential if any agreement was to be reached, a more flexible U.S. position had to be forthcoming (this was probably Shultz's thinking as well). It was at this juncture that the extent of Perle's opposition to an INF agreement became obvious: Perle informed Weinberger that he would prefer to forget the deployments entirely rather than reach an agreement with the Soviets on a zero-plus framework (Talbott 1985, 179). The momentum, however, was against Perle and Weinberger.

At a March 11 NSC meeting, the key issues were the level of specificity and the contents of the soon to be proposed interim solution. Perle and Weinberger wanted the proposal to be kept as vague as possible by not giving any specific numbers for acceptable limits. They also wanted any interim agreement to be predicated on Soviet acceptance of zero as the ultimate goal. Burt and Shultz wanted limits to be specified (300 warheads), and they opposed a requirement that the Soviets accept zero as the eventual limit. As he did in the past, Reagan decided to combine elements of both proposals with no apparent strategic rationale. The United States, he said, would propose equal levels above zero without specifying the numbers (the Perle/Weinberger position) but would not tie an agreement to the eventual elimination of LRINF (the Burt/Shultz position). The proposal was announced in a March 30 speech.

> [W]e are prepared to negotiate an interim agreement in which the United States would substantially reduce its planned deployment of Pershing IIs and ground-launched cruise missiles, provided the Soviet Union reduce the number of its missiles to an equal level on a global scale. (*CPD* 1983, 474)

Even though Reagan emphasized that "the United States views this proposal as a serious initial step toward the total elimination" of these forces, he did not lay this out as a requirement (*CPD* 1983, 474).

The Soviet response was not very favorable. European leaders, especially Kohl, began to push for the resurrection of the "walk in the woods" proposal. Nitze reluctantly raised the issue again in Washington, but to no avail. Although Burt was still looking for a solution, he still objected to the Nitze plan because it eliminated the Pershing IIs. Reagan was worried about the same issue, but for different reasons. Others objected strongly to the absence of global equality. Could a plan be devised to overcome these shortcomings? Burt put forward another proposal. His new version of the zero plus involved proportional reductions in Pershing IIs and GLCMs (i.e., a 50 percent overall reduction would lead to a 50 percent cut in Pershing II deployments). This would be a concession to the Soviets, as they particularly feared the Pershing IIs. More important, it satisfied Burt's concerns about the necessity for deployments in 1983 as well as Reagan's desire to have fast fliers, just like the Soviets.

But the key concession in Burt's latest version of zero plus was his redefinition of the idea of "global equality." This criterion had always entailed the right of the United States to offset Soviet *global* deployments with U.S. missiles *in Europe*. According to Burt's new proposal, however, the United States would agree to deploy only a portion of its INF allotment in Europe, stationing the remainder on its own territory. This was a crucial concession. Remember that global equality was intended to account for possible Soviet redeployments from Asia to Europe. Under Burt's plan, the United States could, of course, transfer its missiles to Europe in response to any Soviet redeployments. In actuality, it would be much easier, logistically and politically, for the Soviets to move their Asian missiles to Eastern Europe than for the United States to move its home-based missiles to Western Europe. Thus, while preserving the facade of global equality, Burt's proposal would have essentially abandoned it. Shultz argued for adoption of the new scheme, and Weinberger opposed it. Reagan sided with Shultz (Talbott 1985, 191–93). The president announced that:

> . . . if the Soviet Union agrees to reductions and limits on a global basis, the United States for its part will not offset the entire Soviet global missile deployment through its deployments in Europe. We would, of course, retain the right to deploy missiles elsewhere. (*CPD* 1983, 1351)

Despite this movement in the U.S. position, the talks appeared to be at a standstill. Deployment of the Pershing IIs was only a few months away, and the Soviets were threatening to leave the talks once U.S. missiles arrived in Europe. Finally, the Soviet attack on a Korean passenger airplane (KAL 007) in late August did not help matters. The administration's response to KAL 007, or lack thereof, is an important instance of a nondecision. Surprisingly, given Reagan's supposed commitment to "linkage" in arms control, he did not even consider breaking off the Geneva talks. Nor is there any evidence that Perle and Weinberger urged such a move: perhaps they wanted the Soviets to bear the onus of ending the talks once the U.S. deployments began in December. In any case, the Pershing IIs arrived on schedule, and, as promised, the Soviets left Geneva without any commitment to return.

### The Second Round, 1985–87: The Shifting Debate

The Soviets did not return to the negotiating table until January, 1985. The new round of talks took place in a context that differed significantly from the first round in several respects. First, Reagan's landslide reelection in November, 1984, destroyed any hopes the Soviets might have entertained for a more accommodating administration. Second, although there was leadership continuity in Washington, an important change occurred in Moscow with Gorbachev's rise to power. Third, an entirely new issue had been introduced beginning with Reagan's announcement of his strategic defense initiative (SDI) in March, 1983, a program Reagan showed no sign of backing away from. These last two developments were to have a profound effect on the future of arms control negotiations and internal policy debates in Washington.

The U.S. position on INF from 1985 to 1987 fluctuated between various formulations of the zero plus put forward in August and September of 1983— equal global ceilings with part of the U.S. allotment stationed in the United States. Debates within the administration about the specifics of the U.S INF proposal ceased. But this did not signal a new consensus on the desirability of reaching an agreement. In fact, it might be slightly misleading to say the debate ceased; a better description might be "shifted." Disagreements over INF were masked by, or transposed onto, conflicts on other issues.

The shift in the nature of the INF debate occurred largely because of the introduction of the issue of SDI. When the new round of talks began in January, 1985, they were so-called umbrella talks in that they were designed to integrate three separate but related issues—INF, strategic systems, and defense/space weapons. The umbrella formula was partly a face-saving device for the Soviets: they could claim that they were technically not returning to the same talks they walked out of in 1983. Shultz had been a leading figure in the push for merging the three sets of negotiations in order to get them going again (Garthoff 1985, 1029; Risse-Kappen 1988, 129). The Soviet position was that progress on INF and strategic issues was dependent on "progress" on defense issues, with "progress" being defined as curtailment of SDI. As long as the Soviets insisted on this linkage, an INF agreement could be indirectly blocked by preventing concessions on SDI. The debate over SDI concessions will be discussed at greater length in the chapters on strategic issues. At this point it is sufficient to point out that Perle and Weinberger were consistent opponents of any flexibility on SDI, while Shultz was one of the primary advocates of accepting restrictions on SDI as part of a "grand compromise" on INF and START. By opposing any give on the issue of strategic defenses, Perle and Weinberger were de facto opposing an INF (and START) treaty.

The remainder of the concessions on INF between 1985 and 1987 were made by the Soviet Union, not the United States. The contents of the U.S. INF proposals did not change. The Soviets dropped their demand for compensation for British and French nuclear forces; they accepted the call for global equality; and they even agreed to the U.S. proposal for complete elimination. When the Soviets eventually "delinked" INF from SDI, the final hurdle had been removed, and the attempt to prevent an INF agreement by holding firm on strategic defense failed. The road to an INF treaty was clear. Gorbachev even went so far as to agree to the elimination of SRINF, just as Perle originally proposed in 1981. By the time the treaty was signed in December, 1987, both Perle and Weinberger had left the administration. Neither ever had to testify in favor of the INF treaty.

### Images and the INF Debate

There are two general sets of issues that are raised by this discussion of the INF debate, each of which will be elaborated at greater length as I examine other issues. The first concerns the relationship between the *content* of a decision maker's image of the Soviet Union and the *content* of his policy positions. That is, do we find that individuals supported policies that were consistent with their beliefs or opposed policies that were inconsistent? The second set of issues deals with the role of images in the sense of whether they are important in a decision maker's *formulation* of policy options or merely his *choice* among options. While it would be rash to draw any firm conclusions on the basis of one set of policy debates, we can attempt a useful "first cut" as to whether our expectations about the image-policy preference relationship are confirmed. We can also look for emerging patterns that might provide clues about the relationship between images and policy preferences.

By focusing on policy *debates*, we are almost inevitably drawn to an emphasis on policy *disagreements*. We should remember, however, that policy debates often take place within a basic framework of agreement. Given the fact that all of the individuals in this study can be classified as hard-liners in a broad sense of the term, we would expect to find consensus on some points, and, indeed, we do. All of the key decision makers in the administration advocated asymmetrical reductions; the contending proposals differed only in the character and extent of these asymmetries. This is, of course, consistent with the perception of dramatic Soviet advantages in this class of weapons. Furthermore, all of the proposals were probably nonnegotiable in the near term. This was certainly recognized by all involved. There seemed to be a general agreement on the need for the alliance to go forward with the deployments before the Soviets would make any meaningful concessions. As a result, there was no constituency in the administration for delaying the deployments, even to forestall a Soviet walkout. This is consistent with the shared belief that only strength and resolve, not unilateral restraint, would produce more reasonable Soviet policies. Thus, to some extent, Perle had a valid point when he complained that his disagreements with Burt were magnified out of proportion.

Despite important similarities in approach, the reports of intense internal debates were not simply the figments of overly dramatic journalistic imaginations. There remained significant areas of disagreement that can be traced to different images of the Soviet Union. The key issues that divided the administration included: (1) how quickly should negotiations with the Soviets be resumed, (2) the commitment to zero INF as the only acceptable result of the talks, (3) the inclusion of Soviet SRINF, and (4) the question of "global equality." Though significant in themselves, these specific debates reflected a more fundamental disagreement over the degree of flexibility the United States should display in its search for an INF treaty.

## Resuming Negotiations

It is reasonable to assume that a decision maker's position on whether to commence or resume arms negotiations would depend on his or her general assessment of the arms control process: is it detrimental, irrelevant, or beneficial to U.S. interests? The more favorable a decision maker's evaluation of the process, the more likely he or she will be to favor negotiations; conversely, the more negative the assessment, the less likely negotiations will be favored. As explained in the previous chapter, a decision maker's evaluation of the arms control process is shaped by a number of factors, the most important being his or her images of the Soviet Union and the United States. In the case of Perle and Weinberger, we found that their very hard-line image of the Soviet Union, which would tend to increase skepticism about the value of negotiations, was compounded by a very dim view of the political capacities of the United States. The result was an almost depressing analysis which all but predicted agreements harmful to U.S. security. Consequently, Perle and Weinberger wanted to delay the resumption of negotiations as long as possible. After all, why should the United States try to reach an agreement with a country whose foreign policy goals and nuclear strategy are so antithetical to those of the United States? Why should the United States resume a process whose dynamics inevitably worked in favor of the Soviet Union?

For Reagan, the picture is more complicated in the sense that it is difficult to tell, on the basis of his images of the Soviet Union and the United States, whether he should have supported or opposed negotiations. This is problematic because of the conflicts in his beliefs that apparently led in different directions. On the one hand, Reagan viewed the Soviet Union as a militarily superior and menacing power bent on world domination and, ultimately, the destruction of the United States. Such an image would seemingly lead Reagan to support Perle and Weinberger. But Reagan differed from Perle and Weinberger in that he apparently did not share their views about the weakness of democracies, and he placed a much greater emphasis on the underlying political and economic weakness of the Soviet system. These Soviet weaknesses, he argued, would eventually lead the Soviets to abandon their more threatening policies, particularly in the face of renewed U.S. strength. When all this is put together, it is still not clear what we get. Such a view could be consistent with a vigorous pursuit of negotiations, assuming that the combination of internal demands and external pressure would lead the Soviets to dramatically alter their objectives. Alternatively, it could also lead to a policy of unrelenting hostility and confrontation designed to hasten the collapse of the Soviet system. Thus, Reagan's image of the Soviet Union is consistent with an extremely wide range of policy options, including his decision to resume INF talks in 1981.

## The Commitment to Zero

The debate over the goal of zero INF illustrates the role of images in two respects: first, it shows how different perceptions of Soviet nuclear strategy and capabilities can shape policy disagreements; and second, it suggests the manner in which images can influence a decision maker's willingness to take "extraneous" factors into account. Regarding the influence of perceptions of Soviet strategy, it is necessary to recall that the Soviet SS-20s were very fast and accurate missiles, which differentiated them from the previous generation of Soviet intermediate range forces. With these capabilities, the SS-20s could be used in a quick strike against NATO military targets—they were counterforce weapons with first-strike potential. If these capabilities are viewed within the framework of an image of the Soviet Union as having a strategy for fighting and winning a nuclear war, the SS-20s become very alarming weapons indeed. In the absence of such a view, the SS-20s, though still not desirable, would not be as threatening. Perceptions of the overall strategic balance would also color a decision maker's assessment of the SS-20s: the Soviet advantage in this type of weapon on the theater level becomes even more troublesome if one believes that the balance of strategic forces also favors the Soviets. That is, if the United States does not have a credible strategic deterrent, its commitment to Europe is less credible, and the Soviet first-strike weapons in Europe are even more ominous.

Perle's and Weinberger's image of the Soviet Union included the belief that Soviet strategy was based upon the notion that a nuclear war could be fought and won. The Soviet nuclear arsenal, particularly its emphasis on counterforce weapons, was viewed as a manifestation of this strategy. The SS-20s only served to confirm these views. In addition, Perle and Weinberger had grave doubts about the U.S. strategic deterrent, claiming that the Soviets either had or were very close to having a disarming first-strike capability. Given these perceptions, we would expect Perle and Weinberger to support policies aimed at reducing Soviet counterforce weapons as much as possible, which is precisely what the zero option would (and did) accomplish. From this perspective, the zero plus had to be opposed because it would have legitimized the presence of Soviet first-strike weapons in Europe and Asia. In contrast, Burt and Shultz did not argue that the Soviets viewed nuclear war as fightable and winnable. Nor did they present a portrait of U.S. strategic forces as inferior to the Soviet Union's, though they did identify important deficiencies. Since they did not share Perle's and Weinberger's views of Soviet strategy and capabilities, Burt and Shultz did not display the same commitment to gutting Soviet counterforce weapons. One must be careful, however, in differentiating Burt and Shultz from Perle and Weinberger. It is not that Burt and Shultz were unconcerned about this new Soviet capability provided by the SS-20s. Undoubtedly, they would have liked to see the SS-20s eliminated. Burt and Shultz did not oppose the zero option because they wanted SS-20s to remain in place; they simply thought that something short of the zero option was both desirable and more possible.

Again, Reagan poses some problems. Our examination of Reagan's image of the Soviet Union revealed some possible contradictions in perceptions of Soviet strategy and capabilities. On many occasions, Reagan stressed his belief that Soviet doctrine was based on the assumption that a nuclear war could be fought and won, and his statements about the Soviets enjoying a "margin of superiority" are well known. But there were other times when he spoke of Soviet leaders as if they were aware of the unacceptable destruction that would result from a nuclear war, vaguely implying that they did not view it as winnable. And his statements about Soviet superiority were mixed with comments suggesting that the United States possessed an adequate and surviv-able nuclear deterrent. Still, the emphasis was clearly on the Soviet Union's war-winning strategy and the superiority of its strategic forces. This should have led Reagan to support the zero option, which he did from October, 1981, until March, 1983. Reagan's position changed gradually throughout 1983, eventually supporting Burt's zero plus, without any changes in the relevant aspects of his image. His willingness to accept some SS-20s in Europe, even without a commitment to eventual zero, was inconsistent with dominant as-pects of his image. But because of the other, admittedly muted, elements of his image, we cannot say that his adoption of the zero plus was without any support in his image.

The problem of establishing consistency between Reagan's beliefs and his policy preferences will be a recurring theme. This is because the nature of Reagan's image of the Soviet Union is such that a variety of policy positions on most issues could find intellectual support. In my theoretical and meth-odological discussions, I stressed that any given image is probably consistent with more than one policy preference, so this is not what makes Reagan stand out. Reagan is unusual because the range of consistent policy positions is often so wide. If we have trouble determining what policies were consistent with Reagan's image of the Soviet Union, it is because his image provides us with unclear and occasionally contradictory guidelines. This is a potentially significant finding. The key point is that if Reagan's image fails to give us guidance, it may not have given him much direction either.

The zero versus zero plus debate was not based solely on different views of Soviet nuclear strategy and capabilities. One of the main arguments used by supporters of the zero plus was that it would meet increasing European demands for a more flexible and reasonable U.S. negotiating position. Burt and Shultz were sensitive to these concerns; Perle and Weinberger were not. There are several plausible explanations for this difference in sensitivity. The most obvious would stress institutional and role factors; representatives of the State Department tend to be more attuned to allied pressures than Defense officials. Images, however, may also be important. We might postulate that decision makers with very hard-line images of the Soviet Union are more likely to view a whole range of issues primarily in East-West terms. Because of the level of threat posed by Soviet objectives, strategy, and capabilities, other considerations are subordinated. As a result, "extraneous" factors such as domestic and international political opinion are less likely to influence policy preferences. A more moderate, less threatening image may decrease the salience of the central adversarial relationship, leading a decision maker to take a wider range of factors into account. Thus, we might hypothesize a closer correspondence between hard-line images and policy preferences than would be the case for more moderate images.

## SRINF and Global Equality

The basic rationale Perle offered for including Soviet SRINF in his initial zero option and for insisting on global equality was that, in the absence of such restrictions, the Soviets would find it much easier to violate and/or circumvent an INF treaty. Perle's overriding concern with blocking every possible avenue of Soviet circumvention is exactly what we would have expected, since Soviet untrustworthiness and duplicity were one of the central features of his image. And since Weinberger emphasized these same points, his support for Perle on these issues is consistent with his image. Burt and Shultz, however, did not have the same extremely negative view of Soviet treaty compliance. The point is not that Burt and Shultz thought it unnecessary to worry about *possible* Soviet violations, but simply that they did not approach arms negotiations as if such violations were *probable* or *inevitable*. Support for including SRINF and demanding global equality would have been consistent with Burt's and Shultz's images of the Soviet Union, but so would compromise on these points. For Perle and Weinberger, any compromise would have been inconsistent with their very strident views of Soviet untrustworthiness.

In this case, it appears as though Reagan supported policies that were inconsistent with his image of the Soviet Union. One of the most prominent, and least ambiguous, themes in Reagan's statements about Soviet behavior was his profound suspicion of Soviet trustworthiness. If Reagan genuinely believed that the Soviets could not be trusted to abide by agreements, he should have supported Perle on both counts. Why, then, did he not go along with the call for including SRINF? Furthermore, why was Reagan willing to support Burt's 1983 plan that would have moved away from strict global equality? There was no change in Reagan's beliefs about Soviet trustworthiness; in fact, his expressions of concern regarding Soviet treaty violations became more frequent later in his administration. Despite this increasing concern, Reagan continued to support variations on Burt's "global equality." At Reykjavík, for example, Reagan agreed to a Soviet proposal of no LRINF in Europe, with 100 warheads stationed in Soviet Asia and the United States (Risse-Kappen 1988, 144).

Why did Reagan support policies that appeared to be inconsistent with his beliefs? Several plausible explanations come immediately to mind. First, we might argue that Reagan really did trust the Soviets to live up to the spirit and letter of agreements. Given the consistency, frequency, and apparent sincerity of Reagan's statements on this issue, it is difficult to accept this explanation. Second, perhaps Reagan was not aware that the Soviets could use SRINF and LRINF redeployments to circumvent a treaty. This possibility has been suggested by several authors, although not with direct reference to this issue. Garthoff, referring to Reagan's support for the zero option, notes that "the American policy community (with the likely significant exception of President Reagan himself) understood the nonnegotiability of the zero-option" (1985, 1024). The basic point being that Reagan, because of his limited knowledge of nuclear issues, was not always cognizant of the implications of the policies he supported. While this explanation might be useful for understanding Reagan's inconsistencies in the more technical and complicated area of strategic weapons, it is not persuasive in this instance. There were several occasions when Reagan demonstrated that he did understand the problems associated with SRINF and LRINF deployments. For example, he explained that "when President Brezhnev offers to stop deployments in Western Europe [Eastern Europe (?)], he fails to mention that these [SS-20s] are mobile missiles. It doesn't matter where you put them, since you can move them anywhere you want" (*CPD* 1982, 302). The final explanation is also the simplest: for whatever reasons (e.g., domestic and international political pressures or a desire to preserve a modest level of administration harmony), Reagan was willing to support policies that he realized were inconsistent with his beliefs about the Soviet Union. Just as he was not particularly troubled by inconsistencies *within* his belief system, Reagan was also not bothered by inconsistencies *between* his beliefs and his policies.

### Negotiating Flexibility

In the previous chapter I discussed the role of images in shaping a decision maker's view of what common interests exist between his or her own country and its adversary. An extremely hard-line image, which stresses the Soviet Union's unlimitedly expansionist goals, military superiority, and nuclear war–winning doctrine, is not the sort of image that is conducive to a perception of mutual interests. The idea that the security of both nations can be advanced simultaneously is difficult to reconcile with such an image. This type of image promotes a zero-sum analysis of the adversarial relationship.

From this perspective, any concessions to the adversary's negotiating position are, almost by definition, inimical to the interests of the United States and dangerous to U.S. national security. A less hard-line image, in which the Soviet Union is not out to destroy the United States or planning to fight and emerge victorious from a nuclear war, is more conducive to the establishment of a limited adversarial relationship. This differs from a zero-sum analysis because it opens the way for perceptions of common interests and the possibility that concessions can be offered that are not necessarily harmful to U.S. security.

In the case of INF we can see how this fundamental disagreement shaped the course of the debate. Perle and Weinberger, whose view of the Soviet Union led them to a zero-sum analysis of East-West relations, opposed every attempt to modify the U.S. position or grant concessions, however modest, to the Soviet position. Burt and Shultz, though unwilling to make concessions on major points of Soviet concern, were willing to accept the idea that concessions could be offered without endangering U.S. security. And once again, Reagan provides a study in contradictions. His image of the Soviet Union's foreign policy and nuclear objectives was more consistent with Perle and Weinberger's zero-sum analysis. Nonetheless, over time, he was willing to accept all the modifications proposed by Burt and Shultz.

## Formulators and Choosers

A final observation from the discussion of the INF debate relates to the role of images in policy formulation and/or choice. An emerging pattern is that Perle and Burt were always the *formulators* of policy options. Weinberger and Shultz appear to have used their subordinates as "policy guides." Whether Shultz and Weinberger would have come up with the same policies if left to their own devices is open to questions. For Burt and Perle, images may be crucial for understanding the formulation of policy options, whereas, for their superiors, images might be important in terms of the choice propensities they introduced. Reagan, on the other hand, did not seem to have had a consistent policy guide. Sometimes he sided with the Perle and Weinberger faction, while at other times he supported Burt and Shultz. Thus, images appear to play a different role, even for people whose beliefs are the same.

There are a number of possible reasons why the role of images might differ across individuals. Though this issue will be dealt with more as we move on, it is useful to at least mention two of the possibilities here. One obvious possibility is role factors. We might hypothesize that lower level officials, whose tasks tend to be more specialized, are the people who spend more of their time dealing with specific issues. As one moves up the ladder from undersecretaries to secretaries, the scope of responsibilities increases, leaving less time to concentrate on specific issues. As demands for their attention and energies increase, upper level officials are forced to rely on subordinates for the details of policy options. A second key factor might be depth of knowledge and experience. Burt and Perle were the two officials of the five in this study who had an intimate knowledge of nuclear questions and a history of thinking about these issues. Shultz and Weinberger entered office as relative novices, though they quickly mastered the nuts and bolts. Reagan entered with very little knowledge and never learned the details. Thus, we might hypothesize that images are more likely to serve a policy formulation role when the decision maker has a great deal of substantive knowledge in a given issue area, which allows him or her to translate his or her beliefs into concrete proposals.

## Conclusions

The most basic observation that can be made is that there was a consistency between the beliefs of Reagan's advisers and their policy preferences, though this may not be the case for Reagan himself. Beneath the level of the president, those who shared a very hard-line image of the Soviet Union invariably lined up on the same side of issues, and they were consistently opposed by those who adhered to a more moderate (or less hard-line) image. In each of the policy debates the Pentagon civilians were active players, and in each instance they were in agreement. They attempted to delay the resumption of talks in 1981. They opposed any concessions on the criterion of zero INF. They fought Nitze's and, later, Burt's attempts to move away from rigid global equality. Perle and Weinberger consistently and adamantly opposed even the most modest concessions proposed by Burt and others at State. Not once did they put forward their own suggestions for modifying the U.S. position, nor did they ever support proposals put forward by others. On those issues that were played out after Shultz entered office (e.g., the move away from zero and the reformulation of global equality), he supported Burt's initiatives, eventually becoming a fairly active advocate on their behalf. And although Shultz was not around for the first debate over the resumption of talks, he did support a quick restart of the talks after the 1983 Soviet walkout. Thus, the lines of battle in the Reagan administration coincided with its intellectual divisions.

# CHAPTER 10

# SALT II and START

The future of the INF deployments and negotiations was not the only issue the Reagan administration inherited from its predecessor; there was also the question of what to do about SALT II. Signed by President Carter but withdrawn from Senate consideration in the wake of the December, 1979, Soviet invasion of Afghanistan, SALT II had been a focal point of Reagan's assault on Carter's foreign policy. Since Reagan denounced the treaty as "fatally flawed," the expectation was that it would have a very short life after January, 1981. The fate of SALT II, however, turned out to be more complicated than anyone expected.

It is not necessary to provide a complete history of SALT II's rather tortured existence during the first six years of the Reagan administration. Although the issue was constantly bubbling beneath the surface, there were two critical periods in the life of SALT II during which the debates reached a climax: from 1981 to 1982, a period of disarray that ultimately led to the euphemistic "no undercut" policy; and 1985 to 1986, when SALT II's opponents finally prevailed and the United States exceeded the treaty's limits.

## Disarray and Dissension, 1981–82

During its first year, the Reagan administration did not have a SALT II policy; it had several. On SALT II, as on most foreign policy issues, Reagan remained detached, dealing with the problem only when there was a pressing need for a decision. Within the foreign policy bureaucracy, the battle raged on with the same cast of characters that was active in the INF debates; Perle and Weinberger were the leading advocates of repudiating the treaty, while Burt and Haig consistently argued for continued compliance. Particularly important were the allies each side gained within the administration. CIA Director William Casey and Secretary of the Navy John Lehman sided with Perle and Weinberger. Lining up in favor of compliance were Admiral Bobby Inman, a deputy of Casey's at the CIA, and the Joint Chiefs of Staff chairman, General David Jones. Outside the administration, the correlation of political forces was with the pro–SALT II faction; most in Congress urged continued adherence, as did the European allies. In contrast to the INF debate, the administration did not do a very good job of keeping its disagreements under wraps. Only one week after entering office a foreshadowing of things to come was provided in a joint appearance by Weinberger and Jones before a congressional committee. The new secretary of defense announced that he opposed SALT II while the chairman of the Joint Chiefs at his side explained why he thought the treaty served U.S. interests.

The more significant episode in terms of the development of administration policy occurred in early March, 1981. In a meeting with reporters on March 3, Navy Secretary Lehman announced that the United States should not consider itself bound by the restrictions of the SALT agreements, I or II (Smith 1988, 576). Although Lehman emphasized that he was speaking for himself, not the administration, Haig and Burt were worried that, in the absence of any official policy statement, Lehman's comments would be taken as more than personal opinion. At their initiative the State Department released a statement the following day that sent a very different signal: "While we are reviewing our SALT policy, we will take no action that would undercut existing agreements so long as the Soviet Union exercises the same restraint" (Talbott 1985, 225). This became the administration's policy, apparently without any decision by the president. As Hedrick Smith explains, "Haig was unilaterally declaring that SALT I and SALT II remained in force. . . . There was no time—and for that matter no inclination at State—to check with the Reagan White House" (1988, 578, 577). Haig and Burt had made U.S. policy.

About two months after the State Department issued its announcement, the issue of SALT II was raised at an NSC meeting when the president asked flatly, "what are we going to do about SALT anyway?" (Smith 1988, 226). In response, Weinberger made the case against continued adherence by claiming that the treaty stood in the way of the administration's modernization program. JCS Chairman Jones offered the same arguments he had made in disagreeing with Weinberger several months earlier: the treaty posed no obstacles to a U.S. buildup. When pressed by Jones to specify which elements of the modernization program were inconsistent with SALT II, Weinberger was at a loss. This, in fact, was the cornerstone of the case for SALT II adherence that would be repeated ad nauseam for the next five years—the treaty permitted the modernization of U.S. forces while it prevented further Soviet increases in key areas, such as increasing the number of warheads on heavy missiles. The logic of this argument carried the day. Reagan decided to continue the no undercut policy laid down by Haig and Burt in March, although no official statement to this effect was released.

The administration lurched along with this policy throughout the remainder of 1981 and into 1982. But this was an uneasy truce within the administration that was only exacerbated by questions that plagued its officials as they tried to explain and defend the no undercut policy. Henry Kissinger, among others, could not understand why it "was safe to adhere to a nonratified agreement but unsafe to ratify what was already being observed" (IISA 1982–83, 26). Although SALT II did not interfere with any major elements of the administration's modernization program, it did require the United States to forgo the deployment of fifty new Minuteman III missiles. This did not sit well with those inside or outside the administration who thought that the United States was strategically inferior to the Soviet Union.

Throughout 1981 and the spring of 1982, Reagan had trouble with questions about his no undercut policy. He could always explain what he did not like about SALT II—it "permitted" or "authorized" a Soviet buildup—but he had difficulty explaining why his administration continued to honor the agreement. At a May, 1982, press conference, for example, the president was asked, "why not push for ratification of that [SALT II] treaty as a first step, then go on to START? After all, a bird in the hand?" Reagan responded:

> Because, Helen, this bird is not a very friendly bird . . . the limitations in that agreement would allow in the life of the treaty for the Soviet Union to just about double their present nuclear capability. It would allow us—and does allow us—to increase ours . . . [the president did not continue with this train of thought]. Now, the parts that we're observing have to do with the monitoring of each other's weaponry, and both sides are doing that. (*CPD* 1982, 619)

There are two interesting aspects of this explanation of the administration's policy. First, beyond pointing out that it legitimized a buildup on both sides, Reagan failed to provide a single reason why ratification would endanger the United States. Second, Reagan displayed confusion about what his administration's policy was. The United States was observing *all* aspects of SALT II, not simply those having to do with monitoring.

Inaccurate and confusing statements by the president were one of several developments in the spring of 1982 that pointed to the need for a clarification of policy. There was congressional pressure for the administration to get its act in order as well as calls for resubmission of the treaty from powerful figures such as Senator Sam Nunn (D-Georgia). In May, 1982, the administration announced its START proposal, which meant that SALT II was no longer the only policy it had. Finally, and probably most important, the administration was facing a decision about dismantling Poseidon submarines to make way for the new Trident system. If the Poseidons were retained while the Tridents were deployed, the United States would exceed SALT II limits.

The issue came to a head at a May 21 NSC meeting. Most of the usual participants were present: the president, Haig, Weinberger, Jones, and NSC adviser Richard Allen. There was one significant substitution: CIA Director

Casey was unable to attend and sent his deputy, Bobby Inman, in his place. This was crucial because Inman was an outspoken and very articulate supporter of SALT II. When the president asked, "what's good about SALT II" Inman had his cue, proceeding to deliver a point-by-point review of the virtues of the treaty. Weinberger continued to oppose adherence, suggesting a policy of "selective compliance," which effectively meant repudiating the agreement (see Newhouse 1989, 342; Talbott 1985, 274). The nature of the division at this meeting was interesting and perhaps critical to the outcome. While Weinberger was elaborating on the dangers of adhering to SALT II, there were three high-ranking military men arguing that U.S. interests were served by living up to the treaty. While we cannot say this was a decisive element in Reagan's decision, it certainly was an impressive array of military brass opposing the secretary of defense, not a group one could accuse of being naive or soft on security issues.

Reagan decided in favor of Haig, Jones, and Inman, announcing on May 30 that the no undercut policy would continue (*CPD* 1982, 367). The key points made by Inman, Jones, and Haig had apparently sunk in: "I learned," the president said to one journalist, "that the Soviet Union has a capacity to increase weaponry much faster than the treaty permitted, and we didn't" (Gelb 1985, 23). By no means, however, was this the end of the SALT II debate. Though he accepted a policy of continued adherence, Reagan was not converted into a firm supporter of SALT II. He still criticized the agreement for authorizing a weapons buildup, particularly on the Soviet side. The opposition to SALT II within the administration was determined and knew that it could play on Reagan's residual unease with the treaty. In a short time, Haig, Inman, and Jones would all be gone. The Poseidon-Trident decision was not the last one that posed hard choices: certain MX basing modes were in conflict with SALT II, as were plans for new bombers equipped with air-launched cruise missiles (ALCMs). To use a cliché, the battle was over, but the war waged on.

## The End of SALT II, 1985–86

If SALT II had been ratified, it would have expired on the last day of 1985; as a result, by the middle of 1985, the administration's no undercut policy was once again in doubt. The situation then was different than 1982 in several key respects. First, the INF and START talks had collapsed in November, 1983, and were not resumed until March, 1985. Second, there was a leadership change in Moscow, where Gorbachev was now in command. Third, Shultz had replaced Haig at State, Admiral Crowe was appointed by Reagan as chairman of the Joint Chiefs (replacing John Vessey, who had replaced Jones), and Burt was now the ambassador to West Germany. Finally, Soviet compliance with SALT II had become a matter of debate after the administration released two reports (in January, 1984 and 1985) detailing Soviet violations and possible violations. Perle and Weinberger remained the leaders of the movement for scrapping SALT II and seized upon these reports, which they had pushed to make harsher and less equivocal, to argue that U.S. compliance was "unilateral," not mutual. The president surely would not like that. Once again, the future of SALT II seemed bleak.

By early June, 1985, another Poseidon-Trident decision had to be made. As usual, Perle and Weinberger pushed for exceeding the SALT II limits. The pro–SALT II banner was taken up by Shultz, who was joined by Nitze and Crowe. Although the new JCS chairman sided with the pro–SALT II forces, he was not the enthusiastic supporter of the treaty that Jones, a Carter appointee, had been. External pressures pointed in the direction of continued compliance: British Prime Minister Thatcher openly and in private expressed her support for adherence, and on June 5 the Senate passed a resolution to this effect by the overwhelming margin of 90 to 5 (Newhouse 1989, 386). All of these factors apparently contributed to the president's decision to dismantle the Poseidon to make room for the new Trident (Jensen 1988, 211).

In March, 1986, the by now infamous Poseidon-Trident trade-off raised its annoying head again. This time, however, there were other key deployment decisions to be made. The trickiest problem concerned the deployment of ALCMs on long-range B-1 bombers; if the current pace continued, the United States would exceed SALT II limits by the end of the year, when the 131st bomber equipped with ALCMs became operational (Haley 1987, 78). The Poseidon and ALCM issues were the subject of an April 21 NSC meeting. The familiar arguments were rehashed. Shultz, Crowe, and Nitze favored staying within the restrictions of SALT II; Weinberger argued for exceeding them by going forward with the Trident and ALCM deployments. "I've never liked SALT and neither have you Mr. President," said Weinberger, playing on Reagan's deeply ingrained skepticism about the treaty. "Never liked it at all," Reagan grumbled (Smith 1988, 591–92). Nitze was livid about Weinberger's presentation, which reportedly involved a number of misleading, but very colorful, charts and tables. Weinberger was "no better than that other shyster lawyer, that dreadful man Dulles," Nitze complained to one colleague (Talbott 1988, 228).

The decision facing Reagan in March, 1986, differed from those in the past because it involved two issues; the submarines, which were an immediate concern, and the ALCM deployments, which were still in the future. Given the nature of the issues before him, Reagan had a golden opportunity to do what he had done so often—give something to each side. The president's decision was announced on April 21: the United States would destroy the Poseidon submarines, staying within SALT II for the time being, but would go ahead with the ALCM deployments, exceeding SALT II by the end of the year (Jensen 1988, 212; Talbott 1988, 228). The "fatally flawed" SALT II treaty had finally used up all of its lives.

## Images and SALT II

In order to understand the debate and divisions in the Reagan administration over SALT II, it is important to realize that the treaty existed on two levels. On one level, SALT II was an arms control agreement containing a variety of provisions regulating the shape and growth of strategic arsenals. On another, perhaps more significant, level, SALT II was a symbol, a lingering reminder of an era in U.S. foreign policy and the process that was at its heart—détente and arms control. SALT II was more than a collection of restrictions; it was a quintessential example of the whole being greater than the sum of its parts. For those who opposed these policies, SALT II was the living embodiment of a decade of misguided foreign policy. If a clean break were to be made with the past, it simply would not do to have SALT II lying around.

### SALT II, the Treaty

The debate over SALT II as an arms control treaty centered on three interrelated issues. First, should the United States allow its weapons procurement and deployment decisions to be dictated by the restrictions of SALT II? Second, to what extent did the agreement inhibit the Soviet strategic buildup? Third, were the Soviets actually abiding by the treaty? The debates over these issues were partially rooted in the decision makers' perceptions of the existing strategic balance, beliefs about Soviet treaty behavior, and their view of the Soviet approach to arms control in general.

There is no doubt that abiding by SALT II did require the United States to forgo certain weapons (e.g., additional Minuteman III missiles) and dismantle others (Poseidon submarines and their Polaris missiles). In the eyes of most, however, these were not terribly imposing concessions. The handful of Minuteman IIIs planned for deployment in the early 1980s would have added only marginally to the capabilities of the U.S. ICBM force, certainly not enough to complicate any possible Soviet attack on the land-based portion of the U.S. triad. The dismantling of the Poseidons was more significant; although old, they were by no means obsolete. However, despite these restrictions, virtually the entire modernization program planned by the Reagan administration could proceed uninterrupted, with the MX as a possible problem.

Since abiding by SALT II did entail some limitations on the U.S. buildup, however minimal, the decision maker's perception of the balance should be an important factor in shaping his or her position on SALT II adherence. We would anticipate that the more unfavorable the balance is perceived to be, the more likely one would be to push for maximum possible deployments, regardless of treaty constraints. A categorical prediction to this effect is not possible, since it is perfectly logical to perceive an imbalance yet still favor compliance, if one thinks the imbalance will worsen in the absence of a treaty. As usual, we are in the realm of expectations and tendencies. One need not assume that the weapons in question would actually correct the imbalance: even if the weapons themselves were not crucial in a strictly military sense, a decision to refrain from going forward with planned deployments and actually getting rid of other weapons would not exactly set the proper example if the United States was in an inferior position.

Consistent with these expectations, Perle and Weinberger, who routinely described the strategic balance in dire terms, argued throughout the Reagan administration that SALT II limits should be ignored and that capable weapons systems should not be deactivated. Burt and Shultz, who saw a situation of rough parity with Soviet advantages in a few areas, favored continued adherence and the necessary tailoring of U.S. forces.

Reagan, however, runs contrary to our expectations about the relationship between perceptions of the strategic balance and his position on SALT II. Although Smith argues that "it took Reagan six years to decide what to do about SALT II," the fact is that, for five years, Reagan decided to abide by the treaty, and throughout this period Reagan claimed that the Soviets enjoyed a "definite margin of superiority" (Smith 1988, 589). Not until 1986 did Reagan decide to abandon SALT II, and by that time his assertions of Soviet strategic superiority had all but disappeared. When he believed the Soviets were superior, Reagan abided by SALT II; when he thought the United States had made progress in reducing the imbalances, he decided to repudiate SALT II. Even at this basic level, Reagan's position on SALT II seems inexplicable in terms of his image of the Soviet Union. A purely political explanation might account for his continuation of the no undercut policy from 1981 to 1986, but it does not explain his reversal in the spring of 1986. The domestic and political pressures for SALT II adherence were as great in 1986 as they were the year before.

The issue of whether or not the United States should abide by SALT II was closely related to the question of what it got in return. In Perle and Weinberger's view the answer was clear—nothing. Perle and Weinberger rejected the heart of the case for continued compliance, questioning whether the agreement restrained the Soviet buildup. In their analysis, the United States got the short end of the stick for two reasons: first, they simply did not believe that the Soviet Union would have signed a treaty that did not conform to previously existing plans; second, when the treaty did pose some obstacle to Soviet plans, the Soviet Union did not hesitate to violate it. The following exchange reflects Weinberger's views.

> *Senator Mathias*: Do you think that the SALT II treaty in any way inhibits the Soviets' strategic weapons program?
> *Secretary Weinberger*: Frankly, no, sir, I do not.
> *Senator Mathias*: Does it induce them, say, to scrap submarines they might otherwise mean to keep?
> *Secretary Weinberger*: Since you put in that qualifying clause, the answer is no. (U.S. Cong. 1981r, 37)

On another occasion, Weinberger claimed, "they dismantled things they had planned to dismantle a long time before" (CBS News 1986b). These statements are revealing. Perle and Weinberger did not deny that the Soviets dismantled submarines in accordance with SALT II; but they did deny that this was motivated by any desire to abide by the treaty. Whenever they were confronted by evidence of Soviet behavior consistent with SALT II, Perle and Weinberger responded that the Soviets would have acted like that even without a treaty. They claimed that the Soviets dismantled the submarines because they were too old, not because SALT II required their destruction. Thus, when asked to speculate about Soviet behavior in the absence of SALT II, Perle responded that "it is likely to be just about the same as Soviet behavior under the constraints" (U.S. Cong. 1985h, 82). After pursuing this line of questioning with Perle about why the Soviets were dismantling various weapons, one senator realized the dilemma.

> I think what we are saying here, Richard, what you are saying here, is a point that essentially of course neither of us can prove. I mean I cannot prove that they dismantled the submarine to keep within SALT II, and you cannot prove that they would have dismantled it had there been no SALT. I mean we are essentially arguing from a data point, and we cannot do a cause and effect. . . . It does seem strange, though, that they would have come to exactly the limits and agreed to that and happened to hit it by just sheer chance. . . . (U.S. Cong. 1986c, 70–71)

Had the Senator been familiar with the present study, he might have pointed out that Perle's interpretation of that data point was influenced by his image of the Soviet Union and Soviet arms control strategy.

As if this were not enough, Perle and Weinberger also concluded that the Soviets had violated SALT II; even the very few limits imposed by the agreement were apparently too much for the Soviets. The two most important violations were the development of a second new ICBM (SALT II limited each side to one) and telemetry encryption (which was restricted, though not prohibited, by SALT II). In official administration reports, these were listed as "possible violations," but there was no ambiguity in Perle's or Weinberger's eyes. According to one member of the Joint Chiefs, "if the evidence [of violations] was ambiguous, they judged it conclusive" (Newhouse 1989, 341). Although Perle claimed that "there [was] no excuse, no rationalization, no obfuscating hypothesis that was not exhaustively explored as one agency or another sought to avoid the most dreaded of all conclusions—that the Soviets were cheating," he was openly dismissive of any attempts to dispute the conclusions or provide explanations other than conscious Soviet cheating (U.S. Cong. 1987e, 4). At one congressional hearing, Perle was preceded by witnesses presenting the results of a Stanford University study on Soviet treaty violations. Their report had concluded that there had been only a few violations that were, on the whole, militarily insignificant. Perle shot back, "presumably 90 percent compliance earns an 'A' as it does on the Stanford campus." In a more serious vein, Perle continued:

> . . . let me acknowledge at once that the Soviets have violated only a few provisions. . . . To be rather more precise, they have violated those provisions that they found inconvenient, those that turned out to be inconsistent with their military plans. (U.S. Cong. 1987e, 4-5)

But in the larger scheme of things, Perle and Weinberger's perception of Soviet violations was only another nail in the coffin; they both opposed adhering to the agreement *before* any of the violations came to light.

Shultz and Burt did not share this view. Burt's original analysis of SALT II (1978) emphasized both the shortcomings and benefits of the agreement. Among the important pluses were the restrictions placed on the growth of the Soviet arsenal. One example was the limits on MIRVing large missiles. Since the Soviet Union's large SS-18 ICBMs were capable of carrying more than ten warheads, which was the limit imposed by SALT II, it would have been easy for the Soviets to place additional warheads on existing missiles. Burt never changed his mind on this point or contradicted any of his earlier kind words for SALT II. He obviously thought that the treaty prevented the Soviets from doing things they would and could have done in the absence of an agreement. Shultz, too, was willing to recognize Soviet actions to stay within the treaty without trying to explain them away as coincidences (see U.S. Cong. 1986g, 321; and U.S. Cong. 1988a, 92).

Unfortunately, Reagan did not comment on any specifics about whether the Soviets were dismantling weapons in order to stay within SALT II limits. He did, however, have a lot to say about the Soviet Union's trustworthiness and treaty record. Going all the way back to Reagan's famous line about the Soviets reserving unto themselves the right to lie, cheat, and steal, the president demonstrated his doubts about Soviet trustworthiness. Interestingly, however, when we look at his comments specifically about treaty behavior, we find a sudden rise in expressions of concern beginning in 1986 and 1987— *after* he decided to exceed SALT II limits.

## SALT II, the Symbol

It is probably a mistake to dwell on arguments about the specifics of SALT II, particularly for Perle and Weinberger. During the debate over its ratification, SALT II took on a significance well beyond its immediate military consequences; it became a symbol of a certain type of superpower relationship. As a symbol, it might not have been very important that the Soviets violated this or that provision or whether they were really constrained by the treaty. Even if the United States benefited in the short term from SALT II adherence (or at least did not suffer as much as it would have without the treaty), Perle and Weinberger were convinced that the overall process that produced the treaty "did violence," in Perle's words, to the ability of the United States to defend itself.

Snyder and Diesing provide some insights on this point. They note that hard-line images tend to lead decision makers to view immediate issues in a broader context.

> Since the opponent is always on the lookout for signs of weakness and opportunity to expand, it is essential [according to the hard-liner] to maintain a general image of determination to resist on all issues. In any particular crisis the preservation of the image is more important than the specific issue at stake. The issue is perceived as a test of strength in the general, long-term confrontation, for which the specific stake is merely the occasion or focus. (1977, 300)

If we wanted to employ the language of political philosophy, we might say that Snyder and Diesing are suggesting that hard-line images promote a form of "rule utilitarianism" in decision making as opposed to the "act utilitarianism" that accompanies more moderate images. That is, because arms control *as a rule* was harmful to the United States, specific agreements had to be opposed, even if they were in the U.S. interest (unless, of course, they *significantly* shifted the strategic balance in favor of the United States, and no one argued that SALT II accomplished that).

In contrast, Snyder and Diesing observe that individuals with moderate enemy images are more inclined to judge specific issues on their own merits

(301). This was certainly true of Burt and Shultz, both of whom saw faults with SALT II but still concluded that, on balance, the United States was better off with the treaty than without it. There may also have been a symbolic element to their support for SALT II adherence: in abiding by the treaty, the administration would not be making a total break with the past; it would be recognizing that something useful did (and could) come from arms control, which was precisely the message Perle and Weinberger did not want to send.

## START: A New Beginning

INF and SALT II, important though they were, can be viewed as sideshows to the big debate over the future of strategic arms control. During the 1976 and 1980 presidential campaigns, Reagan had focused on the eroding strategic balance and the failure of arms control to halt this erosion or reverse the arms race. Specifically, Reagan focused on two issues: first, the so-called window of vulnerability, which was a supposed Soviet ability to eliminate American ICBMs in a first strike while retaining sufficient forces to deter any retaliation; and second, the logically distinct issue of the failure of arms control to achieve real reductions. Although the problems of vulnerability and arsenal growth are not necessarily related—the former is a function of force structure and capabilities, not size—they were thrown into the same basket as if they were connected.

### The Long Delay, 1981–82

It took the Reagan administration almost seventeen months to devise and unveil a strategic arms reduction proposal. During this period, the only thing the administration had to show for itself was a new name for the negotiations, START (Strategic Arms Reduction Talks). While the Congress's and public's clamor for a START proposal was momentarily quieted by the resumption of the INF talks in the fall of 1981, it was only a slight reprieve. In the vacuum created by the lack of any official policy, the nuclear freeze movement seized the initiative in the winter of 81–82, resulting in several freeze resolutions in Congress that the administration opposed even though it had nothing to offer in their place. The Catholic Bishops' pastoral letter only served to further highlight the issue of arms control. The problem, however, was that the administration was deeply divided over the contents of the START proposal.

Arms control negotiations often revolve around differences about the "methodology of control" and the scope of restrictions. The former concerns the unit of measurement for counting and limiting weapons; the latter refers to the issue of which weapons are excluded from, or included in, the agreements (IISA 1982–83, 15). Since the administration promised a clean break with the past, everything was on the table. The most contentious issue was also the most basic—the methodology of control, that is, how would the capabilities of each side be measured and reduced. The key disagreements were again between Perle and Burt and those who followed their leads.

### The Great Debate

I have already noted that, in Perle's view, a successful arms control agreement was one that would significantly shift the strategic balance in favor of the United States or substantially reduce the threat posed by Soviet forces. There is no doubt that the START proposal he put forward would have accomplished just that, and there is also no doubt that it represented a departure from the SALT regime. The key difference between Perle's approach and that embodied in SALT concerned the methodology of control. The traditional approach had been to place limits on launchers and missiles, with few constraints on warheads (e.g., MIRVing limits). According to Perle, these measures failed to address the area of greatest Soviet advantage—throw-weight, which is a rough measure of an arsenal's overall destructive power "based on the payload that each side can deliver against the other's territory" (Barrett 1983, 317). The greater a missile's throw-weight, the larger its warheads can be and the more warheads it can carry. In an era of increasing missile accuracy, many argued that throw-weight was an increasingly irrelevant measure of capabilities because smaller, lighter warheads could do just as well. Others countered that throw-weight was still important in terms of the number of warheads that can be delivered. Perle was particularly concerned with *ballistic missile* throw-weight, in which the Soviets had a tremendous advantage; if bombers and cruise missiles are added to the equation, the two superpowers were basically equal. Thus, in terms of methodology, Perle wanted to focus on throw-weight; in terms of scope, he wanted reductions in ballistic missiles (ICBMs and SLBMs). Weinberger accepted the emphasis on throw-weight, claiming that "the thing you want most to remove, equalize, and balance out in the ultimate analysis is throw-weight" (U.S. Cong. 1983g, 134).

As the administration was attempting to formulate its initial START proposal during 1981–82, Perle suggested a plan for 4,000 ballistic missile warheads (no more than half on ICBMs) and a throw-weight limit on ballistic missiles of 2 million kg. Limitations on other strategic systems such as bombers and cruise missiles would either be forgotten or delayed until a second phase of negotiations (see Talbott 1985, 235). If this proposal had been adopted, START would have been a misnomer for the talks; a better name would have been the Ballistic Missile Reductions Talks, since it did not encompass the full range of strategic systems.

Perle's START proposal revealed the same minimalist-maximalist orientation as his INF zero option. The asymmetrical impact of the demand for equal ballistic missile throw-weight was obvious to anyone conversant in the details of nuclear weapons: only a slight reduction would have been required of the United States (in the neighborhood of 1–5 percent), while the Soviet Union would have had to reduce its throw-weight by more than 60 percent (Talbott 1985, 235). The warhead limits were also dramatically asymmetrical, particularly the 2,000 sublimit for ICBMs: it would have required the Soviets to eliminate approximately 4,170 ICBM warheads, whereas the United States would only have to get rid of 152 (IISA 1982–83, 24).

It is true that the SLBM limits would have fallen more heavily on the United States, which lent a certain surface plausibility to Perle's proposal. But this trade-off was much less attractive when viewed from the Soviet perspective. By zeroing in on ICBMs, Perle was going after the only component of the strategic triad that was a Soviet specialty. This was the leg where the Soviets had channeled most of their financial and technological resources. The United States, on the other hand, "specialized" in all three legs of its more evenly divided triad. Reductions in the SLBM component of the American triad would have left the other two legs untouched. After ballistic missiles were equal, the Soviet Union would have enjoyed no area of advantage, while the United States would retain an immense quantitative and qualitative edge in bombers and cruise missiles.

If accepted, the Perle throw-weight and warhead limits would have "required an abrupt and fundamental change in the structure of the Soviet land-based force" (Haig 1984, 222). In addition to radically restructuring the Soviet arsenal, Perle's proposal would have allowed every new weapon system being planned by the Reagan administration to go forward. Thus, the Soviets would have had to dismantle the heart of their nuclear arsenal while the United States modernized its areas of strength. There was another wrinkle to the use of throw-weight as the unit of measurement. One benefit of using launchers and missiles had been that they were easily verified by national technical means (i.e., nonobtrusive techniques). Counting warheads would require more intrusive means of verification. But the problems of verifying warhead limits would be nothing compared to the difficulty of measuring and estimating throw-weight. It would be hard to think of a measure that is subject to greater variation in estimation. Given Perle's and Weinberger's worries about Soviet cheating, one can only imagine the sorts of verification procedures they would have insisted on.

Perle's nemesis was Burt. Burt provides an interesting case of a decision maker who almost certainly had to tailor his policy preferences to meet the requirements of the policy-making milieu in which he operated. Unlike others in the Reagan administration, Burt had not criticized the SALT agreements for failing to actually reduce nuclear stockpiles. Prior to entering the administration, there is no evidence that Burt was concerned about the absence of genuine reductions. Once he was in the administration, however, he must have realized that Reagan would not accept a proposal that did not call for dramatic reductions. Whether or not he thought it strategically necessary, it was a political prerequisite. Furthermore, given the president's conviction that the Soviets enjoyed a "definite margin of superiority," any successful proposal would have to require greater Soviet reductions (or at least appear to). Thus, Burt must have recognized that, in order to be successful in the competition for the president's support, his proposal would have to meet at least three criteria: (1) it had to be simple; (2) it had to entail dramatic reductions; and (3) the Soviets had to give up more than the United States. For Burt, the trick was to craft a proposal that would be acceptable within the Reagan administration without making it completely unacceptable to the Soviets. This was no easy task.

Burt's first objective was to stop the movement for equal ballistic missile throw-weight. In addition to the problems of verification, the equal throw-weight demand would have been patently unacceptable to the Soviets. Burt wanted to continue with the same methodology of control that had been used for SALT—launchers (silos, missile tubes, and bombers), though he did favor a greater reliance on warheads as well. Burt's original formulation called for a limit of 1,200 ballistic missile launchers with 5,000 warheads, with no more than 2,500 on ICBMs (Talbott 1985, 239–40). Even without the direct throw-weight limits, Burt's proposal was only marginally less one-sided than Perle's. It, too, would have required dramatic cuts at the heart of the Soviet arsenal, ICBMs, while actually permitting the United States to *add* to its ICBM force. Unlike Perle, however, Burt wanted to expand the scope of the negotiations to include other strategic systems—bombers and cruise missiles. These were areas of U.S. advantage where the Soviets would certainly want concessions to compensate for the reductions in ballistic missiles.

Burt explored a number of options designed to make the U.S. proposal more equitable. Chief among these were U.S. concessions in cruise missiles, which, after all, had been sold in the 1970s as important bargaining chips for SALT. Burt wanted the United States to propose SALT-like restrictions on strategic bombers, particularly those equipped with cruise missiles. He also suggested to Haig that the United States consider a complete ban on sea-launched cruise missiles (SLCMs) that would have been very tempting to the Soviets. In the area of ballistic missiles, Burt considered the possibility of trading away the MX missile, which was in terrible political trouble anyway, for SS-18s, the Soviet Union's huge ICBMs with ten warheads. The SS-18/MX swap would have involved two counterforce systems, a stabilizing trade-off. At every turn, however, Burt was rebuffed by Perle, Weinberger, and various combinations of the uniformed military that no longer viewed cruise missiles as bargaining chips. Because of the opposition he encountered, none of these feelers ever reached the stage of concrete proposals. Burt simply could not find enough support; in any case, most of his efforts went into the battle over throw-weight, which raged on until Reagan "decided" (see Talbott 1985, 233–52).

The internal squabbling could not go on forever. There were pressures from Congress, the public, and allies to resume talks on strategic weapons. Reagan was scheduled to visit Western Europe in June, 1982, and his political advisers did not want him hounded by questions about the resumption of strategic arms negotiations. As the need for a decision approached, Reagan's advisers were no closer together. Again, the battle lines were drawn; Perle, Weinberger, and Edward Rowny argued that throw-weight was the most important measure of Soviet power and should be equalized; Burt and Haig opposed any direct limits on throw-weight. The Joint Chiefs eventually sided with the State Department after Burt agreed to lower his launcher limit (1,200 apparently conflicted with the Pentagon's targeting plans). Recognizing that Reagan would be uncomfortable with such irreconcilable dissension in the ranks, Burt cleverly (or deviously, depending on one's point of view) proposed a compromise: divide the START talks into two phases, making launchers and warheads the focus of the first phase, throw-weight the second. The throw-weight forces were suspicious; delaying their cherished goal to some second phase was, they feared, an attempt to kill the idea entirely. They were probably right.

The decision was made at a May 3 NSC meeting in which Reagan opted for the two-phase approach, postponing the goal of equalizing ballistic missile throw-weight. Ironically, in proposing throw-weight as the basic unit of account, Perle and Weinberger most likely hurt their cause. Whereas missiles, launchers, and warheads were easy things to understand and conceptualize, throw-weight was a more technical and slippery concept. The average person could grasp the notion of eliminating one third of each side's missiles or warheads, but what does a 50 percent reduction in throw-weight mean? The problem was that Reagan was not well versed in the technicalities of nuclear arms. He never displayed an understanding of exactly what throw-weight was; reportedly, on one occasion, he even admitted that he never comprehended "what this throw-weight business was all about" (Talbott 1985, 237).

The devil, however, is always in the details, and translating this basic framework into concrete proposals provided yet another opportunity to refight the throw-weight battle. Exactly what happened in the days and weeks following the May 3 NSC meeting remains murky. It is possible, however, to identify the three main issues that were bones of contention and, except in the case of Reagan, to identify where everyone stood. The first issue was whether to include "secret" throw-weight guidelines for the U.S. negotiating team for the first phase, even though an agreement would be sought in terms of launchers and warheads. Perle, Weinberger, and Rowny favored such a stipulation; Burt and Haig opposed it. Somewhere along the way the president apparently agreed to a secret throw-weight directive, though it is not clear when, how, or why he did so (Talbott 1985, 269–70). The second issue concerned limits on Soviet heavy (SS-18) and medium (SS-17 and SS-19) missiles. Perle and Rowny favored a total ban on heavies and restrictions on mediums without any U.S. concessions on the MX; Burt opposed the SS-18 ban without offering the MX in exchange. The final issue was what to do about bombers and cruise missiles. The Pentagon civilians wanted, at a minimum, to delay them to the second phase; Burt and Haig wanted them discussed in the first (see Talbott 1985, 268–69).

The issues were resolved, at least for the moment, and a proposal was accepted by the president at a June 25 NSC meeting and announced at Eureka College on May 9 (*CPD* 1982, 584–90). The Eureka proposal called for a ballistic missile limit of 850 and a warhead limit of 5,000, of which no more than half could be on ICBMs. Direct throw-weight limits were postponed to the second phase, as were limits on bombers and cruise missiles (IISA 1982–83, 24–25). Though not mentioned in the Eureka speech, there were also to be collateral limits on heavy and medium ICBMs; a combined total of 210, with no more than 110 heavies (308 SS-18s were deployed at the time in accordance with SALT II limits) (Jensen 1988, 218). The MX, classified as a medium, would be permitted (the United States had no heavies). The status of the "secret" throw-weight guidelines is unclear: it is difficult to tell whether it was an ironclad rule or merely a suggested goal; in fact, many accounts of the Eureka proposals do not mention it at all (e.g., NAS 1985, 59–61).

The Eureka proposal met with some praise from surprising quarters, including former President Carter (McMahan 1985, 61). Most, however, quickly realized that even without explicit throw-weight limits the proposal was too lopsided. As Haig himself explained, the Eureka plan was "a position that would require such drastic reductions [in the Soviet arsenal] as to suggest that they were unnegotiable" (1984, 273). This was even more so because of the postponement of any discussion of bombers and cruise missiles to the second phase.

## Back to the Drawing Board

This initial proposal did not stay intact very long, and the various factions within the Reagan administration did not give up on their respective goals very easily. After the first round of talks in Geneva led nowhere, the administration put its START policy "under review." The proposals for changes were predictable. Perle, Weinberger, and Rowny wanted the explicit throw-weight limits brought back into phase one. Burt, on the other hand, wanted to move bombers and cruise missiles back into phase one while leaving throw-weight where it was. The U.S. position had been revised in the spring of 1983 to include ceilings on bombers and ALCMs (not SLCMs or GLCMs), but the proposed limits were above current or planned U.S. deployments, so they were meaningless (IISA 1983–84, 32; Jensen 1988, 222–23).

Meanwhile, the MX was in deep trouble on Capitol Hill, largely because of the high "snicker factor" associated with the last basing mode, Dense Pack. A presidential commission headed by General Brent Scowcroft was appointed in January, 1983, to review the MX in the context of the nation's overall strategic posture and arms control strategy. When its report was released in April, 1983, the commission issued only a lukewarm endorsement of the MX (proposing 100 in existing Minuteman silos). More important, the commission essentially concluded that the "window of vulnerability" was a myth, though it used more diplomatic language (see NAS 1985, 61).

As if all of this were not enough for the administration to digest, there was another arms control fad in Congress—build-down. The basic idea was to permit modernization while forcing reductions by requiring old weapons to be retired as new ones came on line at a ratio of greater than 1 to 1. Certain types of weapons could be discouraged by rigging the exchange ratios. A number of very powerful figures had jumped on the build-down bandwagon, including Rep. Les Aspin (D-Wisconsin) and Senators Gore (D-Tennessee), Cohen (R-Maine), and Nunn (D-Georgia).

According to Talbott, Reagan liked the concept of build-down (1985, 306). The Pentagon civilians, however, did not (Jensen 1988, 222). The problem with build-down in their eyes was that it "aggregated" strategic weapons—it did not set specific limits for different categories of weapons. As a result, it would be possible to build more ICBMs by "buying" them with bombers and SLBMs. There might be a penalty in the form of an unfavorable exchange ratio, but it could be done. In the jargon of arms control, such aggregation permitted trade-offs and gave each side freedom to mix: "both countries would have complete freedom to determine the structure of their forces and the nature of the reductions they would make" (IISA 1983–84, 33). The State Department's position on build-down is unclear. Jensen claims that State "remained neutral" (1988, 222). Another account reports that "enthusiasm for, and the status of, build-down among administration officials . . . seems questionable at best" (IISA 1983–84, 33). Talbott notes that Burt was preoccupied with INF in the summer and fall of 1983; but he does identify Shultz, who had laid low on strategic issues up until this point, as the one who successfully persuaded Reagan of the wisdom of allowing trade-offs for different arsenal structures, which is what build-down did (1985, 339).

Indeed, 1983–84 seems to have been a crucial period in the evolution of

Reagan's views on arms control. It was during this period that Reagan, by his own admission, became aware of the fact that the Soviet Union had a very different deployment pattern than the United States. It was also during this time that Reagan's repeated claims of Soviet strategic superiority began to decline significantly; they did not disappear nor were they replaced by evaluations of parity, but assessments of Soviet superiority no longer dominated his discussions of the strategic balance. And in accepting build-down, Reagan was moving closer to an arms control strategy of offsetting asymmetries. By 1985, he was sounding more like Shultz and Burt than Perle or Weinberger (or even himself in 1981). At a January, 1985, press conference, for example, Reagan explained:

> One of the things we made clear to the Soviets is that we recognize there may be differences with regard to the mix of weapons on both sides. And we're prepared to deal with that problem, and when, perhaps, we have something that is an advantage to us, [and] they have something that is an advantage to them, to discuss trade-offs in that area. (*CPD* 1985, 36)

Build-down was incorporated into the U.S. proposal in October, 1983. It did not, however, replace the administration's warhead limits on ICBMs. But build-down's inclusion did signal a willingness to discuss the reduction of bombers and cruise missiles (SLCMs were still excluded) as the Soviet Union reduced its ballistic missiles (NAS 1985, 66). More significantly, Reagan was beginning to think in these terms. In this respect, Burt won. The problem was that throw-weight was also brought into phase one as the two phases were essentially collapsed into one. Specifics of the build-down plan were not proposed; it was simply a possibility that the two sides could explore (IISA 1983–84, 32–33; McMahan 1985, 61). Unfortunately for supporters of build-down, this potentially significant change in the U.S. position occurred at an inopportune moment. The downing of KAL 007 a few weeks earlier and the impending deployment of Pershings and GLCMs in Europe did not exactly create fertile ground for progress in START. Two months later the Soviets walked out of the START talks as threatened.

**Images and START**

Real Reductions

At the outset I noted that the administration proclaimed two goals for strategic arms control—reduce the vulnerability of U.S. forces while achieving genuine reductions. The stress on the need to reduce the vulnerability of U.S.

forces was understandable, given Reagan's perception that the Soviets either had or were close to having a first-strike capability. This was a view shared (and expressed more articulately) by Perle and Weinberger. The administration's insistence on dramatic reductions is more puzzling. There was never any definitive strategic rationale offered by the administration for why reductions were necessary. After all, drastic reductions might actually increase the vulnerability of U.S. forces, depending on how the cuts were distributed.

Why, then, the demand for dramatic reductions? There are several (mutually compatible) explanations, a few of which can be related to images of the Soviet Union. One possibility that is unrelated to images of the Soviet Union is that the attack on the SALT treaties (for not reducing weapons) was merely a convenient excuse for opposing the agreements while appearing to out arms control the arms controllers—a way to oppose SALT while still accepting arms control in principle. Once in office, the administration may have been trapped by its rhetoric into proposing the sort of reductions that SALT had been criticized for not bringing about. Alternatively, there may have been a very simplistic belief by some in the administration (the most likely candidate being Reagan himself) that there was something inherently better about having fewer nuclear weapons, perhaps because it might decrease the risk of war. Neither of these explanations has its roots in images of the Soviet Union.

For Perle and Weinberger, the emphasis on genuine reductions can be related to their beliefs about the Soviet Union. In a particularly interesting response to a question about the administration's emphasis on reductions, Weinberger explained:

> I would prefer proposals that would provide for deep reductions rather than a somewhat less practical proposal that would allow us to build up because a proposal to allow us to build up requires the process we are going through now to try and get the money; a process that the Soviets do not have to go through. So it is important to bear in mind, as I have said many times, the political differences between these systems. (U.S. Cong. 1987g, 67)

This goes back to the discussion in chapter 8 of the influence of Perle and Weinberger's image of the Soviet Union on their analysis of the arms control process. In their view, the process of arms control eroded the will of the United States to increase its defenses, whereas there was no similar diminution of will on the Soviet side. Accordingly, useful arms control had to set limits below U.S. levels, otherwise the Soviets would have the political advantages that would allow them to increase their military advantage.

In my discussion of Perle and Weinberger's overall approach to arms control, I also explained how their pessimistic analysis all but dictated the conclusion that a positive outcome from arms control was not possible. Their analysis of the political pressures in pluralistic societies, however, led them to recognize that democratic governments had to at least appear to be serious about arms control. Thus, a more cynical explanation is that the push for real reductions was a ploy or gamble designed to prevent arms control on the assumption that a worthwhile agreement was impossible with the Soviet Union. As Patrick Glynn hypothesizes, "the foundation of their strategy was the expectation that the Soviets would resist real arms cuts" (1988, 19). The fact that the Soviets actually came around to embracing such reductions does not invalidate the possibility that proposals for deep reductions were put forward in the hope, and with the expectation, that they would not be accepted. A final possibility is suggested by Newhouse, who argues that the aversion to dealing with the Soviet Union was so great in some quarters that "only reductions—deep ones—justified the unnatural act of negotiations with the enemy on so vital a subject" (1989, 344). This is consistent with Perle's comment that the United States should agree to an arms treaty only when it *significantly* shifted the strategic balance. Thus, treaties should not be signed for the marginal gains derived from tinkering with existing nuclear arsenals— it is only wise to accept agreements that transform the relationship.[1]

## Giving and Getting

Aside from the emphasis on dramatic reductions, the most obvious aspect of the Reagan administration's START proposals, including the variations considered within the administration, was their asymmetry. This was true not only in strictly quantitative terms, but also in the sense that reductions focused on those systems the Soviets valued most, the few areas where they were on a technological par with the United States. Given the shared perception of Soviet advantages in strategic weapons, this common call for asymmetrical reductions is not surprising. But this is only the most basic observation that can be made, for although all of the proposals were asymmetrical, they were not equally so.

No doubt the most radically asymmetrical proposal of them all was Perle's demand for equal ballistic missile throw-weight at 2 million kg. While it is true that the result would have been equality on this measure (though not overall because of the U.S. advantage in bombers and cruise missiles), the reductions needed to reach this point would have been anything but equal. The

---

1. It is not possible to look at the issue of reductions in terms of any policy debate within the administration because the issue was really not open to question. But, as I pointed out earlier, Burt had not criticized the SALT agreements for failing to achieve reductions.

lopsidedness of this proposal was even more pronounced because of Perle's and Weinberger's reluctance to include restrictions on those elements of the triad in which the United States enjoyed the advantage. The proposal that the Pentagon civilians supported was consistent not merely with a perception of Soviet advantages in certain strategic weapons, but with a perception of a general Soviet strategic superiority. Recall Perle's observation that the Soviets held the upper hand in virtually all areas of the strategic equation. Since the Soviets were ahead in almost all respects, the United States could not "afford" to pay for Soviet reductions with concessions of its own.

Remember that Burt and Shultz did not perceive any general Soviet superiority. Sure, the Soviets had advantages in some areas, particularly land-based ballistic missiles, but the overall strategic capabilities were roughly balanced (in their view). As I pointed out in chapter 5, Burt and Shultz never used the term *superior* to describe the Soviet arsenal, they did not use the expression "window of vulnerability," and they did not speak as if the Soviets enjoyed advantages across the board. This difference between the Burt and Shultz perception of the strategic balance and the Perle and Weinberger view is important for two reasons. First, since the United States was not entering its negotiations with the Soviet Union from a position of inferiority, there was a possibility for an agreement on somewhat favorable terms. Second, since the situation was one of rough parity, the United States could "afford" to accept restrictions in exchange for the sort of reductions being sought from the Soviet Union.

In fact, Burt's proposals did attempt to balance Soviet reductions and U.S. restrictions. It is true that his proposals were still very asymmetrical, but we have to bear in mind his attempts to expand the scope of the negotiations to include bombers and cruise missiles. Even though these moves were thwarted in their early stages, at least they demonstrated a willingness to put forward more balanced proposals. Despite Shultz's inactivity in this area during his first year in office, he did support efforts to expand the scope of the proposals and make them more equal, as was evident by his role in the build-down episode, in which he persuaded the president to accept the basic logic of what Burt had been trying to accomplish all along.

The proposals, however, were not asymmetrical simply for the purpose of being asymmetrical. Garthoff hit upon the key point in his evaluation of the Eureka plan, explaining that "the United States was not ready to accept a curtailment of its own buildup of counterforce capability comparable to the dramatic reductions in Soviet counterforce capability" (1985, 1025). One of the key criticisms of the administration's proposals, as indicated by Garthoff, was that they would permit all of the new U.S. weapons systems to go forward. The problem was that many of these weapons had counterforce capabilities, the two most important being the MX and Trident D-5 missiles.

The Soviet Union would have been required to dramatically reduce its counterforce weapons, while the United States would actually have been allowed to increase its counterforce weapons.

The administration, however, was not of one mind on how to deal with Soviet and U.S. counterforces. Recall that Burt wanted to offer the MX in exchange for the elimination of the Soviet SS-18s. In the absence of such a swap, Burt was willing to let the Soviets retain a substantial portion of their SS-18 force. Weinberger and Perle rejected both parts of the MX/SS-18 deal, insisting that the United States needed the MX even if the Soviets got rid of their SS-18s. The differences on these points reveal two things: first, Perle and Weinberger were obsessed with cutting Soviet counterforce capabilities; and second, they were relatively unconcerned about the growth of U.S. counterforce capabilities.

Perle's and Weinberger's preoccupation with the Soviet counterforce is consistent with their view that the Soviet Union either had or was very close to having a first-strike capability. Perhaps more important was their perception that this capability was consciously acquired in line with a Soviet nuclear doctrine that stressed strategic superiority and the winnability of nuclear war. This is a powerful combination of perceptions: the Soviets had a strategic doctrine that assumed that they could win a nuclear war; they had a rational and unified decision-making structure, which meant that weapons were deployed to fulfill specific missions flowing from Soviet strategic doctrine; and the Soviets were close to having what they needed for a disarming first strike. This is a constellation of beliefs that would be expected to lead to a determination to radically curtail the Soviet counterforce.

Moreover, Perle and Weinberger were convinced that the Soviets "knew" that the intentions of the United States were peaceful, so they had nothing to worry about when it came to the U.S. counterforce. This point was vividly illustrated in Weinberger's repeated assertions that "a first-strike weapon is a weapon that is used first, and we do not have intentions of doing that" (U.S. Cong. 1983l, 579). When he was asked whether the MX and the D-5 Trident missile would give the United States a first-strike capability, Weinberger responded, "No. I don't think so, sir. Really, I have always had a hard time defining first-strike weapons and first-strike capability. A first-strike weapon is a weapon you use first, but you cannot put labels on them like first, or second, or anything of the kind" (U.S. Cong. 1983o, 116).

Of course, Weinberger had no problem putting these labels on Soviet weapons. By Weinberger's logic, the United States had no first-strike weapons; therefore, why should the Soviets be concerned? After all, "they know perfectly well that we will never launch a first strike" (NBC News, 1983). It was only the Soviets who had such weapons. Why? Because they had a strategic doctrine that anticipated using them first. The circularity here is stunning, as is the influence of Weinberger's Soviet image on his view of the limitation of counterforce in arms control.

Burt and Shultz did not share this obsession with Soviet counterforce, which is not to say that they were unconcerned. Unlike Perle and Weinberger, Burt and Shultz were apparently not convinced that the Soviets had a strategic doctrine that assumed that a nuclear war could be fought and won. They did not portray Soviet decision making as a highly unified and rational process in which every procurement and deployment decision was intended to further some strategic goal. Nor did they think the Soviets were strategically superior to the United States. On the other hand, they did not seem convinced that the Soviet Union accepted the concept of mutual vulnerability and the assumption that a nuclear war could not be fought and won. Burt and Shultz wanted reductions in Soviet counterforce capabilities, and they supported proposals that would have accomplished this, but they were more flexible on the issue than Perle and Weinberger. Burt and Shultz were concerned about the Soviet counterforce, not obsessed with it. It is a subtle but important distinction.

In understanding his policy preferences on the issues of asymmetrical reductions and the treatment of counterforces, Reagan presents some problems. One problem is that many of the issues that were debated in the administration (e.g., Burt's suggestion of a ban on SLCMs and the MX/SS-18 swap) apparently never reached the president's desk. Furthermore, it is sometimes difficult to tell when, or even if, Reagan made certain decisions, even when the result was a change in the administration's negotiating position.

The more problematic issue has to do with Reagan's relative lack of knowledge about the specifics involved in the discussions of START. For the other individuals in this study, one can safely assume that they understood the implications of the proposals they crafted or supported. When Perle wanted equal ballistic missile throw-weight, there is no doubt that he knew exactly what this would do to the Soviet arsenal. Burt was also well aware of what the impact of his proposals would be. For Reagan, we cannot be so certain. When he agreed to seek equal ballistic missile throw-weight, either in phase 2 or informally in phase 1 of the START talks, we cannot assume that Reagan understood what this meant. In addition to his confession that he never really understood the concept of throw-weight, we have his surprising admission that he was unaware of the Soviet reliance on land-based missiles until after the START talks began.[2] Without understanding the basic concepts or knowing the structure of the Soviet strategic arsenal, how could Reagan know what the impact of the various throw-weight, missile, and warhead limits would be?

---

2. This also raises questions about Reagan's understanding of the "window of vulnerability." The window was thought to exist because of the Soviet Union's disproportionate reliance on ICBMs. If Reagan did not realize the extent of this reliance until 1984, why did he think there was a vulnerability problem in 1981?

More than likely, Reagan was attracted to the idea of "equality," be it in throw-weight, missiles, warheads, or whatever other measure was used, even if he was not cognizant of the inequality of the reductions needed to achieve this equality. If the Soviets enjoyed a "definite margin of superiority," any proposal that would result in equality had to be good, especially if the reductions were dramatic. This may be why Reagan was almost never firm in deciding between the options presented to him, often making compromises that had no apparent strategic rationale: since the various proposals were always framed in terms of equality, though at different levels and using different measures, Reagan was unable to differentiate among them in terms of their strategic implications.

This is not gratuitous Reagan bashing. There is an important and very tricky problem here involving the conceptualization of "policy preferences." If Perle put forward proposals that were radically asymmetrical and Reagan supported these proposals without realizing how asymmetrical they were, can we say that they had the same policy preferences? This is why substantive knowledge is a potentially crucial intervening variable shaping the relationship between images and policy preferences: without a detailed knowledge of the issues involved, particularly in a highly technical area like strategic arms control, images may provide only the most general policy guides. In this policy area, as Schwartzmann observes, "Reagan rode far above the details of launchers, warheads, and throw-weight. The issues were simple for him: the Soviets were ahead, they must not gain any advantage" (1988, 172). We might paraphrase this and say that the issues were simple for Reagan: the Soviets were ahead; the two sides should be equal, whatever that meant.

In a rudimentary sense, Reagan was on the right track when he emphasized the need to reduce "fast fliers," that is, ballistic missiles. The desire to decrease these weapons was consistent with his suspicions about Soviet nuclear intentions and his perception of Soviet strategic advantages, because ballistic missiles are counterforce weapons. Reducing these weapons was a potentially important element of "closing" any window of vulnerability and denying a disarming first-strike capability. But it is not enough simply to cut ballistic missile arsenals—they have to be cut in the right way and with a certain distribution of warheads in order to ameliorate the vulnerability.

All of Reagan's proposals would have reduced ballistic missiles; that much is obvious. But it was on the details where Reagan's proposals went awry; this is where the connection between his beliefs about the Soviet Union and his policy preferences became jumbled. The loose connection between Reagan's image and his policies is demonstrated by the fact that the START proposal announced at Eureka College would not have eliminated the window of vulnerability that so exercised the president. In fact, as Sloan and Gray point out:

The most peculiar feature of the Reagan START proposal is that it permits this problem to get worse. . . . The START proposal could lead to a situation in which the Soviet warhead to American silo ratio went from the current 4:1 to 5:1. The ratio of American warheads to Soviet silos could increase from 2:1 to 11:1. Both sides could be faced with the prospect of increased vulnerability of their ICBMs. (1983, 71)

Whatever one's opinion of it, at least Perle's original proposal had the potential for lessening the vulnerability problem because it had no missile limits, only throw-weight and warhead limits, which would have permitted (though not required) a proliferation of missiles. Such a proliferation could have decreased the warhead-to-target ratio, thereby closing the window. Reagan's initial proposal, which combined elements of Perle's and Burt's, called for dramatic reductions in ballistic missiles, but it would have done nothing to close the supposed window of vulnerability because of the distribution of warheads and missiles. This was later pointed out by the Scowcroft Commission when it recommended that a higher limit on missiles be incorporated into the U.S. START position. Perle must have realized this from the beginning, which was why he did not want missile or launcher limits, but it is doubtful that Reagan understood this.

### Philosophies of Arms Control

At an even more fundamental level, the differences among Reagan's advisers over the extent of asymmetrical reductions and the treatment of counterforces reflected a more basic disagreement on overall philosophies of arms control. Generally speaking, there are two approaches to arms control. On the one hand, there is the "balanced" or "offsetting" asymmetries approach, which had been embodied in the SALT agreements. This method "accept[s] certain inequities in certain categories so long as they are balanced by Soviet inferiority in other categories" (Hoover 1986, 103). On the other hand, there is the "equal aggregates" approach, whose standard is that "the two countries should be limited to equal quantities in all the various categories of offensive weapons systems" (102). Strictly enforced, an equal aggregates orientation would lead to a situation in which each side had essentially the same nuclear arsenal in terms of the distribution of forces and capabilities.

In theory, an offsetting asymmetries approach could lead to any number of combinations. In the area of strategic arms control, however, a balanced asymmetries approach translated into Soviet superiority in large, land-based ICBMs. No one denies that this would have been the operational result of such an approach. Proponents of balanced asymmetries were prepared to tolerate a situation in which the Soviet Union retained a nuclear force that was, at least on paper, better suited to carrying out a first strike. Although it is not often recognized by supporters of balanced asymmetries, this rests upon several assumptions about the Soviet Union. It assumes that the Soviets accept the basic logic of mutual assured destruction and, therefore, do not view a nuclear war as winnable. Closely tied to this, it also assumes that the Soviets are not attempting to acquire a disarming first-strike capability. These assumptions were largely accepted by the architects of SALT, perhaps unwittingly in some cases. If one does not agree with these assumptions about the Soviet approach to nuclear weapons, Soviet superiority in ICBMs is intolerable. Even if this superiority is at levels insufficient to actually implement a first strike, it would still be easier for the Soviets to "break out" and acquire the necessary additional forces faster than the United States. The force structure disparities accepted by advocates of balanced asymmetries are only acceptable if they are not viewed as the outcome of fundamentally incompatible nuclear objectives and strategies. If the two countries' strategies are at odds, different types of weapons systems do not really "offset" each other. More bluntly, balanced asymmetries require a certain level of trust in Soviet intentions, something that critics of SALT did not have.

As a result, it should come as no surprise that a key element of the Perle and Weinberger arms control strategy was a rejection of the balanced asymmetries approach that had dominated U.S. policy for the previous decade and its replacement with an equal aggregates approach. In line with this strategy, Perle and Weinberger opposed attempts to broaden the scope of weapons systems encompassed by the START negotiations because this would almost inevitably have led the United States down the path of offsetting asymmetries. They opposed proposals such as build-down that would have allowed the Soviets some freedom and flexibility in determining the structure of their arsenal. What Perle and Weinberger were proposing was a set of limits and sublimits that would have made the Soviet arsenal more like the U.S. arsenal so that the two sides would eventually have the same distribution of offensive weapons systems (provided that the Soviets built up in those areas of U.S. advantage). Perle and Weinberger wanted this because they assumed that existing force structure disparities reflected contending strategic doctrines.

As usual, Burt and Shultz are a little more difficult to figure out. The key problem, which has been pointed out several times already, is that we do not know exactly what Burt and Shultz thought the Soviets were up to. They apparently did not agree with the portrait of Soviet capabilities, strategy, and goals presented by Perle and Weinberger. Burt did express some concerns that the Soviets might exploit their advantages in strategic weapons for political gains in Europe, but this is different from saying the Soviets acquired these advantages as part of a plan to get a first-strike capability. At the same time, there is little evidence that Burt and Shultz accepted the views that provide the intellectual foundation for balanced asymmetries. Because of these uncertainties surrounding their beliefs, we would not necessarily predict that Burt and Shultz would adopt a balanced asymmetries orientation (as we would predict that Perle and Weinberger would favor equal aggregates). In a comparative sense, however, we would anticipate that Burt and Shultz would be more inclined to accept balanced asymmetries, or at least less insistent on equal aggregates, than Perle and Weinberger.

Though it is important to distinguish between the two basic approaches, we must realize that choosing between them is not necessarily an either/or proposition. It is possible to accept a balanced asymmetries approach while simultaneously arguing that inequalities are tolerable only within certain limits. Nonetheless, it is usually possible to identify in which direction a decision maker leans. In fact, we find that Burt and Shultz tended to fall somewhere between the two extremes, with a tendency toward balanced asymmetries. On the one hand, they were not enamored of SALT's tolerance for radically different superpower arsenal structures; but, on the other hand, they also did not feel it necessary for the United States and the Soviet Union to have the same distribution of forces, as did Perle and Weinberger. Burt and Shultz were willing to allow the Soviets an advantage in ICBMs, and they supported proposals that granted some freedom to mix, but they still wanted to reduce the imbalances in key areas. Whereas Perle and Weinberger were determined to prevent the introduction of any balanced asymmetries logic into the U.S. position, Shultz and Burt (particularly the latter) tried to pull the administration in that direction.

One of the more puzzling aspects of the START debate during Reagan's first term was his apparent, if slow, conversion to the notion of offsetting asymmetries in late 1983 (a trend that would continue over the next four years). This was signaled by Reagan's attraction to the concept of build-down after (according to Talbott) Shultz convinced him that trade-offs should be made between the two countries' areas of strength. Soon after this, Reagan began talking in the language of balanced asymmetries—discussing the willingness of the United States to take the Soviet Union's different force structure into account. This seems odd for two reasons. First, Reagan continued to argue that Soviet nuclear doctrine stressed the winnability of nuclear war and that the Soviet Union never accepted the concepts of mutual vulnerability and assured destruction. Second, Reagan had recently found out that the Soviet nuclear arsenal was top-heavy in land-based ICBMs. Presuming that Reagan realized that these weapons are exactly the kind needed to carry out a first strike, he should have been even more alarmed than before. If one believes that the Soviets think they can win a nuclear war *and* one knows that most Soviet weapons are first-strike weapons, the last thing one should want to do is accept the logic of balanced asymmetries.

## Conclusion

In my theoretical and methodological discussions, I explained that it would be unrealistic to expect the type of image analysis undertaken here to account for all the details of decision makers' policy preferences. Knowledge of Perle's beliefs about the Soviet Union, for example, would not lead us to predict that he would propose a ballistic missile warhead limit of 4,000, or that Burt would propose a limit of 1,250 ballistic missiles. Instead, I noted that images are potentially important for understanding a decision maker's policy predispositions and tendencies. They might also be useful for explaining the composition of policy coalitions by allowing us to anticipate where decision makers will stand in relation to each other on key issues. In my examination of the INF debates, I demonstrated that, below the level of the president, the decision makers did adopt policy positions that were consistent with their beliefs about the Soviet Union. Furthermore, individuals who shared the same beliefs invariably lined up on the same side of the issues. We find the same thing in the area of strategic weapons. On the most contentious issues—SALT II compliance, the extent of asymmetrical reductions, the treatment of counterforces, and philosophies of arms control—Perle, Weinberger, Burt, and Shultz had policy preferences that were consistent with their images of the Soviet Union. Again, the exception was Reagan, who supported policies that appeared to be at odds with his beliefs about the Soviet Union. Sometimes there were persuasive political explanations for this lack of congruence, but at other times his position seems genuinely puzzling unless we assume that his lack of knowledge prevented him from realizing the incongruities.

We can also observe the same pattern in terms of policy formulation and choice that we saw on INF. Perle and Burt were the ones who crafted the policy options that became the focus of debate. Weinberger and Shultz adopted the positions put forward by their institutional subordinates and intellectual brethren. Reagan rarely sided with either faction firmly or consistently, displaying a tendency to make decisions through compromise by taking some of the ideas of Burt and Shultz and combining them with those of Perle and Weinberger. The one issue on which Reagan did take the initiative, where his support was firm and unwavering, was the Strategic Defense Initiative. This would be the decisive factor shaping the arms control agenda in Reagan's second term, to which I now turn.

CHAPTER 11

# In the Shadow of SDI

The most important factor that shaped U.S. arms control efforts during Reagan's second term was his Strategic Defense Initiative (SDI). Originally announced in March, 1983, SDI was a versatile program that served the purposes of many individuals. For those who accepted Reagan's vision of a system that would make nuclear weapons obsolete by ushering in a defense-dominated superpower strategic relationship, SDI offered a way out of the strategically uncomfortable and morally questionable predicament of mutually assured destruction. But for those who had doubts about its millennial potential, SDI still had its uses. The technology resulting from an SDI research program might yield a form of defense designed to reinforce deterrence, not transcend it—point defenses or a "leaky" space shield that would complicate any Soviet first-strike calculations. For others, SDI might prove to be the key to untying the Gordian knot of arms control by inducing major Soviet concessions in offensive weapons. Indeed the irony of SDI is that it presented a potentially lethal obstacle to arms control while simultaneously creating an opportunity for undreamed of progress. Exactly which of these courses the Reagan administration would follow proved to be the great drama of arms control after 1984.

## SDI: Opportunity or Obstacle?

Although there were no negotiations between the United States and Soviet Union during 1984, there were still important developments on the arms control front. On the Soviet side, the Kremlin's geriatric leadership was on its last legs: in November, 1984, Mikhail Gorbachev took London by storm, persuading Prime Minister Thatcher that he was a man she could do business with. Of course, she could not have known that, in a few months, she would be doing business with him after Soviet General Secretary Chernenko's death in March, 1985.

On the U.S. side, 1984 began with the administration's report to Congress on Soviet treaty violations. On the political front, Reagan was preoccupied with his reelection campaign, which resulted in a landslide victory. One of the major issues throughout the campaign was SDI. Skeptics and critics who might have hoped that SDI would simply go away were sadly disappointed. If anything, SDI gathered momentum among the general public and within conservative foreign policy circles during the 1984 campaign. Supporters of SDI ran television ads portraying stick-figure children being protected from incoming missiles by a space shield. The soundtrack had one child bragging about how smart her father was for supporting SDI (and, by implication, Ronald Reagan). Most important, SDI continued to hold the imagination of the president, who was fond of comparing it to "a roof that protects a family from the rain" (*CPD* 1986, 989).

Almost as significant as Reagan's attachment to SDI was the newfound enthusiasm for the program exhibited by Perle and Weinberger (the shift was more striking in Weinberger's case). Neither had been particularly thrilled by the idea when the president gave his speech in March, 1983. Perle, who was in Lisbon at the time, spent hours on the phone to Washington doing what he could to get the address delayed or modified (Newhouse 1989, 359–60). Perle's qualms about the speech did not stem from any reverence for the ABM treaty. Almost a year before the announcement of SDI, Perle was asked, "when does the ABM treaty expire?" "I am sorry to say that it does not," he responded. Perle's objections to the speech probably had more to do with its suddenness and sweepingly utopian portrait of SDI. "It seemed unwise to me to launch a program of those dimensions without any advance preparation," Perle observed (Newhouse 1989, 361–62). Furthermore, Perle was skeptical of the whole concept of rendering nuclear weapons obsolete; the idea of a safety dome that would protect populations was, in Perle's words, "the product of millions of American teenagers putting quarters into video machines" (Talbott 1988, 231). In public, he would simply say that the president's vision was a long-term goal. But over the next three years, Perle became one of the key forces behind the so-called broad interpretation of the ABM treaty (known as the "legally correct interpretation" to its supporters), an opponent of making concessions on SDI to secure a START agreement, as well as a cautious advocate of early deployment of strategic defenses.

Weinberger's position on SDI was particularly interesting. Prior to the president's speech, he was never very encouraging about the prospects for strategic defense. Although early on he claimed that "we are going to look very carefully at the possibility of getting improved ballistic missile defenses [because] what we have now we don't believe is good enough," Weinberger was skeptical about the chances for building something good enough in the foreseeable future (U.S. Cong. 1981o, 168). In April, 1982, for example, Weinberger was questioned by Senator Jesse Helms (R-North Carolina), a High Frontier enthusiast, regarding the administration's apparent lack of commitment to pursue defenses. Weinberger assured the senator that "we are doing a great deal of exploration in space-based weapons and lasers and all of the other things out toward the frontier of space." But, he cautioned, "we do not have any indication at this point that it is anything on which we could put our reliance. . . . It would not be for a very long time." Helms continued to press the issue: "would you say that your experts upon whom you rely are unanimous that it is eighteen years away?" Weinberger answered, "I think I was being generous with that estimate. . . . Most people who look at it feel that it is considerably farther off than what I have indicated" (U.S. Cong. 1982j, 46). In line with this, Weinberger reportedly told Reagan that he could not support the ideas expressed in the SDI speech (Talbott 1988, 193). Within a very short time, however, Weinberger would be advocating Perle's broad interpretation of the ABM treaty and adamantly opposing SDI concessions. In addition, Weinberger would become the leading force behind early deployment, a position that became the litmus test used by SDI's supporters to judge an individual's fidelity to the cause (see Board 1987).

How are we to account for this conversion from skeptic to enthusiastic salesman? It cannot be traced to any change in Weinberger's Soviet image, since there was no change. As usual, however, there are number of possible explanations, some more charitable than others. First, it might be that new information about technological breakthroughs persuaded Weinberger that his previous assessment was too pessimistic. Recall that, in his exchange with Senator Helms, Weinberger only questioned the technical feasibility of strategic defenses, not their desirability. Second, Weinberger may have felt compelled to support a program about which his boss (and friend) was obviously so enthusiastic. This may have stemmed from a sense of loyalty or a calculation that his clout with the president would suffer if he did not fall in line on SDI. Finally, one can attribute the change to more crass motives by emphasizing the role SDI could play in blocking a strategic arms agreement. The fact that Weinberger's support for SDI grew in 1984 and 1985, just as the Soviets were making it clear that a START agreement would depend on SDI concessions, lends a certain surface plausibility to this thesis. Although these are not mutually exclusive possibilities, most accounts lean toward the last explanation. Making this point, Newhouse quotes one U.S. diplomat as observing, "it took several months for people like Weinberger and Perle to see [SDI's] potential for mischief" (1989, 363).

"Mischief," of course, is in the eye of the beholder. No doubt that supporters of SDI viewed the situation differently. From their perspective, it must have been the advocates of the so-called grand compromise who were being mischievous by using SDI to advance their own agenda. The basic logic of the grand compromise was to use SDI, or, more accurately, the Soviets' fear of SDI, as the ultimate trump card to get Soviet concessions on ballistic missiles. National Security Adviser McFarlane, Nitze, and Shultz were the key proponents of such a compromise (see Talbott 1988, 250–53). Those favoring an offensive/defensive trade-off found themselves in a very delicate position within the administration. On the one hand, they wanted to exploit the Soviets' obsession with SDI to reach a deal in strategic weapons; but on the other hand, they could not risk appearing to trifle with the president's vision. To do so would be to lessen their influence with Reagan and thereby endanger their cause in the long run. Shultz, Nitze, and McFarlane walked this fine line for the next four years.

## Talks Resume

Before any sort of deal could be reached, however, the negotiations had to be resumed. There were obstacles on both sides. On the U.S. side, the administration was immersed in the campaign, and since a landslide seemed likely despite the absence of any arms control negotiations, there was no pressing political imperative to revive the talks. On the Soviet side, there was no evidence of any willingness to return to Geneva until the summer of 1984, when it must have become obvious that Reagan was going to win the election anyway. Even more ominous in Soviet eyes must have been the steam SDI picked up during the campaign. Thus, the Soviets must have realized that SDI and Reagan were going to be around for a while.

   Throughout 1984, Shultz tried his best to get the talks underway. It is not clear whether Shultz ran into opposition or simply apathy from Perle and Weinberger. In any case, they were opposed to making any changes in the U.S. position to lure the Soviets back to the table. Perle and Weinberger resisted the alterations recommended by Burt and Shultz, which involved additional constraints on bombers and cruise missiles as well as a bit more leniency in treating Soviet ballistic missiles. Reagan also did not like the idea of offering preemptive concessions for the sake of resuming negotiations (Talbott 1985, 343–62). Shultz's efforts finally bore fruit after the November election in a series of talks with the new Soviet Foreign Minister, Eduard Shevardnadze (Shultz, who supposedly did not get along with Gromyko, got on very well with Shevardnadze). At a meeting in Geneva in January, 1985, Shultz and Shevardnadze announced that arms control negotiations, officially dubbed the Nuclear and Space Talks, would resume in March. These would be "umbrella talks" in the sense that they would deal with all three classes of weapons—INF, strategic systems, and defenses—"in their interrelationship." This formulation was sufficiently ambiguous to satisfy every constituency— those who wanted an offensive/defensive trade-off as well as those who wanted a managed transition to a defensive strategic relationship.

   When the negotiations resumed in March, the participants picked up pretty much where they had left off—in a stalemate. The United States entered with the same position it had put forward in October, 1983–1,200 ballistic missile launchers, 5,000 warheads on these missiles (no more than half on ICBMs), sublimits on heavy and medium missiles, and the possibility of limits on ALCMs and bombers equipped with them (IISA 1985–86, 50). Build-down was still in the U.S. proposal, but it was no longer the fad in Washington it had been in 1983. The Soviets did not really have a concrete proposal other than a demand that SDI be banned (IISA 1985–86, 51). Just as the talks were beginning in Geneva, news arrived from Moscow of Chernenko's death. Shortly thereafter it was learned that he was succeeded by the man who had so impressed Thatcher five months earlier, Gorbachev. Within a few months, it became obvious that the new leader's approach to arms control bore little resemblance to his predecessor's, except in his obsession with SDI.

Once Shultz had managed to get the arms talks back on track, he turned his attention to arranging a summit meeting between Reagan and Gorbachev. Although Reagan was certain to be attracted to the idea of meeting the Soviet leader face to face, given his confidence in the value of personal meetings and his own persuasive abilities, others in the administration were not so favorably inclined. According to one U.S. diplomat involved in setting up the meeting: "only a handful of people at State were pushing for it . . . Nancy Reagan and Mike Deaver were very helpful. But Casey, Meese, and Weinberger were Mau-Mauing the enterprise. Reagan himself seemed most interested in finding out whether Gorbachev believed in God" (Newhouse 1989, 386). In the end, Shultz prevailed; a summit set for November in Geneva was announced on July 2.

In addition to the agreement on a summit, there were more positive developments in the summer of 1985. Most important were hints from the Soviet negotiators that they might finally be willing to accept the principle of deep cuts in offensive forces. The concept of 50 percent reductions was officially advanced by Shevardnadze during his September visit to Washington to prepare for the Geneva summit (Jensen 1988, 224). A formal proposal was put forward in Geneva in early October. The cornerstone of the Soviet plan was a limit of 6,000 nuclear "charges" (the Soviet term for warheads on strategic delivery vehicles, including bombers). This was approximately half of existing arsenals. Furthermore, the Soviets proposed a maximum of 60 percent in any one component of strategic arsenals, which would have meant a maximum of 3,600 ICBM warheads (IISA 1985–86, 53). Even without the strings attached to SDI, this was not entirely to the administration's liking. The 6,000 warhead limit would include all warheads aboard bombers (including gravity bombs) but would exempt key Soviet systems (e.g., the Backfire bomber, which the Soviets had always maintained did not have strategic range). In addition, the Soviets wanted a ban on cruise missiles. Still, the Soviets had come a long way in accepting the principle of deep reductions on offensive missiles, as well as agreeing to significant sublimits on ICBMs.

In response to the Soviet proposal, the United States revised its position, accepting the figure of 6,000 nuclear charges. The new proposal called for a limit of 1,250–1,450 ballistic missiles, a maximum of 3,000 ICBM warheads, and a sublimit of 1,500 on heavy ICBMs. In exchange, the United States would accept a limit of 1,500 ALCMs (a 50 percent cut from planned deployments) and 350 strategic bombers (see IISA 1985–86, 54; Talbott 1988, 275). The key concession in this proposal was that it allowed the Soviets to keep more weapons in their area of advantage while the United States would accept some genuine restrictions in its area of advantage: "In this sense," one study concluded, "the U.S. had at last put flesh on the idea of trading off force asymmetries" (IISA 1985–86, 55). From the Soviet perspective, however, the United States was still not willing to trade enough—it would not abandon SDI.

## The Broad and Narrow

The sudden movement by the two sides raised the question of what the United States was going to do about SDI and its apparent conflict with the ABM treaty. The Soviets were adamant in predicating any START agreement on continued U.S. adherence to the ABM treaty for a minimum of twenty years. The universal interpretation of the ABM treaty since its ratification in 1972 was that it permitted only basic laboratory research, which could not be verified in any case, but prohibited any development, testing, or deployment of defensive systems. It is easy to understand why people thought this, given the treaty's injunction that "each side undertakes not to develop, test, or deploy ABM systems which are sea-based, air-based, space-based, or mobile-land based" (for the text, see Labrie 1979, 15–19). Supporters of SDI within the administration countered that this common understanding was mistaken; in fact, they argued, the treaty permitted just about everything short of deployment. This so-called broad interpretation was the brainchild of Perle (Talbott 1988, 233). The irony here was not lost on most: the person who frequently charged the Soviets with taking advantage of loopholes and technicalities to violate the spirit of arms agreements was now doing the same thing. Weinberger quickly agreed with this broad interpretation. It also went over well with Reagan, since he could proceed with SDI without worrying about violating an agreement.

The only major figure who was not pleased by this ABM revisionism was Shultz, and fortunately for him, he had allies outside the administration to compensate for his loneliness within it. Whether Shultz had an opinion about the "correct" interpretation of the ABM treaty is unclear. Undoubtedly, however, he realized that an insistence on the broad interpretation would severely hamper attempts to reach a START (and INF) agreement. Certainly he was not alone in recognizing this. In order to head off a collision with the Soviets, the ABM treaty, and congressional critics, Shultz persuaded Reagan to adopt a compromise position reminiscent of the administration's SALT II policy: the United States would conduct SDI research within the confines of the narrow interpretation of the ABM treaty while it asserted that development and testing would be fully justified (see Newhouse 1989, 301; Talbott 1988, 247). But this was not a long-term solution to the problem: the Soviets and congressional critics would not be satisfied with this for long, and neither would SDI's supporters.

The Geneva summit came and went without any major developments. The talks between the two leaders bogged down into a familiar stalemate: Reagan persisted in emphasizing the value of SDI, denying any aggressive designs; Gorbachev explained that, like Reagan, he had to focus on the other side's capabilities and could not rely on assurances about intentions. The one interesting sidelight was the absence of Perle and Weinberger, who were left back in Washington. On the eve of the summit, a "private" letter from Weinberger to Reagan urging him to stand firm on SDI was leaked to the press, much to the dismay of those in Geneva. Perle and Weinberger, of course, denied any knowledge of the leak; others were suspicious. The summit ended with an agreement to pursue 50 percent reductions and a communiqué in which both sides agreed that a nuclear war could not be fought or won.

## Toward Reykjavík

The nuclear disarmament one-upmanship that reached a crescendo at Reykjavík actually began shortly after the Geneva summit. In January, 1986, the Soviets made their boldest proposal to date: a plan for complete nuclear disarmament by the end of the century. There were two phases to the plan. In the first phase, the two superpowers would reduce their strategic arsenals by 50 percent over five to seven years. The remaining weapons would be eliminated over the next ten years, provided the world's other nuclear powers joined in (IISA 1985–86, 56; Jensen 1988, 225). How much of this was propaganda as opposed to serious proposal is an open question. The important thing was that the Soviets were finally taking the president up on his oft-repeated desire for a total elimination of nuclear weapons. Was Reagan bluffing? Were the Soviets? In order to find out, one major obstacle remained—all this was tied to continued adherence to the ABM treaty as it had been traditionally interpreted.

The United States responded to the Soviet initiative with one of its own, this time from the desks of Perle and Weinberger. Since the Soviets were talking in terms of eliminating nuclear weapons, Perle and Weinberger put a new twist on the idea: they proposed that the two countries agree to the elimination of ballistic missiles. This idea, which would appear again at Reykjavík, became known as Zero Ballistic Missiles (ZBM). Nitze, Shultz, and the uniformed military thought that the concept was silly and unrealistic (Talbott 1988, 308). They might also have added that it was transparently one-sided: if ballistic missiles were eliminated, the Soviets would have almost no nuclear arsenal, whereas the United States would retain a tremendous quantitative and qualitative advantage in bombers and cruise missiles. But the idea was almost certain to appeal to Reagan, since it would eliminate "fast flyers." Reagan suggested the idea to Gorbachev in a letter on July 25 (IISA 1986–87, 55).

This almost dizzying round of new proposals once again brought the question of SDI to the fore. What was the United States going to say about SDI and the ABM treaty? Shultz wanted to continue with the compromise announced the previous year—abide by the narrow interpretation while claiming the broad one was correct. Weinberger and Perle wanted the United States to commit itself unequivocally to the broad interpretation. In his letter containing the ZBM idea, Reagan indicated a willingness to guarantee no deployment of SDI for seven-and-a-half years but accepted no constraints on development and testing. Since nothing would be ready to deploy for more than seven years, this was a pseudoconcession (IISA 1986–87, 56).

### A Chill Wind Blows: The Reykjavík Summit

After a series of letters in the summer of 1986, Gorbachev surprised everyone by suggesting a meeting between the two leaders before the anticipated Washington summit, which was in the works for late 1986 or early 1987. He identified London and Reykjavík (a meeting halfway between the two countries) as possible sites (IISA 1986–87, 58). Gorbachev's motives for urging such a meeting are, of course, a matter of debate. A favorable interpretation is that he concluded that a personal meeting was the only way to break the logjam emerging on START and SDI. A less charitable view is that Gorbachev set Reagan up for a public relations fiasco in order to influence upcoming congressional elections. Moscow might have imagined the headlines: "Reagan and SDI Prevent Disarmament." An additional benefit might have been the damage to the Atlantic alliance caused by fears of Reagan's willingness to contemplate such revolutionary proposals without consultation. Why the administration agreed is also open to speculation, but there might have been hopes of favorable press before the elections to help the president's party. Foreign policy spectacles are always good for a few percentage points in the polls. In any case, the meeting was set for October 11–12 at Reykjavík. The Soviets misled the administration to anticipate fairly informal talks, not real negotiations. In fact, Gorbachev showed up ready to deal (or at least ready to convey the impression that he was ready to deal); the United States did not, but it dealt anyway.

What happened at Hofdi House that weekend has been described as "puzzling," "bizarre," "surreal," and even "lunacy." Margaret Thatcher was appalled—"shook rigid," as one of her aides put it—when she learned that only a few words stood in the way of a complete transformation of the postwar security system (Newhouse 1989, 398). It will probably be years before the complete details are known and even longer before we fully understand the dynamics, personal and interpersonal, that propelled the participants to the brink of complete nuclear disarmament. But despite Haley's contention that the events of that weekend were "without warning," there was substantial continuity in the positions the key U.S. participants took on arms control and strategic defense.

The setting may have been different, and participants of slightly higher rank, but the issues at Reykjavík were the same as those in Geneva. Which weapons would be cut? By how much? How should the cuts be distributed? What, if any, restrictions should be placed on defenses? By this point the idea of dramatic reductions was accepted as a given; in this sense, Reagan's supporters are correct when they note how he reshaped the whole arms control debate. Furthermore, both sides seemed settled on the figure of 50 percent reductions. Exactly what this meant was another matter. Gorbachev opened his meeting with Reagan by proposing just that—a 50 percent across-the-board reduction in strategic arsenals (bombers, ballistic missiles, and cruise missiles) (see Haley 1987, 83; Talbott 1988, 318). The kicker in this scheme was the across-the-board formulation: if both sides halved their arsenals category by category, the existing distribution of capabilities would remain the same, only at lower levels. Reagan and Gorbachev delegated the issue to working groups.

The key U.S. figures were Nitze, Perle, Rowny, and Colonel Robert Linhard, a member of the NSC staff (Weinberger was back in Washington). They immediately saw through the across-the-board formula and reiterated that reductions would have to result in equal ceilings, particularly for ICBMs. It would not suffice to mirror existing inequalities at lower levels. The U.S. leaders insisted on subceilings of the type on the table at Geneva (6,000 warheads, 1,600 launchers, and no more than 3,000 ICBM warheads). Unable to find common ground, the meeting broke up in the early morning.

Nitze appealed to Shultz for the authority to raise the ICBM warhead limit to 3,600. This was more than the United States had or probably ever would have; the Soviet Union had more already and would certainly retain the maximum. The United States could have more SLBMs to compensate, but the Soviets would have a large ICBM advantage. Perle and Rowny opposed this move in the direction of offsetting asymmetries. Shultz, however, gave permission to raise the ICBM warhead ceiling. When the two sides got back together, Nitze discovered that his pleadings were wasted: the Soviets agreed to the principle of equal ceilings, the first time they had done so. Although disagreements remained over how this principle would be translated into concrete numbers, it was a significant concession by the Soviets.

But it was not this agreement on the principle of equal ceilings that made Reykjavík a unique event in the history of arms control; it was the feverish round of arms control proposals that followed. In the next meeting between Reagan and Gorbachev, the president continued his attempts to convert the Soviet leader to the wisdom of SDI. He restated his promise to share the technology (at cost). Gorbachev reminded Reagan that the United States would not even sell certain industrial technologies. Why should he believe that some future U.S. president would (or could) hand over SDI technology (Haley 1987, 84-86)? Gorbachev insisted on an agreement to abide by the ABM treaty (strictly interpreted) for ten years (down from the previous demand of twenty). Reagan stayed with his pledge of seven-and-a-half years (narrowly interpreted). Gorbachev wanted the issue resolved at Reykjavík, predicting that "if this goes back to Geneva, we'll be eating this porridge for years" (Talbott 1988, 322). Again, the issue was delegated to the experts.

Shultz, Perle, and Linhard attempted to break the impasse by resurrecting the ZBM idea contained in Reagan's July 25 letter. This time, however, it was put in the form of a concrete proposal. They suggested two five-year phases. During the first, each side would reduce its strategic arsenal by half while continuing to abide by the ABM treaty. In the second phase, all remaining ballistic missiles would be destroyed and ABM treaty adherence would continue. After the two phases were complete, each side would be free to deploy defenses. "Adherence," however, referred to the broad interpretation; thus, development and testing would be permitted throughout the ten-year disarmament process.

Reagan put this plan on the table when he met with Gorbachev on Sunday afternoon. The Soviet criticisms could have been predicted: the broad interpretation was unacceptable, as was the focus on ballistic missiles. Gorbachev countered with a more detailed version of his January, 1986, proposal, going one step further than Reagan by proposing the elimination of all strategic weapons over the ten years. Reagan's reaction is a matter of controversy. By all secondhand accounts, including the one provided by Donald Regan (1988), Reagan agreed to the elimination of all strategic weapons. Shortly after the return to Washington, however, the administration line was that Reagan only agreed *in principle* to such disarmament as a long-term goal. But, in the end, it all fell through because Reagan would not concede Gorbachev's demand that SDI development and testing be restricted to the laboratory (IISA 1986–87, 64). This, in the president's mind, would have killed SDI. The participants left Hofdi House with dour expressions. The events of the next two years would confirm Gorbachev's prediction about eating the SDI/START porridge for years.

### Back to Earth—And Full Speed Ahead?

For those who experienced the heady days of Reykjavík, the aftermath must have been a rude awakening. Opposition to the agreements almost reached at the summit—both ZBM and complete strategic disarmament—emerged from all quarters. Margaret Thatcher and François Mitterrand made it clear that they would have no part of any grandiose disarmament plan; they intended to keep their weapons, thank you. The Joint Chiefs were stunned that such drastic proposals would be seriously considered without an extensive study of their military ramifications. Weinberger, who had supported ZBM when it was a vague idea in the summer, opposed the elimination of ballistic missiles. After listening to the sobering arguments of European allies and the military, Shultz returned to his initial skepticism of ZBM. Within a few months, ZBM and complete strategic disarmament disappeared from the arms control agendas of the two sides.

After the recriminations about the failure of Reykjavík died down, the two sides made some substantial progress on START, particularly in terms of Soviet acceptance of various subceilings for ICBMs (IISA 1987–88, 41). But again, this progress was impeded by developments on the SDI side of the START equation. In Washington, there was a move afoot to commit the United States unambiguously to the broad interpretation by pressing ahead full speed with a phased, early deployment of a defensive system. Within the administration, the leading advocates of early deployment were Perle and Weinberger, especially the latter. Nitze was proposing a series of talks with the Soviets to determine what was and was not permitted by the ABM treaty. Perle and Weinberger fought Nitze on this; after all, the United States already knew what was allowed. Already suspect in the eyes of SDI's supporters, Shultz did not go to bat for Nitze, and the issue never reached the president.

The renewed push for the broad interpretation and the new plan for a phased deployment of SDI were probably motivated by two concerns. First, as the superpowers moved closer together in START, the only way to forestall an agreement was to drive a wedge into the talks with defense issues. Second, there may have been fears that SDI might not survive the departure of its strongest supporter, the president; as a result, the best way to ensure SDI's future was to get as far along on deployment as possible.

The most forceful advocate of early deployment was Weinberger. In the months after Reykjavík, the secretary of defense began to deliver glowingly optimistic updates about the progress of SDI research to the president (Talbott 1988, 329). Reagan was thrilled that his pet program was progressing so splendidly. Weinberger and Perle urged the president to move away from the ten-year ABM adherence figure that was suggested at Reykjavík in conjunction with the refined ZBM proposal. In this they were successful; the administration announced that it was reverting back to the seven-and-a-half-year pledge contained in Reagan's letter of July 25. Like everyone else in the administration, Weinberger denied that SDI was, or should be, a bargaining chip in the START negotiations. Furthermore, he continued to argue that SDI was going to defend populations, not missile sites or other strategic assets: "we want a system that would destroy weapons and not people, that would protect entire continents. It would not be designed to defend missile sites or anything of the kind, but would protect populations." Weinberger added with a sense of urgency, "we want strategic defense and we want to get it deployed" (U.S. Cong. 1987d, 112, 128).

Although Weinberger anticipated an effective population defense, he did not want to wait until one was available before deploying something. In the winter of 1986–87, Weinberger came out for early or phased deployment of SDI. In an article for a major foreign affairs journal, Weinberger argued:

> The United States can now look forward to a phased introduction of each element of a whole system. This is not a new idea, of course; it has been accepted since the earliest days of the president's program. . . . The administration perceives opportunities to begin describing technologies and concepts for a first phase . . . Phase 1 would yield great benefit. It would enhance deterrence by complicating the USSR's ability to gain a decisive advantage [and,] . . . it would severely restrict the confidence level Soviet leaders could have in a first strike designed to disable Western retaliatory forces and essential communications links. (1987, 16–17)

In addition to the fact that Weinberger advocated a first phase deployment, there were two interesting features of his proposal. First, the initial phase would be designed to strengthen deterrence, not transcend it. Second, while this sort of leaky shield would certainly save lives in the event of a Soviet strike, its primary purpose would be to protect the targets of the first strike—Western retaliatory forces.

Perle was a little bit more restrained, both in terms of the population protection potential of SDI and the decision for early deployment. A year before Weinberger began to push for a phased deployment, Perle explained that:

I think it is likely to be the case that a first generation of SDI, whether it proves to be capable of defending the population or not, it would greatly improve the credibility of our deterrent, and I think it is worth pursuing for that reason alone. . . . If it ultimately leads to the sort of defense that is part of the president's long-term vision, so much the better, but I think one need not assume that in order [to] justify carrying on with our program. (U.S. Cong. 1985o, 72)

Perle did not directly come out in support of an early deployment of the "first generation," as he called it, but the germ of the proposal was there. After Weinberger's article calling for phased deployment was published, Perle was again questioned about the idea, and his response was still cautious.

I support the SDI program of research, development, and testing; and if it is successful, then I would support deployment. In other words, I have no disagreement in principle with deploying a strategic defense . . . [but] any early deployment of SDI, any first generation or probably even second generation or third generation system, is not going to be an impermeable shield stopping all missiles. But a defense that significantly diminished the number of missiles that would reach their targets in the United States would, in the first instance, add significantly to the credibility of our deterrent, in my judgment. (U.S. Cong. 1987c, 88)

Again, this was not an explicit endorsement, but it was close. Perle, however, would not be around long enough to see what came of the idea in the administration. The day after the quoted statement, Perle submitted his resignation, announcing that he would be leaving in the early summer. Five months later, Weinberger would follow suit, citing his wife's poor health as the reason. That Weinberger left only weeks before the signing of the INF treaty was judged to be more than a coincidence by some observers, most of whom were skeptical of the official reason for his departure. The more likely explanation is probably found in Perle's lament that it was "getting to be springtime for arms control around here" (Talbott 1988, 360).

On the surface at least, Shultz managed to stay in step with the rest of the administration. He paid homage to SDI and denied that it was a bargaining chip, but he did so in less adamant terms than others in the administration. For example, on the eve of the Reykjavík summit, Shultz was asked whether restrictions on SDI could be accepted in the context of reductions in offensive forces. He responded that the President's proposal to eliminate ballistic missiles "radically changes what you need to do to defend against them, and I think that's a pretty obvious proposition" (*DSB*, December, 1986, 6). Was Shultz saying that SDI could be compromised in exchange for Soviet concessions on offensive systems? It depends on how you read it. This vague idea that less offensive capabilities would "change" the need for, or requirements of, strategic defense was as close as Shultz would come to saying SDI was negotiable, but it was closer than anyone else in the administration came.

On the issue of early deployment, Shultz was even more cautious than Perle.

> Any such decision must be based on a careful appraisal of where we are in finding out about the feasibility, the survivability, and cost-effectiveness at the margins of such a system. As I said earlier, it is my impression from my contact with the program that it has been going quite well. But I do not have any sense that there is, as I think Admiral Crowe said to this committee, something in the parking lot that you can decide about. (U.S. Cong. 1987c, 818)

This was a lukewarm endorsement to say the least. Asked about the utility of a leaky shield defense, Shultz claimed that this type of system could be "an important contribution *potentially* to the system of deterrence because it makes your capability of avoiding a first strike greater, *assuming* that it works out" (*DSB*, September, 1986, 26; italics added). In a February, 1988, speech, Shultz assured his audience that "we will continue a vigorous SDI program *to see whether* strategic stability *might* rest increasingly on defense-based deterrence . . . because it *may* establish a basis *in the future* for a safer way to secure international peace" (*DSB*, April, 1988, 42; italics added). It was as if SDI was getting less promising by the day. Thus, unlike others in the administration, Shultz was equivocal about the status of SDI as a bargaining chip, while he consistently downplayed the progress being made in SDI research.

Much to the dismay of conservatives, once Perle and Weinberger were gone, the idea of phased deployment of SDI apparently disappeared from the administration's agenda. Perle was replaced by Frank Gaffney, who largely shared his views but lacked Perle's political skills. More important, however, was Weinberger's replacement by Frank Carlucci, who had been serving as Reagan's national security adviser. Carlucci had never been enthralled by SDI or impressed by technological advances in the field. Thus, by the end of 1987, Reagan was surrounded by advisers whose commitment to SDI did not match his own.

Despite these changes, Reagan's support for SDI never wavered. He was firm in arguing that "SDI is not now, nor will it ever become, a mere bargaining chip. I've said for a long time that the doctrine of mutual assured destruction, what's called MAD, is downright immoral" (*CPD* 1987, 321). Reagan was willing to talk about SDI in the context of a leaky shield whose purpose was to introduce uncertainty into Soviet first-strike calculations. For example, in a 1988 interview, Reagan explained that "even before it becomes leak proof, strategic defense will strengthen deterrence. It can make anyone who might think about disabling the West with a first strike think again" (*CPD* 1988, 245). Unlike Weinberger, however, Reagan did not speak explicitly in terms of a plan for phased or early deployment. Indeed, there is no evidence that Reagan ever made a decision about whether or not to plan for this type of deployment. The Reagan years ended with SDI in limbo and START stuck in neutral.

**Images, START, and SDI**

**START under SDI**

Unfortunately for our purposes, the available accounts of arms control during Reagan's second term tend to focus on the internal debates over SDI; relatively little attention is devoted to what transpired before and during some of the shifts in the administration's START position. As a result, changes in policy in this area are often presented without any account of the debates that accompanied them. There are at least two reasons for this. First, once the initial set of debates had been "resolved" between 1981 and 1983, the administration's START policy did not change much until the dramatic events surrounding Reykjavík. As was the case with INF, the more important changes were in the Soviet position, not the U.S. position. Second, the main issue was no longer START per se, but rather SDI and its relationship to START, so the focus of the disagreements within the administration shifted.

What we do have suggests that the trends that emerged from 1981 to 1983 continued. Perle and Weinberger were still committed to equalizing ballistic missile throw-weight, and this remained part of the administration's formal proposal, even though not very much was heard about it. Attempts to expand the scope of the talks by including areas of U.S. strategic strength were opposed. Perle and Weinberger resisted efforts to pull the U.S. position further in the direction of offsetting asymmetries. Overall, there was no noticeable change in the Pentagon civilians' approach to START.

Shultz's involvement and interest in arms control issues increased substantially during Reagan's second term, and he was obviously more comfortable with some of the complex and technical matters that he avoided during his first two years in office, though he was still not as conversant as Perle. Despite his newfound confidence and increasing activism, Shultz did not become a policy leader in the sense of putting forward new ideas. With Burt out of the picture, Shultz relied more on Nitze, who generally sided with Burt in the INF and START battles of the early Reagan years. It was Shultz who tried to bring the two sides back together during 1984, even though others in the administration seemed not to care. Shultz continued to support efforts to include U.S. concessions on bombers and cruise missiles in exchange for Soviet reductions in ballistic missiles. He sided with Nitze in his attempts to move the U.S. position further in the direction of offsetting asymmetries, which involved a more lenient treatment of Soviet ICBMs. Though it is still difficult to identify an underlying strategic logic motivating Shultz's efforts to revise the U.S. position, he was clearly interested in moving the situation along. The difficulty of identifying any guiding strategic logic behind Shultz's efforts is consistent with my analysis of his overall approach to arms control (chap. 8).

Because of the somewhat limited coverage of the debates surrounding the evolution of the administration's START position toward a balanced asymmetries orientation, it is difficult to say when, how, or even whether Reagan was involved in the more important decisions. Presumably, he approved of them; in which case, he continued to move in the direction indicated by his support for build-down in 1983; that is, toward allowing trade-offs in the superpowers' areas of strength. But we should be careful not to exaggerate this shift—the basics of the administration's policy remained the same. This seems to run counter to the widespread perception that there was a significant alteration of the president's approach to arms control during the first half of his second term. If there were any dramatic changes in Reagan's approach, it was in the realm of intangibles, such as his enthusiasm for negotiations and summits and perhaps even an increased desire to reach an agreement; but there were no radical alterations in the content of the administration's START policies.

## Zero Ballistic Missiles

The exception to this was, of course, the series of proposals considered during the Reykjavík summit and the months leading up to it. The proposals that were bandied about during this period were so grandiose and incredible that it is difficult to know what to make of them. It is hard to distinguish between sincere proposals and silly propaganda; it is impossible to tell where genuine policy preferences ended and negotiating ploys began; and it is difficult to tell who took what proposals seriously (this applies equally to the United States and the Soviet Union).

The most dramatic new U.S. proposal in 1986 was the plan to eliminate all ballistic missiles, ZBM. Proposed by Perle and initially supported by Weinberger, ZBM was certainly bold. In many respects, it was consistent with Perle's previous proposals and his image of the Soviet Union. The emphasis on asymmetrical reductions, ballistic missiles, and counterforces carried the underlying premises of his earlier ideas to their logical extremes. On another level, however, it is hard to square ZBM with Perle's beliefs about Soviet treaty behavior. One of the key criticisms of a plan such as ZBM was that it would greatly increase the benefits to be derived from cheating. For a country as vast as the Soviet Union, it would be nearly impossible to guarantee that a few dozen ballistic missiles were not hidden away somewhere. If fifty ballistic missiles suddenly appeared in the midst of some future crisis, the Soviet Union would have a substantial advantage (the Joint Chiefs were quick to point this out upon the delegation's return to Washington). Given Perle's deeply ingrained suspicions about Soviet trustworthiness, it is difficult to imagine why he would want to risk this (Perle's earlier proposals would have reduced Soviet ballistic missiles, but they would have left virtually all U.S. ICBMs intact. In this situation, it would have been necessary to hide a lot of missiles in order to achieve an advantage by cheating). Perhaps more important, ZBM had something else in common with Perle's other proposals—it was certain to be unacceptable to the Soviets. Perle must have known this. According to Smith, Perle even predicted to one colleague that "the Soviets will save us; they'll never accept" (1988, 643). He was right, they didn't.

Shultz's position on ZBM is slightly confusing. Talbott reports that he did not like the idea very much when it was first proposed by Perle during the summer. But it does not seem as though he was opposed to it outright; he simply thought it was an unrealistic, and therefore counterproductive, attempt to match the Soviet Union's dramatic proposals for complete disarmament. His support for ZBM at Reykjavík was momentary—shortly after returning to Washington, he reverted to his original skepticism. Why did he sign onto ZBM at the summit? It seems as though he was motivated by a desire to keep the momentum of the talks going. The United States had to offer something in response to Gorbachev's proposals. There was not much time to be very creative. As Smith speculates, "Shultz, whose knowledge of arms issues [was] limited, felt a momentous opportunity was at hand and was eager to seize it" (1988, 643). Perle revived ZBM. Shultz did not have any better ideas at the moment, so why not go for it? Shultz, as he was prone to do, was simply "moving the situation along."

Reagan's support for ZBM is consistent with his preoccupation with fast flyers, as it would have eliminated all of them. As a result, ZBM is consistent with his image of the Soviet Union in that it focused on those weapons the Soviets would use to strike first. But there is the same problem for Reagan that we discussed with regard to Perle: the apparent inconsistency of supporting a proposal that increases the strategic incentive to cheat when one thinks the other party cannot be trusted. And if Reagan really did agree to Gorbachev's proposal for total strategic disarmament, the inconsistency grows even larger because of the strategic windfall that would accrue to the nation that retained only a handful of any kind of strategic weapons. Reagan, however, had an answer to this: that is why SDI was needed, even in the face of a dramatic reduction or elimination of ballistic missiles—"it will underwrite all of us against Soviet cheating" (*CPD* 1987, 1375; see also *CPD* 1986, 1378, 1387, 1393).

## Images and SDI as a Defense

The debate over SDI centered on two issues, the system's technical feasibility and its strategic desirability. These are logically distinct issues—one can argue that defenses are desirable but not feasible or, conversely, feasible but not desirable. Though logically separate, the two may be cognitively intertwined. There is some support for the thesis that people tend to evaluate more favorably the feasibility of doing those things they find desirable, whereas they tend to underestimate the feasibility of doing those things they find undesirable. Jervis discusses such "irrational consistency," labeling it "intellectual overkill" (1976, 128–42). On the question of desirability, there were two "minidebates"—was it necessary to construct a potentially very expensive system to protect the United States against a Soviet nuclear attack, and would the deployment of such a system be destabilizing? It is reasonable to expect images to play a role in how a decision maker answers both questions.

Defenses are not needed if there is nothing to defend against. Defenses become more necessary as the imminence and seriousness of the threat increases. These seem like fairly basic assumptions. As a result, we would expect a decision maker's position on SDI to be related to his or her perception of the threat posed by the Soviet Union. In this case, the most important aspects of his or her image are likely to be beliefs about the Soviet Union's nuclear capabilities, objectives, and doctrine. That is, if the Soviet Union is thought to possess the ability and willingness to launch an attack, the decision maker should favor moving ahead with defenses; if the Soviet Union does not have the ability or willingness to attack, the decision maker should be more likely to oppose a move toward defenses. (Because a decision maker might deem defense desirable, but not feasible, this expectation cannot be ironclad).

Given this basic prediction, there are no surprises in the Reagan administration. There is no need to rehash the various decision makers' perceptions of the Soviet Union's nuclear capabilities, objectives, and doctrine yet again. Suffice it to point out that those who believed the Soviet Union was strategically superior (or nearly so), was striving to acquire a first strike, and viewed nuclear war as winnable (i.e., Reagan, Perle, and Weinberger), favored SDI in some form and opposed any concessions.

These, however, are the easy cases. What if we have a decision maker who is not quite sure about Soviet intentions? Shultz might fall into this category. In a case like this, there are problems. As we have indicated several times before, the first problem is that we do not have a very clear picture of Shultz's views regarding Soviet nuclear intentions. Whether this stems from shortcomings of the evidence or a genuine uncertainty on Shultz's part we cannot know for sure. The second problem is that we do not know exactly what his position on SDI was. He was obviously more willing to consider limitations on SDI than Perle, Weinberger, and Reagan, and Shultz was not an advocate of early deployment. Furthermore, he tried to keep the United States committed to the ABM treaty. But how far was he willing to go in negotiating limits on SDI? What did he mean when he said that less offense "changes" the requirements for defense? The only definite conclusions we can reach for Shultz are negative: he did not accept the view of Soviet capabilities and intentions presented by Perle, Weinberger, and Reagan. Consistent with this, he did not share their view of the need for SDI. Precisely how great his disagreement with them was remains a mystery.

The other aspect of SDI's desirability concerns its impact on nuclear stability. The criticism was that SDI would be destabilizing because the Soviets would perceive it as an attempt to render their retaliatory forces impotent, thereby allowing the United States to attack (or threaten to attack) with impunity. Thus, a decision maker's evaluation of the effect of SDI on strategic stability should be related to his or her beliefs about how the Soviets view the United States. If the Soviets are thought to fear the United States, then SDI should be deemed destabilizing; if the Soviets "know" that the United States poses no threat, then SDI would not be destabilizing. I have already shown that Perle and Weinberger were convinced that the Soviets did not view the United States as threat; they thought the Soviets were fully aware of the peaceful intentions of the United States. Consistent with this, they never betrayed any concerns about the destabilizing potential of strategic defenses (in U.S. hands, that is).

Reagan presents an interesting case. On some occasions, Reagan seemed to agree with Perle and Weinberger's view that Soviet protests about the U.S. threat were merely smokescreens designed to rationalize the Soviet military buildup. But at other times, he spoke of the Soviet-U.S. rivalry as being propelled by *mutual* suspicions, which suggested that the Soviets did fear the United States, perhaps unjustifiably. Reagan was fond of asking, "how is Moscow threatened if other nations are defended" (*CPD* 1985, 1287). Addressing the issue of whether the Soviets had anything to fear, he argued that SDI was "an innocent technology that threatens no one" (*CPD* 1987, 1337). The day before declaring SDI to be an innocent technology, however, he warned that "if we leave the Soviets with a monopoly in this vital area, our security will be gravely jeopardized" (*CPD* 1987, 1333). But if it was an "innocent technology," why would U.S. security be endangered should the

Soviets get defenses first? Paraphrasing Reagan himself; how is the United States threatened if the Soviet Union is defended? The answer, of course, is that it is not the technology that is innocent, but the country possessing it, the United States. Because the Soviets were not innocent, defensive technology in their hands would be threatening.

There were times when Reagan admitted that, in the abstract, defenses had offensive uses. In a fascinating interview with Soviet journalists, Reagan recognized that "if someone was developing such a defensive system and going to couple it with their own nuclear weapons, offensive weapons, yes, that could put them in a position where they might be more likely to dare a first strike" (*CPD* 1985, 1343). But when it came to specifics about the United States, Reagan had a difficult time accepting the idea that his country might actually be viewed as a threat: "I don't think anyone in the world can honestly believe that the United States is interested in such a thing or would ever put itself in such a position" (*CPD* 1985, 172). Nonetheless, Reagan's pledge to share SDI technology with the Soviets seemed to be an implicit recognition that unilateral U.S. deployment of strategic defenses might be destabilizing. Reagan never seemed to make up his mind whether the deployment of SDI was destabilizing, which is consistent with his uncertainty about how the Soviets viewed the United States.

### SDI as a Tactic

There are those who will say that our attention is misplaced if we focus on SDI as a military program designed to meet a perceived Soviet threat. The real threat that SDI was intended to deal with was not the Soviet Union, but arms control. SDI was designed to shoot down not incoming missiles but rather the arms control process itself. This goes back to the charge that Perle and Weinberger used SDI for "mischief." Of course, it is possible that they supported SDI both as a military and a political weapon. Even if Perle and Weinberger did promote SDI primarily as a means to prevent a START agreement, they could have done so while actually wanting to move forward with SDI for security reasons. In a sense, two birds could be killed with the same stone—the Soviet threat and the arms control threat.

Even if SDI were mainly a device to kill arms control, it might still be related to a decision maker's image of the Soviet Union indirectly, through the influence of that image on his or her analysis of the arms control process. Recall from our examination of the role of images in shaping a decision maker's evaluation of arms control in general (chap. 8) that Perle's and Weinberger's image was such that they viewed the prospects for a favorable outcome from arms negotiations to be negligible at best. The incompatibility of the two countries' goals, objectives, and strategies was so great that common interests were virtually nonexistent. Furthermore, the relative political capacities of the two systems were such that agreements would almost inevitably be detrimental to U.S. interests. Thus, the use of SDI as a means to halt the progress toward an agreement is consistent with their view of the dynamics of arms control, which, in turn, was shaped by their image of the Soviet Union.

Shultz's image of the Soviet Union did not preclude the identification of common interests; in fact, he pointed to common interests in reducing the risks of war. He did not analyze the two countries' political capacities in a manner that led him to the conclusion that the dynamics of negotiations invariably favored the Soviets. Even if he did not have a very clear view of what positive outcomes could come from arms control, at least his image of the Soviet Union (and the United States) left him open to the notion that something worthwhile could be achieved that was in the interests, and consistent with the goals, of both countries. What does this mean in terms of using SDI as a tactic or tool? Not much. But given the fact that SDI was a force in the administration, something Shultz had to deal with even if he would have preferred not to, we would be inclined to predict that he would use it to move the process of arms control forward, not thwart it.

### Conclusion: Images, Morality, and SDI

Trying to find specific links between a decision maker's beliefs and his or her position on SDI might be a mistake in cases where the impact of his or her image is more general. Whether people like to dwell on it or not, the reality of the present nuclear situation is that every country is completely vulnerable to instantaneous destruction. This is an uncomfortable thought, particularly when the primary source of vulnerability is the nuclear arsenal of a nation viewed as an adversary. By all accounts, Reagan had long been uneasy with the concept of mutual (particularly U.S.) vulnerability. A perceptive Pentagon official put his finger on a telling point:

> This is a president who is well attuned to the American viscera. Somewhere in the American viscera we don't want to believe that some son-of-a-bitch on the other side can destroy us. . . . It has nothing to do with military planning . . . it's just a gut reaction that comes from the deepest, deepest recesses of the American viscera that Reagan is attuned with. (Kull 1988, 235–36)

The idea that the United States existed, on a daily basis, at the sufferance of the evil empire may have been more than Reagan could handle. In this sense, Reagan's image was not the specific determinant of his support for SDI, but it introduced a general and overwhelming sense of unease with being vulnerable to a nation that "reserved unto itself the right to lie, steal, and cheat or commit any crime to further its cause." Surely this was intolerable.

Images of the Soviet Union may be even less important for Reagan in the area of strategic defenses than on the other issues we have examined because of the heavy moralistic element in his support for SDI. It would be hard to imagine a moral equation that would lead someone to prefer throw-weight limits over launcher and warhead limits. SDI is different in this respect. For those whose support for SDI transcended strategic and tactical considerations, images of the Soviet Union may be of little importance. One is tempted to conclude that this was the case for Reagan. More than anyone else in his administration, Reagan emphasized the immorality of mutual assured destruction and portrayed SDI as the means of delivering the world from a moral quandary. This rationale for SDI is essentially unrelated to images of the Soviet Union, which may be why Reagan's commitment to SDI remained unchanged despite his softening image of the Soviet Union. In addition to this skepticism about the ethical propriety of nuclear deterrence, one senses in Reagan the quintessentially U.S. faith in technological solutions to complex political and social problems. A few scientific advances could make all the troubling strategic and moral dilemmas that political leaders had grappled with for decades simply disappear. Furthermore, Reagan's enthusiastic support for SDI displayed a traditional U.S. unilateralism. As Alford explains:

> SDI promises total autonomy, total independence. We need not depend on the good will of the Soviets. Neither need we depend upon their rational self-interest, or even their sanity. We need not depend upon the Soviets at all. We can guarantee ourselves total security, without the cooperation of anyone else. We shall need no one. Indeed, we do not even have to rely on our *own* rationality, restraint, or sanity, only our cleverness. (1988, 585)

According to this analysis, SDI was not simply the result of too many kids putting quarters into video machines (Reagan, after all, did not play video games), but rather a manifestation of a deeply ingrained part of the U.S. psyche, a psyche that Reagan embodied.

# Part 4
# Conclusions and Summary

CHAPTER 12

# Conclusions and Summary

In a review of an influential book dealing with the relationship between the economic and political decline of great powers, one critic observed that "the concern to be arresting and interesting draws [the author] in one direction; the concern to be true to the evidence, to recognize the autonomy of noneconomic forces, in the other." The dilemma, according to the reviewer, is that the more "arresting" and "interesting" conclusions are "unsustainable" because "who can demonstrate convincingly that everything is reducible to economics," while the "softer, pluralistic version is true but banal . . . for who can dispute that among all the factors at work the economic is extremely important" (Harries 1988, 33).

Though I am not concerned with the particulars of economic well-being and hegemonic decline, the general point is relevant. One of the perennial pitfalls of conclusions is the tendency for plausible explanations to be presented as compelling and for important variables to be deemed all-important. Of course, this is to be avoided. But on another level, the criticism misses the mark. The assumption that "soft" and "pluralistic" conclusions are "banal" and "uninteresting" is misguided. The complexity of social phenomena necessitates soft, pluralistic conclusions. If one is looking for simple, monocausal explanations, social science is not the place to be. The goal of social science research is to explain how, why, and under what conditions certain phenomena are related. The purpose of this study was not to provide the "arresting" conclusion that images of the enemy are the only, or even the most important, determinant of a decision maker's policy preferences; rather, the objective was to increase our understanding of why, how, and under what circumstances images influence policy formulation and choice.

## Images and Policy Preferences

One thing is clear from my study of the arms control debates in the Reagan administration: the relationship between images and policy preferences was not the same for all of the individuals involved. What exactly do I mean by "relationship"? On the most basic level, the one that was stressed in the empirical sections of this study, there is the relationship between the *content* of a decision maker's images and the *substance* of his or her policy proposals. In general, I have shown that for Perle, Weinberger, Burt, and Shultz, their policy preferences were consistent with their beliefs about the Soviet Union. There is, however, a great deal more to it than that. In addition to differences in the content of images and policy preferences, there were also differences in the *tightness* of the relationship. Furthermore, there may even have been differences in the *direction* of the relationship, though this is difficult to establish empirically.

What do I mean by "tightness"? Another way of expressing it would be "degree of correspondence" or "tightness of fit." An image-policy preference relationship is tight if the latter appears to follow logically and inevitably from the former. The relationship is loose if the decision maker's policy preferences are consistent with his or her image but would not necessarily have been anticipated or predicted on the basis of that image. Given the type of content analysis used in this study and the manner in which policy preferences have been identified, it is difficult to imagine a very precise or quantitative measure of tightness.

By "direction" of the relationship I mean whether images shape policy preferences or vice versa. Policy preferences can influence or shape images in two senses. One possibility is that a decision maker will acquire new beliefs or abandon old ones in order to justify (to himself or herself and others) policies adopted for other reasons (e.g., international or domestic political pressures). Alternatively, we can imagine a decision maker who has a belief system containing a variety of inconsistent beliefs, some of which become more prominent and salient following the adoption of particular policies. In this case, it is not a matter of creating new beliefs or eliminating old ones, but rather mobilizing previously existing beliefs that coexist with other, contradictory beliefs. Unfortunately, this is almost impossible to demonstrate conclusively. Without a very detailed record of a decision maker's beliefs during the period in which he or she is making decisions, it is difficult to tell what happened first—the adoption of a policy preference or the adjustment or reshuffling of beliefs. This would require an information-processing approach (see chap. 4) that necessitates access to governmental and archival sources not available to us (and even that might be insufficient). The basic problem is familiar to all social scientists—establishing causality. As Rosati explains:

> . . . three conditions must be fulfilled in order to have a causal relation-
> ship between beliefs and behavior: covariation (beliefs and behavior
> must be related over time), temporal precedence (changes in beliefs must
> precede changes in behavior), and nonspuriousness (no other factors
> beyond beliefs can be responsible for the behavior). (1987, 166)

These observations remain valid when we replace "behavior" with "policy preferences." But since these conditions will most likely not be met beyond a reasonable doubt, we should not wait until they are before we consider the nature of the image–policy preference relationship and the factors that influence it.

## Image Characteristics

The obvious place to begin a survey of the variables that might influence the role of images in shaping policy preferences is the image itself. That is, some types of images may have a greater impact on policy preferences than others. Images can be differentiated along three dimensions: content, "fullness," and degree of internal consistency. The underlying thesis is that "full," consistent, hard-line images will play a more significant role in a decision maker's formulation and choice of policy than incomplete, inconsistent, moderate images. I have dealt with some of these issues throughout my empirical discussion, but others were only touched upon.

In much of the literature on images, there is an often unstated assumption that decision makers with hard-line images are more likely to be guided by their beliefs than those with more moderate images, though there has been little systematic work testing this proposition. One of the most ambitious attempts to assess the relative importance of different types of images is Snyder and Diesing's study of decision making in international crises (the scope of their work, however, is much broader than a focus on images). They concluded that individuals with hard-line images are less flexible in terms of their approach to dealing with the adversary. "Flexibility" in this context refers to the decision maker's willingness to consider and accept policy alternatives. In a bargaining situation such as a crisis or arms negotiations, flexibility is a function of the range of policies an individual is prepared to support—the broader the range, the greater the flexibility. As the range of acceptable policies expands, a decision maker will be more likely to adjust his or her policies in order to resolve the crises or reach an agreement. An image that places severe constraints on the range of policies an individual will seriously consider can be said to have a more significant effect on policy preferences than an image that leads to a wide range of policy options.

In several places, I have already discussed why hard-line images tend to restrict policy options and promote inflexibility. It is because such images involve a view of the enemy as uniformly hostile, unalterably antagonistic, pursuing fundamentally incompatible goals, and constantly on the lookout for signs of weakness that can be exploited. Given the hard-liner's perception of the opponent's objectives and strategy, there will be very little, if any, room for reasonable compromise in the first place, and any moves in the direction of the opponent's position would, almost by definition, be inimical to one's own country's security interests and would signal a lack of resolve or will. Because the level of perceived threat is so high and the dangers of compromise are so great, the hard-liner is unlikely to propose compromises and is likely to resist pressures to revise policies in order to reach an agreement. The greater the perception of threat, the less likely a decision maker will be to allow other, nonstrategic considerations to intrude on his or her choice and formulation of policies. Hard-liners will focus on the central adversarial relationship to the exclusion of other considerations because the gravity of the threat is thought to be so great. Thus, the relationship between images and policy preferences may be tightest when a decision maker adheres to a hard-line image.

We can also differentiate images on the basis of their "fullness." An image is full if it contains beliefs about all those aspects of the opponent and his or her behavior that might be important for setting policies in a given issue area. Again, Snyder and Diesing are helpful in drawing a distinction between "two levels or components of an image: a background or long-term component, which is how the two parties view each other in general . . . and an immediate component, which comprises how they see each other in the crisis itself" (1977, 291). The background image includes such elements as the opponent's general foreign policy objectives, trustworthiness, and likely response to policies of firmness or accommodation. Given our focus on arms control, the immediate image consists of the decision maker's beliefs about Soviet nuclear capabilities, objectives, doctrine, and treaty behavior. It is possible for a decision maker to have a consistent and well-developed background image and a less consistent and poorly formed immediate image.

In general, it seems reasonable to hypothesize a closer correspondence between full images and policy preferences than would be the case for incomplete images. When a decision maker is dealing with specific policy issues, particularly those as complex and technical as arms control, background images will provide only broad and vague policy guidelines. The details of policy preferences are filled in by the beliefs in the immediate image. There is support for the thesis that we are better able to predict the behavior of an individual toward an object when his or her beliefs about that object are specific rather than general (Fishbien and Ajzen 1975). In the absence of firm, specific beliefs, the details of policies will be determined by other factors. For example, an image of the Soviet Union as an expansionist power driven by ideology does not offer many clues for an arms control strategy. On the other hand, if a decision maker has definite beliefs about those aspects of the opponent that are directly relevant to issues of nuclear arms control, his or her image will offer more guidance. As Stephen Walker observes with respect to operational codes in general, "the less developed an individual's operational code, the less relevant is operational code analysis in understanding his/her foreign policy decisions" (1988, 10).

Finally, in addition to an image's content and fullness, we can also expect its internal consistency to be an important determinant of its impact on policy preferences. The basic logic is much the same as it was for fullness. Just as incomplete images will not offer a decision maker many policy clues, neither will inconsistent images. Perhaps it is more accurate to say that inconsistent and incoherent images will offer too much guidance in the sense that they will lead the decision maker in different, even contradictory, directions. When some elements of an individual's image draw him or her toward one set of policies and other elements lead him or her to another set, we cannot look to his or her image for an explanation of why he or she chose one policy over the other. Thus, an inconsistent or incoherent image will result in less clear policy guidelines; as a result, the influence of other cognitive and noncognitive factors will increase because policy choices will not be determined by the image.

## Cognitive Styles

In my earlier discussion of theory and research, which might lead us to expect variation among individuals in terms of the importance of images in shaping policy preferences, I noted that people differ in their overall cognitive styles (chap. 3). Goldstein and Blackman define cognitive style as "the characteristic ways in which individuals conceptually organize the environment" (1978, 2). Modifying this a little, I will define a cognitive style as an individual's mode of structuring his or her beliefs and managing incoming information, particularly when it contradicts previously existing beliefs. Because cognitive styles involve the organization of beliefs and the processing of information, differences in cognitive style will influence the nature of a person's images as well as their behavior. Recognizing that people do not perform these tasks in the same manner, a number of attempts have been made to understand the origins and implications of distinct cognitive styles. Undoubtedly the most famous and influential exploration of these issues was Milton Rokeach's work on "open" and "closed" minds (1960), cognitive styles that he traced to more fundamental psychological needs and motivations. Most of the other schemes that have been advanced over the years rely heavily on his pioneering work. Surveying the variety of cognitive styles identified in the literature, it is possible to identify four key cognitive elements that distinguish the various styles: complexity, consistency, tolerance, and flexibility. We can describe an individual's style by answering a series of questions embodying these components. First, to what extent is the subject motivated to establish, preserve, or restore consistency among the elements of his or her belief system? Second, are the individual's beliefs complex or simple?[1] Third, how does the person deal with belief-discrepant information—does he or she recognize and accept it, or ignore and reject it? Finally, does the decision maker exhibit a willingness to alter his or her beliefs in the face of contradictory information? Using these questions, it would be possible to devise a large number of cognitive styles, but the situation is not as chaotic as it might at first appear. Since the elements of cognitive styles are probably interrelated, some combinations are unlikely to occur. For example, it is difficult to imagine an individual who has a high tolerance for belief-discrepant information yet refuses to adjust his or her beliefs in response to such information. Still, it is easy to imagine more than two cognitive styles.

It is not necessary for us to proceed in a deductive fashion and devise an exhaustive list of styles based upon these four criteria. But drawing upon the work of Rokeach (1960), Larson (1985), Steinbruner (1974), Hermann (1988), and the results of this study, we can begin by identifying three styles that are found in the literature and appear to have some parallels with the subjects of this project. The first style, which is included in some form in all of the schemes, can be labeled "ideological." This is yet another variant of Rokeach's "dogmatic," "closed" mind. An ideological cognitive style rests upon a set of firm and simple beliefs. An ideologue's belief system is composed of blacks and whites and is lacking in ambiguity, uncertainty, and qualifications. The elements of an ideologue's belief system are internally consistent and mutually reinforcing. Furthermore, ideologues have a low tolerance for information that challenges their beliefs, and, therefore, they tend to ignore or explain away uncomfortable information. Largely because of this treatment of belief-discrepant information, an ideologue's beliefs will be rigid in the sense of being constant over time. Thus, an ideological cognitive style is characterized by a high level of consistency (both internally and over time), low complexity, and a low tolerance for belief-discrepant information.

An ideological style is usually contrasted with some form of intellectual cognitive style. In one respect, intellectuals have something in common with ideologues—their belief systems will display a substantial degree of consistency. As "systemizers of ideas," to use Larson's terminology, intellectuals want their beliefs to "make sense," to "fit." But unlike ideologues, intellec-

---

1. Cognitive complexity is not a matter of the number of beliefs a person holds, but rather the degree of "differentiation" within his or her belief system. The gist of what I mean by complexity can be conveyed by looking at the manner in which it has typically been measured. Hermann (1983) operationalizes complexity by using a form of content analysis that determines the relative frequency with which an individual uses words such as *may, possibly, sometimes,* and *tends to.* The frequent use of such words indicates a high level of differentiation, whereas words such as *always, only, never,* and *without a doubt* indicate simplicity.

tuals are cognitively complex; that is, their views will be more nuanced and qualified, allowing for a certain element of ambiguity. Everything does not have to fit into neat categories and everything does not have to have an ironclad answer and explanation. Moreover, intellectuals will display a greater willingness to recognize information and interpretations that run counter to their beliefs, though we would not anticipate their uncritical acceptance. Finally, because of this greater tolerance for belief-discrepant information, intellectuals will be more prone to alter their beliefs, but the changes will be gradual and ordered, not chaotic and sudden (the possibility of cognitive change carries with it the potential for inconsistencies as belief systems are undergoing revision). Thus, an intellectual cognitive style will be characterized by complexity, substantial consistency, a higher tolerance for belief-discrepant information, and flexibility.

These two styles are not particularly novel, since they have roots in previous schemes and grow out of orthodox attitude theory, which assumes that there is a certain coherence to people's belief structures. Drawing upon a body of cognitive theory that challenges the basic tenets of prevailing cognitive paradigms, Larson argues that there are "people who are not introspective and spend little time reflecting on their own beliefs and are not bothered by gaping inconsistencies between their statements or thoughts from one moment to another" (1985, 33). Larson claims that this is characteristic of "practical" or "pragmatic politicians," especially those elected to high office, and explains why this might be the case.

> Their career success depend[s] on successfully molding their political opinions and personality to the expectations of voters and influential people. An elected politician generally has little time to acquire expertise on more than one or two issues; foreign policy questions typically win few votes at home. Consequently, the foreign policy positions [and opinions] of politicians fluctuate with the political winds. (1985, 49–50)

Larson recognizes that this is very similar to Steinbruner's "uncommitted thinking syndrome," in which an individual is able to maintain a variety of inconsistent "belief patterns" simultaneously. Uncommitted thinkers are not guided by one set of mutually reinforcing beliefs, but rather "will tend at different times to adopt *different* belief patterns for the same decision problem . . . . The signature of the uncommitted thinker," according to Steinbruner, is a tendency to "oscillat[e] between groups of advisers—siding with one on one issue and with another on the next and then back again" (1974, 131).

The implications of this for other aspects of cognitive style are uncertain. On the question of complexity, there is no persuasive reason to assume any necessary connection: it seems plausible that there can be substantial inconsistencies in either simple or complex belief systems. The issue of tolerance for belief-discrepant information is complicated by the presence of a range of inconsistent beliefs within the same cognitive structure. If an individual is able to maintain a variety of inconsistent beliefs, this would seem to expand the range of information that would find support somewhere within the belief system.

The issue of flexibility is transformed slightly. It would not appear to be a matter of changing beliefs, but rather "activating" those elements of the belief system that are consistent with new information or situations. That is, the result will be "an oscillation over time *between* a number of belief patterns" (Steinbruner 1974, 130; italics added). This is a little different than saying a person's beliefs are *flexible*; it might be more accurate to say that they are *variable*.

What does this discussion of cognitive styles have to do with the role of images in shaping policy preferences? Its relevance is found in Margaret Hermann's contention that the difference among the styles boils down to one key factor—an individual's sensitivity to situational or contextual information and cues.[2] That is, some people are "top-down" information processors in the sense that they look at the world and ask, "what do my beliefs tell me about the situation?" Others, however, are "bottom-up" information processors who ask, "what does this situation tell me about my beliefs?" Ideologues are an extreme version of top-down information processing; uncommitted thinkers or practical politicians exhibit bottom-up information processing. Using different terminology, we can say that ideologues are inner directed, whereas pragmatic politicians are situationally driven. Intellectuals would fall somewhere between the extremes. Intellectuals do have consistent ideas that guide them in interpreting situations and making policy choices. As a result, they do ask "what do my beliefs tell me about this situation?" But at the same time, they also look to the situation to "test" the adequacy of their ideas, and if the situation presents information that is at odds with their beliefs, they are willing to adjust them.

This is directly relevant to my study because images are collections of beliefs. For top-down information processors, images are likely to be dominant, perhaps even predominant, factors in shaping policy preferences. In the case of intellectuals, images should also be important, but perhaps less so than for ideologues for three reasons: first, a greater tolerance for belief-discrepant information will expand the informational base upon which decisions are made; second, cognitive complexity is less conducive to rigid and ironclad

---

2. This point is made briefly in Hermann (1988). It was suggested to me when Margaret Hermann served as discussant for my paper presented at the ISA/Midwest annual conference at Ohio State University in November, 1988.

policy positions; and third, there is always the possibility of alterations in images in response to situational developments. The impact of images will be least for practical politicians, who are more likely to be guided by situational forces (e.g., domestic public opinion, international political pressures, and the advice they receive from those around them). Various elements of their belief system will then be mobilized to justify policy preferences that were adopted for other reasons.

The important empirical question is posed by Hermann: "how do we decide when a [decision maker] is more principled or more pragmatic—that is, relatively insensitive versus sensitive to contextual clues" (1988, 8)? Her suggestion is to see whether an individual's beliefs are generally consistent with his or her behavior. Since behavior (e.g., behavioral predispositions or policy preferences) is our dependent variable, this would be methodologically improper. To avoid an empirical tautology, we need to identify cognitive styles independently of behavior and policy preferences. Thus, we need to return to the style characteristics of consistency, complexity, tolerance, and flexibility or variability.

## Knowledge and Interest

A final point, one that seems almost too obvious to mention, is that the importance of a decision maker's image will also depend on his or her knowledge of, and interest in, particular policy questions. We need to remember that images do not simply "lead to" policy preferences; it takes some effort to translate beliefs into concrete policy proposals. This may not be the case for very dramatic and grandiose proposals such as complete nuclear disarmament, since it is not difficult to tell what the effects would be; but in most cases it is not easy to figure out the implications of complicated arms control proposals. Furthermore, policy evaluation and formulation require not only time and effort, but also substantive knowledge. Believing that someone means you harm does not allow you to translate this belief into actions that will protect you unless you know what weapons your potential attacker has at his or her disposal. In the absence of such knowledge, a person who perceives a threat might choose an option that fails to protect him or her or even puts him or her at greater risk. Thus, we would expect the tightness of the relationship between images and policy preferences to increase as the decision maker's knowledge and interest rise.

## The Reagan Administration

Toward the end of Reagan's first term, Robert Dallek concluded that the administration "lack[ed] intellectual range" because "Reagan's national security and foreign policy advisers all share[d] these [hard-line] attitudes toward Soviet communism *in one degree or another*" (1984, 186, 134; italics added). Despite this significant qualifier, Dallek lumped Shultz, Weinberger, and Perle together as "Reaganites." Gregg Herken was also impressed by the similarities among Reagan's advisers: "however ideologically disparate they might be on other issues, all of Reagan's appointees and advisers seemed to be united in their criticisms of the military and political status quo inherited by the administration" (1985, 317). Others, however, were more impressed by the administration's divisions. Vincent Davis, for example, argued that there was "abundant evidence suggest[ing] not only a lack of coordination but also a far more profound lack of basic consensus on some fundamental issues facing U.S. foreign/defense policymakers" (1986, 35–36). Although Dallek, Herken, and Davis were not addressing arms control per se, this disagreement is reflected in most of the literature on the Reagan administration. Who is right? Of course, they all are. From one perspective, the Reagan administration was nothing but a bunch of hard-liners whose differences were dwarfed by their similarities; but from another, the administration was a conglomeration of pragmatic and ideological hard-liners (or whatever other labels one wants to use) whose differences were very important. To some, this might be a distinction without a difference, but my study has shown that these divisions existed and were reflected in significant debates over arms control.

## Image Characteristics

Dallek's statement that all of Reagan's advisers shared the same image of the Soviet Union to some degree is correct, but he misses the point. We all share the same views about the Soviet Union *to some degree*, but eventually matters of degree become differences of kind: the summer differs from the winter, literally, by only a matter of degrees, but the two seasons are sufficiently different that we give them distinct names. Certainly it would be possible to exaggerate the differences in the Reagan administration. Other administrations probably had similar, if not greater, disagreements: the divisions between Vance and Brzezinski in the Carter administration being a prime example. Broadly speaking, all of the decision makers in this study were hard-liners. They shared a perception of the Soviet Union as an expansionist power that posed threats to U.S. interests. They were convinced that U.S. strength and resolve were prerequisites for Soviet accommodation and restraint; conversely, there was agreement that U.S. restraint would be exploited. All thought that ideology played some role in shaping Soviet foreign policy. They all harbored some doubts about the Soviet Union's trustworthiness and treaty behavior. And there was a shared perception that the Soviet Union enjoyed certain military advantages, both in conventional and nuclear weapons. In line with these commonalities, there was agreement on the broad outlines of U.S. policy. Everyone thought that a U.S.

military buildup was essential to redress existing imbalances and to provide the needed incentive for reductions in Soviet strategic weapons. All thought that these reductions would have to be asymmetrical, falling most heavily on Soviet ICBMs. There was common ground in the Reagan administration.

Beyond the very general level of images and policy preferences, however, there was significant variation in the content of images and the substance of policy preferences. There is an important difference between hard-line images and inherent-bad-faith or diabolical enemy images. The latter two entail a view of "one's opponent as being fundamentally hostile [and] encour-. ages the actor to define situations of possible interaction with the opponent as posing dangers to his side" (George 1979, 102). A "regular" hard-line image also emphasizes conflicts of interest and the need to meet challenges with firmness and strength, but it does not define the conflict in apocalyptic and zero-sum terms. Perle's and Weinberger's images were of the diabolical variety. Weinberger, more than Perle, remained committed to the idea that the Soviet Union was an ideologically inspired power pursuing the goal of global revolution and domination. On more specific issues relating to nuclear weapons and strategy, Perle and Weinberger adhered to those views that prevailed in conservative foreign policy circles and the Committee on the Present Danger. According to this analysis, the Soviet Union was determined to achieve strategic superiority over the United States in the sense of a disarming first-strike capability. This goal was in line with Soviet strategic doctrine and its emphasis on nuclear war winnability and damage limitation. The SALT process, which previous administrations had assumed would institutionalize a situation of mutual vulnerability and strategic stability, was merely a convenient vehicle for the Soviets to pursue superiority while lulling the West into a false sense of security. Such were the dynamics of arms control between a totalitarian state and a liberal democracy. The agreements reached during the 1970s restrained only the United States; in every case the Soviets either got what they wanted or simply proceeded to violate agreements.

In terms of image content, Perle's and Weinberger's views of the Soviet Union were about as hard-line as one could get; it is difficult to imagine a collection of beliefs that would be less conducive to negotiation, compromise, and diplomatic solutions. According to the analysis that flowed from this image, successful arms control would have required that the Soviets abandon fundamental foreign policy and strategic objectives that Perle and Weinberger claimed had been the driving Soviet policy for almost two decades. Not only was this an extremely hard-line image, it was also full in that it contained firm beliefs about every aspect of Soviet behavior that could be expected to influence a decision maker's arms control policies. Moreover, all the elements of their image were mutually reinforcing in the sense that they pointed in the same policy direction.

Despite the similarities with Perle and Weinberger that led me to classify Burt and Shultz as hard-liners, there were significant differences in outlook. On the whole, the most striking thing about Burt and Shultz is what they did not say. Unlike Weinberger (and Reagan), neither Burt nor Shultz spoke of Soviet expansionist designs in terms of a desire for global domination. Although Burt and Shultz were concerned about Soviet treaty violations, they did not paint a picture of across-the-board and routine Soviet violations, and they did believe that the Soviets were restrained by existing agreements in militarily significant ways. What stands out most is the absence of the litany of charges about Soviet behavior that were the cornerstones of the neoconservative assault on SALT and détente. Burt and Shultz did not argue that Soviet nuclear doctrine was based upon the notion that a nuclear war could be fought and won, which was a staple with Perle, Weinberger, and Reagan. They did not claim that the Soviets were determined to acquire the ability to launch a disarming first strike, though Burt did say the Soviets were prepared to exploit perceptions of Soviet advantages and U.S. vulnerability. Perhaps Burt's and Shultz's most blatant disagreement with others in the administration was their view of the strategic balance. Not only did they never use expressions like "the window of vulnerability," but they indicated that the situation was one of rough parity, with the United States possessing an adequate deterrent. While it may not be wise to rely too heavily on what people do not say, these omissions are particularly telling. On some of these issues, Burt and Shultz contradicted the claims of the president, though they were careful not to do so directly. Furthermore, failure to toe the line on these points did little to increase their stock among the administration's more conservative supporters, most of whom already had their suspicions about Burt and Shultz (and with good reason, apparently).

The evidence suggests that Burt's and Shultz's images were not as full as Perle's and Weinberger's. The reader will recall the number of times that I had to caution that we could not tell exactly what Burt and Shultz thought about certain issues. This is the reason I had to rely so heavily on what they did not say in comparison to Perle and Weinberger. In Shultz's case, this is not very surprising, since there is no evidence that he devoted much attention to strategic questions prior to becoming secretary of state. Even after he joined the administration, Shultz was slow to get involved in strategic issues. This incompleteness is somewhat more surprising for Burt, given his extensive experience. It may be that the evidence, not their images, is incomplete. This seems plausible for Burt because of the relative lack of evidence. In Shultz's case, however, we have an adequate array of documents, and he had many opportunities to express his views. Still, we have to conclude that their images were not as fully developed or crystallized as Perle's and Weinberger's. There are also some problems in judging the consistency of their images. Although there were no obvious inconsistencies, it is difficult to say whether their beliefs were mutually reinforcing in the sense that they pointed in the same policy direction. The problem is that it is hard to say in what policy direction their beliefs pointed in the first place.

The basic outlines of Reagan's image clearly put him closer to Perle and Weinberger than Burt and Shultz. Of the five people in this study, only Reagan and Weinberger were outspoken in their belief that the Soviet Union was an ideologically motivated power bent on global domination. Reagan was convinced that this objective was dictated by the writings of Marx and Lenin, which he assumed Soviet leaders followed religiously. Reagan joined Weinberger and Perle in claiming that the Soviets had a "definite margin of superiority" in strategic weapons (until 1984). Furthermore, Reagan concluded that this was consistent with a Soviet doctrine of nuclear war winnability. Reagan's profound mistrust of the Soviet Union was evident in his early comments about Soviet "lying" and "cheating" as well his later statements about Soviet treaty violations. Reagan seemed fairly confident in these beliefs. But once we move beyond the level of dramatic assertions, we run into some problems. When Reagan was pressed into explaining the window of vulnerability and its implications, he was unable to do so. When he looked at the possible ramifications of a nuclear war, Reagan seemed to indicate that the Soviets were aware of the unacceptable levels of destruction that would inevitably result. When pushed on the question of whether the Soviets might view the United States as a threat, Reagan waffled. It was as if Reagan had a repertoire of statements that reflected his underlying fear and suspicion of the Soviet Union and communism, though he did not really comprehend the implications of what he was saying. This became clearer as the discussion became more detailed. One gets the impression that many of Reagan's assertions were more incantations and reiterations of charges he had picked up from sources who shared his basic feelings about the Soviet Union than genuine expressions of established beliefs.

It is hard to judge the fullness of Reagan's image. On the one hand, he did express views on just about every aspect of the Soviet Union I have identified as potentially important for shaping policy preferences in arms control. On the other hand, there are doubts about the nature of these beliefs. For example, when Reagan said that the Soviets believed they could fight and win a nuclear war, did he believe this in the same sense that Perle believed it? This is a difficult point to put one's finger on, but it has to do with a person's level or depth of belief. Many components of Reagan's image were *not* based "on a network of supporting assumptions and examples" (Larson 1985, 346). It is like someone who believes that a new acquaintance cannot be trusted, but is unable to explain exactly why as opposed to someone who has the same belief based on years of observing that person's behavior. That is, there is a difference between a superficial attachment to ideas and adherence to beliefs accompanied by knowledge, comprehension, and understanding. One is reminded of Gabriel Almond's observation that most U.S. citizens do not have a fully formed and well-grounded set of beliefs about foreign affairs, but rather a collection of "superficial psychic states" (1950, 69). Many of Reagan's beliefs, particularly concerning unfamiliar issues of nuclear weapons and strategy, appear to fall into the category of superficial ideas. It was more like a mantra than a fully formed image.[3]

It would be inaccurate to say that Reagan's image was incoherent or riddled with inconsistencies; it was not. But there were tensions that had potential policy relevance. First, there was his confusing view of the strategic balance. On the one hand, he claimed there was a window of vulnerability and that the Soviets enjoyed a definite margin of superiority. On the other hand, he recognized that the United States had sufficient forces to deter a Soviet attack; that is, it had an invulnerable retaliatory force. This raises questions about what Reagan meant by "superiority," which he never really clarified. This is not simply a matter of semantics—a decision maker's view of the strategic balance can have important ramifications for arms control policy, especially when one thinks the enemy respects only firmness and strength and is ready to pounce on weaknesses. First, there are implications in terms of the need for a buildup and the extent of asymmetrical reductions required for successful arms control: in the absence of an adequate deterrent, the need for a strategic buildup and asymmetrical reductions is more acute. Furthermore, given Reagan's beliefs about the typical Soviet responses to firmness and weakness, it matters whether the United States enters arms talks from a position of vulnerability and inferiority or with the knowledge that its deterrent is secure. If the United States is not inferior and its nuclear deterrent is credible, the prospects for successful arms control should be greater than if it is vulnerable to a disarming Soviet first strike.

Most intriguing, however, was Reagan's view of what motivated the Soviet half of the arms race. At times, Reagan portrayed the Soviet buildup as the inevitable outcome of internal drives—a menacing strategic doctrine and ideologically motivated quest for military superiority and global domination. On other occasions, he claimed the arms race was a result of unwarranted suspicions that could be cleared up by communication and understanding. These are incompatible views that lead in very different policy directions. The first view would imply that the tools of negotiation and diplomacy are unlikely to result in a change in Soviet objectives—what are needed are overwhelming

---

3. The use of mantra is borrowed from Stockman (1986), who used it to describe Reagan's anecdotal economic philosophy.

strength and the forces to deny Soviet objectives. The second view would lead to the conclusion that negotiations and diplomacy are not only useful, but essential. Thus, we cannot say that the various components of Reagan's image were consistent in the sense of being mutually reinforcing in their policy implications.

## Cognitive Styles

There seems to be little doubt about which cognitive style best describes Perle and Weinberger. Virtually all accounts of the Reagan administration identify them as ideologues. Admittedly, this is usually done without an explicit definition of the term, but my research indicates that all the telltale signs were there. Perle's and Weinberger's thoughts about foreign policy and U.S.-Soviet relations were consistent and mutually reinforcing. The most obvious example was the way in which their analysis of the political and psychological weaknesses of liberal democracies buttressed the gloomy assessment of arms control produced by their beliefs about Soviet objectives. All elements of their belief systems seemed to converge to one point—a profound skepticism about the utility of negotiation, diplomacy, and compromise with the Soviet Union. There was a manifest lack of complexity and nuance in their analysis of Soviet and U.S. foreign policy; they had concrete, black-and-white explanations for everything. *Maybe*, *perhaps*, and *possibly* were words seldom used in their discussions of U.S.-Soviets relations.

   Their interpretations were not open to reasonable challenge: all the evidence supported their conclusions. For example, on the question of Soviet strategic doctrine, they claimed that all indications pointed to a Soviet belief that a nuclear war could be fought and won—there was no other possible explanation, Perle argued, for Soviet reliance on ICBMs and civil defense. Even after Gorbachev signed a communiqué at the 1985 Geneva summit stating that a nuclear war could not be fought or won, Weinberger claimed there were no indications that the Soviets had abandoned this belief. There were few gray areas in their analysis. When it came to Soviet treaty violations, for example, Perle and Weinberger portrayed as naive or uninformed anyone who tried to explain Soviet behavior as something other than conscious attempts to cheat and achieve strategic advantages. All of this is in line with Hermann's "top-down" information processing style. Perle and Weinberger consistently imposed their beliefs on evidence and information; they did not use it to test the accuracy of their images. Everything had a simple and straightforward explanation; interpretations and information that contradicted their views were either dismissed or ignored. And in the face of dramatic changes in the Soviet Union, their analysis of Soviet foreign and strategic policy remained unchanged. As Perle himself confessed in 1987, "I have held the same view of the world since I learned it from Scoop Jackson in the 1970s" (U.S. Cong. 1987a, 91).

Burt and Shultz would appear to fall under the rubric of intellectuals. In classifying them, however, we are faced with problems that arise from our inability to identify clearly what they thought about some issues. It is hard to tell how they dealt with belief-discrepant information and interpretations because we do not know exactly what some of their beliefs were. We can say that they were not dismissive or contemptuous of arguments and explanations that differed from their own, but this may be more a matter of personal style and tact than a willingness to accept alternatives. Their behavior, however, was not indicative of pure "top-down" information processors; Burt and Shultz did not try to fit every piece of information into their previously existing beliefs.

Uncertainty about some of their beliefs also makes it difficult to speak with confidence about how well their overall belief system fit together. I did not, however, identify any competing belief patterns. Ironically, these problems support my classification of Burt and Shultz as intellectuals. One of the reasons why I did not face similar problems for Perle and Weinberger was the simplicity and stridency of their views: when someone thinks in simplistic, black-and-white terms, it is easy to figure out what they believed. But if a decision maker thinks in more nuanced and qualified terms, and if he or she is willing to live with a certain level of uncertainty and ambiguity, the task of deciphering his or her beliefs is more difficult (recall Smith's observation that Shultz's world is painted in shades of gray). Thus, the fact that Burt and Shultz did not have neat, clear-cut, and simple explanations for everything is indicative of a more intellectual cognitive style.

Reagan is much more difficult to categorize in my scheme of cognitive styles. The problem is reflected in the literature on Reagan and his administration—observers do not seem to know what to make of him. Dallek's analysis (1984) is a good example of the confusion; he seems to conclude that Reagan was both an ideologue and a political pragmatist. On some of the criteria for cognitive styles, Reagan fit the mold of an ideologue. In a sensitive analysis of Reagan's foreign policy views, Betty Glad showed that his cognitive style was characterized by "dichotomizing," "black-and-white thinking," and a "rigidity of perception." "For him," she concluded, "there are no ambiguities about the nature of the enemy . . . no question about the 'facts' which support [his image]" (Glad 1983, 33, 51). Supporting Glad's thesis, Margaret Hermann employed a form of systematic content analysis and concluded that Reagan was among the least cognitively complex political leaders she had studied (1983).

In contrast, however, one is struck by similarities between Larson's descriptions of Truman, whom she classified as a practical politician, and Reagan. The following observations are illustrative.

> Truman had a limited understanding of foreign affairs. (Larson 1985, 126)
>
> [Truman was] a consummate politician and proud of it. . . . [He] had acute political instincts. (129)
>
> [Truman's] beliefs about world order were a contradictory mishmash of political realism and lofty idealism. He enjoyed spinning "golden dreams" about world peace. (131)
>
> His method of administration suited his cognitive style. He read official reports rapidly but superficially, skipping over details. Truman preferred to let others handle the particulars, leaving him free to concentrate on the broad issues. (145)
>
> Truman was not an ideologue or a systemizer of ideas. Many of his beliefs were inconsistent, and the situation determined which of his many convictions became salient to Truman at the particular moment. (149)
>
> Whereas Roosevelt had strong, consistent ideas about the appropriate strategy and tactics for dealing with the Soviets, Truman's belief system was blank on many issues, and very loosely connected. (335)

We could replace "Truman" with "Reagan" in each of these quotations without raising any eyebrows. Even Reagan's most ardent supporters do not claim that he was very knowledgeable about world affairs or a particularly diligent participant in the policy-making process. As Stanley Hoffmann (not an admirer) observed, Reagan was a "president with markedly little interest in foreign affairs who [was] content to receive a series of minimemos summarizing foreign and defense problems and . . . a foreign policy paper of ten pages or more only about once a month" (1981, 22). I have already shown that Reagan's harsh image of the Soviet Union was accompanied by a very idealistic and liberal view of the nature of political conflict and a belief in an underlying harmony of interests. And the charge that Reagan was guided by the political situation, not his beliefs, has been leveled for years. In assessing the Reagan presidency, two observers made this argument in very blunt terms.

> At the beginning of his administration, Reagan knew exactly one thing about the Soviet Union: it was the "evil empire," the bad guys. And you fight bad guys at every step. What rendered Reagan suddenly conciliatory in midadministration wasn't any dramatic change in Soviet behavior; the mystical revelation that visited him at Reykjavík—that suddenly we could trust the Soviets to destroy their nuclear arsenal and not

keep a single warhead in secret storage—came long before they began withdrawing from Afghanistan or talking plausibly about a less offensive military posture. What changed Reagan's tune, rather, was the cue he's always responded to: applause. Mikhail Gorbachev had been winning global acclaim by talking peace, and Reagan wanted some of the action. It's that simple. (TRB 1989, 6)

Reagan's greatest political skill was his obedience. Conservatives who puzzle over why he failed to cash in his popularity chips for real policy changes have simply gotten it the wrong way round: Reagan produced policies for the popularity chips. When Americans wanted taxes cut, he did so. When they wanted him to stand up to the Soviets, he obliged. When they hankered for détente, he offered them Geneva, then Reykjavík, and finally Moscow. (Sullivan 1989, 20)

Even Glad, who basically viewed Reagan as an ideologue, was a little suspicious: "one could argue that Reagan's views have had an instrumental value for him . . . each time Reagan moved to the right in his early career . . . he allied himself with strong forces in his environment and advanced his career" (1983, 66). Plausible as all this might be, it is really not "that simple." Despite the identifiable professional or career interests to be advanced by adopting a hard-line image of the Soviet Union in the 1940s and 1950s, Glad notes that:

. . . if one looks carefully at these events, it is clear that Reagan is not simply a passive product of his environment. . . . He made choices . . . and these suited *his own personal bent as well as his interests*. . . . Even his anticommunism, popular as it was in the American culture, did not necessitate his particular version of it. There were somewhat more discriminating frameworks around. (1983, 67, italics added)

Similarly, even though the public may have "hankered" for détente in the mid- and late 1980s, Reagan did not have to go around talking about eliminating nuclear weapons and the possibility of everlasting peace if all young people got to know one another; there were, to use Glad's words, "more discriminating frameworks around."

Reagan was an ideologue if we look at his beliefs solely from the standpoint of his cognitive complexity. But he was not an ideologue when it came to consistency—all his beliefs and convictions were not mutually reinforcing in their policy implications. Reagan's beliefs about international affairs and U.S.-Soviet relations were a combination of two uncomplicated (hence the failure to find cognitive complexity) mind-sets or belief patterns. On the one hand, there was a simplistic, Manichean view of the superpower rivalry and the challenge of communism; on the other hand, there was a liberal faith in the value of education, reason, and communication as the means to overcome conflicts that arise from the failure to recognize that all people have the same basic interests. The latter set of beliefs slipped into his analysis of Soviet behavior on questions such as the Soviet view of the United States and the driving force behind the arms race (i.e., mutual suspicion). Both of these mind-sets were simple and largely internally consistent, but when taken together, there were definite conflicts: they were not necessarily logically inconsistent, but they certainly did not lead in the same policy direction.

So where does Reagan fit? No one has made the case that he was an intellectual, and there is nothing in my study or previous work to support such a classification; in fact, Glad's and Hermann's work on Reagan's cognitive complexity strongly undermines such a conclusion. The presence of nonreinforcing beliefs about the Soviet Union, U.S.-Soviet relations, and international politics in general would seem to preclude a classification as an ideologue. But one is also uncomfortable with a view of Reagan as a practical politician who had no cognitive anchors and was able to mold his beliefs to the needs of the moment. He was not an "uncommitted thinker" in that sense. But in a way, the label "uncommitted thinking syndrome" is misleading, since Steinbruner defines it in terms of *oscillating* between different belief patterns, which does not imply that one is totally uncommitted. Reagan was committed to certain beliefs; they just happened to be very different. Although he may not exactly fit the description of an "uncommitted thinker" or "practical politician," he resembled these types more than he did the ideological or intellectual types.

## Knowledge and Interest

If we had to rank our subjects according to their level of interest in and knowledge about nuclear weapons and arms control from the most interested and knowledgeable to the least, we would come up with the following list: Perle, Burt, Weinberger, Shultz, and Reagan. Certainly no one would quarrel with placing Burt and Perle at the top of the list; both knew the subject inside out, and their behavior in and out of the Reagan administration demonstrated their longstanding interest in nuclear arms control and strategy. Weinberger probably enjoyed the edge over Shultz on both counts. Even if he was not very knowledgeable before becoming secretary of defense, he was a very quick study, mastering the details in no time. By his own admission, Shultz had never been terribly interested in arms control issues, and his knowledge, though it increased throughout his five years as secretary of state (as did his interest), was never comparable to that of Perle, Burt, or Weinberger. Reagan's knowledge of the issues was clearly the least of the five. As Lou Cannon, a journalist who followed Reagan's career for more than two decades, noted, "in both press conferences and private meetings with advisers, Reagan was most at sea when the topic turned to foreign affairs" (1982, 373). Reagan's interest seemed to vary. Early in his presidency, most of Reagan's attention was devoted to domestic economic issues of tax and budget cuts, but, in the last few years, U.S.- Soviet relations and arms control became dominant concerns.

## Images and Policy Debates
## in the Reagan Administration

Robert Jervis claims that "differing perceptions of the other states' intentions often underlie policy debates. In the frequent cases where the participants do not realize that they differ on this crucial point, the dispute is apt to be vituperative and counterproductive" (1976, 58). It is unclear whether Reagan's advisers realized the extent of their differences on this point, but there is little reason to believe their debates would have been more enlightening if they had. Nonetheless, Jervis's basic observation is supported by my study. Of course it would be simplistic to argue that all aspects of the debate had their roots in conflicting images. The administration was divided by personality conflicts as well; there was no love lost between Perle and Burt or Shultz and Weinberger. And undoubtedly there were elements of traditional bureaucratic/institutional rivalries. But it would be equally simplistic to think that the debates can be understood without reference to underlying intellectual differences.

Although we can say that Jervis is right in this case, I wanted to do more than find out whether the overall debate was influenced by conflicting images. My goal was to see how images shaped policy preferences at the level of the individual decision maker. As expected, the impact of images varied. In some cases, the influence of the decision maker's beliefs about the Soviet Union appeared to be the dominant factor shaping their policies, while in other cases the relationship was weaker. That is, the relative potency of images was clearly not the same. I can illustrate this by asking how well we could have anticipated or predicted each decision maker's policy preferences on the basis of what we know about their images.

Much of the discussion in the empirical portion of this study revolved around Perle and Weinberger and their policy preferences. There are a variety of reasons for this. First, it was Perle and Weinberger who set the terms of debate; much of Burt's and Haig's (and Shultz's) efforts were devoted to preventing the adoption of the Pentagon's agenda. My account reflected the centrality of Perle and Weinberger. Second, and more important for my purposes, the connection between images and policy preferences was very tight in their cases. Virtually without exception, their policy positions appeared to be the inevitable and logical outgrowth of their beliefs about the Soviet Union—its capabilities, strategy, objectives, and doctrine. On SALT II, START, INF, SDI, and arms control in general, Perle put forward exactly the sort of policies we would have anticipated, and Weinberger supported him down the line. As I have pointed out before, this is not to say that we would have predicted specifics, such as the number of warheads and missiles, but the outlines of their policies were not merely shaped by their images; they mirrored them.

Given my previous observations, the reasons for the tightness of the image–policy preference relationship in Perle's and Weinberger's cases seem clear. On each of the key variables—image characteristics, cognitive style, and interest/knowledge—Perle and Weinberger displayed those features that should increase the importance of images. They adhered to extremely hard-line and consistent images that restricted the range of acceptable options, promoted inflexibility, and inhibited compromise in negotiations. Since their images were full, they offered guidance on the specific issues of nuclear weapons and strategy. An ideological cognitive style increased the salience of their images, primarily because of the way they reacted to information and interpretations that challenged their views. In addition, other elements of their foreign policy belief systems (e.g., the diplomatic weakness of democracies) supported the policy implications of their images. Finally, Perle possessed the knowledge and interest needed to translate his beliefs into concrete policy proposals. While Weinberger may have lacked Perle's knowledge and interest, at least initially, he was a quick learner, and he was fortunate to have Perle around to craft policy proposals he could support. Overall, one is struck by how closely Perle's and Weinberger's policies followed their Soviet images. One is tempted to conclude that if we could choose only one thing about Perle and Weinberger we would want to know in order to understand their arms control proposals, it would be their beliefs about the Soviet Union.

Shultz and Burt provided some of the more frustrating aspects of the empirical discussion. On many issues, it seemed as though the most interesting thing we could say about them was that they were not Perle and Weinberger. That is, it was clear that their beliefs about the Soviet Union would not lead them to insist on the type of proposals put forward by the Pentagon civilians, but it was less clear why they adopted their policy preferences. Perle's and Weinberger's positions appeared to have been carefully deduced from their beliefs about the Soviet Union. Burt's and Shultz's policy preferences were consistent with their images, but it is not possible to say that they flowed logically and inevitably from them. If all we knew about Burt and Shultz were their views of the Soviet Union, one doubts whether we could have anticipated their policy preferences with any accuracy, though we would not have been surprised by them either. This points to a much looser image–policy preference relationship than we found for Perle and Weinberger.

From another angle, however, we would not expect to be able to anticipate their policy preferences with the same precision that was possible for Perle and Weinberger. More moderate images, a nuanced and complex cognitive style, and, at least in Shultz's case, a lower level of knowledge and interest would suggest a less dominant role for Burt's and Shultz's images.

The absence of extremely hard-line images meant that Burt and Shultz were more amenable to the idea that there was a range of common interests that could serve as the basis for agreement because the conflict was not viewed in zero-sum terms. When the conflict is not viewed in apocalyptic, zero-sum terms, all concessions are not considered imprudent accommodations to an enemy whose goals are fundamentally at odds with those of the United States. As a result, the range of acceptable policies will be greater. Not only were Burt's and Shultz's images more moderate, but they were somewhat incomplete and ambiguous, particularly concerning issues of Soviet nuclear objectives and doctrine. These elements of Perle's and Weinberger's images were crucial for shaping their arms control proposals. Burt's and Shultz's images did not offer the same degree of detailed policy guidance.

Unlike Perle and Weinberger, Burt and Shultz did not have a set of simple and firm beliefs about everything. They did not claim that all the evidence supported their interpretations. They tolerated some ambiguity and uncertainty when it came to understanding and explaining the Soviet Union and its behavior. This sort of thought pattern indicates an intellectual cognitive style that is more likely to promote policy flexibility. This is in contrast to an ideological style, which tends to produce one set of policies that are rigid, reflecting simple and ironclad beliefs about which ideologues have no doubts. A more intellectual style leads to greater caution and flexibility; when there is more flexibility, the connection between images and policy preferences will be looser.

On a superficial level, Reagan had much in common with Perle and Weinberger, particularly with respect to his harsh views of the Soviet Union. Reagan's talk about world domination, a Soviet belief in nuclear war winnability, and Soviet untrustworthiness was rivaled only by Weinberger's. And there were indications of an ideological style, especially when we look at cognitive complexity. On this basis, we would expect his image to have a similarly dominant influence on his policy preferences. In fact, this was not the case. It would have been almost impossible to predict Reagan's policy choices in the area of arms control with much accuracy solely on the basis of his beliefs about the Soviet Union. In fact, there are several issues on which his policies ran counter to what one would have expected (e.g., SALT II and the move toward offsetting asymmetries in START).

The reasons for this are clear once we move beyond a superficial analysis and look at Reagan's image, overall foreign policy belief system, and level of knowledge about and interest in arms control issues. Unlike Perle and Weinberger, as I have already pointed out, Reagan's image was not very well developed, he only had a rudimentary knowledge of the issues involved, his interest fluctuated, and, perhaps most important, his image did not receive support from other elements of his belief system. The poorly developed nature of Reagan's beliefs was demonstrated by his frequent inability to explain them in any depth. This, in turn, revealed Reagan's lack of substantive knowledge, which is important for two reasons. First, as Jervis explains, "those with extensive knowledge—and, presumably, well-grounded beliefs—might be more likely to maintain their beliefs in the face of extensive knowledge that indicates they are incorrect" (1980, 88). Second, without sufficient knowledge, it is impossible to convert one's ideas into policies or accurately evaluate alternatives. As a result, an uninformed decision maker may support policies that contradict his or her beliefs without even realizing it (e.g., Reagan's support for a START proposal that would probably have increased the vulnerability of U.S. forces).

Despite the rhetoric of the 1980 presidential campaign and Reagan's harsh criticism of SALT and détente, "Reagan came into office lacking any master plan for foreign policy" (Smith 1988, 578). He certainly did not have any blueprint for arms control other than vague calls for real reductions, negotiations from strength, closing the window of vulnerability, and establishing "equality." One is reminded of Ronald Steel's observation that Reagan did not have a Soviet policy; he had an anticommunist policy *stance* (1981, 22). The same can be said with respect to arms control. His arms control stance was to get real reductions from a position of strength and close the window of vulnerability. When it came time to translate this stance into policies, Reagan had to rely on his subordinates, whose proposals he was ill equipped to judge. As Smith observes, "on foreign policy Reagan would set a general course, but his understanding was so hazy and simplistic that he was at the mercy of his aides" (1988, 627). In a none too flattering account of his years in the Reagan administration, David Stockman cites numerous examples of Reagan's dependence on advisers. Time and time again Reagan would "decide" by combining elements of the proposals in front of him without any apparent rationale (though he preferred that such compromises be made before questions reached him). Reagan combined proposals in this manner so often that the index to Stockman's memoirs actually contains the entry "Reagan . . . split the difference pencil work of" (1986, 419). Although Stockman concentrated on economic policy, we found the same thing in arms control. But even if Reagan's image and knowledge were only sufficient to provide him with an arms control stance, why did he not consistently side with those who shared his image, who had the same stance? After all, Weinberger routinely adopted the position of the person to whom he was intellectually closest (i.e., Perle); why did Reagan not do the same and side with Weinberger?

Lack of knowledge and interest was only one reason Reagan failed consistently to support those policies that best "fit" his image. In order to understand aspects of Reagan's arms control policy that make little sense in the context of his beliefs about the Soviet Union, one must look to his broader foreign policy belief system. As I have shown, Reagan's hard-line image coexisted with a simplistic, liberal optimism that negotiation and communication could strip away surface conflicts and reveal a basic commonality of interests. There was nothing comparable for Perle and Weinberger (or Shultz and Burt). Perle's and Weinberger's belief systems were characterized by cognitive reinforcement; Reagan's exhibited cognitive competition. Using Steinbruner's terminology, we can say that Reagan had two belief patterns that were relevant to problems of arms control. Thus, it is not only the superficiality of many of Reagan's beliefs about the Soviet Union and his lack of substantive knowledge that explain the loose connection between his image and policy preferences; we must also take into account the presence of a competing belief pattern.

This helps us understand some things. Recall that my examination of Reagan's image of the Soviet Union failed to exhibit any dramatic change. Yes, Reagan did argue that the new Soviet leadership no longer proclaimed the goal of global domination; this hardly indicates the emergence of an extremely moderate image. Furthermore, in some respects (i.e., regarding Soviet treaty violations), his image seemed to become more hard-line. How do we reconcile this with the general impression that there was a fairly dramatic change in Reagan's views of the Soviet Union? It seems as though this widespread perception of change was the result of Reagan's shift in emphasis to another belief pattern, not a major overhaul of his Soviet image.

This also explains why we really did not find a dramatic change in the substance of the administration's arms control proposals (except for those related to the Reykjavík summit). The common perception that Reagan's Soviet image had changed substantially during his second term is often accompanied by the belief that U.S. arms control policy also changed. In fact, when I analyzed INF and START, the changes after 1983 were really not that great, certainly not significant enough to suggest any major policy reversal (the real changes were on the Soviet side). Any change was primarily in the realm of intangibles, such as a desire for summits and an eagerness to reach an agreement. That is, there was change in the administration's policy orientation or stance, not the specific details of proposals. Indeed, given what has been observed about Reagan's lack of substantive knowledge and the simplistic, vague, and superficial nature of his belief patterns, we would not expect shifts between these patterns to produce changes in the details of policy.

Where does this leave us in terms of the relationship between Reagan's image and his policies (or policy stances)? In comparison to the others in his administration, his image was least important for understanding his policy choices. In fact, the most accurate mode of prediction would have been to take Perle's and Burt's proposals and combine them in some fashion. There were several reasons for the relative lack of potency of Reagan's image—the poorly developed nature of his image, the presence of a competing, policy-relevant belief pattern within his overall cognitive structure, and Reagan's lack of substantive knowledge.

But was his image irrelevant for understanding his policies? Was he a practical politician who responded to the demands of the moment by altering his beliefs and policies? Were his beliefs merely useful epiphenomena that allowed Reagan to follow the demands of the electorate? Some may think so, but it is more complicated than that. Recall Glad's observation that Reagan's early adoption of a very hard-line image suited his career interests *as well as* his own personal bent. Even if the shift in Reagan's belief pattern was motivated, consciously or unconsciously, by political imperatives, it is significant that there was a belief pattern in place to shift to. It is not an either/or proposition—political calculations may be part of the explanation for the increasing prominence of Reagan's liberal, optimist mind-set, but once the shift was underway, it had an influence on Reagan's approach to arms control. However, for reasons already discussed, it did not result in a dramatic change in the specifics of the U.S. position. Neither Reagan's image of the Soviet Union nor his optimistic belief pattern was sufficiently precise or well grounded to provide a high degree of policy guidance. The result was a more upbeat approach to arms control in general—a new arms control stance—without major revisions of policy specifics.

## Conclusion

It is rare in the social sciences that we find two variables that are related in the same manner in all situations. It is also rare to study variables that are never related, since the initial interest is usually sparked by observing cases where the variables were related. As a result, we often find that, in some cases, the expected relationship was found, whereas in others it is not. In addition, we normally find that the nature of the relationship varies. The goal of social science is to determine why two phenomena are related in some cases but not others. If the relationship varies, we want to find the reasons for the variation.

That is, we are concerned with delineating boundary conditions: parameters within which variables are related and the factors that make the relationship vary. These boundary conditions or parameters are essentially antecedent or intervening variables that affect the relationship—X will be strongly related to Y, if $a$, $b$, and $c$. We want to identify $a$, $b$, and $c$.

I did not begin this study expecting to find no relationship between images and policy preferences in any of the cases. I was open to the possibility, but it would have been very surprising indeed. Nor did I expect to find that images had the same influence on policy preferences for each of the individuals. I expected to discover that the nature and strength of the relationship were different for the various individuals, which is what was found. But if this was all I could say in conclusion, I would only be where I started; in which case, why do all the work? Fortunately, this is not all I have to say. I have been able to delineate some of the boundary conditions (i.e., variables) that help us understand why images are strongly related to policy preferences in some cases, weakly in others, and not at all in yet others, though I do not pretend to have identified all the factors that influence the image-policy preference relationship.

Drawing upon existing theory and the results of my research, I have identified three basic factors that influence the nature and strength of the image–policy preference relationship: characteristics of the image itself, cognitive style, and substantive knowledge and interest. Undoubtedly these are not the only factors that can influence the relationship, but there are persuasive theoretical reasons to expect differences in these variables to alter the connection between images and policy preferences.

At the level of the image itself, it appears as though the impact of images on policy preferences is a function of their content, fullness, and consistency. My research speaks primarily to the first two characteristics, because I did not have anyone whose image was very inconsistent. In general, hard-line images will exert a greater influence on policy preferences than more moderate images. The evidence for Perle, Weinberger, Shultz, and Burt substantiates this basic thesis. But it is not only a matter of content—if it were, we would expect a close connection between Reagan's image and policies, which I did not find. We need to look at the fullness of a decision maker's image, as well as how well grounded his or her beliefs are. When a decision maker has a full image that rests upon a network of supporting assumptions and facts, his or her image will be more influential than if it were incomplete or superficial. The evidence in the case of Reagan, particularly when compared to Perle and Weinberger, supports this conclusion.

In terms of cognitive style, I have highlighted the differences between ideologues, intellectuals, and uncommitted thinkers, suggesting that images should be most influential for the first type and least influential for the last type. There are several reasons this might be the case. First, as Hermann points out, these different types entail varying levels of sensitivity to contextual cues. Those who are least sensitive (i.e., ideologues) are more likely to be guided by their beliefs, whereas those who are most sensitive (e.g., uncommitted thinkers or practical politicians) are more likely to be guided by the imperatives of the situation. Second, ideologues and intellectuals have cognitive structures composed of consistent and mutually reinforcing (or at least not contradictory) beliefs; they are not drawn in different directions by the elements of their belief systems. Practical politicians or uncommitted thinkers, on the other hand, tolerate inconsistencies in their cognitive structures; as a result, they often have competing belief patterns that lead to different policies. Lacking consistent cognitive guidelines, uncommitted thinkers are more likely to be influenced by features of their environment (e.g., advice from aides, the latest piece of dramatic information, their most recent personal experiences, international or domestic political pressures). My results appear to be consistent with these propositions.

Finally, the influence of images is also a function of the decision maker's substantive knowledge and interest. These factors become more important as we view specific policies on very complex issues. Images will be more important in the sense of shaping the details of policy preferences as a decision maker's level of knowledge and interest rises. If a decision maker does not have sufficient knowledge and interest to translate his or her beliefs into policies, the impact of images will be low; the implications of images will get "lost" in the processes of moving to specific policies. The problem might not be that great if the decision maker can rely on someone who shares his or her beliefs to develop concrete policy options. In this case, there might be very tight correspondence between images and policy preferences despite the decision maker's personal lack of knowledge and interest.

This last point suggests that images are important beyond the level of the individual decision maker; they might be crucial determinants of policy coalitions. In this study, I found that those who shared the same basic beliefs about the Soviet Union were generally on the same side of the arms control debates. It was not that they sat down and discussed their beliefs and agreed to support the same policies; indeed, they were probably not even cognizant of the fact that they adhered to the same images. But even when there were alternative sources of policy guidance (e.g., Weinberger could have relied on the Joint Chiefs instead of Perle for arms control advice), the decision makers lined up according to their images. The exception was Reagan, who did not consistently side with the hard-liners; instead, he fluctuated back and forth between the two coalitions, adopting compromises that made little strategic sense.

Thus, it is significant that Reagan was not a reliable member of either policy coalition, which is what Steinbruner predicted we would see for an uncommitted thinker.

I do not want to exaggerate the importance of images. It would be unrealistic to claim that I could have predicted all the twists and turns in the Reagan administration's arms control debates on the basis of what we know about the different decision makers' images of the Soviet Union. No one variable would give us enough information to do this. Obviously knowledge of the decision maker's image would have been more useful in some cases than others—that is, for some individuals, images exerted a greater influence on policy preferences. Understanding why this is so was the goal of this study. I wanted to explore why, how, and under what circumstances images influenced policy preferences. I hope that I have moved a substantial distance toward that goal.

# Bibliography

Abelson, R. 1972. Are Attitudes Necessary? In *Attitudes, Conflict, and Social Change,* ed. B. King and E. McGinnies, 19–33. New York: Academic Press.

Abelson, R. 1976. Script Processing in Attitude Formation and Decision Making. In *Cognition and Social Behavior,* ed. J. Carroll and J. Payne, 33–45. Hillsdale, N.J.: Lawrence Erlbaum.

Ajzen, I. 1982. On Behaving in Accordance with One's Beliefs. In *Consistency in Social Behavior: The Ontario Symposium,* ed. M. Zanna, E. T. Higgins, and C. P. Herman, 2:173–86. Hillsdale, N.J.: Lawrence Erlbaum.

Ajzen, I., and M. Fishbein. 1980. *Understanding Attitudes and Predicting Social Behavior.* Englewood Cliffs, N.J.: Prentice Hall.

Alford, C. F. 1988. Mastery and Retreat: Psychological Sources of the Appeal of Ronald Reagan. *Political Psychology* 9:571–89.

Allison, G. 1971. *The Essence of Decision.* Boston: Little, Brown.

Almond, G. 1950. *The American People and Foreign Policy.* New York: Praeger.

Aronson, E. 1968. Dissonance Theory: Progress and Problems. In *Theories of Cognitive Consistency: A Sourcebook,* ed. R. Abelson, E. Aronson, W. McGuire, T. Newcomb, M. Rosenberg, and P. Tannenbaum, 5–27. Chicago: Rand McNally.

Aronson, E. 1978. The Theory of Cognitive Dissonance: A Current Perspective. In *Cognitive Theories in Social Psychology,* ed. L. Berkowitz, 181–211. San Francisco: Academic Press.

Barrett, L. 1983. *Gambling With History: Ronald Reagan in the White House.* New York: Doubleday.

Bem, D. 1967. Self-Perception: An Alternative Interpretation of Cognitive Dissonance Phenomena. *Psychological Review* 74:183–200.

Bem, D. 1972. Self-Perception Theory. In *Advances in Experimental Social Psychology,* ed. L. Berkowitz, 221–82. San Francisco: Academic Press.

Bem, D. 1978. Self-Perception Theory. In *Cognitive Theories in Social Psychology,* ed. L. Berkowitz, 221–82. San Francisco: Academic Press.

Bem, D. 1982. Persons, Situations, and Template Matching: Theme and Variation. In *Consistency in Social Behavior: The Ontario Symposium,* ed. M. Zanna, E. T. Higgins, and C. P. Herman, 2:173–86. Hillsdale, N.J.: Lawrence Erlbaum.

Bem, D., and H. K. McConnell. 1970. Testing the Self-Perception Explanation of Dissonance Phenomena. *Journal of Personality and Social Psychology* 14:23–30.

Berelson, B. 1952. *Content Analysis in Communications Research.* Glencoe, Ill.: Free Press.

251

Board, W. 1987. Space Weapons Plan Now Being Weighed Was Assailed in 82. *New York Times*, May 4.

Boulding, K. 1956. *The Image*. Ann Arbor: University of Michigan Press.

Brady, L. 1978. The Situation and Foreign Policy. In *Why Nations Act,* ed. M. East, S. Salamore, and C. Hermann, 173–90. Beverly Hills: Sage.

Brownstein, R., and N. Easton. 1983. *Reagan's Ruling Class: Portraits of the President's Top One Hundred Officials*. New York: Macmillan.

Burgess, P. 1968. *Elite Images and Foreign Policy Outcomes*. Columbus: Ohio State University Press.

Cannon, L. 1980. Reagan Asserts U.S. Security in Jeopardy. *Washington Post*, August 21.

Cannon, L. 1982. *Reagan*. New York: Perigree.

Carmines, E. 1986. The Analysis of Covariance Structure Models. In *New Tools for Social Scientists,* ed. W. D. Berry and M. S. Lewis-Beck, 23–55. Beverly Hills: Sage.

Carney, T. 1972. *Content Analysis*. Winnipeg: University of Manitoba Press.

Christiansen, B. 1959. *Attitudes toward Foreign Affairs as a Function of Personality*. Oslo: University of Oslo Press.

Cottam, M. 1986. *Foreign Policy Decision Making: The Influence of Cognition*. Boulder, Colo.: Westview.

Cottam, R. 1977. *Foreign Policy Motivation*. Pittsburgh: University of Pittsburgh Press.

Dallek, R. 1984. *Ronald Reagan: The Politics of Symbolism*. Cambridge: Harvard University Press.

Dallin, A., and G. Lapidus. 1987. Reagan and the Russians: American Policy toward the Soviet Union. In *Eagle Resurgent? The Reagan Era in American Foreign Policy,* ed. K. Oye, R. Lieber, and D. Rothchild, 193–254. Boston: Little, Brown.

Davis, V. 1986. The Reagan Defense Program. In *The Reagan Defense Progam: An Interim Assessment,* ed. S. Cimbala, 23–62. Willimington, Del.: Scholarly Resources.

Duetsch, M., and R. Merritt. 1965. Effects of Events on National and International Images. In *International Behavior,* ed. H. Kelman, 130–87. New York: The Free Press.

Edwards, A. 1987. *Early Reagan*. New York: Morrow.

Festinger, L. 1957. *A Theory of Cognitive Dissonance*. Stanford: Stanford University Press.

Fishbein, M., and I. Ajzen. 1975. *Belief, Attitude, Intention, and Behavior*. Boston: Addison-Wesley.

Gamson, W. A., and A. Modigliani. 1971. *Untangling the Cold War*. Boston: Little, Brown.

Garthoff, R. 1985. *Détente and Confrontation*. Washington, D.C.: Brookings.

Gelb, L. 1985. The Mind of the President. *New York Times Magazine,* October 6.

George, A. 1969. The "Operational Code": A Neglected Approach to the Study of Political Leaders and Decision Making. *International Studies Quarterly* 13:190–222.

George, A. 1979. The Causal Nexus between Cognitive Beliefs and Decision Making Behavior: The "Operational Code." In *Psychological Models in International Politics,* ed. L. Falkowski, 95–124. Boulder, Colo.: Westview.

Glad, B. 1983, Black-and-White Thinking: Ronald Reagan's Approach to Foreign Policy. *Political Psychology* 4:33–76.

Glass, D. G. 1968. Individual Differences and the Resolution of Cognitive Inconsistencies. In *Theories of Cognitive Consistency: A Sourcebook,* ed. R. Abelson, E. Aronson, W. McGuire, T. Newcomb, M. Rosenberg, and P. Tannenbaum, 615–23. Chicago: Rand McNally.

Glynn, P. 1988. Reagan's Rush to Disarm. *Commentary,* March.

Goldstein, K., and S. Blackman. 1978. *Cognitive Style.* New York: Wiley.

Guertner, G. 1988. Three Images of Soviet Arms Control Compliance. Photocopy.

Gwertzman, B. 1983. The Shultz Method: How the New Secretary is Trying to Stabilize Foreign Policy. *New York Times Magazine,* January 2.

Haig, A. 1984. *Caveat: Realism, Reagan, and Foreign Policy.* New York: Macmillan.

Haley, P.E. 1987. You Could Have Said Yes: Lessons from Reykjavík. Orbis 31:75–97.

Harries, O. 1988. The Rise of American Decline. *Commentary,* May.

Herken, G. 1985. *Counsels of War.* New York: Knopf.

Hermann, M. 1983. Assessing Personality at a Distance: A Profile of Ronald Reagan. *Mershon Center Quarterly Report* 7:1–7.

Hermann, M. 1988. How Predominant Leaders Shape Foreign Policy Decisions. Presented at the Midwest annual meeting of the International Studies Association, Columbus, Ohio.

Herrmann, R. 1985. American Perceptions of Soviet Foreign Policy: Reconsidering Three Competing Perspectives. *Political Psychology* 6:375–411.

Herrmann, R. 1986. The Power of Perceptions in Foreign Policy Decision Making: Do Views of the Soviet Union Determine the Policy Choices of American Leaders? *American Journal of Political Science* 30:841–75.

Herrmann, R. 1988. The Empirical Challenge of the Cognitive Revolution: A Strategy for Drawing Inferences about Perceptions. *International Studies Quarterly* 32:175–203.

Hoffmann, S. 1988. Review of 1999: *Victory without War. New Republic,* May 23.

Holsti, O. 1962. The Belief System and National Images: A Case Study. *Journal of Conflict Resolution* 6:244–52.

Holsti, O. 1969. *Content Analysis for the Social Sciences and Humanities.* Reading, Mass.: Addison-Wesley.

Holsti, O. 1970. The "Operational Code" Approach to the Study of Political Leaders: John Foster Dulles' Philosophical and Instrumental Beliefs. *Canadian Journal of Political Science* 3:123–57.

Holsti, O. 1976. Foreign Policy Viewed Cognitively. In *The Structure of Decision,* ed. R. Axelrod, 18–54. Princeton: Princeton University Press.

Holsti, O. 1977a. Foreign Policy Decision-Making Viewed Cognitively. In *Thought and Action in Foreign Policy,* ed. G. M. Bonham and M. Shapiro, 1–74. Basel: Birkhauser Verlag.

Holsti, O. 1977b. *The "Operational Code" as an Approach to the Analysis of Belief*

*Systems*. Final report to the National Science Foundation, Grant No. Soc75-15368.

Holsti, O. 1982. The Operational Code Approach: Problems and Some Solutions. In *Cognitive Dynamics and International Politics*, ed. C. Jonsson, 75–90. New York: St. Martin's.

Hoopes, T. 1973. *The Devil and John Foster Dulles*. Boston: Little, Brown.

Hoover, R. 1986. Strategic Arms Limitation and U.S. Decision Making. In *Technology, Strategy and Arms Control*, ed. W. F. Hanrieder, 93–111. Boulder, Colo.: Westview.

IISA. (International Institute for Security Affairs) 1982–83. *Strategic Survey*. London: IISA.

IISA. 1983–84. *Strategic Survey*. London: IISA.

IISA. 1984–85. *Strategic Survey*. London: IISA.

IISA. 1985–86. *Strategic Survey*. London: IISA

IISA. 1986–87. *Strategic Survey*. London: IISA.

IISA. 1987–88. *Strategic Survey*. London: IISA.

Jensen, L. 1988. *Bargaining for National Security*. Columbia: University of South Carolina Press.

Jervis, R. 1970. *The Logic of Images in International Politics*. Princeton: Princeton University Press.

Jervis, R. 1976. *Perception and Misperception in International Politics*. Princeton: Princeton University Press.

Jervis, R. 1980. Political Decision Making: Recent Contributions. *Political Psychology* 2:86–101.

Johnson, J., and R. Joslyn. 1986. *Political Science Research Methods*. Washington, D.C.: CQ Press.

Jonsson, C. 1984. *Superpower*. New York: St. Martin's.

Jonsson, C., ed. 1982. *Cognitive Dynamics and International Politics*. New York: St. Martin's.

Kennan, G. 1977. *The Cloud of Danger*. Boston: Little, Brown.

Kondrake, M. 1983. Nowhere Man. *The New Republic*, May 16.

Krippendorff, K. 1980. *Content Analysis*. Beverly Hills: Sage.

Kull, S. 1988. *Minds at War: Nuclear Reality and the Inner Conflicts of Defense Policymakers*. New York: Basic Books.

Labrie, R. 1979. *SALT Book: Key Documents and Issues, 1972–1979*. Washington, D.C.: American Enterprise Institute.

Larson, D. 1985. *The Origins of Containment: A Psychological Explanation*. Princeton: Princeton University Press.

Larson, D. 1988. Problems of Content Analysis in Foreign Policy Research: Notes from the Study of the Origins of Cold War Belief Systems. *International Studies Quarterly* 32:241–55.

Leng, R. 1984. Reagan and the Russians. *American Political Science Review* 78:338-55.

McMahan, J. 1985. *Reagan and the World*. London: Pluto Press.

Mandelbaum, M., and S. Talbott. 1984. *Reagan and the Russians*. New York: Vintage.

Miller, L. 1987. Schmidt, Carter, Reagan, and Double Dependencies. *War and Society* 5:89–105.

Miller, G., and M. Rokeach. 1969. Individual Differences and Tolerance for Inconsistency. In *Theories of Cognitive Consistency: A Sourcebook,* ed. R. Abelson, E. Aronson, W. McGuire, T. Newcomb, M. Rosenberg, and P. Tannenbaum, 624–33. Chicago: Rand McNally.

Mills, J. 1968. Interest in Supporting and Discrepant Information. In *Theories of Cognitive Consistency: A Sourcebook,* ed. R. Abelson, E. Aronson, W. McGuire, T. Newcomb, M. Rosenberg, and P. Tannenbaum, 771–76. Chicago: Rand McNally.

Morgenthau, H. 1967. *Politics among Nations.* New York: Knopf.

Nachmias, D., and C. Nachmias. 1987. *Research Methods in the Social Sciences.* New York: St. Martin's.

NAS. (National Academy of Sciences) 1985. *Nuclear Arms Control: Background and Issues.* Washington D.C.: National Academy Press.

Newhouse, J. 1989. *Peace and War in the Nuclear Age.* New York: Knopf.

Osgood, R. ed. 1981. *Containment, Soviet Behavior, and Grand Strategy.* Berkeley: Institute for International Studies.

Pettman, R. 1975. *Human Behavior and World Politics.* New York: St. Martin's.

Pilisuk, M. 1968. Depth, Centrality, and Tolerance in Cognitive Consistency. In *Theories of Cognitive Consistency: A Sourcebook,* ed. R. Abelson, E. Aronson, W. McGuire, T. Newcomb, M. Rosenberg, and P. Tannenbaum, 693–99. Chicago: Rand McNally.

Pipes, R. 1982. Why the Soviet Union Thinks It Can Fight and Win a Nuclear War. In *The Defense Policies of Nations*, ed. P. Murray and P. Viotti, 134–46. Baltimore: Johns Hopkins University Press.

Pranger, R. 1979. *Six Perspectives on Soviet Foreign Policy Intentions.* Washington, D.C.: American Enterprise Institute.

Rapoport, A. 1960. *Fights, Games, and Debates.* Ann Arbor: University of Michigan Press.

Regan, D. 1988. *For the Record: From Wall Street to Washington.* San Francisco: Harcourt, Brace Jovanovich.

Risse-Kappen, T. 1988. *The Zero Option.* Boulder, Colo.: Westview.

Rokeach, M. 1960. *The Open and Closed Mind.* New York: Basic Books.

Rosati, J. 1982. *The Carter Administration's Image of the International System.* Ph.D. diss. American University.

Rosati, J. 1984. The Impact of Beliefs on Behavior: The Foreign Policy of the Carter Administration. In *Foreign Policy Decision Making,* ed. D. Sylvan and S. Chan, 157–91. New York: Praeger.

Rosati, J. 1987. *The Carter Administration's Quest for Global Community: Beliefs and Their Impact on Behavior.* Columbia: University of South Carolina Press.

Sarnoff, I. 1968. Psychoanalytic Theory and Cognitive Dissonance. In *Theories of Cognitive Consistency: A Sourcebook,* ed. R. Abelson, E. Aronson, W. McGuire, T. Newcomb, M. Rosenberg, and P. Tannenbaum, 192–200. Chicago: Rand McNally.

Schwartzmann, D. 1988. *Games of Chicken: Four Decades of U.S. Nuclear Policy.* New York: Praeger.

Scott, W. 1965. Psychological and Social Correlates of International Images. In *International Behavior,* ed. H. Kelman, 70–103. New York: Holt, Rinehart and Winston.

Sears, D. 1968. The Paradox of De Facto Selective Exposure Without Preferences for Supportive Information. In *Theories of Cognitive Consistency: A Sourcebook,* ed. R. Abelson, E. Aronson, W. McGuire, T. Newcomb, M. Rosenberg, and P. Tannenbaum, 777–87. Chicago: Rand McNally.

Secord, P., and C. Blackman. 1964. *Social Psychology.* New York: McGraw-Hill.

Sjoblom, G. 1982. Some Problems of the Operational Code Approach. In *Cognitive Dynamics and World Politics,* ed. C. Jonsson, 37–74 . New York: St. Martin's.

Sloan, S., and R. Gray. 1984. *Nuclear Strategy and Arms Control.* Washington, D.C.: Foreign Policy Association.

Smith, H. 1988. *The Power Game.* New York: Random House.

Snyder, G., and P. Diesing. 1977. *Conflict Among Nations.* Princeton: Princeton University Press.

Snyder, M. 1982. When Believing Means Doing: Creating Links between Attitudes and Behavior. In *Consistency in Social Behavior,* ed. M. Zanna, E. T. Higgins, and C. P. Herman, 105–30. Hillsdale, N.J.: Lawrence Erlbaum.

Starr, H. 1984. *Henry Kissinger: Perceptions of International Politics.* Lexington: University of Kentucky Press.

Steel, R. 1981. Cold War, Cold Comfort. *New Republic,* April 11.

Steinbruner, J. 1974. *The Cybernetic Theory of Decision.* Princeton: Princeton University Press.

Stockman, D. 1986. *The Triumph of Politics.* New York: Harper and Row.

Stoessinger, J. 1976. *Henry Kissinger: The Anguish of Power.* New York: Norton.

Stuart, D., and H. Starr. 1981–82. The Inherent Bad Faith Model Reconsidered. *Political Psychology* 2:1–33.

Sullivan, A. 1989. Mr. Average. *New Republic,* January 9 and 16.

Talbott, S. 1985. *Deadly Gambits: The Reagan Administration and the Stalemate in Nuclear Arms Control.* New York: Vintage.

Talbott, S. 1988. *The Master of the Game.* New York: Vintage.

Tannenbaum, P., and R. Gengel. 1986. Generalization of Attitude Change through Congruity. *Journal of Personality and Social Psychology* 3:233–38.

TRB. 1989. Legacy? What Legacy? *New Republic,* January 9 and 16.

Triandis, H. 1971. *Attitudes and Attitude Change.* New York: Wiley.

Walker, S. 1977. The Interface between Beliefs and Behavior: Henry Kissinger's Operational Code and the Vietnam War. *Journal of Conflict Resolution* 21:129–68.

Walker, S. 1988. The Impact of Personality Structure and Cognitive Processes on American Foreign Policy Decision Makers. Presented at the annual meeting of the American Political Science Association, Washington, D.C.

Walker, S. 1990. The Evolution of Operational Code Analysis. *Political Psychology* 11:403–18.

Waltz, K. 1959. *Man, the State, and War.* New York: Columbia University Press.

White, R. 1968. *Nobody Wanted War.* New York: Doubleday.

White, R. 1984. *Fearful Warriors.* New York: Free Press.

Wills, G. 1987. *Reagan's America: Innocents at Home.* New York: Doubleday.

Wohlstetter, R. 1962. *Pearl Harbor: Warning and Decision.* Stanford: Stanford University Press.

Yergin, D. 1977. *Shattered Peace.* New York: Houghton Mifflin.

Zanna, M., and J. Olson. 1982. Individual Differences in Attitudinal Relations. In *Consistency in Social Behavior: The Ontario Symposium,* ed. M. Zanna, E. T. Higgins, and C. P. Herman, 75–104. Hillsdale, N.J.: Lawrence Erlbaum.

**Burt Documents**

Congressional Testimony

U.S. Congress. 1981a. House. Subcommittee of the Committee on Foreign Affairs. *Hearings on Foreign Assistance Legislation for FY 1982.* 97th Cong., 1st sess. March 23.

U.S. Congress. 1981b. Senate. Committee on Foreign Relations. *Hearings on Yellow Rain.* 97th Cong., 1st sess. October 10.

U.S. Congress. 1981c. House. Subcommittee of the Committee on Foreign Affairs. *Hearings on U.S. Arms Transfer Policy in Latin America.* 97th Cong., 1st sess. October 22.

U.S. Congress. 1982a. House. Subcommittee of the Committee on Foreign Affairs. *Overview of Nuclear Arms Control and Defense Strategy in NATO.* 97th Cong., 2nd sess. February 23.

U.S. Congress. 1982b. House. Committee on Armed Services. *Hearings on Military Posture.* 97th Cong., 2nd sess. February 23.

U.S. Congress. 1982c. Senate. Armed Services Committee. *Hearings on DOD Authorizations for Appropriations for FY 1982.* 97th Cong., 2nd sess. March 22.

U.S. Congress. 1982d. House. Subcommittee of the Committee on Foreign Affairs. *Hearings on Foreign Policy and Arms Control Implications of Chemical Weapons.* 97th Cong., 2nd sess. March 30.

U.S. Congress. 1982e. House. Committee on Foreign Affairs. *Hearings on Strategic Arms Control and U.S. National Security Policy.* 97th Cong., 2nd sess. April 2.

U.S. Congress. 1983a. House. Subcommittee of the Committee on Foreign Affairs. *Hearings on Developments in Europe, March, 1983.* 98th Cong., 1st sess. March 7.

U.S. Congress. 1983b. Senate. Committee on Foreign Relations. *Hearings on Security and Development Assistance for 1984.* 98th Cong., 1st sess. March 9.

U.S. Congress. 1983c. House. Subcommittee of the Armed Services Committee. *Hearings on Arms Control and Disarmament Activities.* 98th Cong., 1st sess. March 9.

U.S. Congress. 1983d. House. Committee in Foreign Affairs. *Hearings on Foreign Assistance Legislation for FY 1984–85 (pt. 3).* 98th Cong., 1st sess. March 16.

U.S. Congress. 1983e. House. Subcommittee of the Committee on Foreign Affairs. *Hearings on Developments in Europe, March, 1983.* 98th Cong., 1st sess. May 18.

U.S. Congress. 1983f. House. Subcommittee of the Committee on Foreign Affairs. *Hearings on Developments in Europe, August, 1983.* 98th Cong., 1st sess. August 1.

U.S. Congress. 1983g. House. Subcommittee of the Committee on Foreign Affairs. *Hearings on Developments in Europe, September, 1983.* 98th Cong., 1st sess. September 22.

U.S. Congress. 1984a. House. Subcommittee of the Committee on Foreign Affairs. *Hearings on Foreign Assistance Legislation for FY 1985.* 98th Cong., 2nd sess. February 6.

U.S. Congress. 1984b. House. Committee on Foreign Affairs. *Hearings on Foreign Assistance Legislation for FY 1985.* 98th Cong., 2nd sess. February 7.

U.S. Congress. 1984c. Senate. Committee on Foreign Relations. *Hearings on Security and Development Assistance for 1985.* 98th Cong., 2nd sess. March 7.

U.S. Congress. 1984d. House. Subcommittee of the Committee on Foreign Affairs. *Hearings on Developments in Europe, March, 1984.* 98th Cong., 2nd sess. March 20.

U.S. Congress. 1984e. House. Subcommittee of the Committee on Foreign Affairs. *Hearings on Developments in Europe, June, 1984.* 98th Cong., 2nd sess. June 24.

U.S. Congress. 1985a. Senate. Committee on Foreign Relations. *Hearings on Commitments, Consensus, and U.S. Foreign Policy.* 99th Cong., 1st sess. February 25.

U.S. Congress. 1985b. Senate. Subcommittee of the Committee on Foreign Relations. *Hearings on Security and Development Assistance for 1986.* 99th Cong., 1st sess. March 22.

U.S. Congress. 1985c. House. Subcommittee of the Committee on Foreign Affairs. *Hearings on Developments in Europe, March, 1985.* 99th Cong., 1st sess. March 27.

U.S. Congress. 1985d. House. Subcommittee of the Committee on Foreign Affairs. *Hearings on Developments in Europe, May, 1985.* 99th Cong., 1st sess. May 22.

Speeches

Transcripts of 5 Burt speeches were contained in the *Department of State Bulletin.*

Interviews

NBC News. 1983. "Meet the Press," March 20.

Articles

1976. The Cruise Missile and Arms Control. *Survival,* January/February.

1978. The Scope and Limits of SALT. *Foreign Affairs,* July.

1979. The Future of Arms Control: A Glass Half Full. *Foreign Policy,* Fall.

1988. Strength and Strategy: U.S. Security in the 1990s. *Washington Quarterly,* Spring.

## Perle Documents

### Congressional Testimony

U.S. Congress. 1981a. Senate. Committee on Armed Services. *Hearings on the Nomination of Richard Perle.* 97th Cong., 1st sess. July 6.

U.S. Congress. 1981b. Senate. Committee on Foreign Relations. *Hearings on International Security Policy.* 97th Cong., 1st sess. July 27.

U.S. Congress. 1981c. House. Subcommittee of the Committee on Foreign Affairs. *Hearings on Export Controls on Oil and Gas Equipment.* 97th Cong., 1st sess. November 12.

U.S. Congress. 1981d. Senate. Committee on Armed Services. *Hearings on Arms Control Policy, Planning, and Negotiations.* 97th Cong., 1st sess. December 1.

U.S. Congress. 1981e. Senate. Committee on Banking, Housing, and Urban Affairs. *Hearings on the Proposed Trans-Siberian Pipeline.* 97th Cong., 1st sess. December 12.

U.S. Congress. 1982a. House. Subcommittee of the Committee on Foreign Affairs. *Hearings on Nuclear Arms Control.* 97th Cong., 2nd sess. February 23.

U.S. Congress. 1982b. House. Committee on Armed Services. *Hearings on Military Posture.* 97th Cong., 2nd sess. February 23.

U.S. Congress. 1982c. Senate. Committee on Armed Services. *Hearings on Strategy and Nuclear Forces.* 97th Cong., 2nd sess. March 1.

U.S. Congress. 1982d. House. Subcommittee of the Armed Services Committee. *Hearings on Military Posture and H. R. 5968.* 97th Cong., 2nd sess. March 2.

U.S. Congress. 1982e. House. Committee on Armed Services. *Hearings on Military Posture.* 97th Cong., 2nd sess. March 12.

U.S. Congress. 1982f. Senate. Subcommittee of the Committee on Foreign Relations. *Hearings on U.S. and Soviet Civil Defense Programs.* 97th Cong., 2nd sess. March 16.

U.S. Congress. 1982g. Senate. Committee on Armed Services. *Hearings on Strategic and Theater Nuclear Forces.* 97th Cong., 2nd sess. March 17.

U.S. Congress. 1982h. Senate. Armed Services Committee. *Hearings on Department of Defense Authorizations for Appropriations for FY 1983.* 97th Cong., 2nd sess. March 22.

U.S. Congress. 1982i. Senate. Armed Services Committee. *Hearings on Department of Defense Authorizations for Appropriations.* 97th Cong., 2nd sess. March 28.

U.S. Congress. 1982j. Senate. Subcommittee of the Committee on Foreign Relations. *Hearings on Arms Control.* 97th Cong., 2nd sess. March 31.

U.S. Congress. 1982k. House. Committee on Foreign Affairs. *Hearings on Strategy, Arms Control, and U.S. National Security Policy.* 97th Cong., 2nd sess. April 2.

U.S. Congress. 1982l. Senate. Committee on Foreign Relations. *Hearings on Strategic Arms Control and U.S. National Security Policy.* 97th Cong., 2nd sess. April 15.

U.S. Congress. 1982m. Senate. Committee on Appropriations. *Hearings on Department of Defense Appropriations FY 1983.* 97th Cong., 2nd sess. April 22.

U.S. Congress. 1983a. House. Committee on Foreign Affairs. *Hearings on Resolution Calling for a Mutual and Verifiable Nuclear Freeze.* 98th Cong., 1st sess. February 17.

U.S. Congress. 1983b. House. Subcommittee of the Committee on Appropriations. *Hearings on Military Construction for FY 1984.* 98th Cong., 1st sess. March 3.

U.S. Congress. 1983c. Senate. Committee on Foreign Relations. *Hearings on Security and Development Assistance.* 98th Cong., 1st sess. March 9.

U.S. Congress. 1983d. Senate. Subcommittee of the Committee on Appropriations. *Hearings on Military Posture.* 98th Cong., 1st sess. March 12.

U.S. Congress. 1983e. Senate. Committee on Armed Services. *Hearings on Department of Defense Authorizations for FY 1984.* 98th Cong., 1st sess. March 15.

U.S. Congress. 1983f. House. Subcommittee of the Committee on Foreign Affairs. *Hearings on Foreign Assistance Legislation for FY 1984–85.* 98th Cong., 1st sess. March 16.

U.S. Congress. 1983g. Senate. Committee on Foreign Relations. *Hearings on Security and Development Assistance.* 98th Cong., 1st sess. July 12.

U.S. Congress. 1983h. House. Subcommittee of the Committee on Armed Services. *Hearings on the People Protection Act.* 98th Cong., 1st sess. November 10.

U.S. Congress. 1984a. Senate. Committee on Foreign Relations. *Hearings on Security and Development Assistance.* 98th Cong., 2nd sess. March 7.

U.S. Congress. 1984b. Senate. Committee on Armed Services. *Hearings on Soviet Treaty Violations.* 98th Cong., 2nd sess. March 14.

U.S. Congress. 1984c. Senate. Committee on Armed Services. *Hearings on Department of Defense Authorizations for Appropriations for FY 1985.* 98th Cong., 2nd sess. March 15.

U.S. Congress. 1984d. Senate. Committee on Appropriations. *Hearings on SALT II Violations.* 98th Cong., 2nd sess. March 28.

U.S. Congress. 1984e. Senate. Committee on Armed Services. *Hearings on Department of Defense Authorizations for Appropriations for FY 1985.* 98th Cong., 2nd sess. April 12.

U.S. Congress. 1984f. Senate. Committee on Foreign Relations. *Hearings on the Strategic Defense and Anti-Satellite Weapons.* 98th Cong., 2nd sess. April 25.

U.S. Congress. 1984g. Senate. Committee on Appropriations. *Hearings on Department of Defense Authorizations for FY 1984.* 98th Cong., 2nd sess. May 10.

U.S. Congress. 1984h. House. Committee on Foreign Affairs. *Hearings on the Role of Arms Control in U.S. Defense Policy.* 98th Cong., 2nd sess. June 20.

U.S. Congress. 1984i. House. Subcommittee of the Committee on Foreign Affairs. *Hearings on Political and Military Issues in the Atlantic Alliance.* 98th Cong., 2nd sess. October 1.

U.S. Congress. 1985a. Senate. Committee on Armed Services. *Hearings on Soviet Treaty Violations.* 99th Cong., 1st sess. February 20.

U.S. Congress. 1985b. House. Subcommittee of the Committee on Foreign Affairs.

*Hearings on Foreign Assistance Legislation for FY 1986–87*. 99th Cong., 1st sess. February 21.

U.S. Congress. 1985c. Senate. Committee on Foreign Relations. *Hearings on Commitments, Consensus, and U.S. Foreign Policy*. 99th Cong., 1st sess. February 25 and November 12.

U.S. Congress. 1985d. House. Subcommittee of the Committee on Armed Services. *Hearings on Arms Control and Disarmament Activity*. 99th Cong., 1st sess. March 9.

U.S. Congress. 1985e. Senate. Committee on Armed Services. *Hearings on Department of Defense Authorization for Appropriations for FY 1986*. 99th Cong., 1st sess. March 13.

U.S. Congress. 1985f. House and Senate. Subcommittee of the Committee on Science and Technology and the Committee on the Interior and Insular Affairs. *Hearings on Nuclear Winter*. 99th Cong., 1st sess. March 14.

U.S. Congress. 1985g. House. Subcommittee of the Committee on Foreign Affairs. *Hearings on U.S. and Multilateral Export Controls*. 99th Cong., 1st sess. April 23.

U.S. Congress. 1985h. Senate. Committee on Armed Services. *Hearings on Soviet Treaty Violations*. 99th Cong., 1st sess. May 7.

U.S. Congress. 1985i. House. Subcommittee of the Committee on Appropriations. *Hearings on Foreign Assistance Program for 1986*. 99th Cong., 1st sess. May 9.

U.S. Congress. 1985j. House. Special Panel of the Committee on Armed Services. *Hearings on the Review of Arms Control and Disarmament Activities*. 99th Cong., 1st sess. September 18.

U.S. Congress. 1985k. Senate. Committee on Armed Services. *Hearings on Nuclear Winter and Its Implications*. 99th Cong., 1st sess. October 3.

U.S. Congress. 1985l. Senate. Subcommittee of the Committee on Governmental Affairs. *Hearings on Foreign Missions Action and Espionage in the U.S.* 99th Cong., 1st sess. October 22.

U.S. Congress. 1985m. Senate. Subcommittee of the Committee on Armed Services. *Hearings on the Strategic Defense Initiative*. 99th Cong., 1st sess. November 6.

U.S. Congress. 1985n. House. Subcommittee of the Committee on Foreign Affairs. *Hearings on Technology Transfer and the SDI Agreement*. 99th Cong., 1st sess. December 10.

U.S. Congress. 1986a. Senate. Committee on Armed Services. *Hearings on Authorizations for Appropriations for FY 1987*. 99th Cong., 2nd sess. March 25.

U.S. Congress. 1986b. Senate. Committee on Armed Services. *Hearings on Nuclear Testing Issues*. 99th Cong., 2nd sess. April 26.

U.S. Congress. 1986c. Senate. Committee on Armed Services. *Hearings on Nuclear Testing Issues*. 99th Cong., 2nd sess. May 5.

U.S. Congress. 1986d. House. Panel of the Committee on Armed Services. *Hearings on U.S. Nuclear Forces and Arms Control Policy*. 99th Cong., 2nd sess. June 5.

U.S. Congress. 1986e. House. Panel of the Committee on Armed Services. *Hearings on the Process and Implications of the Iceland Summit.* 99th Cong., 2nd sess. November 21.

U.S. Congress. 1987a. House. Subcommittee of the Committee on Foreign Affairs. *Hearings on Foreign Assistance Legislation for FY 1988–89.* 100th Cong., 1st sess. March 3.

U.S. Congress. 1987b. Senate. Committee on Governmental Affairs. *Hearings on Nuclear Nonproliferation and U.S. National Security.* 100th Cong., 1st sess. March 5.

U.S. Congress. 1987c. House. Panel of the Committee on Armed Services. *Hearings on National Security Policy.* 100th Cong., 1st sess. March 11.

U.S. Congress. 1987d. House. Subcommittee of the Committee of Foreign Affairs. *Hearings on Soviet Compliance with Arms Control Agreements.* 100th Cong., 1st sess. March 12.

U.S. Congress. 1987e. Senate. Committee on Banking, Housing, and Urban Affairs. *Hearings on the Export-Import Bank and Export Promotion.* 100th Cong., 1st sess. March 12.

U.S. Congress. 1987f. House and Senate. Committee on Foreign Affairs and the Committee of the Judiciary. *Hearings on the ABM Treaty and the Constitution.* 100th Cong., 1st sess. March 26.

U.S. Congress. 1987g. House. Committee of Science, Space, and Technology. *Hearings on the National Academy of Science Report on International Technology Transfer.* 100th Cong., 1st sess. April 23.

## Interviews

NBC News. 1983. "Meet the Press." April 17.

CBS News. 1983. "Face the Nation." November 27.

CBS News. 1985. "Face the Nation." September 29.

## Articles/Editorials

1979. Echoes of the 1930s. *Strategic Review,* Winter.

1983. Technology and the Quiet War. *Strategic Review,* Winter.

1984. Soviet Military Technology. *Current,* Winter.

1987a. America's Failure of Nerve in Nicaragua. *U.S. News and World Report,* August 10.

1987b. The Dangers of Detente II. *U.S. News and World Report,* November 23.

1987c. The Political Trials of SDI. *U.S. News and World Report,* September 14.

1987d. The Real Stakes in the Persian Gulf. *U.S. News and World Report,* October 26.

1987e. Reykjavík as a Watershed in U.S.-Soviet Arms Control. *International Security,* Summer.

1988. What's Wrong with the INF Treaty. *U.S. News and World Report,* March 21.

## Shultz Documents

## Congressional Testimony

U.S. Congress. 1982a. Senate. Committee on Foreign Relations. *Hearings on the*

*Nomination of George Pratt Shultz to be Secretary of State.* 97th Cong., 2nd sess. July 13.

U.S. Congress. 1982b. Senate. Committee on Finance. *Hearings on the Caribbean Basin Initiative.* 97th Cong., 2nd sess. August 2.

U.S. Congress. 1983a. Senate. Committee on the Budget. *Hearings on the First Concurrent Resolution on the Budget for FY 1984.* 98th Cong., 1st sess. February 2.

U.S. Congress. 1983b. Senate. Committee on Foreign Relations. *Hearings on the Global Economic Outlook.* 98th Cong., 1st sess. February 15.

U.S. Congress. 1983c. House. Committee on Foreign Affairs. *Hearings on Foreign Assistance Legislation for FYs 1984–85 I.* 98th Cong., 1st sess. February 16.

U.S. Congress. 1983d. House. Committee on Foreign Affairs. *Hearings on the Authorization for Appropriations for FY 1984–85.* 98th Cong., 1st sess. February 23.

U.S. Congress. 1983e. Senate. Committee on Appropriations. *Hearings on Foreign Assistance Legislation for FY 1984.* 98th Cong., 1st sess. February 28.

U.S. Congress. 1983f. House. Subcommittee of the Committee on Appropriations. *Hearings on Foreign Assistance Legislation for FY 1984.* 98th Cong., 1st sess. March 16.

U.S. Congress. 1983g. Senate. Subcommittee of the Committee on Appropriations. *Hearings on El Salvador Military and Economic Assistance.* 98th Cong., 1st sess. March 22.

U.S. Congress. 1983h. Senate. Committee on Finance. *Hearings on the Caribbean Basin Initiative.* 98th Cong., 1st sess. April 13.

U.S. Congress. 1983i. Senate. Armed Services Committee. *Hearings on MX Basing Mode and Related Issues.* 98th Cong., 1st sess. April 20.

U.S. Congress. 1983j. Senate. Committee on Appropriations. *Hearings on Commerce, Justice, and State and Related Area Appropriations for FY 1984.* 98th Cong., 1st sess. April 21.

U.S. Congress. 1984a. House. Committee on Foreign Affairs. *Hearings on Foreign Assistance Legislation for FY 1985 I.* 98th Cong., 2nd sess. February 9.

U.S. Congress. 1984b. Senate. Committee on the Budget. *Hearings on the First Concurrent Resolution on the Budget for FY 1985.* 98th Cong., 2nd sess. February 21.

U.S. Congress. 1984c. Senate. Committee on Foreign Relations. *Hearings on Security and Development Assistance.* 98th Cong., 2nd sess. February 22.

U.S. Congress. 1984d. House. Subcommittee of the Committee on Appropriations. *Hearings on Foreign Assistance and Related Programs for 1985.* 98th Cong., 2nd sess. March 6.

U.S. Congress. 1984e. House. Committee on Appropriations. *Hearings on Departments of Commerce, State, and Justice Appropriations for 1985.* 98th Cong., 2nd sess. March 27.

U.S. Congress. 1984f. Senate. Subcommittee of the Committee on the Judiciary. *Hearings on the Annual Refugee Consultation for 1985.* 98th Cong., 2nd sess. September 11.

U.S. Congress. 1985a. Senate. Committee on Foreign Relations. *Hearings on Commitments, Consensus, and U.S. Foreign Policy.* 99th Cong., 1st sess. January 31.

U.S. Congress. 1985b. Senate. Committee on the Budget. *Hearings on the First Concurrent Resolution on the Budget for FY 1986.* 99th Cong., 1st sess. February 19.

U.S. Congress. 1985c. House. Committee on Foreign Affairs. *Hearings on Foreign Assistance Legislation for FYs 1986–87.* 99th Cong., 1st sess. February 19.

U.S. Congress. 1985d. Senate. Armed Services Committee. *Hearings on DOD Authorization for Appropriations for FY 1986.* 99th Cong., 1st sess. February 26.

U.S. Congress. 1985e. House. Committee on Foreign Affairs. *Hearings on the Authorization for Appropriations for FY 1986–87.* 99th Cong., 1st sess. February 27.

U.S. Congress. 1985f. House. Committee on Appropriations. *Hearings on Foreign Assistance and Development Assistance and Related Programs for 1986.* 99th Cong., 1st sess. March 2.

U.S. Congress. 1985g. Senate. Committee on Appropriations. *Hearings on Foreign Assistance and Related Programs for FY 1986.* 99th Cong., 1st sess. March 7.

U.S. Congress. 1985h. Senate. Committee of Foreign Relations. *Hearings on Security and Development Assistance for 1986.* 99th Cong., 1st sess. March 15.

U.S. Congress. 1985i. House. Committee on Foreign Affairs. *Hearings on Legislation to Combat Terrorism.* 99th Cong., 1st sess. June 13.

U.S. Congress. 1985j. House. Committee on Foreign Affairs. *Hearings on Arms Sales to Jordan and the Middle East Peace Process.* 99th Cong., 1st sess. October 7.

U.S. Congress. 1986a. House. Committee on Foreign Affairs. *Hearings on the Foreign Assistance Budget for FY 1987.* 99th Cong., 2nd sess. February 5.

U.S. Congress. 1986b. Senate. Committee on the Budget. *Hearings on the Concurrent Resolution on the Budget for FY 1987.* 99th Cong., 2nd sess. February 19.

U.S. Congress. 1986c. Senate. Committee on Foreign Relations. *Hearings on U.S. Policy Toward Nicaragua.* 99th Cong., 2nd sess. February 27.

U.S. Congress. 1986d. House. Subcommittee of the Committee on Appropriations. *Hearings on Foreign Assistance Legislation for 1987.* 99th Cong., 2nd sess. March 4.

U.S. Congress. 1986e. House. Committee on Appropriations. *Hearings on Departments of Commerce, Justice, and State Appropriations for 1987.* 99th Cong., 2nd sess. March 12.

U.S. Congress. 1986f. Senate. Committee on Appropriations. *Hearings on Foreign Assistance and Related Programs for FY 1987.* 99th Cong., 2nd sess. March 13.

U.S. Congress. 1986g. Senate. Committee on Appropriations. *Hearings on Justice, State, and Judiciary and Related Agencies Appropriations for FY 1987.* 99th Cong., 2nd sess. March 19.

U.S. Congress. 1987a. Senate. Committee on the Budget. *Hearings on the Concurrent Resolution on the Budget for FY 1988.* 100th Cong., 1st sess. January 23.

U.S. Congress. 1987b. House. Committee on the Budget. *Hearings on the Revised Budget Proposal for 1988.* 100th Cong., 1st sess. January 28.

U.S. Congress. 1987c. Senate. Armed Services Committee. *Hearings on National Security Strategy.* 100th Cong., 1st sess. February 3.

U.S. Congress. 1987d. House. Committee on Appropriations. *Hearings on DOD Appropriations for 1988.* 100th Cong., 1st sess. February 11.

U.S. Congress. 1987e. Senate. Committee on Foreign Relations. *Hearings on Security and Development Assistance.* 100th Cong., 1st sess. February 24.

U.S. Congress. 1987f. House. Committee on Appropriations. *Hearings on Foreign Assistance and Related Programs for 1988.* 100th Cong., 1st sess. March 11.

U.S. Congress. 1987g. House. Committee on Appropriations. *Hearings on Departments of Commerce, Justice, State, and the Judiciary and Related Agency Appropriations for 1988.* 100th Cong., 1st sess. March 19.

U.S. Congress. 1987h. Senate. Committee on Appropriations. *Hearings on Commerce, State, Justice and the Judiciary, and Related Agency Appropriations for 1988.* 100th Cong., 1st sess. March 25.

U.S. Congress. 1987i. Senate. Committee on Appropriations. *Hearings on Foreign Assistance and Related Appropriations for FY 1988.* 100th Cong., 1st sess. August 7.

U.S. Congress. 1988a. Senate. Committee on Foreign Relations. *Hearings on the INF Treaty.* 100th Cong., 2nd sess. January 25.

U.S. Congress. 1988b. House. Committee on Foreign Affairs. *Hearings on the Review of U.S. Foreign and National Security Policy.* 100th Cong., 2nd sess. February 2.

U.S. Congress. 1988c. House. Subcommittee of the Committee on Appropriations. *Hearings on Foreign Operations, Export Financing, and Related Programs for 1989.* 100th Cong., 2nd sess. March 10.

U.S. Congress. 1988d. Senate. Committee on Foreign Relations. *Hearings on the INF Treaty.* 100th Cong., 2nd sess. March 14.

U.S. Congress. 1988e. House. Committee on the Budget. *Hearings on the Concurrent Resolution of the Budget for FY 1989.* 100th Cong., 2nd sess. March 17.

U.S. Congress. 1988f. House. Subcommittee of the Committee on Appropriations. *Hearings on Departments of Commerce, Justice, and State and Related Agency Appropriations for 1989.* 100th Cong., 2nd sess. May 4.

### Interviews, Press Conferences, Speeches

All of Shultz's speeches, media interviews and news conferences are in the Department of State Bulletin, which is published monthly by the Department of State. There were a total of 101 of these in which something was coded about Shultz's image of the Soviet Union.

### Other

1985. New Realities and New Ways of Thinking. *Foreign Affairs,* Spring.

## Weinberger Documents

### Congressional Testimony

U.S. Congress. 1981a. Senate. Armed Services Committee. *Hearings on the Nomination of Caspar W. Weinberger.* 97th Cong., 1st sess. January 6.

U.S. Congress. 1981b. Senate. Armed Services Committee. *Hearings on the DOD Authorization for Appropriations.* 97th Cong., 1st sess. January 28.

U.S. Congress. 1981c. Senate. Armed Services Committee. *Hearings on the DOD Authorization for Appropriations.* 97th Cong., 1st sess. March 4.

U.S. Congress. 1981d. House. Subcommittee of the Committee on Appropriations. *Hearings on DOD Appropriations for 1982.* 97th Cong., 1st sess. March 9.

U.S. Congress. 1981e. House. Committee on Armed Services. *Hearings on Military Posture.* 97th Cong., 1st sess. March 10.

U.S. Congress. 1981f. House. Subcommittee of the Committee on Appropriations. *Hearings on DOD Appropriations for 1982.* 97th Cong., 1st sess. March 18.

U.S. Congress. 1981g. House. Subcommittee of the Committee on Appropriations. *Hearings on DOD Appropriations for 1982.* 97th Cong., 1st sess. March 19.

U.S. Congress. 1981h. House. Committee on the Budget. *Hearings on Budget Issues of 1982.* 97th Cong., 1st sess. March 20.

U.S. Congress. 1981i. Senate. Armed Services Committee. *Hearings on FY 1981 DOD Supplemental Authorizations.* 97th Cong., 1st sess. March 23.

U.S. Congress. 1981j. Senate. Committee on the Budget. *Hearings on the First Concurrent Resolution on the Budget, FY 1982.* 97th Cong., 1st sess. April 4.

U.S. Congress. 1981k. House. Committee on Armed Services. *Hearings on Multiyear Procurement.* 97th Cong., 1st sess. June 23.

U.S. Congress. 1981l. House. Committee on the Budget. *Hearings on the Economic Outlook for the 2d Budget Resolution.* 97th Cong., 1st sess. September 23.

U.S. Congress. 1981m. House. Subcommittee of the Committee on Appropriations. *DOD Appropriations for FY 1982.* 97th Cong., 1st sess. September 24.

U.S. Congress. 1981n. Senate. Committee on Armed Services. *Hearings on the Modernization of the U.S. Strategic Deterrent.* 97th Cong., 1st sess. October 5 and November 5.

U.S. Congress. 1981o. House. Subcommittee of the Committee on Appropriations. *Hearings on DOD Appropriations for 1982.* 97th Cong., 1st sess. October 5.

U.S. Congress. 1981p. House. Committee on Armed Services. *Hearings on Military Posture and HR 5968.* 97th Cong., 1st sess. October 6.

U.S. Congress. 1981q. Senate. Subcommittee of the Committee on Appropriations. *Hearings on DOD Appropriations for FY 1982.* 97th Cong., 1st sess. October 28.

U.S. Congress. 1981r. Senate. Committee on Foreign Relations. *Hearings on Strategic Weapons Proposals.* 97th Cong., 1st sess. November 3.

U.S. Congress. 1981s. House. Subcommittee of the Committee on Appropriations. *Hearings on Military Construction Programs for 1982.* 97th Cong., 1st sess. November 5.

U.S. Congress. 1982a. Senate. Armed Services Committee. *Hearings on DOD Authorization for Appropriations for FY 1983.* 97th Cong., 2nd sess. February 2.

U.S. Congress. 1982b. House. Committee on Armed Services. *Hearings on Military Posture.* 97th Cong., 2nd sess. February 3.

U.S. Congress. 1982c. House. Subcommittee of the Committee on Appropriations. *Hearings on DOD Appropriations for 1983.* 97th Cong., 2nd sess. February 24.

U.S. Congress. 1982d. Senate. Subcommittee of the Committee on Appropriations.

*Hearings on Military Construction Appropriations for 1983.* 97th Cong., 2nd sess. February 24.

U.S. Congress. 1982e. House. Committee on Appropriations. *Hearings on DOD Appropriations for 1983.* 97th Cong., 2nd sess. February 25.

U.S. Congress. 1982f. House. Committee on Budget. *Hearings on the First Concurrent Resolution on the Budget for FY 1983.* 97th Cong., 2nd sess. March 3.

U.S. Congress. 1982g. House. Committee on the Budget. *Hearings on Budget Issues of 1983.* 97th Cong., 2nd sess. March 4.

U.S. Congress. 1982h. House. Committee on Foreign Affairs. *Hearings on Role of International Security Assistance in U.S. Defense Policy.* 97th Cong., 2nd sess. March 10.

U.S. Congress. 1982i. Senate. Committee on Foreign Relations. *Hearings on Nuclear Arms Reductions Proposals.* 97th Cong., 2nd sess. April 29.

U.S. Congress. 1982j. Senate. Subcommittee of the Committee on Appropriations. *Hearings on DOD Appropriations for FY 1983.* 97th Cong., 2nd sess. May 2.

U.S. Congress. 1982k. Senate. Armed Services Committee. *Hearings on the DOD Authorization for Appropriations for FY 1983.* 97th Cong., 2nd sess. May 10.

U.S. Congress. 1982l. House. Committee on Armed Services. *Hearings on Military Posture.* 97th Cong., 2nd sess. May 13.

U.S. Congress. 1982m. House. Subcommittee of the Committee on Appropriations. *Hearings on Supplemental Appropriations for 1982.* 97th Cong., 2nd sess. May 18.

U.S. Congress. 1982n. House. Subcommittee of the Committee on Appropriations. *Hearings on DOD Appropriations for FY 1983.* 97th Cong., 2nd sess. August 17.

U.S. Congress. 1982o. Senate. Armed Service Committee. *Hearings on the MX Missile & Associated Basing Modes.* 97th Cong., 2nd sess. December 8.

U.S. Congress. 1982p. Senate. Committee on Foreign Relations. *Hearings on U.S. Strategic Doctrine.* 97th Cong., 2nd sess. December 14.

U.S. Congress. 1983a. Senate. Armed Service Committee. *Hearings on the DOD Authorization for Appropriations for FY 1984.* 98th Cong., 1st sess. February 1.

U.S. Congress. 1983b. Senate. Armed Services Committee. *Hearings on the DOD Authorization for Appropriations for FY 1984.* 98th Cong., 1st sess. February 3.

U.S. Congress. 1983c. House. Subcommittee of the Committee on Appropriations. *Hearings on DOD Appropriations for 1984.* 98th Cong., 1st sess. February 8.

U.S. Congress. 1983d. House. Committee on the Budget. *Hearings on Defense and Budget Policy Overview.* 98th Cong., 1st sess. February 16.

U.S. Congress. 1983e. House. Committee on Foreign Affairs. *Hearings on Foreign Assistance Legislation for FY 1984–85 I.* 98th Cong., 1st sess. February 22.

U.S. Congress. 1983f. Senate. Committee on Appropriations. *Hearings on DOD Appropriations for FY 1984.* 98th Cong., 1st sess. February 23.

U.S. Congress. 1983g. Senate. Armed Services Committee. *Hearings on the MX Missile and Related Issues.* 98th Cong., 1st sess. April 20.

U.S. Congress. 1983h. House. Committee on Armed Services. *Hearings on the DOD Authorization for Appropriations for FY 1984.* 98th Cong., 1st sess. April 21.

U.S. Congress. 1983i. House. Subcommittee of the Committee on Appropriations.

*Hearings on Supplementary Appropriations for 1983–84.* 98th Cong., 1st sess. April 26.

U.S. Congress. 1983j. House. Subcommittee of the Committee on Appropriations. *Hearings on DOD Appropriations for 1984.* 98th Cong., 1st sess. May 3.

U.S. Congress. 1983k. House. Committee on Appropriations. *Hearings on the FY 1983 Supplemental Request for DOD.* 98th Cong., 1st sess. May 5.

U.S. Congress. 1983l. House. Subcommittee of the Committee on Appropriations. *Hearings on Military Construction for 1984.* 98th Cong., 1st sess. May 5.

U.S. Congress 1983m. Senate. Committee on Appropriations. *Hearings on the Resolution for Funding the MX Missile.* 98th Cong., 1st sess. May 5.

U.S. Congress. 1983n. House. Committee on Foreign Affairs. *Hearings on the Review of Arms Control Implications of the President's Commission on Strategic Nuclear Forces.* 98th Cong., 1st sess. May 17.

U.S. Congress. 1983o. House. Committee on Foreign Affairs. *Hearings on the Review of Arms Control Implications of the President's Commission on Strategic Nuclear Forces.* 98th Cong., 1st sess. May 24.

U.S. Congress. 1984a. Senate. Armed Services Committee. *Hearings on the DOD Authorization for Appropriations for FY 1985.* 98th Cong., 2nd sess. February 1.

U.S. Congress. 1984b. House. Committee on Armed Services. *Hearings on the DOD Authorization for Appropriations for FY 1985.* 98th Cong., 2nd sess. February 2.

U.S. Congress. 1984c. Senate. Committee on the Budget. *Hearings on the First Concurrent Resolution on the Budget for FY 1985.* 98th Cong., 2nd sess. February 6.

U.S. Congress. 1984d. House. Committee on Foreign Affairs. *Hearings on Foreign Assistance Legislation for FY 1985 I.* 98th Cong., 2nd sess. February 9.

U.S. Congress. 1984e. House. Committee on the Budget. *Hearings on Views of Budget Proposals for FY 1985.* 98th Cong., 2nd sess. February 21.

U.S. Congress. 1984f. House. Committee on Appropriations. *Hearings on DOD Appropriations for 1985.* 98th Cong., 2nd sess. March 1.

U.S. Congress. 1984g. Senate. Armed Services Committee. *Hearings on Recommended FY 1985 Defense Funding Reductions.* 98th Cong., 2nd sess. May 3.

U.S. Congress. 1984h. Senate. Committee on Appropriations. *Hearings on DOD Appropriations for FY 1985.* 98th Cong., 2nd sess. May 24.

U.S. Congress. 1985a. Senate. Committee on Foreign Relations. *Hearings on Commitments, Consensus, and U.S. Foreign Policy.* 99th Cong., 1st sess. January 31.

U.S. Congress. 1985b. House. Committee on Foreign Affairs. *Hearings on Foreign Assistance Legislation for FYs 1986–87.* 99th Cong., 1st sess. February 2.

U.S. Congress. 1985c. Senate. Committee on Armed Services. *Hearings on the DOD Authorization for Appropriations for FY 1986.* 99th Cong., 1st sess. February 4.

U.S. Congress. 1985d. Senate. Committee on the Budget. *Hearings on the First Concurrent Resolution on the Budget FY 1986.* 99th Cong., 1st sess. February 7.

U.S. Congress. 1985e. House. Committee on Appropriations. *Hearings on the DOD Appropriations for 1986.* 99th Cong., 1st sess. February 7.

U.S. Congress. 1985f. Senate. Armed Services Committee. *Hearings on the DOD Authorization for Appropriations for FY 1986.* 99th Cong., 1st sess. February 26.

U.S. Congress. 1985g. Senate. Subcommittee of the Committee on Appropriations. *Hearings on the MX-Peacekeeper Missile Program.* 99th Cong., 1st sess. March 7.

U.S. Congress. 1985h. House. Committee on the Budget. *Hearings on Views of the Budget Proposal for FY 1986.* 99th Cong., 1st sess. March 7.

U.S. Congress. 1985i. House. Committee on Armed Services. *Hearings on the MX Missile and SDI.* 99th Cong., 1st sess. March 13.

U.S. Congress. 1985j. Senate. Committee on Appropriations. *Hearings on DOD Appropriations for FY 1986.* 99th Cong., 1st sess. June 25 and 26.

U.S. Congress. 1986a. Senate. Armed Services Committee. *Hearings on the DOD Authorization for Appropriations for FY 1987.* 99th Cong., 2nd sess. February 5.

U.S. Congress. 1986b. Senate. Committee on the Budget. *Hearings on the Concurrent Resolution on the Budget for FY 1987.* 99th Cong., 2nd sess. February 6.

U.S. Congress. 1986c. House. Committee on the Budget. *Hearings on the Impact of the President's 1987 Budget.* 99th Cong., 2nd sess. February 7.

U.S. Congress. 1986d. House. Committee on Foreign Affairs. *Hearings on Foreign Assistance Legislation for FY 1987.* 99th Cong., 2nd sess. February 19.

U.S. Congress. 1986e. House. Committee on Armed Services. Full Committee Consideration of H.J. Resolution 540. 99th Cong., 2nd sess. March 5.

U.S. Congress. 1986f. House. Committee on Appropriations. *Hearings on DOD Appropriations for 1987.* 99th Cong., 2nd sess. April 26.

U.S. Congress. 1986g. House. Subcommittee on Appropriations. *Hearings on DOD Appropriations for 1987.* 99th Cong., 2nd sess. April 26.

U.S. Congress. 1987a. Senate. Armed Services Committee. *Hearings on the National Security Strategy.* 100th Cong., 1st sess. January 12.

U.S. Congress. 1987b. Senate. Committee on the Budget. *Hearings on the Concurrent Resolution for the Budget for FY 1988.* 100th Cong., 1st sess. January 13.

U.S. Congress. 1987c. House. Committee on the Budget. *Hearings on the Review of Budget Proposals for FY 1988.* 100th Cong., 1st sess. January 21.

U.S. Congress. 1987d. Senate. Committee on Appropriations. *Hearings on DOD Appropriations for 1988.* 100th Cong., 1st sess. February 4.

U.S. Congress. 1987e. Senate. Armed Services Committee. *Hearings on the DOD Authorization for Appropriations for 1988.* 100th Cong., 1st sess. February 17.

U.S. Congress. 1987f. House. Committee on Foreign Affairs. *Hearings on Foreign Assistance Legislation for 1987–88 I.* 100th Cong., 1st sess. February 18.

U.S. Congress. 1987g. House. Committee on Armed Services. *Hearings on the National Defense Authorization Act for FY 1988–89.* 100th Cong., 1st sess. March 24.

U.S. Congress. 1987h. House. Committee on Foreign Affairs. *Hearings on the Overview of the Situation in the Persian Gulf.* 100th Cong., 1st sess. June 10.

### Articles/Speeches

1984a. Facing the Challenge of Arms Control. *Vital Speeches of the Day,* January 1.

1984b. Peace Through Strength and Dialogue: Ballistic Missile Defense. *Vital Speeches of the Day,* December 1.

1986a. Low Intensity Warfare. *Vital Speeches of the Day,* February 15.
1986b. United States Defenses. *Vital Speeches of the Day,* March 1.
1986c. U.S. Defense Strategy. *Foreign Policy,* Spring.
1987. Why Offense Needs Defense. *Foreign Policy,* Fall.
1988. Arms Reductions and Deterrence. *Foreign Policy,* Fall.

Interviews
CBS News. 1981a. "Face the Nation." March 8.
CBS News. 1981b. "Face the Nation." October 4.
CBS News. 1982. "Face the Nation." August 22.
CBS News. 1983a. "Face the Nation." March 13.
CBS News. 1983b. "Face the Nation." June 12.
CBS News. 1983c. "Face the Nation." October 23.
CBS News. 1985. "Face the Nation." September 15.
CBS News. 1986a. "Face the Nation." March 2.
CBS News. 1986b. "Face the Nation." June 1.
NBC News. 1981a. "Meet the Press." March 8.
NBC News. 1981b. "Meet the Press." May 17.
NBC News. 1981c. "Meet the Press." October 4.
NBC News. 1981d. "Meet the Press." November 22.
NBC News. 1983. "Meet the Press." March 27.
NBC News. 1985. "Meet the Press." May 19.

# Index

Abelson, Robert, 39
Acheson, Dean, 38–39
Air Launched Cruise Missiles (ALCM), 134, 174–76, 187, 203, 205
Ajzen, Icek, 37
Alford, C. Fred, 220
Allen, Richard, 173
Allison, Graham, 21
Almond, Gabriel, 236
Anti-Ballistic Missile (ABM) Treaty, 63, 109, 200–201, 205; "broad" and "narrow" interpretations of, 200, 204–5; discussions at Reykjavík, 208–10; Perle on, 76, 200, 204, 206; Reagan on, 109, 204–6; Shultz on, 205, 217; Weinberger on, 77, 201, 204, 206, 209
Arms Control and Disarmament Agency (ACDA), 131
Aspin, Les, 187

Backfire Bomber, 203
Bem, Daryl J., 39
Berelson, Bernard, 44
Bingham, Jeffrey, 126
Blackman, S., 227
B-1 Bomber, 175
Brezhnev, Leonid, 146, 167–68
Brown, Harold, 95, 137
Brown, Seyom, 6
Brzezinski, Zbigniew, 118, 232
Build-down proposal, 187–88
Burgess, Philip, 11–12, 35–36
Burt, Richard, 5–7, 44, 53, 84, 99–100, 162, 165–66, 224, 241–42; approach to arms control, 133–40; cog-

nitive style of, 238; on common interests with the USSR, 136–37, 147; on democracies and negotiations, 135–36; on INF, 138; on need for INF deployments, 92; as policy formulator, 168–69; on SALT II, 133–35, 171–72, 179, 181; and Soviet perceptions of the U.S., 98–99; on START, 138, 183–85, 192–93, 196–97; strength of image-policy preference relationship, 243–47; view of Soviet decision making, 98–99; view of Soviet foreign policy goals, 85–87, 234; view of Soviet nuclear capabilities, 177, 191, 193, 196–97, 234; view of Soviet nuclear doctrine and objectives, 91, 164, 193, 196–97, 234; view of Soviet policy motivation, 89; view of Soviet response to U.S. policies, 94–95; view of Soviet treaty compliance, 96–97, 166; walk in the woods proposal, 155–57; zero plus option, 152–54, 169

Cannon, Lou, 102, 242
Carlucci, Frank, 212
Carmines, Edward, 52
Carney, Thomas, 43, 50
Carter, Jimmy, 9, 118, 149–50, 152, 171
Casey, William, 171, 203
Chernenko, Konstantin, 199, 203
Christiansen, Bjorn, 2
Cognitive style, 227–31, 248–49; Burt's, 238; definition of, 227; ideological, 228, 243; intellectual, 228–

Cognitive style (*continued*)
29; Perle's, 237–38, 243; Reagan's,
238–41; Shultz's, 238; uncommitted
thinking syndrome, 229–30; Weinberger's, 237–38, 243
Cohen, William, 187
Committee on the Present Danger, 35,
63, 83, 233
Consistency (balance) theory, 28–30, 38
Content analysis, 43–44; coding
scheme, 44–49; composite reliability
coefficient, 56–67; evaluative assertion analysis, 51–52; recording and
context units, 49–52; reliability tests,
54–57; representational versus instrumental communication, 52–54; validity issues, 52–53
Cottam, Richard, 14–15, 17
Cranston, Alan, 71
Crowe, William, 174–75

Dallek, Robert, 84, 102, 231–32, 238
Davis, Vincent, 232
Deaver, Michael, 203
Dense Pack (MX basing mode), 187
Diabolical enemy image, 81, 100, 233
Diesing, Paul, 12, 14–15, 123, 180–
81, 225–26
Dual track decision (1979), 149, 152
Dulles, John Foster, 3, 18, 33, 81,
101–2, 175

Eagleburger, Lawrence, 6, 150–51, 157
Eureka Plan, 191, 194

Festinger, Leon, 28–30
Fishbein, Martin, 37

Gaffney, Frank, 212
Gamson, William A., 100
Garthoff, Raymond, 167
Gelb, Leslie, 120
Gengel, R., 28
George, Alexander, 4–5, 34, 36, 58–60
Glad, Betty, 101, 238, 240–41, 247

Goldstein, K., 227
Gorbachev, Mikhail, 67–69, 98–99,
104–5, 107–8, 115, 117, 120, 146,
161, 174, 199, 203, 237, 240; at
Reykjavík summit, 206–9, 215
Gore, Albert, 187
Gray, Robert, 194–95
Gromyko, Andrei, 202
Guertner, Gary, 21
Gwertzman, Bernard, 139

Haig, Alexander, 6, 83–84, 112, 155,
157, 172–74, 184–86, 242; on be-
ginning INF negotiations, 150; zero
option, 150–52; and zero plus option,
152–54
Haley, P. Edward, 207
Helms, Jesse, 83, 200–201
Herken, Greg, 232
Hermann, Margaret, 228, 230–31,
237–38, 241, 249
Herrmann, Richard, 2, 100
Holsti, Ole, 5, 7, 14–15, 20, 45, 50,
81
Humphrey, Gordon, 83

Images (national/enemy), 4; characteristics of, 225–27, 232–37, 248; and
cognitive style, 227–31, 237–41,
248–49; components of, 13–15, 25,
45–49; decision processes, 14, 21–
22, 25, 48; definitions of, 12–13, 24,
45; diabolical enemy image, 81, 100,
233; hard-line images, 25–26; inherent bad faith model, 81, 100; intentions, 14–17, 25, 45–46; and
interpretation, 32–33, 41; linkages to
policy preferences, 34–41, 58–60;
and memory/recall, 33–34, 41; military capabilities, 14, 20–21, 25, 46–
47; moderate images, 25–26; nuclear
doctrine and objectives, 17, 25, 46;
and operational codes, 4–5; and perception, 30–32, 41; and policy analy-
sis/evaluation, 34–37, 41; policy